SOCIAL SCIENCES & HISTORY DIVISION

# THE CHICAGO PUBLIC LIBRARY

**McCarthy and McCarthyism in Wisconsin**

# McCarthy and McCarthyism in Wisconsin

Michael O'Brien

University of Missouri Press
Columbia & London
1980

Copyright © 1980 by The Curators of the University of Missouri
Library of Congress Catalog Number 80–16792
Printed and bound in the United States of America
University of Missouri Press, Columbia, Missouri 65211

Library of Congress Cataloging in Publication Data

O'Brien, Michael, 1943–
  McCarthy and McCarthyism in Wisconsin.

  Bibliography: p. 250
  Includes index.
  1. McCarthy, Joseph Raymond, 1908–1957. 2. Wisconsin—Politics and govern-
ment. 3. Legislators—United States—Biography. 4. United States. Congress.
Senate—Biography. I. Title.
E748.M143027     973.9′092′4 [B]     80–16792
ISBN 0–8262–0319–1

Certain portions of this book have appeared previously in similar form in the
following articles by the author:

"The Anti McCarthy Campaign in Wisconsin: 1951–1952," *Wisconsin Magazine of
History* 56:2 (Winter 1972–1973): 91–108. Copyright © 1973 by the State Historical
Society of Wisconsin. Reprinted by permission.

"Young Joe McCarthy: 1908–1944,"*Wisconsin Magazine of History* (Spring 1980).
Copyright © 1980 by the State Historical Society of Wisconsin. Reprinted by
permission.

"McCarthy and McCarthyism: The Cedric Parker Case, November, 1949," in
Robert Griffith and Athan Theoharis, eds., *The Specter: Original Essays on the Cold
War and the Origins of McCarthyism.* Copyright © 1974 by New Viewpoints. Re-
printed by permission.

"Robert Fleming, Senator McCarthy, and the Myth of the Marine Hero," *Journalism
Quarterly* 50:1 (Spring 1973): 48–53. Reprinted by permission.

For my mother
Margaret O'Brien

# Preface

It has been almost thirty years since Sen. Joseph R. McCarthy announced in a speech at Wheeling, West Virginia, that a large number of Communists worked in the U.S. State Department, thereby thrusting himself into the national spotlight, polarizing political rhetoric for a decade, and contributing a new "ism" to the lexicon of American politics. Since then, countless historians and observers have subjected him and his anti-Communist crusade to analysis, exploring McCarthy's senatorial career, his impact on national politics and the cold war, his relationship to the labor movement, civil liberties, the press, the Catholic church, and so on. The picture that emerges is a strangely disembodied one, however, for it largely disconnects McCarthy from the Wisconsin environment that produced him. Much of his career in Wisconsin remains shrouded in myth, or, at best, glossed over with generalities. But Joe McCarthy learned his political trade in Wisconsin. The traits he so prominently displayed to the nation as a red-hunting senator were first refined in Wisconsin where McCarthy was a student, lawyer, judge, soldier, and aspiring politician.

Joe McCarthy aroused in the nation more intense feelings of loathing and admiration than any other contemporary political figure. The same was true in Wisconsin, and, by relating his life and his political career to the Wisconsin scene, we can see, in microcosm, many of the forces that produced this unique phenomenon. McCarthy's opponents in the state were persistent, often shrill, and ultimately successful. At critical moments, though, the anti-McCarthy movement suffered a frustrating series of disagreements, problems, and setbacks. McCarthy's most important backing in Wisconsin came from the Republican party and most newspapers. Particularly from 1950 to 1952, he advanced their cause as a slugging fighter against the Democratic Truman administration. During his red-hunting years, his public appearances electrified audiences in Wisconsin. McCarthyites detected unique traits in their hero, and they admired those traits to an exceptional degree.

Wisconsin newspapers played a critical role in McCarthy's rise to fame. Long before he began to lash the Truman administration, McCarthy had learned to master the art of press-agentry. The state press helped to transform a mediocre judge into a wise and prudent one and a dutiful marine intelligence officer into a glamorous tail gunner and war hero. In the Quaker Dairy case of 1941 and the Cedric Parker incident of 1949, state newspapers saved him from political disaster. Like all his Wisconsin admirers, the press showed remarkable indifference to the moral implications of his personal and legislative record.

In one important respect, McCarthy's impact on Wisconsin was limited.

While much of the nation after World War II succumbed to serious encroachments on civil liberties (the movement McCarthy symbolized), Wisconsin for the most part defeated legislative assaults on basic freedoms. Nowhere was concern for subversive thought and activity more steadily manifest than in education. While other parts of the country enforced censorship, enacted loyalty oaths, conducted legislative investigations, and fired teachers, powerful forces in Wisconsin worked to blunt or defuse assaults on academic freedom. The state that provided the nation with a senator and an "ism" symbolizing serious infringement on basic freedoms ironically preserved those freedoms better than other parts of the country.

## Acknowledgments

This book was written in two stages. The first dealt with all aspects of McCarthy's political career with respect to Wisconsin from 1946 to 1957. Recently, however, I decided to extend my analysis to McCarthy's early career because previous studies were either superficial or inaccurate. This new section, which comprises the first three chapters, is not intended to be a comprehensive early biography. Rather, I seek to explain the major facets of McCarthy's life before 1946—his educational, legal, judicial, military, and political careers—so his subsequent political prominence can be better understood.

I am delighted to have the opportunity to express my deep gratitude to all those who made this book possible. I am indebted to Philip D. Lagerquist of the Harry S. Truman Library, John Wickman of the Dwight D. Eisenhower Library, and Maurice Rosenblatt who guided me through the papers of the National Committee for an Effective Congress. Of the many pleasant and efficient archivists and librarians at the State Historical Society of Wisconsin, I am particularly grateful for the assistance of Gerald Ham, Margaret Hofstad, Josephine Harper, Barbara Kaiser, and Pat Quinn. Leslie H. Fishel, Jr., former head of the society, made helpful suggestions for locating historical material. Paul Chao, former librarian at the University of Wisconsin Center–Fox Valley, also found important material for me.

I appreciate the counsel of Prof. Richard Dalfiume, whose encouragement and advice during the initial stage of this project were more important than he realized. Prof. E. David Cronon supervised the study as my Ph.D. dissertation, and his suggestions, criticism, and knowledge of Wisconsin history added immeasurably to its quality.

In writing this book I relied heavily on the counsel and criticism of the following friends, critics, and scholars: Robert Zieger, William Skelton, Athan Theoharis, Robert Griffith, Mitchell Lechter, Donald Hrubesky, Donald Castonia, John Cooper, and Paul Hass. I wish to thank Dean Rue Johnson and the staff of the University of Wisconsin Center–Fox Valley for their many acts of kind assistance. A sabbatical leave from the University of

Wisconsin allowed me time to complete this project. My typist, Kathleen Yunkers, was not only proficient at her primary task but was a fine critic as well.

Last, I thank my wife Sally. In addition to her patience and encouragement, she typed many early drafts of the manuscript. I owe more to her than to anyone else. Also, thanks to Tim, Sean, Jeremy, and Carey for many reasons.


M.O'B.
Menasha, Wisconsin
April 1980

# Contents

# Chapter 1

# Young Joe McCarthy

Joseph R. McCarthy's rise to prominence in Wisconsin was a consequence of his extraordinary personality, media coverage, powerful political forces, and fortuitous circumstances. Like many successful politicians, McCarthy benefited from accidents of time and circumstance: vulnerable opponents, a financial windfall in the stock market, and that great adventure of mid-century, World War II. He swiftly exploited every advantage. He was dynamic, ambitious, and industrious; also opportunistic, cynical, and unethical. His mind was perceptive but shallow. With friends and voters, he was amiable and charming; with opponents, devious and ruthless. His more sinister qualities did nothing to obstruct his political career because McCarthy was a shrewd press agent and because newspapers— the dominant news medium of his time—were both naive and irresponsible. As a result, his virtues were magnified and his vices ignored. After 1944, when he was able to link his ambitions and undoubted abilities with the goals and potent resources of conservative Wisconsin Republicans, he was propelled into the U.S. Senate.

Most of the formative influences on his childhood remain obscure or conjectural. He was very reticent about his early life, especially about his life before age twenty. Richard Rovere, a McCarthy biographer, perceptively remarked that, while Senator McCarthy found himself endlessly interesting and summoned up the fanciest rhetoric when discussing himself, his self-absorption seldom extended to his childhood. He never talked publicly about his parents and would only discuss his background in very broad outline. Rovere noted that McCarthy never said, as most politicians would who could, "how much fun it was and how splendid for the development of character to have been brought up in a family of [seven] children, a family that had, indeed, started in a log cabin."[1] McCarthy's childhood may have been so tormented that he did not wish to recall it, but there is no evidence to indicate that it was sad or painful. Perhaps his failure to do what the conventional politician would have done was simply another manifestation of his altogether eccentric personality.

Joe's grandfather, Stephen McCarthy, was born in Ireland in 1821. Sometime around 1850, he left County Tipperary for New York State, where for most of the decade he labored as a farmhand. In 1855, without having seen the property, he purchased land in the town of Center in Outagamie County, Wisconsin, at the northern tip of Lake Winnebago.

1

With his hard-earned money, he also purchased a team of oxen and a wagon and migrated to Wisconsin three years later. He built a log cabin, sent for his mother in Ireland, and settled down to clear a farm from the wilderness. Fellow townsmen respected him enough to select him to community offices. In 1862 he married Margaret Stoffel, twenty-one years his junior, whose parents had emigrated from Bavaria. The couple had six sons and four daughters. Two of the daughters became nuns, implying a devout Catholic family.[2] At least three of Stephen's sons and probably a brother settled on nearby farms, making the section heavily populated with the McCarthy clan. The McCarthys were an island of Hibernians in a sea of German and Dutch farmers, and their enclave was known locally as "the Irish Settlement."[3]

Timothy, one of Stephen's sons (and Joe's father), built a log cabin and cleared 142 acres in the farm community of Grand Chute. The rolling property with its wooded ridges was a short distance south of the town of Center. Timothy married Bridget Tierney, whose parents had also come from Ireland. They had three daughters and four sons. Joe, three parts Irish, one part German, was the fifth child. By the time of his birth on 14 November 1908, the McCarthy family fortunes had improved enough for them to live in an eight-room, white clapboard house.[4]

Timothy was a small, quick, wiry man who managed his finances frugally and worked hard and swiftly. His children helped with the chores, and he demanded that they perform them correctly. Sloppy workmanship was a cardinal sin. He was also cautious and suspicious and advised his children to be careful of people who might take advantage of them. "Don't sign nothing unless you know what you're signing," he emphatically warned Stephen, his oldest son. He brooked no nonsense from his children, but he was especially strict on only two points: going to church regularly and not keeping late hours. "In his nervous, fast ways," recalled Joe's brother Howard, "Joe took after his Dad. In his persistence, he took after mother." Bridget was a large, big-boned woman, abrim with kindly devotion for her family. She not only babied Joe, as most historical accounts have related; she babied all her children.[5]

When Joe was about eleven, the family raised corn, barley, cabbage, oats, and hay. The McCarthys also had chickens, five horses, and about twenty-five cows. In summer months, they rose before 5:30 A.M., worked until noon, broke for lunch, and then worked until supper. They picked corn, hauled hay and grain, fed the chickens and horses, fed and milked the cows, and filled the silo.[6] Joe was a particularly diligent worker. Often he impatiently awaited the next chore. "Joe worked like the devil," a neighboring farmer recalled. "I remember one day when he was helpin' Tim load hay into the barn. We was usin' a team of horses and a rope and pulley to hoist the hay up. Joe's job was leadin' the horses. He had to lead them across the yard and through a ditch and clear to the road. The ditch was near fulla water, but Joe plowed right into it, up to his knees, leadin' them horses. Never even slowed down. One of his boots came off in the mud and I remember he didn't go pick up that boot till all the hay was in. Joe was always like that—a hard worker."[7]

Occasional visits with neighbors and regular Sunday worship interrupted the continual round of work. In a logging sleigh in winter and a two-horse surrey in summer, the McCarthys faithfully drove the seven miles to St. Mary's Church in Appleton. Timothy enrolled his four boys in the parish Holy Name Society and relied on the priest for their moral guidance. Before bed each evening, the family gathered to pray the rosary.[8]

Joe was barrel-chested and short-armed, with thick eyebrows and heavy lips. His brothers and sisters recalled him as always busy, ambitious, restless, and self-confident. He enjoyed practical jokes. He was not abnormally shy or introverted. Around adults, all the McCarthy children were shy, but Joe less so than the others. At the dinner table, with company present, most of the children were afraid to talk, but not Joe. "He'd always speak up, no matter what the subject might be," his sister Anna Mae recalled.[9]

Joe attended the Underhill Country School, about a mile from home, where all eight grades studied and recited together in one small, bare room. Students of German background heavily outnumbered the McCarthys. The students walked to class except when a farmer picked up the children as he made his delivery to the cheese factory next to the school. As his children grew, Timothy made the journey easier by buying bikes for them. At school Joe studied geography, reading, spelling, history, and arithmetic. He did well enough to complete two grades in one year. He developed a keen interest in reading, especially adventure stories and westerns. He devoured magazines from home and books from the school. "He was always reading library books," his sister Olive said. "Sometimes he'd read till late at night—and then get up at five-thirty to do his chores in the barn." He could look at a page in a book and know it almost by heart in a matter of minutes.[10]

Joe and his brothers had little free time. However, after school and work, they played the usual games of hide-and-seek and tag, frolicked in the hay mound, fished and cavorted in a nearby creek, and skated on it in the winter. The family had a set of boxing gloves, and Joe developed a fascination for boxing. Once he and Stephen challenged their father to a boxing match. Timothy beat each of them, one at a time (though not maliciously), until Bridget made him stop. On a Sunday afternoon when Joe was about thirteen, Steve allowed Joe to ride his new motorcycle. With careless enthusiasm he crashed and broke his ankle—the first in a series of major injuries to his legs. During their adolescence, the McCarthy children attended square dances at nearby Stephensville. Timothy and Bridget and other parents warned their children to avoid temptation at such gatherings, and watchful chaperones enforced the rule. The youngsters knew how far they could go sexually, which was not very far.[11]

Joe graduated from grade school at fourteen. Like most local farm boys, he did not continue on to high school. The Appleton school was too far away, and boys were eager to begin earning money. Joe worked for his father for a while, then struck out on his own in 1923. With $65 earned doing part-time labor for an uncle and probably with the added financial assistance of his father and other relatives, he rented land from his father and began his own chicken business. He invested in fifty baby chicks and built (mostly by himself) a new chicken coop, ninety feet long and thirty feet wide. He insulated it, installed a coal burner, and laid a concrete floor. He hovered over his brood day and night, primarily to prevent inquisitive friends and relatives from entering the building and disturbing the health of his chickens. For five years he worked the business and made it thrive. At its peak, his flock consisted of two thousand laying hens and from ten to twenty thousand broilers. Before he was legally old enough to drive, he bought a truck and began hauling his goods to the Chicago market. He became something of an authority on poultry diseases, feed, and marketing, and his picture appeared in poultry magazines.[12]

Then various misfortunes beset the business. On his way to Chicago with an extra heavy load, his truck swayed around a bend in the road and tipped over, scattering chickens, feathers, and splintered crates over the roadside. Another time, while trying to corner the market, he bought his brooders too early in the spring, and many died. One last misfortune was fatal to his business. On a cold night in 1928, emerging from the warm, moist chicken house, Joe took a chill, and a few days later was flat on his back with pneumonia. In desperation, he hired a couple of neighbor boys to care for the chickens until he was back on his feet, but they were inexperienced and either slow or careless. Within a few weeks almost his entire flock died, and Joe's five years of hard work died with it.[13]

Although the primary influences on McCarthy's childhood remain locked in mystery and probably will continue so, some confident critics, relying on the research of enterprising journalists, assumed they had discovered the key. Shy, ugly, and awkward—so this interpretation contends—Joe McCarthy listened to the advice of his overprotective mother to be somebody, rebelled against his domineering father, and entered adulthood brash, ruthless, and insatiably ambitious.

The symptoms are mostly accurate (though narrowly defined), but speculation on the cause of the malady is based on insufficient and sometimes contradictory data. Not enough is known about the child-rearing practices of Joe McCarthy's parents, peer influences, or the progress of his emotional and intellectual growth. The same is true of his moral and ethical training. In terms of what is known about his class, religion, upbringing, and education, there seems to be little that sets Joseph Raymond McCarthy apart from his boyhood peers in and around "the Irish Settlement."[14] It is clear, however, that a sudden and quite dramatic change occurred in McCarthy's life just about the time he was achieving his majority—when he moved from rural Grand Chute to the little Waupaca County village of Manawa in the spring of 1929.

\*　　\*　　\*　　\*

McCarthy tried to rebuild his chicken business, but his heart was not in it. Shortly thereafter, probably in the summer of 1928, he took a job as a clerk in a Cash-Way grocery store in downtown Appleton. Cash-Way was a locally owned chain of nineteen stores in the Fox River valley. When he overheard the district manager tell the manager that there was an opening for a man to head a new store in Manawa, Joe volunteered and got the job.[15] He and his sister Olive moved to Manawa (population seven hundred), rented rooms at Mrs. Frank Osterloth's home near the Little Wolf High School, and got ready for the grand opening of the Cash-Way on 11 May 1929.

During the week of the store's opening, McCarthy filled the *Manawa Advocate* with exuberant advertising. He thanked the "folks" for their welcome and for the "wonderful crowds" that "thronged" the store on opening day. Cash-Way, he promised, would be a "thrift center," not merely a branch store but a "local institution." His ads became more mundane thereafter as he and Olive labored long hours making the store prosper.[16]

McCarthy was intensely ambitious. "I never saw anybody so steamed up," an acquaintance recalled. "He just couldn't ever relax; he worked at everything he did. He was pushing all the time." He quickly became a popular town figure, the center of attention. Jovial and friendly, he stood at the store entrance greeting everyone and trading wisecracks and pleasantries.[17]

The Cash-Way prospered, but what initially must have seemed a promising business opportunity soon began to pall. The job was too dull for McCarthy's temperament; it lacked a future. During the summer he decided to enroll in high school. The decision was a turning point in his life. Timothy McCarthy had encouraged his sons to acquire a high-school education, but none of them had heeded his advice. Perhaps Joe now recognized the wisdom of his father's counsel. Mrs. Osterloth, the kind German landlady whom he later called his "second mother," had warned him he would never get ahead without a high-school diploma. With his maturity, intelligence, and confidence, he certainly believed he could handle the course work. He was so confident of his ability, and so disturbed by the prospect of sitting with thirteen- and fourteen-year-old freshmen, that he devised a plan to "get it over quickly."[18]

The normal load for a student at Little Wolf High was four courses per year, with sixteen necessary for graduation. Just before school opened,

McCarthy approached the principal, Leo Hershberger, and asked if he could take six subjects the first semester with the understanding that he would finish the following semester if he did not fall down in his work. Hershberger refused. McCarthy persisted. The principal studied him carefully. Husky, awkward, but personally ingratiating, McCarthy obviously wanted to make something of himself. Impressed with the young man's intensity and determination, Hershberger agreed to sign him up and to help him all he could.[19]

When classes commenced on 9 September the forty-three other freshmen applauded and snickered as twenty-year-old Joe McCarthy sat down with them in the assembly hall. "The day I first walked into that classroom and sat down with those kids," McCarthy recalled years later, "I would have sold out for two cents on the dollar." For the first two months, he added burdens to his already overloaded schedule. Besides his course work, he continued to work at the Cash-Way after school and plunged into extracurricular activities. The freshman class elected him vice-president. He also headed a citizenship class and helped to plan the Halloween party. By late October 1929, he was filled with the sense of urgency, the need to complete the courses fast. Therefore, he dropped out of most outside activities. When an executive from Cash-Way visited Manawa, he insisted that McCarthy devote full-time either to school or to the store. McCarthy quit Cash-Way.[20]

From November to June, McCarthy concentrated on his course work. Little Wolf High used the three-level assignment system. Teachers typed out an assignment for each unit of work in each course, mimeographed it, and distributed a copy to each student in the class. The student then decided whether he or she wished to fulfill the requirements for a grade of A, B, or C. There was little group discussion or instruction. Each student worked quietly alone, going to the instructor for help only when he or she could not find the answer to a specific question. After finishing an assignment, the student took it to the teacher, who graded it immediately. Examinations were generally true-false and short-answer questions. After passing the test at the chosen level, the student moved on to the next mimeographed sheet.[21]

Rising at five in the morning, McCarthy ate breakfast and then began studying until school started. From eight until twelve he plugged away at one assignment after another, filling it out, having it graded, and taking an exam. (He always tried for an A.) Then he started another assignment. At noon he gulped down his lunch and returned to study until 5:00 P.M. After supper he usually studied until 10:00 P.M., often until midnight, and occasionally until 3:00 in the morning. In addition, he studied on many weekends and during vacations. He followed this schedule rigorously, month after month. He always paid attention in class and did not fool around like his younger classmates. He seldom mingled with other students, but, when he did, he was always friendly and good-natured.[22]

Hershberger, worried that his star pupil might suffer a nervous break-down, suggested that McCarthy get some physical exercise. McCarthy agreed and asked him to arrange late-afternoon boxing sessions with some of the boys. McCarthy promised to teach them to box. When he tired of boxing, he jogged around the block, showered, and went home to resume studying.[23]

With his hard work and the cooperation of his teachers and Hershberger, McCarthy shot far ahead of his fellow freshmen. At Thanksgiving he joined the sophomore class. At midyear he became a junior. In mid-March, after he had been in school only seven months, Hershberger announced that McCarthy would graduate in June. McCarthy made the honor roll each quarter, twice achieving the second highest grade in the class. He received his best grades in history, science, social problems, and math, but only fair marks in Latin and English.[24]

Some writers have alleged that McCarthy connived to complete one of his courses. According to the story, a young female instructor refused to go along with the crusade to help Joe through school and would not give him the final exam. McCarthy cunningly warmed up to her and invited her to the prom, after which she revised her objection and gave him the test. The tale is mostly embellished. He once dated Mildred Berger, the commercial teacher, and his classmates kidded him about doing so for a grade. But there is no evidence that that was his motive.[25]

When he entered high school, McCarthy had only a vague intention of going on to college. By March 1930, however, he had decided to enroll and had narrowed his choices to Marquette University and the University of Wisconsin. At that point he discoverd that he needed advanced algebra to clear the hurdle into college. Little Wolf High School had no such course. He solved the problem by enrolling in a correspondence course at the University of Wisconsin. Hershberger gave him the final examination in his home; he received a 93.

Acceptance by any college proved to be a major problem because McCarthy had not spent four years at an accredited high school. For Marquette, Hershberger completed the forms himself, and to the question "Did you attend four years of high school?" he wrote, "Yes." Marquette accepted McCarthy in electrical engineering.[26]

McCarthy spent some of his spare time in Manawa playing poker with young professional men in town, or as a dinner guest of a friend. Several nights a week he earned pin money as an usher at a movie house. He dutifully attended Sunday mass at Sacred Heart Church. He went to the annual prom with Vivian Moss, a shy high-school senior who had trans-ferred from Nebraska. Occasionally, he spent weekends on the farm in Grand Chute.[27] For the most part, he was as tireless in his enthusiasm for leisure activities as he was for his studies. Few people ever saw him relax. One friend thought he seemed impatient with the twenty-four-hour day and wanted to pack more into it. He was too old to be eligible for varsity sports, but, once in a while, he practiced with the basketball team. He tried to be a good player, rather than just play at it, but was too awkward and rough for basketball and could not learn or ignored the rules.

One Sunday afternoon, probably the weekend before high school opened, McCarthy, Olive, and two friends took their first airplane ride. It was the kind of arrangement where each paid according to weight. The others were reluctant and fearful, but McCarthy told the pilot to "Give 'er the works." The plane looped all over the sky, and he loved every minute of it.

McCarthy could not swim—and never did learn—but he tried anyway. On one occasion, at the Casino on the Waupaca Chain of Lakes, he repeatedly jumped off a high diving board with an inner tube around his waist. Each time he bruised himself terribly, ending the day black and blue. George Kelley, a classmate who witnessed the scene, could not understand what compelled him to do it.[28]

On 6 June 1930, McCarthy graduated from high school. At the ceremonies Hershberger singled him out for special tribute and recounted his accomplishment. It had been a difficult but rewarding year for McCarthy, and he often referred to it in his later political campaign literature. He exaggerated when he told a friend after graduation that he had lost sixty pounds during his ordeal, but he was thinner and noticeably nervous, and he had overcome physical setbacks during the year. He underwent eye surgery in August and had dislocated an ankle in March.[29]

McCarthy's substantial success stemmed from many factors. Compared to his fellow students, he was more mature, worldly wise, and intensely motivated. Hershberger wrote in McCarthy's school record that Joe completed the requirement by "will power, unusual ability, and concentrated work!" Hershberger insisted that no teacher gave him any breaks but that McCarthy devoted four times as many hours to study each day as most other students. (This was mostly true, but the teachers and Hershberger undoubtedly cut some corners for him.) His academic program, with its self-paced learning and emphasis on memorization, ideally suited his superior qualities of perseverance, determination, and comprehension.[30]

McCarthy's year in Manawa rewarded him in other ways as well. He had become a town celebrity. During the year, the junior class nominated him for "most lovable man" in town. The weekly newspaper regularly reported his activities, both in school and out. He made the front page three times in one week. In March, the *Milwaukee Journal* wrote a feature story about the scholastic prodigy from Manawa, highlighting his perseverance and grit. He had every reason to leave Manawa strong and self-confident.[31]

. But McCarthy's education at Manawa lacked both depth and breadth. The school offered no art instruction, and Joe had no time to take music or speech. He took no part in journalism or drama; he apparently did not have to write essays or research papers. His program efficiently avoided class discussion, and, consequently, he did not learn to exchange ideas or to appreciate other viewpoints. Nor did he have time to analyze or reflect on his study. His goals were purely instrumental. He wanted to "get it over quickly," as he told the *Milwaukee Journal*. One could argue that most of his classmates held the same view of education and had similar experiences. But they, at least, had four years to absorb some of the finer points of education. Joe never had the time.

As McCarthy prepared for Marquette University, he told his brother Stephen that he intended to repeat his high-school feat and graduate from college in one year. He was probably kidding. If he was serious, the rigors of college soon forced him to lower his expectation. He spent five years at Marquette: two in engineering (1930–1932) and three in law (1932–1935).

McCarthy probably did not thoughtfully consider his plans in engineering. The profession must have appeared profitable and adventurous; the president, Herbert Hoover, had been an engineer. At Marquette, McCarthy talked for a time about going to South America for the money and adventure of some large engineering project. He took part in some of the activities of Sigma Phi Delta, the engineering fraternity, but never joined or made friends among engineers. In the first semester of his freshman year, his grades were not outstanding: C's in inorganic chemistry and English; B's in algebra, drawing, and elementary engineering.[32]

McCarthy never explained his decision to forsake engineering for law. Presumably, he came face to face with the realization that he could not complete the difficult engineering requirements with the meager mathematics and science he had crammed into his head at Manawa. Engineering demanded absolutes, precision, and the prospect of working with tools and machines. In law, he could express himself and work with people. Many of the friends he met in campus activities were also preparing to study law. He naturally inclined toward the company of law students, many of whom were boisterous, congenial, and garrulous like himself.[33]

McCarthy's family gave him some assistance, but primarily he worked his way through college. With job opportunities so scarce, many Marquette students had difficulty remaining in school. Before the Great Depression, about 30 percent of students found part-time jobs; by the beginning of 1932, only 10 percent could find work. The following fall, half the job applicants had to be turned down, and, consequently, Marquette lost five hundred prospective students.

Joe always managed to find work. He held jobs as short-order cook, dishwasher, and construction worker. One summer he sold a caulking compound for windows and doors. A friend, too bashful to join his enterprise, recalled that McCarthy had a forceful sales personality and had no reticence about trekking door-to-door. His principal means of support from 1932 to 1935 were jobs at Standard Oil gas stations, primarily at a large station at 16th and Wisconsin Avenue in Milwaukee. (His brother William, who worked for Standard Oil, may have found the jobs for him.)

He worked afternoons and evenings, forty to sixty hours a week, and for about thirty-five cents an hour he pumped gas, serviced autos, and sold tires. On one occasion he proudly claimed an award for selling the most tires in the Milwaukee district.[34]

Joe was always busy, always ambitious at Marquette. Sports absorbed much of his energy the first three years. He tried out for the freshman football team in the fall of 1930, but he had no skill or background in the sport and soon dropped out. He then returned to boxing, which more closely suited his interest and experience. (The sport also allowed him to waive the physical-education requirement for engineers.)

Marquette had introduced boxing to its intramural program in 1918 and, in 1930, hired Curtis Brown to teach classes and to arrange two boxing exhibitions each year. Brown was a small man with a badly scarred face from a career as a professional boxer. He stressed physical conditioning in his classes. Boxers came to class twice a week and returned to the gym on their own for extra training as exhibitions neared.[35]

Older and more mature than most of the fighters, McCarthy brought to the sport a little experience, fierce determination, and a powerful round-house right (a fellow boxer called it a "swinging gate"). He had little polish or technique, but under Brown's coaching he improved substantially, though he never became a stylish fighter. Before the first exhibition, Brown described his freshman prospect as a "husky, hard hitting middleweight" who promised an "evening's work for any foe." On 20 March 1931, Brown matched McCarthy with an opponent with similar qualities but even less finesse. Nine hundred spectators watched McCarthy batter Al Razor to the canvas three times in the first round and go on to win a decision. The fight boosted him to the status of a campus celebrity. The school paper, *The Marquette Tribune,* said that he had "dynamite in both hands" and noted that he had graduated from high school in one year, which "disproves the assertion that brawn, not brains, makes good boxers." The following month, however, he lost to Frank Didier, a deliberate veteran boxer, who kept him at bay throughout the fight and claimed the decision.[36]

As a sophomore, McCarthy moved up to the heavyweight class. In March 1932, before a crowd of twenty-five hundred people, he lost a decision to Stanley Balcerzak. Afterward, Coach Brown accepted part of the blame for McCarthy's defeat, claiming that he had mismatched the fighters; Balcerzak's large weight advantage and longer reach had prevented McCarthy from displaying his talent. Brown planned to find McCarthy a more suitable opponent the next time.

But the loss to Balcerzak hurt McCarthy's pride. Despite his disadvantage, he insisted on a rematch to even the score. Brown consented. At the 2 May bout, both fighters came out swinging and continued flailing at each other for a full minute, though neither landed a solid blow. Near the end of the second round, McCarthy hooked a right to Balcerzak's chin and dropped him for a count of nine. In the final round, Balcerzak entangled himself in the ropes. McCarthy waited, according to *The Marquette Tribune*, and then "launched himself across the ring in a flurry of gloves. Balcerzak let go with a right that started on Thirteenth Street, and slowed McCarthy down to a walk."

McCarthy won the decision. His record at Marquette had been modest: two victories and two defeats. By upsetting Balcerzak, however, he claimed the school's heavyweight championship. He had also gained respect by defeating an outstanding Milwaukee boxer in an off-campus bout.[37]

Brown resigned in the fall of 1932. With the university in serious financial difficulties and unwilling to hire a salaried replacement, the boxing program appeared doomed. McCarthy volunteered to coach, working for nothing or perhaps for a small stipend. He obviously did not have Brown's credentials, but school officials welcomed the opportunity to continue a popular program and appointed him coach.

For a first-year law student with a heavy work schedule at a gas station, boxing consumed much time. Nevertheless, McCarthy relished the job. In October 1932, he described his coaching philosophy to the student newspaper. "I want to teach the boys how to avoid punishment rather than take it," he explained. "I also want to develop in them a sense of self-confidence." He had difficulty teaching defensive boxing techniques, since he had never learned them himself. But increased self-confidence was probably the most significant dividend of his own boxing career.[38]

Basically, McCarthy copied Brown's procedures. He conducted classes, taught fundamentals, supervised training, and arranged two exhibitions. At first he thought he had plenty of squad members and would have to select exhibition participants on the basis of "survival of the fittest." Later, however, he had a shortage of heavyweights and tried to recruit football players.

McCarthy's selection as coach surprised veteran Marquette boxers who thought him unqualified. Indeed, some of his instructions fortified their apprehensions. For example, to use the right hand effectively, right-handed boxers are supposed to move to their left. With his emphasis on defensive strategy, however, McCarthy reversed the movement, instructing his right-handed boxers to move to their right so that right-handed opponents could not hit them. This perplexed the veterans. If the boxer followed his coach's advice, he could not land his own right and had to abandon all previous instruction and practice. (In the ring, William Schmit and Bernard O'Connor, both seasoned boxers, ignored McCarthy's instruction and reverted to customary style. McCarthy did not object.)

Although McCarthy's coaching was not as professional as Brown's, he won the respect of his pupils. He was sincere, concerned, and sympathetic. "He did not have a mean bone in his body," recalled Schmit. Occasionally, he tutored boxers with academic problems. When one of his finest fighters, Joe Kores, was knocked out in a sparring session, McCarthy anxiously hovered over him until he regained consciousness and then sat with him for an hour. Although Kores assured his coach that he was fine, McCarthy insisted on taking him home. He coached only one season, since law, work, and other interests demanded his time, but at the end of the year, *The Marquette Tribune* commended him on the success of the boxing program.[39]

McCarthy made another venture into extracurricular activities to overcome a serious weakness in speech, a problem that had been apparent in Manawa: he stuttered when he got excited. Probably in McCarthy's sophomore year at Marquette, Hershberger had invited him to address a student assembly at Hortonville High School where Hershberger was then principal. He gave the speech, but was so nervous and tongue-tied that he later sought to improve his technique and confidence.

So he joined the Franklin Club, the oldest society on campus and one that sponsored forensic development among students of average ability. The club held oratorical contests and debates with the varsity debate squad. Club leaders never selected McCarthy for major contests because he lacked polish and the proper demeanor on the platform. Nonetheless, he debated tenaciously and gained experience.[40]

McCarthy also plunged into campus politics, where he learned the art of personal campaigning that proved valuable after graduation. A friend, Richard Drew, ran for "most popular fraternity man" on campus; McCarthy worked as one of his campaign managers, and Drew won. McCarthy was less successful the first time he tried for office himself. After only a few months in the Franklin Club, he decided to run for president. He campaigned hard, buttonholing members and making lavish promises. But old-timers complained loudly that a newcomer should not be so presumptuous. At the election meeting, Charles Curran easily defeated him. Rankled, McCarthy walked out of the meeting. He was more shrewd and successful in his second run for office. At the first assembly of the freshman law class in the fall of 1932, class officers needed to be elected. McCarthy had anticipated the election and had campaigned vigorously for class president. Curran was his opponent again. In the interest of goodwill, he and Curran agreed that each would vote for the other at the election. The first ballot ended in a tie. In the second, McCarthy won by two votes. One person had switched his ballot, and Curran thought he knew who. "Joe, did you vote for yourself?" Curran asked. McCarthy smiled and answered: "Sure, you wanted me to vote for the best man, didn't you?" Curran might have been angry, but McCarthy's almost irresistible friendliness quickly healed the breach between them. When Curran's father died in 1933, McCarthy won Curran's lasting gratitude by leaving his job and driving two-thirds of the way across the state to Mauston to attend the funeral.[41]

McCarthy no doubt ran for campus offices because he was ambitious, but he also craved acceptance and sincerely thought he had something to offer. (He may have run for class president to influence the faculty's opinion of him, since Marquette professors supposedly favored class officers.) In any case, his performance as class president made no impression on his fellow students. Most of them did not care about such activities, and few could later recall that he accomplished anything, or even that he had held office. However, the office apparently thrust him into the chairmanship of the end-of-the-year law banquet, a major annual event at which the freshman class honored the graduating seniors. At the banquet, McCarthy welcomed guests that included Wisconsin's lieutenant governor and five state supreme court justices.[42]

McCarthy had a wide circle of acquaintances at Marquette. Some thought him overbearing and insincere, but most liked him. He was witty, cheerful, and pleasant, and he flattered people constantly. However, except for Curran, he made no friends among serious, dedicated students. His companions were mostly athletes and law students with social interests and average scholastic ability, many of whom later assisted his political career. One of his closest friends was Thomas Korb, who briefly worked for him in Washington and who remained a close political adviser. At Marquette, he and Korb double-dated and had gas-station jobs, law, and sports in common. At the gas station, McCarthy serviced the auto of Otis Gomillion, and the two developed a close relationship. Gomillion later served as McCarthy's bodyguard. McCarthy met Arlo McKinnon, a Milwaukee lawyer, when he coached one of McKinnon's relatives. McKinnon grew to admire him and substantially assisted his race against Alexander Wiley in 1944. Four of McCarthy's acquaintances at Marquette later worked for the FBI. Some of them—perhaps all of them—supplied him with information during his anti-Communist crusade.[43]

McCarthy led a conventional social life. He joined friends at parties and restaurants, and, in his freshman year, he and three others sneaked into a downtown burlesque theater to watch the semi-striptease. In law school, he dated a couple of times a month. He had a serious relationship with beautiful, red-headed Mildred Byrnes. He talked about her often and seemed troubled over what seems to have been a difficult courtship. He continued to see her after graduation and invited her to Shawano one weekend. Soon after, they broke up.[44]

In the last two years of law school, most of McCarthy's social life centered on the activities of his fraternity, Delta Theta Phi, a national legal fraternity that he joined in the fall of 1933. The local chapter had over thirty members, and he served as an officer for a while. The fraternity sponsored educational programs at which judges and lawyers spoke on topics ranging from the reading of abstracts to the trial of kidnapper Bruno Hauptmann. It was essentially a social fraternity, however, which sponsored parties, picnics, stag smokers, and trips to football games.

McCarthy lived with about nine brothers at the fraternity house, first on West Kilbourn Avenue and then in larger quarters on North 12th Street. He was the messiest person in the house, leaving clothes strewn throughout his room. He had little time for most fraternity activities, not even for bull sessions, the popular pastime at the house; he preferred poker or cribbage to dating. Sometimes, on days off, he started playing poker at one in the afternoon and continued past midnight. When the game broke up, occasionally he and Francis Reiske, a fraternity brother, played two-handed poker through the night until classes began the next morning.[45]

Marquette scheduled law classes only in the mornings, an arrangement that suited McCarthy because of his afternoon and evening job. There were few luminaries among the Marquette faculty, and intellectual excitement on campus was negligible. His instructors ranged from Harold Hallows, a demanding but interesting and learned professor of equity (later a justice of the Wisconsin Supreme Court), to Father Hugh McMahon, a naive, ineffective instructor of ethics (Catholic natural law). McCarthy and other students baited the old priest with difficult questions and mimicked his speech defect.

McCarthy was a mediocre law student. He complained to a friend that he wanted to be a good trial lawyer, but that work at the gas station handicapped him. To a degree this was true. When business slackened at the station, he occasionally studied. Otherwise, except when exams approached, he studied very little. He showed little inclination to study even when he had the opportunity. He did not have the time, the inclination, or the ability to take part in the *Marquette Law Review* or moot court. He had less academic preparation than most of his classmates, most of whom had had four years of high school. Many also had three years of undergraduate work; two of the best students in his class had five-year engineering degrees. Sometimes he looked sleepy in class, either from work or an all-night poker session.[46]

To compensate, Joe asked academic favors of friends. Some of them wearied of his constant borrowing of notes and case summaries. But, if called on in class, he responded adequately. ("He never prepared for class," a fellow student recalled, "but always seemed to be able to get the answers.") For some classes, such as torts, he bought "canned" briefs, even though professors frowned on this almost universal practice. McCarthy's principal salvation was his remarkable memory. Some classmates described his memory as photographic; others called it a blotter or a sponge. He quickly grasped both the fundamentals and the details of a subject and spewed them forth in cram sessions and exams.[47]

Most professors held only one exam, at the end of each semester. About ten days before exams, students cut back on working hours, stopped social activities, paged through the briefs and past examinations on file at the fraternity house, and gathered in small discussion groups. McCarthy followed the same routine. He asked to join a group consisting of the most dedicated, brilliant students, including the *Law Review* editor, Robert Harland. The members knew that McCarthy could contribute nothing, but, unwilling to reject a genial colleague, they allowed him to sit in. They insisted, however, that he sit quietly and not disturb them. McCarthy agreed, attended their sessions, and just listened. In other study groups with average students, he contributed substantially. He could do so because of his exceptional memory, and, perhaps, because he brought back significant insights from Harland's group.[48]

McCarthy graduated in the spring of 1935. On 13 June, he was admitted to the Wisconsin bar. His timing was doubly fortunate. His class was one of the last to be allowed admittance to law school with only two years of undergraduate preparation, and his was the first Marquette law class that had only to pass courses to be admitted to the bar and did not have to take the state bar examination.

McCarthy left Marquette University proud and confident. Despite severe economic pressure, he had gained a law degree faster than most of his classmates, had cultivated numerous friendships, and had gained fame as a campus athlete and coach. (In the next few years, he returned to the campus many times to see friends and to attend football games.) In his academic work, particularly exams, McCarthy had put his quick, perceptive mind to effective use, but he was substantially less diligent than he had been in Manawa. To McCarthy, education remained simply a means to an end; it failed to stimulate new questions, new ideas, or new perspectives. His classwork had been telescoped into a five-year sequence, sandwiched between jobs and extracurricular activities. In later years, he never mentioned any stimulating professors or discussed ideas he had encountered in college. Engineering and law students did not have to write research papers, and his Marquette career did nothing to improve his ability to write with style, distinction, or clarity. He spent little time in the library, and neither his high-school nor his college education revived his youthful zest for reading. He never read any of the great books of the Western world with their supposedly timeless example and inspiration. "I don't know that Joe ever read a book in the entire time I knew him," recalled his close friend, Urban Van Susteren. "He scanned the newspapers, but he learned from people."[49]

# Chapter 2

# First Steps and Missteps in Public Life

Six hours after McCarthy was sworn in as a member of the state bar, he opened a law office on Main Street in Waupaca, Wisconsin, thereby setting up shop ahead of a Marquette classmate and winning a bet. Waupaca, a town of five thousand people and the seat of Waupaca County, offered political opportunities for a newcomer; McCarthy also evidently hoped to draw business from nearby Manawa, where he still had friends.

When he arrived, he had made no arrangements for housing, so he stopped off at the office of Dr. William Remmel, a Waupaca dentist and a former poker-playing friend in Manawa. Remmel agreed to provide him with a room, even though McCarthy told him he had no money for rent. The arrangement worked well enough for a time—McCarthy teased and flattered Mrs. Remmel and played with their new baby—though he may eventually have overstayed his welcome.[1]

At his office, McCarthy shared a waiting room with William Rudersdorf, also a dentist. (Rudersdorf had the most clients.) McCarthy worked industriously, but, like most new lawyers—especially those starting out during the depression—he had little business. He spent part of his time at the courthouse watching court proceedings and learning the techniques of other lawyers. He had only four court cases during his stay in Waupaca, but he built a modest reputation when he won a substantial judgment for a girl who had been scarred in an automobile accident. Another lawyer, representing the spouse of another passenger who died in the same accident, got nothing. McCarthy, though, probably had more business than the four cases litigated at the Waupaca courthouse. He may have advised businesses, for example, or closed real-estate transactions. His tax return indicated that he earned $777.81 in the six months he practiced during 1935.[2]

McCarthy gambled often in Waupaca, as he did throughout his adult life. Before he went to Washington, he played cribbage and sheephead (a popular card game in Wisconsin); on vacations, he bet on the horses in Kentucky and played the slot machines in Biloxi, Mississippi. But poker was his game, and he did particularly well at it in Waupaca.

One Saturday afternoon, McCarthy told Remmel that he was not making enough money in his law practice and wanted to enter a high-stakes poker game at Ben Johnson's Bar about a mile west of town. McCarthy confessed that he had no money for the game; he even owed Remmel $50 back rent. But he proposed a deal. If Remmel would forgive the past rent and lend him another $50, McCarthy would give him the title to his car. Remmel agreed, gave McCarthy the money, and took the car. McCarthy told Remmel that he planned to win by remaining sober and holding his own in the game until midnight. By that time, with his opponents approaching drunkenness, he would start winning.

On Sunday morning, as the Remmels prepared for church, McCarthy returned with a roll of bills that, as Remmel recalled, would "knock you dead" in those days. McCarthy found a calendar, counted off the weeks, paid Remmel all his past rent and some for the future, and returned the borrowed $50. He then took his car back and, because he could not make it to church, gave Remmel $5 for the church collection.[3]

Much has been written about MCarthy's cutthroat poker methods, and there was undoubtedly much in his personality that made poker's daring strategy and bluffing attractive to him. "McCarthy had the guts of a burglar," a fellow Waupaca lawyer recalled. "He was brutal. He'd take all the fun out of the game because he took it so seriously." In high-stakes games, he would often sit quietly counting his chips and then, suddenly, shove them all in the pot and say, "I'll bet $104.75." Many players would fold because he had bet his whole pile. If someone called his bet and perhaps raised him a quarter, he would come back and raise him another $104.75, using the money in his pocket. One man who played with him found it nerve-wracking to be raised, reraised, and reraised at seven-card stud, when McCarthy had not even looked at his hole cards. "You get to the point," a friend recalled, "where you don't care what McCarthy's got in the hole—all you know is that it's too costly to stay in the game." He was so shifty, clever, and bold that a few players privately thought he cheated.[4]

Usually, he gambled with friends for smaller stakes, but he used the same daring tactics in those social games that made them fun and exciting.[5] McCarthy's gambling served other purposes than making money and fulfilling his elusive psychological needs. These poker sessions made and cemented friendships; many of his poker-playing friends later became his most ardent campaign supporters.

To get his name before the public, McCarthy labored for Waupaca civic functions. He served as general chairman of the Lions Club's Annual Harvest Day, a major community function, and sold tickets for the President's Birthday Ball, a charity event. In the basement of a tavern, he also helped to organize a Matt and Mitt Club, complete with showers and lockers, to keep "older, younger men" in shape.[6] He also played softball once a week where, as an outfielder, he was awkward and ill-coordinated. Jack Anderson and Ronald May have recounted McCarthy's hilarious performance at the town's annual benefit ball, a happy-go-lucky affair in which the players rode donkeys throughout the game. When a batter hit the ball, he had to mount the donkey and ride to first base; the fielders had to do the same when they chased the ball. When an opposing player hit the ball to McCarthy's sector of the outfield, he mounted his donkey and tore off after it. Then the donkey stopped and refused to move. McCarthy cursed and fumed. Finally, with the crowd laughing at his frustration, he grabbed the donkey around its midsection and carried it bodily over to the ball.[7]

McCarthy stayed in Waupaca only eight months. Financially and professionally, he did about as well there as other new lawyers during the depression years. Besides making friends and gaining experience, he also attracted the attention of Michael Eberlein, one of the most outstanding trial lawyers in northeastern Wisconsin.

Before World War I, Eberlein had formed a partnership with Albert Larson in Shawano, a town the size of Waupaca forty miles to the north. Larson died in 1931, and practicing alone became a burden for Eberlein. His son would not complete law school until 1939; meanwhile, he needed help, and searched the area for a hardworking, aggressive lawyer like himself. At least one other young prospect refused Eberlein's offer. One day in February 1936, Eberlein watched McCarthy perform in the courtroom, and, impressed by his aggressive manner, he stopped by his office to talk. McCarthy painted a picture of himself as a brilliant young lawyer with an ever-widening reputation in Waupaca County. Eberlein listened, knowing full well the details of McCarthy's meager practice. Finally he interrupted: "Why don't you close up this dump and come to work for me?" McCarthy shot back: "Why don't you close up that dump of yours and come to work for me?" Eberlein laughed and told McCarthy to think it over. McCarthy did and agreed to come. He moved to Shawano several weeks later.[8]

McCarthy told friends that he could not pass up the opportunity to earn $2,400 a year and to learn from a seasoned, successful, and highly respected lawyer. Eberlein developed a paternal affection for McCarthy, gave him tips on the law, introduced him to clients, and helped him to manage his money. He recalled later that McCarthy had a poor business head: "He never could save. It went fast or faster than he got it." So that McCarthy would not squander his earnings, Eberlein worked out a special arrangement with him. He paid him half his salary—$100 a month—at the beginning of every month and held the other half to give him in a lump sum of $1,200 at the end of the year.[9]

Politically, the law firm of Eberlein and McCarthy was strangely bipartisan. Early in his career, Eberlein had been friendly with the La Follette Progressives when they were in the Republican party. Later he had been a leader among conservative Wisconsin Republicans, the dominant faction in Shawano County. In 1930, Eberlein contended for the party's nomination for attorney general, and in 1940 he would run for the U.S. Senate. His arrogant and overbearing manner, however, repelled some Republicans and forestalled further success.[10]

"When I move to Shawano," McCarthy told the Waupaca newspaper upon his departure, "I'll have to make a hasty transition from a Young Democrat to a Young Republican." But he was only kidding. He was too independent to allow Eberlein to dictate to him; besides, in 1936, he championed Franklin D. Roosevelt. His roots in Democratic politics were shallow, a matter of ethnic tradition and environment. Democrats predominated among the Irish settlers of rural Outagamie County. Two of McCarthy's uncles—the only two whose politics are known—had been Democrats. McCarthy's father had also been a Democrat, though apparently not an avid one; Stephen McCarthy, oldest of the McCarthy boys, could not recall that his father had ever discussed the subject. At Marquette, Joe McCarthy had remained on the periphery of Democratic politics. He and fellow law students had attended a Young Democrat convention in Milwaukee, but the attractions were a free meal and pretty girls, not politics. His interest in the Democratic party burgeoned in Waupaca and stemmed both from his political ambitions and his admiration for Franklin D. Roosevelt and the New Deal. He particularly supported Roosevelt's work-relief programs.[11]

State Democratic politics, however, never attracted him. The Wisconsin Democratic organization in the 1930s was a German-Irish-Polish marching society, with a Catholic base, led by conservatives awaiting New Deal patronage. In 1932 the combination of La Follette Progressive support, worsening economic conditions, and Roosevelt's landslide victory gave Democrats control of the governorship, the assembly, five congressional seats, and a senatorship. But Wisconsin's Democrats did not thrive on success. In 1934 they lost the governorship, and, thereafter, Wisconsin politics reverted to battles between conservative Republicans and La Follette Progressives. The Progressives had formed a third party in 1934 that attracted mostly liberal and radical voters who supported Roosevelt nationally.[12]

When McCarthy arrived in Shawano, he entered a political situation dominated by Republicans and La Follette Progressives. Democrats lacked leadership, enthusiasm, and any hope of victory. The meager Democratic organization usually labored unsuccessfully even to complete the local ticket. Funds were so scarce that the party could not afford headquarters during campaigns. As the 1936 election approached, however, Roosevelt's leadership and the expected coattails effect sparked a modest revival of enthusiasm and hope. Therefore, in July 1936, McCarthy announced his candidacy for the Democratic nomination for district attorney. He told a friend that he was realistic about his prospects, but, if by chance he won, he hoped to gain valuable trial experience.[13] Since political interest and activity heighten during a presidental election year, McCarthy had an excellent opportunity to fill the leadership vacuum among local Democrats. Besides, he could advertise his name in the community and thereby enhance his law practice. In short, he had nothing to lose.

McCarthy's involvement in Democratic politics in 1936 was extensive and intense. He tested his political savvy and learned valuable, though cynical, political tactics. Shortly after he announced his candidacy, Democrats elected him chairman of the Young Democrats of the Seventh Congressional District, a useful position for anyone interested in running for Congress later. In this role, he helped to organize Young Democrats in Waupaca County and probably in other areas.[14] Because he had lived in Shawano County only six months, however, he had not had time to make the necessary contacts and to promote his own candidacy, and, as a result, he finished a dismal third in the September primary.

He became an effective organizer, probably the best that Shawano Democrats had had in years. His reputation increased to such an extent that the Roosevelt organization appointed him chairman in charge of fund raising in the county. Local Democrats also elected him treasurer of their county organization, and, for a while, he even played a major role in dispensing New Deal patronage. A Shawano County lawyer claimed that McCarthy decided who would receive work-relief jobs from the Works Progress Administration, and that his first question about an applicant was "Is the man a Democrat?"[15]

After the primary, however, McCarthy concentrated primarily on attacking the national Republican ticket and on promoting his own campaign. He repeatedly blasted Republicans for offering no alternative to New Deal programs and for allying with the most callous, reactionary elements in the party. At a Democratic rally in Aniwa on 8 October, McCarthy called Alf Landon "William Randolph Hearst's puppet from Kansas." "Landon admits he doesn't know what's wrong but claims that many mistakes are being made," McCarthy asserted. "Landon wants to give the farmer a little more of everything but doesn't say how he'll do it." Such a position, he concluded, is "hare-brained, illogical, and senseless."[16]

Ironically, that same evening, Eberlein was the featured speaker at a Republican rally in nearby Bonduel, where he criticized the New Deal for discouraging work as an ideal for youth, squandering taxpayers' money, and ruining private enterprise. The firm of Eberlein and McCarthy survived such political division because of Eberlein's tolerance and McCarthy's teasing, and because neither of them mixed politics with law.[17]

McCarthy continued to hammer at Republicans in a series of speeches throughout October—fourteen of them in a two-day period. On 30 October, at a rally attended by 450 people, he reiterated his attack on Landon and warmly endorsed Roosevelt. He sarcastically paraphrased his version of the Republican–Landon platform: "In 1932 we had no idea what should be done—then we were helpless. . . . How we would remedy those mistakes even today, we don't know. All we can promise definitely is that we will tear down the structure which is being built, but what we will give you in its place, we don't know. But vote for us." McCarthy concluded: "Of all the brainless, halfbaked, cockeyed pleas which have ever been made to a voting public, that absolutely tops the pinnacle of them all in asininity." The alternative was Franklin D. Roosevelt, "every drop of whose blood and every faculty of whose mind and body is devoted to that great noble, unselfish task . . . of serving all the American people."[18]

McCarthy organized his own campaign from his law office. For the predominantly agricultural community, his campaign biography stressed that he was just an "ordinary farm boy" proficient at diagnosing and curing poultry diseases. He also campaigned as a man of principle—a person who opposed dishonesty and extravagance in local government. Louis Cattau, the Progressive incumbent, campaigned on his record. The Republican candidate, Ed Aschenbrenner, vigorously worked the theme that Cattau had tolerated vice and gambling in the county, but Cattau successfully fended off the charge.

In August, McCarthy had unveiled a moderate and reasonable platform. Claiming that there was insufficient work in the county for a full-time district attorney, he proposed that the county board change the office to a part-time position. This had been done in other Wisconsin communities, he said, and would save Shawano taxpayers $1,500 a year. He campaigned on this theme until the results of the primary election convinced him he needed a more personal, hard-hitting, and dramatic approach. On primary election day, 17 September 1936, he had finished third behind Cattau, who polled 3,014 votes, and Aschenbrenner, who got 692. McCarthy tallied a mere 577.

McCarthy now researched Cattau's background and, a few weeks before the November election, changed his strategy. In a pamphlet, he accused Cattau of holding a second job even though a 1930 county board ordinance specifically forbade the district attorney to engage in the private practice of law. "The county is now paying the District Attorney $3,000 per year, and approximately another $1,000 per year to his secretary" and fringe benefits, McCarthy said, yet Cattau used his time and the services to draw another $40-a-month from another "association."[19]

The charge stung Cattau, forcing him to respond in a large advertisement in the local newspaper. He accused McCarthy of being an unscrupulous politician who grossly misstated the facts. He identified his other job as secretary to the Shawano County Fair, an association of which he was proud. "Why wasn't Mr. McCarthy fair and state that fact in his pamphlet rather than to insinuate some other connection?" Cattau claimed he worked for the county fair only during his free time, and that the job did not violate the spirit of the county board resolution.[20] McCarthy's charge was devious, exaggerated, and tardy, but Cattau's action had indeed violated the spirit of the ordinance and probably its letter as well. Moreover, McCarthy had done something that Aschenbrenner had been unable to do: force Cattau to the defensive.

By October, McCarthy must have realized that he had no hope for victory. This itself became a useful campaign theme. At a rally at Almon on 14 October, McCarthy emphasized that a "candidate for a county office has a duty to the voters above and beyond selfish promotion of his own candidacy—a duty to help clear away the smoke screen and help every voter to base his vote upon facts and reason rather than unreason and fallacy." If he succeeded in doing this, he said, "the question of whether or not I personally am elected will, in my mind, fade into insignificance." As he took his seat, the crowd responded with a standing ovation.[21]

As expected, McCarthy lost in the general election. Cattau polled 6,175 votes; McCarthy, 3,422; Aschenbrenner, 2,842. Roosevelt swept 71 percent of the two-party presidential vote in the county, and a Republican incumbent retained his seat in the state senate. Otherwise, voters unanimously endorsed the La Follette–Progressive ticket. Roosevelt's coattails pulled Democrats to second-place finishes in many local contests. McCarthy, with 28 percent of the three-party vote, did better in the county than did Democratic candidates for governor (18 percent) and register of deeds (18 percent), but worse than party aspirants for county clerk (35 percent) and assembly (32 percent). Considering his third-place finish in the September primary and his brief residence in the county, McCarthy's showing was respectable.

More important, he had learned a great deal about politics and campaigning. He learned to organize and plan strategy, and he found that a hard-hitting, personal assault hurt an incumbent opponent, suited his political style, and enhanced his campaign more than a moderate, conventional approach to issues. He also gained knowledge of newspaper practices, and how the press could be exploited. They printed his charges verbatim and made no attempt to evaluate them; the only newspaper source for a campaign profile was the candidate himself. McCarthy took advantage of this: when he moved to Shawano, he lied. He enhanced his credentials by telling the newspapers that he had several years' experience with the Milwaukee law firm of Brennan, Lucas, and McDonough.[22]

The campaign also taught him that he could successfully sell his personality and stir audiences with his oratory. McCarthy loaded his speeches with repetitious and extravagant language, but he delivered them with such apparent sincerity and such dynamism that they sparked enthusiastic response. Grover Meisner, the Democratic assembly candidate and the most prominent Shawano Democrat, campaigned alongside McCarthy throughout 1936, and he remembered that McCarthy could "make you believe blackbirds were white." Meisner also remembered him as a "foxy Irishman" with a cynical approach to politics. Early in the campaign, McCarthy asked Meisner to read a speech he had prepared. Meisner read it, and then asked McCarthy if he believed what he had written. "Hell no," McCarthy responded, "I don't believe in all that. But if you want to get anywhere in politics, you've got to feed the public what they want to hear and not what you believe."[23]

Finally, McCarthy learned that he probably could not win an election in Shawano on the Democratic ticket. It took him a while to reach that decision. He dropped out of most party activities after the election, though, in February 1938, he and other Shawano Democrats went to Fond du Lac to hear Sen. Alben Barkley address a fund-raising banquet for Wisconsin Sen. F. Ryan Duffy.[24]

After the election, McCarthy again concentrated on his law practice but only had mixed results. Some lawyers remembered him as honorable and upright; all conceded his workmanlike approach and his aggressive, flamboyant courtroom manner. He tried to impress jurors with his personality and style. For example, most lawyers in Shawano wore suits in the courtroom at all times, but, if the jurors took off their coats on a hot summer day, McCarthy would do the same.[25]

McCarthy never developed a deep understanding of law. Often he was unprepared for a jury case and tried to compensate with style. Eberlein performed the difficult legal research for the firm. McCarthy's only speech on a legal subject in Shawano suited the Lions Club gathering and his own interest in trial law, but was otherwise conventional. (He described various types of legal procedures, identified cases where people had been convicted of crimes but were later proven innocent, and suggested rectifying miscarriages of justice.)[26]

His most publicized case occurred in 1938. Reuben Long had been arrested by a warden for poaching on the nearby Menominee Indian reservation. The Menominee were permitted by federal law to fish and hunt on the reservation in all seasons, but the warden apparently arrested Long because he was only one-quarter Menominee. A county court assigned Long's defense to McCarthy, who dramatically told the local newspaper that he wanted to make the incident a major test case before the Wisconsin Supreme Court to establish once and for all "who is an Indian." Such a determination, he said, would allow wardens to dispose of such cases more efficiently in the future. Nothing further became of the case. Either he lost interest in the subject after the initial publicity or a court quietly dropped it.[27]

McCarthy had a reputation among some lawyers as an ambulance chaser. A lawyer friend of McCarthy claimed that the accusation was made by competing lawyers jealous of McCarthy's properly zealous solicitation of good cases. Substantial evidence, however, suggests that it was more than that. A lawyer in Waupaca described McCarthy as "about the worst ambulance chaser that ever hit the country." In both Waupaca and Shawano, he would hear or read about an accident, rush out to the victim's home or to the hospital, and try to convince him that he should sue and could win a substantial judgment. Such action clearly violated the legal code of ethics and, if exposed (admittedly a rare occurence), could have led to disbarment.[28]

McCarthy spent much of his free time joining organizations and cultivating an astonishingly large number of friends. He was very popular in Shawano. People liked him; he liked people. He had the legendary Irish wit, and he loved to play practical jokes on his friends. As he walked down Main Street, he would shake hands and joke with passersby; he would open business doors to salute the cleaning lady and all the secretaries. As a bachelor he particularly attracted women with his charm, compliments, and rugged appearance. He dated frequently but had no serious relationships.

McCarthy was also generous. He gave topcoats and suits to John Reed, a recent high-school graduate whom he had befriended. ("I was the best dressed man in Shawano," Reed recalled.) On one occasion, the son of a former client asked him for money so that he and his mother could visit a sick relative in Antigo. McCarthy pulled all the money out of his wallet and gave it to the boy on the spot.[29]

For seven dollars a week, McCarthy roomed and boarded at Mrs. Edith Green's home in Shawano. Of Swiss ancestry, Mrs. Green was motherly, much like Mrs. Osterloth in Manawa. Her home became a haven for young professional men, mostly lawyers and teachers. Five men lived there, and three more joined them for Mrs. Green's family-style meals. The men socialized and often played cards. Because of community pressure, the teachers felt uncomfortable drinking in town so McCarthy would join them for convivial evenings in nearby Clintonville.[30]

Of course, not everyone liked Joe McCarthy. He was too aggressive and too opinionated for some. Others resented his sponging of drinks, meals, and money. He made life miserable for one resident at Mrs. Green's—a prim and proper man whom McCarthy teased so relentlessly that he often fled the dinner table. Furthermore, as McCarthy's political ambitions increased, his friendliness became less relaxed and more calculating. His brash and pushy method of making friends and contacts at cocktail parties infuriated his fellow lawyers in Shawano, who never supported him politically. Some called him a "four-flusher." Nevertheless, within an hour of his arrival at a party, he knew everyone's first name, and most thought him a great fellow.[31]

McCarthy gave only a few speeches in the community. Most noteworthy was his address to the Junior Women's Club of Shawano on the subject of Americanization. He traced the rise and decline of civilizations, concluding that Americans should try to dispel the illusion of grandeur because they were not any greater than the people of any other nation. (This somber theme, quite different from McCarthy's subsequent 110 percent Americanism, appears inexplicably open-minded, almost unpatriotic by Shawano standards.)[32]

McCarthy met many people through his participation in community service organizations. Usually he joined organizations in a capacity that permitted him to expand contacts with people. Thus he chaired a committee that sold tickets for the President's Birthday Ball; chaired committees to solicit funds for the Boy Scouts and the Red Cross; and served as secretary-treasurer of the Holy Name Society. For one year, he served as scoutmaster for a troop of forty boys sponsored by the Holy Name Society of Sacred Heart Church.[33]

Early in 1939, McCarthy assembled his friends and acquaintances, made new ones, and, with an army of volunteers, embarked on one of the most vigorous campaigns ever conducted in northeastern Wisconsin.

McCarthy probably would have liked to run for office in the election of November 1938. But to run as a Democrat in Shawano County, he may have sensed, would have resulted in another defeat and a reputation as a two-time loser. Instead he watched quietly from the sidelines as Republicans swept to victory in Wisconsin, in the process permanently disabling the La Follette Progressives. The same result occurred locally. The Democrats in Shawano did not threaten in any races. They held no rallies, raised little money, garnered no publicity, and lacked any semblance of organization. The Democrats did not even bother to put up anyone for precinct committeemen. The Democratic candidate for governor received less than 5 percent of the three-party vote in Shawano, and Meisner, the assembly candidate, finished fourth behind an independent.[34]

The 1938 election confirmed McCarthy's suspicions that the Democratic party offered no hope for his future. He probably still admired Roosevelt, but he had tired of bucking the prevailing Republican tide. Waupaca had been a Republican county with a Republican newspaper. After 1938, Shawano was solidly Republican. One of its two newspapers was nonpartisan, but the editor of the other chaired the local Republican organization. The same situation would prevail in Outagamie County when McCarthy moved there in 1940. Like Eberlein, most of his friends in Shawano were Republicans.

But McCarthy did not change his political affiliation immediately. Such blatant opportunism would have exposed him to ridicule. An attractive alternative arose shortly after the 1938 election. He could run for judge of the Tenth Judicial Circuit, a nonpartisan office. The position paid $8,000 a year, three times his starting salary with Eberlein. Victory would satisfy his ambitions while he gained time to reassess his political affiliation. McCarthy's future in the law firm was uncertain at the time. Eberlein's son was about to graduate from law school and join his father, and McCarthy may have reasoned that his stature in the firm would diminish. The circumstances surrounding an earlier judicial contest in Shawano County may also have inspired him. An old Shawano County judge had been defeated for reelection by a young lawyer in a vigorous campaign in which the young challenger made the incumbent's age the major issue. McCarthy told an acquaintance that he planned to win by using the same strategy. He quietly began to buy campaign literature in early September 1938, announcing his candidacy for judge in late December.[35]

Most accounts of the campaign contend that McCarthy's announcement surprised Eberlein, who had desperately wanted to run himself and had often told McCarthy of his intentions. Outraged and humiliated by his partner's precipitous action, so the story goes, Eberlein had no choice but to bow out of the contest, and soon afterward severed his relations with McCarthy. Only after 1946, when McCarthy promoted Eberlein to fill his vacant seat, did Eberlein forgive him and warmly support him.[36]

This account, usually cited to illustrate McCarthy's ruthlessness, is mostly distorted. True, McCarthy may have grown impatient with Eberlein's political vacillation. Despite his prominence among Wisconsin Republicans, Eberlein had not run for office since 1930. Newspapers speculated that he would run for governor in 1938, especially after Republicans named him to keynote the state GOP convention that year, but he never entered the race. If it is true that McCarthy repeatedly had had to listen to old Eberlein pour out his heart on the subject of his political ambitions, including those for circuit judge, McCarthy may have concluded, with good reason, that Eberlein was irresolute and would once again pass up the opportunity.

Actually, it is unclear whether Eberlein wanted to run, and equally unclear whether McCarthy knew Eberlein's intentions. Eberlein was momentarily peeved that McCarthy had not consulted him about his candidacy; he had learned of it secondhand. He subsequently suggested that McCarthy take a leave of absence and conduct his campaign elsewhere—a suggestion he made not in anger, but because he thought there might be a conflict of interest if McCarthy won. The tension between the two men quickly subsided. Eberlein supplied McCarthy's campaign with office equipment and small amounts of money and regularly called his office to inquire about the progress of "my boy's" campaign.[37]

The Tenth Judicial Circuit was long and narrow, with Shawano County in the middle, Langlade County to the north, and Outagamie County to the south. As the campaign opened, the political prophets expected another triumph for the incumbent, Judge Edgar Werner. Werner had held the position for twenty-four years, easily defeating all challengers. With his name, recognition, and long service, he was expected to draw heavily from all three counties in the district, particularly from Outagamie, his residence and the most populous of the three. Werner gave many speeches during the campaign; his advertisements stressed his honesty, impartiality, and efficiency. A third challenger, A. M. Whiting, a municipal judge and former district attorney from Antigo, campaigned little but advertised his legal knowledge and varied experience extensively. Observers expected him to carry his home county, Langlade, the smallest one in the district. McCarthy might carry Shawano County but was considered too young, inexperienced, and unknown to have much weight elsewhere. His campaign would receive no assistance from newspaper endorsements. The Antigo paper endorsed Whiting, and the *Appleton Post-Crescent* supported Judge Werner.[38]

These cogent predictions proved erroneous. Werner was a decent man who looked like a judge, but his many liabilities made his reelection less certain than it seemed. Werner had won little respect from lawyers in his circuit. He had been reversed by the Wisconsin Supreme Court many times and conducted his work so inefficiently that his court had a huge backlog of cases. His pompous, condescending manner particularly alienated young attorneys. To them, Werner typified older judges who seemed preoccupied with their own convenience and not with the practical needs of lawyers. Werner traveled his circuit infrequently, seriously handicapping lawyers in Langlade and Shawano counties. McCarthy capitalized on these weaknesses, assuring attorneys that he would work hard, consider their problems, and regularly travel the circuit.[39]

Werner spoke frequently to groups in his district, but he chose abstract and boring topics. He addressed the Shawano Women's Club on one of his favorite themes: "Know Thyself." "Life is an unfoldment of power within," he said. "What the individual is or attains depends on what he thinks. . . . The world within is in your power, and the world without is reflected in the world within." The effect was deadening.[40]

Werner looked and acted his sixty-six years. One day during the campaign, as lawyers at the Shawano courthouse mused about McCarthy's liability of youth, an old Swedish janitor overheard them and interjected: "I tell you something. Joe McCarthy, he get older. Judge Werner, he never get any younger." Many others agreed. McCarthy was fortunate that he lived in the Tenth Judicial Circuit. He could not have picked a more vulnerable opponent.[41]

Candidates traditionally did not discuss issues in a judicial campaign of this type. Little was expected of them other than that they promise to enforce the law and uphold justice. All three candidates promised to do that. Had this been the extent of the campaign, Werner probably would have been victorious again. But McCarthy broke with conventions, organized a massive personal campaign, and made age a major issue.

McCarthy moved out of Eberlein's office into a small one on Main Street in Shawano, where he established headquarters for the three-month campaign. He hired Dottie Druckery, who served as his personal secretary and sole paid employee, for the duration of the campaign. When she arrived from Oshkosh in early January 1939 to assume her duties, she was shocked to find a desk, a chair, and no other furniture, not even a typewriter. McCarthy had to borrow a typewriter and other furniture from Eberlein.[42]

McCarthy held no organizational meetings. Instead, he carefully planned campaign strategy himself. He intended to charm the voters with his personality and to remind them of Judge Werner's age. He equipped himself with the necessary campaign tools: a new 1939 Oldsmobile, a portable dictaphone that plugged into the car battery, and thousands of form letters printed by a Green Bay firm to look amazingly like original ones. McCarthy's most famous and effective literature was a postcard with a picture of a little boy holding a baseball glove captioned, "Let's Play Ball." The boy was supposed to attract the voters' attention to the personal message on the other side. (Some voters thought he was McCarthy's son.) He assembled poll lists and telephone directories from all three counties.[43] As well as any man who ever ran for office in Wisconsin, McCarthy understood that political destinies are determined by the numerous and humble as well as by the few and powerful. In this campaign, he would rely on men with sunburned necks who talked politics and sports on small-town golf courses or in Elks clubs, and on women who discussed food prices at the Cash-Way or Super Valu.

How he financed his campaign is not altogether clear. His tax returns suggest that he borrowed money from three banks in Shawano County and from his father and brother William. The First National Bank of Tigerton loaned him the largest amount. (His closest friend in the county was Anthony Swanke, a member of the family that owned the bank and just about every other major business in Tigerton; presumably Swanke helped McCarthy obtain the loan.) In all, McCarthy spent $1,221.58 in the campaign, which about equaled the combined expenditures of Werner and Whiting.[44]

McCarthy's most intimate campaign advisers were professional people: Anthony Swanke, Henry Van Straten (superintendent of schools in Outagamie County), and attorneys Gerald Jolin, James Durfee, Urban Van Susteren, Gerard Van Hoof, and Francis Werner. They armed McCarthy with detailed information about voters in or near their home communities. Jolin scouted in Appleton, Van Hoof and Van Susteren in the Dutch community of Little Chute, Durfee in Antigo, Swanke in Tigerton, and so on. McCarthy recorded their information in a notebook, and early each morning, thoroughly briefed, he set out on the campaign trail with John Reed, his driver.[45]

Anderson and May have vividly described a McCarthy visit with one farmer. "He didn't know me from Adam," the farmer recalled. "But somehow he had learned my name. When I first noticed him, he was outside petting the dog. By the time I got to the front door, he was handing my daughter a lollipop, and then Indian-wrestling with my boy."

The farmer first pegged McCarthy as a salesman, "but when he grabbed my hand and introduced himself, I remember his name from a letter he sent me, saying he wanted to beat old man Werner 'cause the judge was too old for the job." McCarthy seemed more interested in the farmer's livestock, poultry, and crops than the election. "He wanted to know if I'd let him milk a cow; said he wanted to keep his hand in. He milked good." But what really floored the farmer was McCarthy's remark: "Say, Bill, how's that sick mare of yours? Any better?"

The two men went to the barn to examine the animal. "He treated that mare like his own flesh and blood," the farmer recalled. "He acted as if it was the saddest thing in the world that my mare was sick. And he promised he'd do all he could to help." Shortly after the visit, the farmer got a letter from McCarthy outlining all the various ways to cure sick horses and wishing good luck to him, his family, his dog, his crops, and his livestock. "Did I vote for him?" the farmer asked. "Sure I voted for him. Wouldn't you, after that?"

The farmer learned later that McCarthy had stopped at a neighboring farm and inquired how to cure a sick mare and had then passed the information along in his letter. This small deception did not matter; the farmer probably would have voted for him anyway.[46]

Obviously McCarthy did not have time to be this thorough with every family in the district. After a typical visit, he returned to the car and, while Reed drove to the next house, he plugged in the recorder and dictated a personal message. After a day of campaigning, he returned to headquarters and continued dictating into the evening. The next morning he gave the dictaphone cylinders to Miss Druckery, who wrote postcards to all the people he had visited. (This averaged about thirty-five cards a day.) McCarthy insisted that the cards be written neatly and that every one of them contain a slightly different message.[47]

This approach, though brilliantly effective, could still reach only a fraction of the voters. McCarthy organized an army of volunteers to reach the rest. People worked for him because they liked him and thought his ambition laudable. He was a persistent recruiter with an unusual capacity for motivating people. Van Susteren, who was to become McCarthy's closest friend in the Fox River valley, first met McCarthy during the campaign. Jolin introduced him at the Rainbow Gardens in Appleton, where McCarthy was campaigning. "Since he was a friend of Jolin's, I told him I thought I could help him in my hometown [Little Chute]. He said 'Great.' " Van Susteren never gave his offer another thought. Early the next morning, his mother woke him and told him there was some guy named McCarthy at the door. "I hadn't really meant it the night before," Van Susteren later confessed, "but what could I do?" He and McCarthy spent the entire day meeting people in Little Chute.[48]

Besides lawyer friends (and their secretaries), McCarthy recruited his brothers and sisters, sixty or seventy housewives and young women in Shawano, poker friends, and some of the residents of Mrs. Green's boardinghouse. As he campaigned, he dropped off postcards for volunteers to distribute. If the volunteer lacked experience, McCarthy tore off a page from a telephone directory, instructed the recruit to write a personal note to each person on the page, sign Joe McCarthy's name, and mail the cards. Most volunteers wrote hundreds of cards.

McCarthy addressed any group that allowed him to speak: service clubs, Republican and Democratic meetings, informal gatherings in kitchens and parlors. His message was always the same: Judge Werner was seventy-three years old and would be eighty when the new term ended, he had lied about his true age, and he had earned a couple hundred thousand dollars at the expense of the taxpayers.[49]

In newspaper advertisements in late February, McCarthy stated that Werner had denied that he was seventy-three years old. "In fairness to him," McCarthy said, "I want it definitely understood that I take no issue with him as to when he was born. As far as I am concerned, his word is final on this question." But Werner's word was not final, McCarthy's ad continued. "My only reason for calling attention to the number of years . . . was to suggest that after he has served over 35 years in public office . . . at a total income of $170,000 to $200,000 it might be well for him to retire voluntarily." He suggested that in "kindness" and "fairness" to Werner, voters should not burden the judge with another term.[50]

On the Saturday before the election, McCarthy returned to the subject in large newspaper ads. "What about this Age Question?" he asked. He insisted that Werner had pressed the issue. He claimed that, according to various sources, Werner had been born in 1866 (*Martindale Hubbell Law Directory*), in 1870 (a thirty-nine-year-old Shawano newspaper article), and in 1872 (Werner's own statement). "Two of the three claims as to his age must be wrong," McCarthy charged, insinuating that Werner had lied. "If as a candidate [for district attorney] 39 years ago, he gave the correct information to the paper, the claim which he makes today must be false. Certainly, I cannot know which if any of the three claims is correct." In view of Werner's "indecision," McCarthy continued, "his repeated attacks on me for using the best available authority are certainly ill-timed and unfair."[51]

McCarthy won a stunning upset in the April election. He captured 15,164 votes (42.8 percent), followed by Werner's 11,219 (31.7 percent) and Whiting's 9,049 (25.5 percent). The totals confirmed McCarthy's decision to concede the city of Appleton, which he lost to Werner by over 300 votes. Whiting carried Langlade County with a hefty 58.8 percent of the vote, but there McCarthy finished second in twenty-one of twenty-four wards (and first in one ward). McCarthy dominated elsewhere. He won the rest of Outagamie County—the rural areas and small towns—by 1,500 votes. He carried Little Chute with 76 percent and Kimberly with 64 percent. He almost captured a majority in Shawano County (48.3 percent) and did particularly well in the city of Shawano with 58 percent. In general, he did best in areas where his campaign organization was strong and where he was personally known. McCarthy's victory astonished area newspapers. They credited his personal campaigning and clever postcards. A prominent political reporter confused the partisan meaning of his triumph by describing him as a "youthful progressive" whose election delighted the La Follette Progressives.[52]

McCarthy's attack on Werner subsequently became the most controversial aspect of the campaign. He had supported his accusation with some evidence. Werner's income had been approximately as McCarthy had claimed: he had earned about $174,000 during his twenty-four years as judge. Simple calculation makes that a modest income (about $7,250 per year), but this, of course, was not McCarthy's intention. He wanted to leave the impression that Werner had fed at the public trough all those years. A McCarthy biographer assumed that McCarthy's use of the age issued proved that he had matured into an uncommonly bold liar. "After all," wrote Richard Rovere, "Judge Werner's real age was verifiable—a matter of public record." In fact, the record was not so easily verified. Just as he had done in his campaign against Cattau, McCarthy found records that seemed to substantiate his charge. The *Martindale Hubbell Law Directory*, the standard biographical source for lawyers, listed Werner's birth as 1866 in all editions from 1922 to 1939. That would have made Werner, as McCarthy claimed, seventy-three years old in 1939. McCarthy could have simply accepted Werner's claim to be sixty-six, based on the birth certificate that Werner produced during the campaign, but McCarthy was about as interested in absolute truth as a trial lawyer in court is. He vigorously presented his evidence to the voters, slanted it to his advantage, insinuated that the defense had distorted the truth, and won his case. It was not his fault that his opponent put up such a poor defense.[53]

McCarthy had been mischievously successful in leaving the impression that Werner had started the controversy by claiming different birth dates. Actually, Werner probably had no knowledge of the error in the law directory or of the old Shawano newspaper article; certainly he had not wanted to make age an issue. Meanwhile, McCarthy had repeatedly reminded voters that Werner was, indeed, old. Newspapers abdicated their role and thereby assisted McCarthy. They neither reported nor commented on the age controversy that swirled in their own advertising columns, nor informed readers of Werner's correct age.[54]

After the election, Fred F. Wettengel, Judge Werner's friend from Appleton, petitioned the Wisconsin attorney general to prosecute McCarthy for misrepresenting Werner's age and for spending more money than the statutory allowance. Early in 1940, however, the attorney general dismissed the case. Republican Gov. Julius Heil announced: "I have examined the petition and do not find any material allegations."[55]

\*     \*     \*     \*

After winning the election McCarthy practiced law in Shawano for the remainder of the year as he waited to assume his judicial duties in January 1940. So that he would not embarrass himself, judges outside the Tenth District allowed him to gain experience by trying cases in their courts. He decided to maintain official chambers in Outagamie County because most of the cases were tried there and the courthouse had more office space. He moved to Appleton and bought a two-bedroom house. For a while he considered hiring his brother William as court reporter, but he changed his mind, apparently because William lacked education and experience, and hired Pat Howlett, Judge Werner's reporter.[56]

Some attorneys remained skeptical of McCarthy's qualifications but accepted him with sufferance. When he appeared in Shawano for the first time, the local bar association sent him congratulations and flowers. He appeared confident as he set out to conduct an efficient, accommodating, and modernized court. He scheduled cases in Shawano on the first and third Monday mornings of each month; those same afternoons he would spend in Antigo. The remainder of each month he held court at the Appleton courthouse.[57]

When he assumed his duties, the court had a backlog of 250 cases, and McCarthy gained a valuable reputation for efficiency and hard work by disposing of them quickly. In his first forty-four days on the bench, he tried 44 cases. While most judges opened court at 9:00 A.M., McCarthy started his at 8:00 A.M. and sometimes earlier. He worked until noon, returned early in the afternoon, and continued hearing cases until supper. Returning at 7:00 P.M., he frequently charged the jury as late as 9:00 P.M. and sometimes kept court in session past midnight.

His incredible pace worked hardship on all participants. One attorney found himself making a final argument to the jury at 10:30 P.M. When he saw a juror nod and doze, he knew it was time to quit. After one long siege of heavy work, reporter Howlett completed typing notes at 2:00 A.M. and arrived in court the same morning at 8:05 A.M.—five minutes late. As Howlett took his seat, McCarthy turned to the clerk and announced that he had fined his reporter one dollar a minute, the same as he did tardy lawyers. Howlett quit instantly and walked out of the courtroom. When McCarthy came off the bench to talk with him in chambers, Howlett complained of overwork and of being abused. He said he refused to take any more. McCarthy must have realized that he had worked everyone too hard, including himself. He walked back into court, dismissed the jury, and announced he was taking a two-week vacation. Howlett remained on the job.[58]

As a judge, McCarthy was not as competent, wise, and prudent as his supporters and campaign literature later claimed. Nor did he always conduct court in the breezy, injudicious, and unethical manner that his critics contended. He brought many assets to his job and fewer, but more profound, liabilities. Contemporary observers, however, magnified his virtues and overlooked his defects.

McCarthy's strengths on the bench were mostly the strengths of his intellect and personality. He was confident, good-natured, hardworking, and quick. Even lawyers skeptical of much of his judicial conduct conceded his brilliant capacity to rapidly grasp the details of cases and the fundamentals of laws and procedures. In his four years as judge, he had a low percentage of reversals by the Wisconsin Supreme Court, and, with notable exceptions, he tried cases in a reasonable and impartial manner. He treated young first offenders with leniency and sympathy, paternalistically lecturing them and their parents on correct behavior and discipline. Many lawyers liked him because he was modern and accommodating. Other judges used a calendar that often produced a situation where an attorney had no idea when his case would be heard. If his case was fifth on the calendar, for example, he might have to wait two hours, two weeks, or two months. McCarthy, however, established definite trial dates that permitted lawyers to plan their schedules. Older, experienced judges fined lawyers for being late for court. McCarthy showed no timidity on this score because of his youth and inexperience. Nor did he allow examination that was unfair or irrelevant.[59]

On the other hand, McCarthy's understanding of the law remained shallow, and he never had anything profound to say on the subject of law. In difficult, controversial cases, he tried to compensate by requiring attorneys to provide him with briefs at the beginning and end of the trial. Occasionally, he was vindictive and unfair. If he did not like an attorney, a party in a case, or the case itself, he let the jury know in subtle ways—by the tone of his voice, by facial expressions, or by one sharp, crucial question put to a witness that expressed the bench's view.[60]

McCarthy was always prepared to serve as peacemaker, and he often summoned opposing counsel to his chambers and tried to talk them into settling out of court. He was always willing to try anything that expedited the business of the law. Some lawyers, however, felt that, if they did not settle a case in pretrial, McCarthy would make them regret it in the trial. This practice particularly irritated Andrew Parnell, a prominent Appleton trial lawyer. On one occasion, according to Parnell, McCarthy attempted to make both sides settle a case. When Parnell refused and won a jury settlement, McCarthy set the verdict aside in the "interest of justice," a procedure a judge could use without explanation. But Parnell thought that the judge had acted for spite not justice and was punishing him for not settling earlier.[61]

McCarthy differed most distinctly from other judges in the way he handled divorces. Sometimes he handled uncontested divorces in the same manner as other judges and required the same amount of evidence. More often, apparently as a practical way of expediting justice, he cut through legal niceties and granted them in five minutes. Normally, in divorce proceedings, the court required the lawyer for the plaintiff to prove the allegations in the examination. Then, to fulfill a legal requirement, a resident witness was called to attest that the petitioner had lived in the county the requisite length of time. McCarthy bypassed part of this procedure. He did not require proof; he merely asked if the allegations were true. If the answer was yes, he called the resident witness and granted the divorce. Sometimes he carried his shortcuts to ludicrous extremes. According to most accounts, he tried one divorce case without a clerk present and granted another while walking up the courthouse steps. He granted hundreds of quick divorces, but, even though people joked about his procedures, he never provoked public criticism until 1946 when he granted quick, uncontested divorces to political supporters.[62]

Unlike most judges, McCarthy socialized with lawyers practicing in his court. He golfed, lunched, vacationed, and played cards with them. They liked this easygoing, affable judge. He also joked with jurors, addressed many by their first name, and, if he knew one particularly well, introduced the juror to the rest of the court. (Most of his joking was harmless enough, but occasionally he embarrassed a court participant. For example, after long hours of testimony, McCarthy would declare a recess with the remark that "Curly down there gets tired." The jury would then laugh at bald Pat Howlett.) McCarthy also told yarns to impress the jury. One day he told them he had acquired his marvelous suntan the past weekend when he flew his own airplane to Florida. (Actually, he had spent the weekend under a sunlamp at home.) Women particularly enjoyed the judge's style. Young women who worked at the courthouse sometimes took their coffee breaks in McCarthy's courtroom, especially during divorce proceedings, because he was likely to be so colorful.[63]

In addition to his informal courtroom manner, McCarthy's political ambitions distinguished him from other judges. In the summer of 1941, McCarthy announced to John Wyngaard, a political columnist from Madison, and to his friends Durfee and Van Susteren, that he intended to run for the U.S. Senate. To accomplish this goal, he needed exposure throughout Wisconsin. His quick disposal of cases in his own district enabled him to try cases elsewhere. At that time, there was no court administrator to assign cases to outside judges. If a judge wanted extra work, he could request to hear cases in other jurisdictions. McCarthy requested to hear cases all over the state, making sure that his presence was well publicized.

Occasionally, he went to extreme measures to keep an out-of-town commitment. Once, he finished trying a case in Antigo at 1:00 A.M. and announced to Howlett that they would drive through eight inches of snow to Racine for a case early the same morning. Howlett refused to go, but McCarthy made the three-hundred-mile drive through a raging blizzard, borrowed a reporter, and began trying cases next morning. McCarthy sought to make friends wherever he traveled. On trips to other circuits, he made a point of looking up lawyers, judges, and newsmen. If he went to a northern Wisconsin cottage for a week, he always made certain everyone knew him. He realized that every new acquaintance he charmed would be an asset for the future.[64]

Typically, the case that most clearly exposed McCarthy's judicial weaknesses also promoted his political career. The history of the Quaker Dairy case has been reviewed many times, with the emphasis on McCarthy's destruction of part of the court transcript and the resulting censure of his action by the Wisconsin Supreme Court. What has been overlooked are the circumstances surrounding the case, the reasons for McCarthy's behavior, and the insight the incident gives into McCarthy's judicial and political temperament.

Quaker Dairy was a milk distributorship founded in Outagamie County in 1938. Its president, Ben Cherkasky, hoped to undercut competition by cutting milk prices through a cash-and-carry method of distribution rather than the more prevalent credit-and-delivery system. Some consumers had publicly supported his price-cutting practices. Nonetheless, his company came under investigation by the Wisconsin Department of Agriculture and was charged under the Milk Control Act, a state marketing law, with controlling milk prices. (The law had been born out of the pressure of economic disaster in the depression; the legislature hoped it would end cutthroat competition, bankruptcy for milk distributors, and absurdly low prices for producers.) When state investigators uncovered a pattern of violations at the Quaker Dairy, departmental lawyers filed suit in McCarthy's court in November 1940, requesting an injunction to make the company obey the law.[65]

McCarthy's first reaction was moderate and responsible. He delayed issuing an injunction, pending an early trial. His action inadvertently assisted Cherkasky, who at that point had no adequate defense. On 9 April 1941, McCarthy set trial for mid-April. On the same day, after learning of McCarthy's action, Cherkasky used a devious legal maneuver to delay proceedings further. Dispensing with the services of his Green Bay attorney, he retained Mark Catlin, Jr., a Republican assemblyman from Appleton. Under an obscure Wisconsin statute, a lawyer-legislator could ask for postponement of a trial until the current session of the legislature ended. Catlin immediately claimed that prerogative, for of course Cherkasky had retained him precisely for that reason. McCarthy had no alternative and postponed the trial indefinitely.[66]

McCarthy, burdened with many cases, had paid little attention to this one. He even misplaced important records of the case in his pile of mail. But the Wisconsin Department of Agriculture persisted. Led by Gilbert Lappley, the competent and determined counsel for the department's Milk Control Division, the department pestered McCarthy (and even helped him find the misplaced records) until, on 20 May, the judge issued a temporary injunction preventing Quaker Dairy from violating the law.

A few days later, Cherkasky went to the judge's chambers and pleaded with McCarthy to suspend the ruling. He apparently argued that he had invested much money in his business, had established his market of supplies, and had developed a large clientele. The injunction threatened to ruin his business. McCarthy listened sympathetically, and Cherkasky apparently convinced him that the law was ridiculous. On 25 May, without advising Lappley, McCarthy reversed his ruling and suspended the injunction.

A week later he went further. After Cherkasky swore that the law hurt his business and told McCarthy that he had been "reliably informed" that the legislature was about to annul or repeal the milk-marketing law, McCarthy ordered the Department of Agriculture to show cause before him on 7 June 1941 why the temporary injunction should not be stayed "pending the outcome of proposed legislation" in the legislature. Meanwhile, on 6 June, the legislature adjourned, and Catlin bowed out as attorney in favor of the original Green Bay firm, assisted now by Parnell. [67]

McCarthy's actions at the 7 June hearing nearly ruined his budding political career. As the proceedings opened, defense attorney Parnell correctly noted that the legislature had adjourned without extending the milk law beyond 1941. Therefore, he argued, the injunction should not be continued, because the defendant's actions would be legal after 31 December 1941. In the meantime, an injunction would ruin the company. Lappley attacked this contention. He pointed out that the law was still on the books. He probably argued further that the future expiration of the law did not exonerate Quaker Dairy for past violations.

But McCarthy agreed completely with Parnell, and Lappley, frustrated and adamant, requested an early trial in order to appeal the judge's ruling. Thus confronted, McCarthy subjected all the participants to a rambling discourse about his thoughts on the Quaker Dairy case. He first complimented Lappley for his diligence in pressing the state's case; indeed, he apparently agreed that the Wisconsin Department of Agriculture, as a matter of strict law, was entitled to judgments. Nevertheless, McCarthy continued, since the law was about to expire, a trial would be (as Lappley recalled his words) "a waste of the court's time." McCarthy therefore denied relief to the state and directed that the complaint against Quaker Dairy be dismissed. Finally, as if to show his impartiality, McCarthy castigated Cherkasky for his "deliberate and reprehensible" action in hiring Catlin for the sole purpose of delaying a hearing in McCarthy's court.

Shortly after concluding this lecture, McCarthy walked over to his court reporter, Howlett, and ordered him to "tear out the remarks." Howlett refused. "There's the book," he said. "You tear it out if you want to." McCarthy picked up Howlett's book and tore out one sheet. Howlett was astounded: he had never seen a judge destroy a reporter's stenographic record. [68]

Three days after the hearing, undaunted by McCarthy's ruling and discourse, Lappley petitioned the Wisconsin Supreme Court for a writ of mandamus, an extraordinary legal remedy to compel an inferior court to perform its legal duty. Lappley reviewed the history of the case and told the high court that he had no other recourse because McCarthy's action was "not a matter of judicial error" but a "direct refusal to uphold and support the laws of Wisconsin." [69]

The next few days were the nadir of McCarthy's judicial career. The Wisconsin Supreme Court responded immediately to Lappley's complaint and heard his petition on 14 June. Meanwhile, it issued a writ of certiorari to the clerk of the circuit court, requiring him to return all records of the case to the supreme court. When the records arrived, minus the missing page, the supreme court demanded an explanation. In a sworn affidavit, McCarthy answered evasively that he had destroyed the notes because he deemed their contents "improper and immaterial." The missing record merely complimented Lappley, he said, and did not represent his views of "the right of the plaintiff to an immediate trial." He refused to admit that he had said that a trial would be a waste of time, nor did he mention his criticism of Cherkasky and Catlin.

The supreme court's deadline of 14 June forced McCarthy to prepare a hasty defense that, considering his untenable position, was necessarily unsubstantial. He accepted most of Lappley's contentions but offered three corrections. He had used his discretion to set aside the injunction, he said, solely because it would "work an irreparable hardship" on the defendants. Lappley had made no written request for an immediate trial, McCarthy argued, and because the court's calendar was so crowded, he could not schedule one until fall. Finally, he reiterated his sworn statement that the missing court record was merely intended as general remarks praising Lappley and questioning the wisdom of holding a trial in view of the fact that the law was to expire.[70]

On 18 June 1941, speaking for the Wisconsin Supreme Court, Justice Marvin Rosenberry brushed aside McCarthy's defense and subjected him to a scathing rebuke. The justice first singled out Cherkasky and Catlin for their "devious" and "most unusual" procedure in delaying court proceedings. Then, turning to the judge's action, Rosenberry said that McCarthy should not have suspended the operation of the law solely because it would work a hardship if enforced. By doing so, McCarthy had assumed a legislative function. He should not have based his decision on discretion but on "justice according to law." To do otherwise would result in advantage to people who disobey the law and disadvantage to those who obey it. McCarthy's action constituted an "abuse of judicial power."

Nor did Justice Rosenberry accept McCarthy's excuse for destroying the stenographic transcript. This was "highly improper." Records indicate that McCarthy's remarks did indeed bear on the only debatable issue in the case, namely, McCarthy's reasons for not holding a trial. Under the circumstances, said Rosenberry, destruction of evidence "could only be open to the inference that the evidence destroyed contained statements of fact contrary to the position taken by the person destroying the evidence." Rosenberry ordered the writ of mandamus and required McCarthy to reinstate the injunction and to hear the case again.[71]

The court's ruling momentarily stunned McCarthy. Rosenberry telephoned his order on 18 June, and, without waiting for the writ to be formally served, McCarthy complied immediately, reinstating the 20 May injunction and scheduling a new hearing for 25 June.[72]

Newspapers throughout Wisconsin reported the supreme court's action but paid only passing notice to the court's criticism of McCarthy. Most news accounts focused on the court's strong criticism of Catlin, who was then the most prominent person associated with the case. Lappley and other Department of Agriculture lawyers considered asking for a change of venue because they feared the high court's sharp criticism would bias McCarthy against them. (Subsequent events wholly justified those fears.) But Ralph Ammon, director of the Department of Agriculture, opposed the idea. He told his lawyers to proceed in McCarthy's court and not to presume prejudice.[73]

Meanwhile, McCarthy, seething with anger, vented his feelings on Lappley. At the hearing on 25 June, both sides presented oral arguments. McCarthy then requested written briefs within ten days, promising a decision on 8 July. At the close of formal proceedings, however, he subjected Lappley to a vigorous tongue-lashing. He blamed him for dragging Catlin's name into the Wisconsin Supreme Court proceedings and promised to prepare a record to be sent to that court correcting any mistaken impressions. (He never followed through on this promise.) He allowed Parnell to dictate a lengthy statement into the record. Then, as Lappley recalled the scene a few months later, "I was asked for a statement but upon commencing to set forth my position was limited to a categorical answer of 'yes' or 'no' as to whether the statements of judge and counsel were true."[74]

In preparing for McCarthy's decision, Parnell wrote a forceful, imaginative brief containing the new argument that the Department of Agriculture had the power only to regulate milk in order to eliminate unfair methods of competition or unfair trade practices. It had no "arbitrary or unlimited power to fix prices." Quaker Dairy, Parnell argued, simply had a different method of distribution that eliminated delivery and credit costs, which was not illegal.

Lappley was pressed to meet the ten-day deadline. He prepared a lengthy brief that attempted to establish the department's authority, but his argument lacked focus, structure, and a cogent conclusion. Just before McCarthy's decision, Lappley replied more effectively to Parnell's brief, arguing that cash-and-carry was legal, but that the real issue was the selling price of milk, which should be the same for all producers, regardless of their system of distribution. The facts, he said, established that Quaker Dairy had a price differential that was not warranted.[75]

Lappley probably wasted his time preparing both briefs. McCarthy had already made up his mind and did not seriously consider Lappley's arguments. On 8 July, he agreed completely with Parnell, saying the Wisconsin Department of Agriculture had failed to prove that the cash-and-carry method of distribution was unfair competition and an unfair trade practice.

Then, in a flight into fantasy, McCarthy expounded at length beyond "any technical rules of law." He assumed the mantle of champion of the poor consumer against the insensitive, oppressive, and bureaucratic Department of Agriculture. By the "rules of common sense," McCarthy argued, it "is ridiculous in the extreme" that the department should "dictate" to those in the "lower income brackets" that they must pay "for a delivery service which they don't want, a service which they don't need, and service which they can ill-afford." The department favored milk dealers and the credit delivery service; consequently, the poor suffered. The court was obligated, he said, to "carefully and jealously guard the rights of the unrepresented and inarticulate." The Milk Control Act had been prompted by the emergency of economic imbalance and unemployment, McCarthy argued, but that emergency was now over. Employment and wages were at a high point, and there was a milk shortage. Yet the department "arbitrarily refused to even consider whether or not the emergency has ended." The department's milk order was "invalid . . . arbitrary, unreasonable, and capricious." He thereupon dismissed the complaint and set aside the injunction.[76]

Most of McCarthy's decision was based on no evidence whatsoever; it sprang from his vivid imagination. The defense had introduced no evidence that only the poor bought at the Quaker Dairy, nor that the Department of Agriculture favored milk dealers and the credit-delivery service. The record was barren of any evidence that the department failed to consider the "rights of the unrepresented and inarticulate groups."[77]

Nevertheless, McCarthy's decision was a publicity triumph, the most favorable he achieved as a judge. He probably notified the local newspaper and the wire service himself. The *Appleton Post-Crescent* carried his decision on its front page, including his ringing defense of poor consumers, the unrepresented, and the inarticulate. Wyngaard, the widely syndicated state columnist, praised McCarthy's decision. He agreed that the depression was over and that price restrictions were inconsistent and no longer necessary. McCarthy's decision had been "effective and significant" and struck the department in a "vulnerable spot." Two days after the decision, Cherkasky advertised that housewives could save money on milk at his store because the "court had declared the milk order invalid."[78]

The Department of Agriculture did not appeal McCarthy's ruling. The milk industry, both producers and dealers, petitioned for a hearing to remove the milk order, arguing that uncontrolled competition was better than their taking a loss by being the only ones submitting to control. The director apparently had a choice between appealing to the Wisconsin Supreme Court while the milk industry was slowly crushed, or allowing producers and dealers to use their own economic weapons in their struggle for self-preservation. With enforcement thwarted, Ammon chose to withdraw the order. On 12 July, when the department suspended enforcement of the milk order in the Appleton area, the local press credited McCarthy's decision.[79]

McCarthy had acted responsibly in the early months of the case. He followed correct procedure, showed no bias, and tried to conduct the case efficiently. The turning point occurred when Cherkasky successfully played on his sympathies and convinced him that the law was absurd. When Lappley persisted, McCarthy lost his judicial sense, and the high court censured him. Thereafter, McCarthy's political instincts predominated, and he won a stunning triumph—stunning not only for the favorable press coverage, but because he successfully placed the Department of Agriculture in a defensive position. Lappley later noted that McCarthy's ruling fortified the prevailing view that the department was capricious, favorable to producers and manufacturers, and unfriendly to consumers.[80]

Why McCarthy destroyed the transcript on 7 June remains a mystery. Obviously he had said something he regretted and, acting impulsively, had obliterated the record. The remark could not have been his innocuous compliment of Lappley; more likely, as critics have long assumed, he regretted saying that a trial was a "waste of the court's time." Another possibility was his implicit criticism of Catlin for conspiring to delay his court. By 1941 McCarthy had probably decided to run for office on the Republican ticket. Catlin was the most powerful Republican in the Fox River valley and one of the most powerful in the state; he had served as party floor leader during the 1941 session of the legislature. Tough, irascible, and intensely partisan, Catlin already disliked McCarthy for having misrepresented Werner's age in the 1939 election. (Catlin and his father had supported Werner.) McCarthy may have sensed that alienating Catlin would hurt his own future in the Republican party. That he never mentioned his criticism of Catlin to the supreme court and subsequently admonished Lappley for doing so adds credence to this possibility.[81]

The case had tragic effects on Lappley. A less sensitive lawyer would have forgotten the case, but Lappley was distressed. In October 1941, with the Department of Agriculture under a barrage of criticism, he defended his position to superiors and speculated that McCarthy's decision was an "attempt to build up a record that might be of some help in the not too distant future." He began to brood. According to one source, he even took his savings out of the bank to buy radio time to tell his side of the story. Finally, he was fired.[82]

The Quaker Dairy case ended much more favorably for McCarthy, who had snatched a triumph of publicity from the jaws of a judicial defeat. His censure by the Wisconsin Supreme Court, far from being a personal disaster or blot on his record, became part of the legend that McCarthy was an extraordinary judge who was compassionate as well as wise. To be sure, he was fortunate that the high court's rebuke received so little coverage in the press at the time. Had Lappley succeeded in persuading the public to listen to him, had the wire services publicized McCarthy's censure, and had the progressive supporters of Sen. Robert M. La Follette, Jr., but known of it, McCarthy could not successfully have portrayed himself as an able and prudent jurist. As it turned out, by the time Wisconsin's liberal press first publicized the Quaker Dairy case and the high court censure—in the autumn of 1946—McCarthy had already defeated La Follette for the Republican senatorial nomination by some five thousand votes.

# Chapter 3

# The Birth of "Tail-Gunner Joe"

Shortly after becoming judge, McCarthy began thinking of running for the U.S. Senate, and he told friends of his plans in 1941. Most of them had been too impressed with his 1939 judicial campaign not to take him seriously. John Wyngaard suggested that McCarthy run for governor instead, but the idea did not interest him. Perhaps the esteem in which Wisconsinites had held Fighting Bob La Follette impressed McCarthy as a youth and riveted his attention on national politics. Whatever the case, he decided to seek office as a Republican. Republicans were the winning party in Wisconsin, and McCarthy wanted to win.[1]

In 1941, Republicans occupied all the state constitutional offices and one U.S. Senate position. Six of Wisconsin's ten congressmen were also Republicans. McCarthy's assemblyman, state senator, and congressman were all Republicans. The same was true of the county offices where he worked at the Outagamie courthouse. All the major newspapers of the Fox River valley, and most in the state, promoted Republican candidates. In conversations with friends, McCarthy never pretended that his switch to the Republican party was anything but opportunism. He merely laughed when they kidded him.

McCarthy's inflated ambition did not match his political base. In 1941 he could depend on strong support from the three counties that had elected him judge and where people regarded him as a folk hero. He also had made some contacts by trying cases all over the state. In Milwaukee, where he had often accepted extra work and where college friends resided, he had enough support to establish an organization. Most valuable were his contacts among newsmen. By upsetting Judge Werner, he had won the respect of John Reidl, managing editor of the *Appleton Post-Crescent,* a deeply religious Catholic and "Mr. Republican" in Outagamie County. Reidl advised McCarthy and probably reinforced his intention to seek office on the Republican ticket. McCarthy had also befriended Wyngaard, whose column reached a statewide audience. McCarthy had met another journalist, Rex Karney, when they both lived in Shawano. After Karney took over political reporting for the Madison *Wisconsin State Journal,* he vigorously promoted McCarthy's 1944 and 1946 campaigns in Wisconsin's capital city, where McCarthy badly needed assistance. All three newsmen enjoyed McCarthy's warm personality and his Horatio Alger background, driving ambition, and dynamic campaign style.

Overall, McCarthy's political strengths were not substantial. He lacked funds to conduct an expensive statewide campaign. His public image outside his district was colorless; most people in Wisconsin had never heard of him. The nonpartisan nature of his job restricted opportunities to speak out on partisan issues and to win acceptance by the Republican party, although later he overcame this handicap. Some of his political supporters were Democrats. For example, Gerald Jolin, McCarthy's principal adviser in the early 1940s, had run for the Appleton assembly seat in 1938 as a Democrat. He lost badly to Mark Catlin, Jr., but continued his Democratic involvement as a member of the central committee of the state Democratic party. McCarthy's relationship with Jolin and other Democrats, combined with his candidacy as a Democrat in 1936, in fact led state Republican leaders to wonder if he was still a New Dealer at heart.[2] But Joe McCarthy, the canny poker player, was used to bucking long odds. America had gone to war in the winter of 1941–1942, and new vistas were opening up for ambitious young men.

After Pearl Harbor, McCarthy contemplated entering military service, though he had no clear idea of what to do. He did not have to join because he was exempt as a judge. Naive at first about the advantages of enlisting, he worried that it might even hurt him politically. Perhaps he feared he would be required to resign his judicial position and return from the war with no job and no political base. The chorus of praise that greeted the enlistment of fellow politician, Carl F. Zeidler, convinced McCarthy to consider the possibility more thoroughly. Zeidler had recently won a stunning upset over incumbent Daniel Hoan for mayor of Milwaukee. Tall, blond, and magnetic, Zeidler spoke for Wisconsin's large German population, and crowds loved him. In the initial burst of patriotic fervor after Pearl Harbor, Zeidler enlisted in the navy. To McCarthy's chagrin, Wisconsin newspapers prominently pictured the handsome ensign in his navy uniform. He may have discerned in Zeidler a potential Republican rival, but, more likely, he simply envied the mayor's acclaim. (Carl Zeidler would be killed in the war; his brother Frank later became mayor of Milwaukee.)

McCarthy had no understanding of the legendary exploits of the marines, and he initially planned to join the army. Urban Van Susteren ridiculed his naiveté. "If you want to be a politician," Van Susteren advised him, "be a hero—join the marines." McCarthy quickly accepted the advice. Meanwhile, the board of state circuit judges agreed to grant him a leave of absence and decided not to seek a replacement. McCarthy arranged for Judges Arold Murphy, Henry Hughes, and Gerald Boileau to take over his duties.[3]

On 2 June 1942, McCarthy wrote Maj. Saxon Holt, marine recruiting officer in Milwaukee, setting forth his qualifications for a commission in the Marine Corps. The next day, he met with Holt in Milwaukee and announced his intentions to newsmen. With a sure sense for the vote-getting comment, McCarthy told them he had offered to enlist "as a private, an officer or anything else. . . . I want to join for the duration." He was "more interested in a gun than a commission." He knew that he could expect to be commissioned, but he convinced Major Holt that he would, indeed, be willing to serve as a private. "Sure, here was a fellow who was ready to give up $8,000 a year to work for us at $21 a month," Holt told the *Milwaukee Journal*. "But the Marine Corps puts a man where it figures he'll do the best job. I've sent his case to Washington. They'll decide whether he should be a private or not." The Marine Corps presently granted McCarthy a commission.[4]

All this brought McCarthy much praise. Although he was thirty-three and automatically deferred, he had enlisted voluntarily in the toughest branch of the armed forces. The *Post-Crescent* told readers that McCarthy had enlisted as a buck private with no promise of a commission or special favors. His action "breathes the spirit that founded America, developed its rugged slopes, harnessed its ceaseless energies and is not only willing but anxious to protect it."

McCarthy's decision worked some hardship on other circuit judges, but probably not as much as is usually assumed. In early July 1942, Murphy, chairman of the board of circuit judges, urged him to reconsider, arguing that his value as a judge far exceeded his value as a marine, but McCarthy rejected his plea. The war reduced activity in McCarthy's court. With so many men in service and with heavy rationing restricting automobile travel, fewer traffic accidents occurred, and the court's workload decreased.[5] Because of cases pending in his court, McCarthy asked that his induction be delayed until he dispensed with the work. On 10 July, he indicated his readiness; on 29 July, the marines commissioned him a first lieutenant. He took his oath on 4 August 1942.

He served in the marines for thirty months. He first reported to Quantico, Virginia, for basic training with eighteen- and nineteen-year-old enlistees. "They keep us busy as the devil," he wrote his former secretary, "but I like it a lot." He took further training at stations in Pennsylvania, North Carolina, and California until April 1943, when he embarked for Hawaii with the Fourth Marine Air Base Defense Wing. From then until he left the marines at the height of the Pacific war, he served on Pacific islands, though always after they had been taken from the Japanese. He quickly adopted the vengeful attitude toward the enemy that was common in the Pacific. Informing a friend of Japanese propaganda claims that the United States had been attacking Japanese hospital ships, he wrote: "Hope to hell we sink them all." He went on to say that the Japanese medical corps had strict orders not to treat enemy prisoners but to kill them immediately: "I can't see why we should spare their medical or hospital ships."[6]

McCarthy's official job, which never changed, was at a desk as an intelligence officer. Each day, he would interrogate pilots on their return from scouting and bombing missions, evaluate the success of their missions, and correlate the information with plans for future air strikes. He also went out of his way to get duty as a defense counsel in court-martial cases. He was good company, and his poker playing, jaunty self-confidence, and resourcefulness as a scrounger of food and beer made him popular with fellow soldiers. Officially, he was rated good to excellent as an officer, and, although he never earned the top rating of outstanding, he performed his duties efficiently and responsibly. The Marine Corps promoted him to captain.

McCarthy's record glowed with praise from superior officers. The tributes served as part of the basis for McCarthy's later claim to have been a tail gunner who had flown many combat missions and had been injured in the line of duty. His most prestigious award came in the form of a citation from Adm. Chester Nimitz, who praised him for "meritorious and efficient performance of duty as an observer and rear gunner of a dive bomber." Nimitz also noted McCarthy's combat missions and "severe leg injury." Maj. Gen. H. R. Harmon, army commander in the Solomons, and Maj. Gen. Field Harris, another of McCarthy's commanders, added their praise. Harris assured McCarthy that the "Marine Corps will not forget the fine contribution you have made."[7]

The basis for the Nimitz citation and the other testimonials was a pivotal letter of recommendation of 19 February 1944, which bore what purported to be the signature of Maj. Glenn A. Todd, then McCarthy's commanding officer. The letter praised McCarthy's "outstanding devotion to duty and achievement." It described McCarthy's efforts to improve dive-bombing efficiency and emphasized his success as personal adviser to squadron personnel, a role that greatly contributed to the "high morale of the squadron." He had arranged for practice operations against U.S. anti-aircraft units and then viewed the operations from the gun emplacements and from the rear of an aircraft. "Upon suggestion of the commanding officer," the letter said, McCarthy had "checked out" as a rear-seat gunner. "On 22 June 1943 Captain McCarthy suffered a broken and burned foot and leg," but he refused hospitalization and "continued doing an excellent job as intelligence officer, working on crutches." Although he was not a combat officer, the letter continued, McCarthy acted as a rear-seat gunner in a dive bomber, "performing the duties of an aerial photographer and observer." (Historian Thomas C. Reeves has shown that Major Todd neither wrote nor signed this letter. McCarthy apparently wrote it himself, forged Todd's signature, and sent it through channels to Admiral Nimitz, who routinely signed thousands of such documents.)[8]

Intelligence work definitely did not satisfy McCarthy's search for adventure and glory. He itched to fly in combat with his fingers on the machine guns. Intelligence officers sometimes volunteered to go on bombing missions in order to check the accuracy of reports and to familiarize themselves with actual conditions. McCarthy volunteered to fly as gunner in an

SBD dive bomber. One of his pilots subsequently recalled that "the judge sure loved to shoot those guns; he was really eager in that rear seat." He strafed areas after the bombs had been released and shot at some specific targets such as supply and fuel dumps, barges, and bridges. At Bougainville he and a pilot badly damaged a Japanese truck convoy, and on several occasions the plane in which he was flying was under fire. Officially he never served as a tail gunner; on dangerous missions, such as that over the Japanese stronghold of Rabaul, pilots did not want an intelligence officer sitting behind them. Nonetheless, McCarthy, distorting his record for political purposes, would later falsely claim that he had flown fourteen, seventeen, thirty, or thirty-two combat missions. Major Todd would later certify that McCarthy took part in eleven strike/flights.[9]

McCarthy was injured in the war, but, again, he and partisan journalists distorted the nature of his injury. His critics have always insisted that McCarthy's only war injury occurred in an accident aboard the seaplane tender *Chandeleur*. The forged Todd letter, establishing 22 June 1943 as the date of McCarthy's injury, led newsmen in the early 1950s to marine records and eyewitness accounts that placed McCarthy aboard the seaplane tender *Chandeleur* on that day. The ship was used as a troop transport carrying McCarthy's squadron and another toward the Pacific war area. When the ship crossed the equator, in keeping with naval tradition, neophyte seamen who were crossing the line for the first time were hazed by the ship's veterans. Since rank meant nothing, McCarthy joined in the horseplay. Barefoot, with a bucket attached to his leg, he was climbing down a ladder when he slipped, fell backward, and broke a bone in his left leg. Doctors put the foot in a cast, but he refused to stay in sick bay and hobbled around on crutches. Fellow officers kidded him about his "wound," and McCarthy joked about it himself. Yet the injury embarrassed him considerably, and he begged others never to reveal how he sustained it. Later, when the cast was about to be removed, a corpsman used acid rather than vinegar to soften the plaster of Paris before cutting it, causing a chemical burn on McCarthy's leg that left a fairly large scar.[10]

After the war, McCarthy never stated categorically that he had been wounded, but pro-McCarthy newspapers often left the impression that he had. After 1951, critical accounts of the *Chandeleur* accident forced him to defend himself. He admitted hurting his foot in the hazing ceremony, but he described it as a minor injury and denied that it had anything to do with a bucket or a ladder. He claimed that he had injured himself on two other occasions. A minor injury occurred when a plane broke loose on an aircraft carrier and cracked open his nose. (He had in fact traveled aboard an aircraft carrier and may have hurt himself in the manner he described.) He consistently asserted after 1951 that he received his only serious injury when a plane "ground-looped" after coming back from a scouting mission, and he "smashed" his foot and "broke" his ankle. "I always made it clear that it was no combat wound," he said. This account was apparently a lie. The only casualty sustained by McCarthy's squadron in over eight thousand hours of flying occurred in the fall of 1943 when a plane did ground-loop, and the pilot broke his arm. But McCarthy was not the pilot; he was not even aboard the plane.[11]

Usually, McCarthy talked of his war injury with reluctance, probably because he wanted to hide the truth. He limped noticeably on the campaign trail in 1944, as could be expected, since the war had inflicted the third major injury to his legs. When he campaigned at the Badger Village at the University of Wisconsin, and a member of the audience asked him why he wore built-up shoes, McCarthy allegedly shot back: "Because I've got 10 pounds of shrapnel in my leg." His remark was not an example of his propensity to distort and dramatize the nature of his war injury; it was simply one of his quick, flippant answers designed to put off questioners. He responded similarly at an appearance in Shawano in 1944. When someone asked him how he was wounded, he responded: "Helping a pregnant woman off a submarine." Everyone laughed, and he had again ended the line of questioning.[12]

The most important fact of McCarthy's military career was the extraordinary amount of publicity he received. In late 1943 and early 1944, he was the hero of a steady flow of local-boy-makes-good stories that found their way into Wisconsin newspapers. He garnered the publicity partly because he was an elected official and partly because he cultivated excellent rapport with public-relations officers in the Pacific. He had pictures taken of himself in various poses: in a dive bomber; wearing a flying helmet; and festooned with web belts, pistols, and knives. The pictures were later displayed in his campaign literature.

The first news story dealing with McCarthy's service was an Associated Press account of July 1943 that said that he had suffered injuries to his leg and face "in the line of duty" and would remain in the hospital for eight weeks. (This report probably referred to the injury aboard the *Chandeleur.*) The next story was the most bizarre. In the fall of 1943, it said, McCarthy and friends decided to search out the king of a tropical island. They found the king, but, because of the language barrier, the group had to communicate in pantomime. The visit consisted of "smiles and silence" until the king passed out cigars and McCarthy and his friends departed.[13]

On 14 November 1943, the *Appleton Post-Crescent* featured McCarthy holding court as an intelligence officer. Bare-chested in a dilapidated shack, the story said, McCarthy quizzed returning pilots: "All right, what kind of hell did you give the Japs today?" He had seen "plenty of action," had "qualified" as a rear gunner and radio man, and had flown with "dive bombers until an order grounded him." The order did not stop his search for action, however, for he had also finagled trips on a submarine and a PT boat.[14]

The next story probably won McCarthy thousands of future votes. Joe was on Munda Island and his squadron was performing dull duty, bombing runways on old airfields to make sure the Japanese did not return. Bored fliers decided to see how many flights they could make in one day, and he joined the fun and rode as a tail gunner. Lt. Penn Kimball, a public-relations officer, wrote the standard form story about the group's "record breaking day of bombing," filling in the names of the men who took part and sending it to their hometown newspapers. Splashed under photographs of a smiling Judge McCarthy, looking rakish in a Devil Dog helmet and flying gear, the story appeared in Wisconsin newspapers in late January 1944. Kimball made the flights as dramatic as possible. Chauffeured by three different pilots, the article said, McCarthy "shed his judicial restraint to strafe Jap ground positions with 4,700 rounds of ammunition after the planes . . . had dive bombed an enemy anti-aircraft emplacement, plastered a Jap bivouac area, and knocked out a field gun shelling American troops on Bougainville." McCarthy showed no ill-effects from the long siege of combat: "The first seven or eight hours were the hardest," he was quoted as saying. The report continued that he was a "veteran of a dozen raids" against Japanese installations and had ridden through "some of the heaviest concentrations of Jap anti-aircraft fire in the area without a scratch." Kimball's article delighted McCarthy, who was planning his campaign for the Senate in 1944 by the time it appeared. Later he greeted Kimball with a handful of clippings from Wisconsin newspapers. "This is worth 50,000 votes to me," he said, inviting Kimball for a drink to celebrate.[15]

A few months later, shortly before McCarthy announced his candidacy, a final major story again featured his flying exploits. A veteran of "14 dive bombing attacks," the *Wisconsin State Journal* reported, McCarthy had worked hard to prove to pilots that he was a "dependable rear seat gunner." "After all," McCarthy said, "one can't blame these pilots for hesitating to leave the back of their neck exposed to a Jap Zero by having a gunner in back of them who couldn't hit a barn if he was inside it." Now when he interrogated pilots he had experience. "This explains," the marine correspondent wrote, "why he is one of the most popular officers in the squadron with the pilots and gunners." All of this newspaper acclaim gave McCarthy a statewide appeal he had previously lacked. Modest and unassuming, brave and competent, Judge McCarthy had clearly served his country manfully both as intelligence officer and aerial gunner.[16]

\*　　\*　　\*　　\*

Throughout his tour in the Pacific, McCarthy had anticipated his campaign for the Senate and had written Wisconsin friends inquiring about the state political scene. The publicity he received back home strengthened his resolve to run. Late in 1943, he arranged for the nucleus of a campaign organization consisting of his brother Howard, his sister Olive and her husband Roman Kornelly, and Gerald Jolin. Centered in Appleton, they recruited volunteers and prepared a direct-mail campaign similar to the one in 1939. McCarthy's correspondence and Jolin's recruiting sparked the creation of another, more professional, organization in Milwaukee led by Arlo McKinnon and his law partner, Charles Kersten, a future congressman from Whitefish Bay. On the recommendation of his Milwaukee supporters, McCarthy hired James Colby to head his campaign. Colby, who worked for the *Milwaukee Sentinel*, a Hearst publication, had acquired political experience in a Milwaukee mayoral campaign in 1943. McCarthy expected him to handle publicity and to raise funds.[17]

Wisconsin did not require voters to register by party affiliation, and in primary elections they could cast ballots for candidates of either party—a feature that historically has tended to benefit mavericks and underdogs. Joe McCarthy was very much the underdog. His principal opponent, Alexander Wiley, had been a lawyer and businessman in Chippewa Falls before he defeated Democrat F. Ryan Duffy for the Senate in the Republican landslide in 1938. Some Republicans regarded Wiley as a charming and delightful humbug, but his status as an incumbent portended easy victory in the primary election. The other Republican challengers were Leathem D. Smith, a fifty-eight-year-old shipping executive from Sturgeon Bay, and Perry Stearns, an unknown Milwaukee lawyer. The major challenge to Wiley was expected to come from Smith, who was wealthy and well known and who had run for the Senate once before, many years earlier. Most experts underestimated McCarthy's candidacy. Besides his war record, which McCarthy embroidered and newspapers glamorized, he also had acquired the funds with which to conduct an effective statewide campaign.

An obsessive preoccupation with money ran like a thread through McCarthy's career. The quick gain, the fast dollar, fascinated him in the same way that poker did. His income-tax returns reveal a tangled series of endless deals and complicated financial maneuvers. His private financial affairs were compounded of mysterious borrowings, unexplained bad debts, speculations in the bonds of bankrupt railroads, and other wildcatting operations. He had pulled off his most successful speculative venture during the war. He apparently invested about $7,000 in defaulted railroad stocks, pyramided his investment, and in 1943 reaped a profit of $42,353.92. He financed his campaign against Wiley with part of this money. He could not do so openly, because a state statute limited to $5,000 the amount a candidate could contribute to his own campaign. He did it covertly, therefore, by funnelling $17,600 through his relatives. Campaign records listed contributions of $10,600 from his brother Howard, $3,000 from his brother-in-law Roman Kornelly, and $4,000 from his father Timothy. None of the three could have afforded to make such contributions without assistance. A quarrel over money also led to a break between McCarthy and Jolin. While in the Pacific, McCarthy had given Jolin the power of attorney to handle his finances. McCarthy became disturbed at the way Jolin handled the job. They argued, and Jolin bowed out of the campaign.[18]

In mid-March 1944, McCarthy's friends floated rumors in the press that he might run for the Senate. The *Post-Crescent* quickly endorsed the idea, stating that he was "impregnated with mother wit and quick, penetrating ability gloved in prudence." A month later, on 25 April, in an exchange of letters with Colby, McCarthy formally announced his candidacy. "You understand . . . that I shall take no part in the campaign," McCarthy wrote, saying that he did not expect to be home before the election. "I cannot, because of military regulations, discuss political issues. But I do have a program, and this I will submit to the people." Meanwhile, McCarthy concluded on a note of self-sacrifice: "I must, of necessity, leave this campaign to my friends and the voters of Wisconsin, because I shall continue on out here, doing to the best of my ability those tasks assigned to me."[19]

McCarthy's announcement referred to one of the two legal restrictions on his campaign. Military regulations forbade servicemen to participate in politics. But a serviceman was permitted to run for office if he made no political speeches and took no political stands. (Later, when he came home to campaign, McCarthy ignored this ruling except when he found it useful.) Another, more serious restriction concerned his legal right to run for office at all. Article VII, Section 10, of the Wisconsin Constitution stated clearly that a circuit judge "shall hold no office of public trust, except a judicial office, during the term for which he was elected." Because of this statute, Secretary of State Fred Zimmerman questioned McCarthy's right to run. But in early June 1944, Atty. Gen. John Martin, citing a 1922 precedent, ruled that McCarthy's name should be allowed on the ballot.[20]

At the state Republican convention in Milwaukee in early May 1944, the major controversy involved whether the Republican Voluntary Committee (RVC) should endorse candidates. The RVC was an extralegal organization founded in 1925 that allowed the party to avoid the financial limitation that the state's corrupt practices act placed on the campaign expenditures of the statutory organization. Unlike the official party, the RVC could support candidates in the primary, and each election year the committee decided whether to endorse candidates. Supporters argued that endorsement was necessary for party discipline and responsibility and would prevent a Progressive intruder from slipping in and winning the Republican primary. McCarthy's managers labored against endorsement, knowing that, if the convention voted for it, the delegates would endorse the incumbent Wiley.

At the convention, Kersten ridiculed the idea that Progressives would sneak into the Republican primary. Nineteen forty-four was going to be a Republican year, he told delegates, and neither Democrats nor Progressives had any hope of victory. "We're not afraid of the people," Kersten yelled at one point. "They will vote Republican, and for new, vigorous young men whom the Republican party needs to win." But when he mentioned McCarthy as an example of this new vigor, someone in the rear of the convention hollered, "A Democrat!" This brought a roar of laughter from the delegates. Nevertheless, McCarthy's forces contributed their votes to the victorious side. The convention decided not to endorse.[21]

McCarthy had not been expected home, but he wangled a leave in early July 1944 and campaigned furiously during the month before the 15 August primary. At most stops he gave short, informal speeches and newspaper interviews, but he declined to answer questions on specific issues, citing the military restriction. Reporters did not press him for answers. At a public forum in Milwaukee, McKinnon introduced him and explained that he could not discuss the issues. McCarthy then told the gathering: "I wish I could discuss the importance of getting and holding bases in the Southwest Pacific, the importance of oil and the importance of maintaining a strong army and navy . . . but I may not do so." He continued that he was "in the same position as the boy who wrote home that censorship prevented him from saying it was raining and that he was in a foxhole."[22]

Actually, McCarthy turned the military restriction to his advantage. Having spent two years in the Pacific and not being especially gifted at understanding complex problems, he might not have effectively answered tough questions about demobilization, education, labor agitation, postwar monetary policy, or other pressing issues. His military status gave him a convenient excuse not to answer. On other occasions, when he controlled the forum, McCarthy addressed several issues in a general, but oblique, manner. He defended labor from the charge that its agitation caused shortages of war materials. He also argued that the country could never pay its fighting men with money. They were not interested in doles or bonuses, but in postwar jobs: "The most valuable and effective boost to our fighters' morale would be an assurance that these men can work when they return after the war."

McCarthy supported an international tribunal backed by force. As a circuit judge, he said, "my judgements would not have been worth the paper they consumed without the authoritative presence of the sheriff's department." The Milwaukee Journal praised this stand: "If anyone has put this as clearly, as simply, and as forcibly, it has escaped our notice."

In a guest editorial in the Wisconsin State Journal on the eve of the election, McCarthy combined homespun phrases with a subtle explanation of his political positions. He used the terminology "we" when referring to soldiers and never dissociated himself from the enlisted man. He scorned the dangers of dive bombing. "There is a strange, a remarkable feeling of security as you sit in the gunner's seat of a dive bomber," he said.[23]

McCarthy looked impressive campaigning. Tanned and rugged, he always wore his marine uniform with his citation from Admiral Nimitz, three battle stars, a presidential unit citation, and other ribbons. Repeatedly asked about his "fourteen combat missions," he jocularly responded: "All I can say is that I've ruined a hell of a lot of coconut trees." In a two-hour visit to Shawano, he pumped hands and talked about the Pacific. It was a happy reunion for a conquering hero. "Captain, judge, gunner, he was the same friendly, snappy Joe McCarthy of half a decade ago," the local editor mused.[24]

Newspapers both limited and assisted McCarthy's campaign. Many papers, especially those in the smaller cities and rural areas of the western part of the state, ignored him, preventing him from achieving recognition. Toward the end of the campaign, the Madison *Capital Times* struck a sour note when it investigated his financial backing, discovered the large contributions from relatives, and wondered where, in fact, the money had come from. But this story did not arouse concern in other papers.[25]

McCarthy received extensive promotion from newspapers in the Fox River valley, from Rex Karney in the *Wisconsin State Journal* and, to a lesser extent, from the *Milwaukee Journal*. Wyngaard's statewide column repeatedly assisted him by discussing his dynamic personality and campaign style. McCarthy was a "personable, dynamic kind of fellow, a political Horatio Alger," the first in a long caravan of soldier candidates, Wyngaard wrote, adding that restrictions on his campaign prevented McCarthy from engaging in his "brilliant, furious campaign style." Wyngaard's praise was so elaborate that McCarthy reprinted it in his major campaign leaflet.[26]

Newspapers that covered McCarthy's campaign also assisted it by their shallow, inaccurate stories. None discussed the legality of his candidacy in terms of either his judgeship or his military status. Nor did they clear up discrepancies in his version of his service record; most of them simply said he had been a tail gunner and had flown many combat missions. Only the *Milwaukee Journal* mentioned that he had once been a Democrat. Old Judge Werner would have appreciated the irony that McCarthy's age was often reported incorrectly. (Although frequently listed as thirty-five in 1944—his correct age—he was also described as being twenty-eight or twenty-nine when he had been elected judge in 1939.) One newspaper praised him as the "youngest circuit judge in America." McCarthy was thirty when he was elected judge. Although certainly one of the youngest in the nation, he and the newspapers accentuated the fact by subtracting one or two years from his age.[27]

The McCarthy campaign came to a whirlwind finish. Harry H. Meyer, mayor of Shawano, and Andrew Parnell, the Appleton attorney, endorsed him in statewide radio advertisements. Colby prepared an effective campaign brochure featuring laudatory newspaper stories under a picture of McCarthy posed as a tail gunner. Colby used the literature in direct mailings and in newspaper ads. In the last days before the primary, supporters mailed out 2.5 million pieces of literature to 88,000 Wisconsin families—perhaps the "most ambitious" direct-mail campaign "ever undertaken for any candidate," a reporter speculated.[28]

As expected, Senator Wiley triumphed in the primary, capturing 153,570 votes (or 52.7 percent of the Republican vote). But McCarthy took a strong second with 79,380 (27.3 percent) and almost doubled Leathem Smith's total of 44,195 (15.2 percent). McCarthy captured the majority of votes in the three counties comprising his judicial circuit (Langlade, Shawano, and Outagamie). In eight Fox River valley counties near his home, he won 41.3 percent of the Republican total. Voters knew him there, and he had a strong organization and newspaper endorsement. He did slightly better than his state average in populous Milwaukee County (28.4 percent), where he had organized support, and in Dane County (35.2 percent), where Madison's *Wisconsin State Journal* had publicized his effort. In the remaining sixty-one counties of the state, McCarthy received only 22.5 percent of the Republican vote. Because he had no organization and little recognition, McCarthy did poorly in La Crosse (18.1 percent), in Eau Claire (15.1 percent), and in other western counties.

Of all the losing candidates in the state election, McCarthy most impressed political observers. His campaign had been determined and imaginative. He was " a magnetic personality, a great back slapper and a good natured Irishman," a county GOP chairman told Wiley after the election. Wyngaard predicted that McCarthy was in a strong position to win in 1946.[29]

Yet McCarthy still had major problems. Most Wisconsin voters still did not know him. He had no organized backing from the Republican establishment, his principal barrier to gaining statewide acceptance. Republican leaders, including party chieftain Thomas Coleman, suspected him of being a Democrat. Some puzzled over the source of McCarthy's financial backing. His campaign committee had reported spending $19,809, but the real expenditure may have approached $50,000. Even Colby apparently did not know the source of McCarthy's campaign funds. "Did the money come from the Republicans or from New Dealers?" some Republicans wondered. Did this upstart threaten to develop a personal machine to rival the RVC? Conservative Republicans were easily reminded of McCarthy's recent conversion to Republicanism. His campaign in 1944 did nothing to allay those fears. He had not attacked Roosevelt or the New Deal and had praised organized labor. A Republican leader in Outagamie County speculated that Democrats and New Dealers "voted for him . . . because they felt he is more of a Roosevelt supporter than otherwise."[30]

McCarthy returned to his marine duties after the election. In October 1944, three months after his previous leave, he applied for another sixty-day leave, explaining that he had judicial problems at home that needed his attention. When the marines refused and McCarthy persisted, the marines gave him the choice of staying or resigning. He thereupon resigned his commission, which the corps accepted on 20 February 1945.

That spring, he won uncontested reelection as judge and prepared to run again for the U.S. Senate. In 1946 Young Bob La Follette's Senate seat would be contested, and conservative Republicans would need a candidate. As usual, Joe McCarthy would be quick to exploit the opportunity. He never stopped running.

# Chapter 4

# The 1946 Election

---

Few Wisconsin elections have been as eventful as the 1946 Senate contest. The election brought Joe McCarthy into the national spotlight, brought an end to the La Follette dynasty, destroyed the last remnants of the Progressive party, and rejuvenated and liberalized the Democrats, thereby returning Wisconsin to two-party politics.

McCarthy's success was inextricably linked with the personal and political decline of Robert M. La Follette, Jr. Young Bob's father was Fighting Bob La Follette, the famous Wisconsin Progressive; his brother Philip was governor of Wisconsin for three terms in the 1930s. Young Bob had served with distinction in the Senate since 1925. In 1946, a magazine gave him an award of $10,000 for distinguished congressional service as a result of his work on the Legislative Reorganization Act that bore his name. Young Bob was gentle and introspective, polished and judicious, with a deliberate and studied platform manner, fine critical intelligence, and high moral purpose. But he lacked his father's magnetism and insurgency and his brother's spell-binding speaking ability. Although better liked than his abrasive brother, Young Bob had little interest in political organization or political niceties. His infrequent visits to Wisconsin after 1940 gave his constituents the impression that he did not care about their interests. In 1945, his sister-in-law complained bitterly that Bob continued to pursue the same course of "making 'the record' but ignoring the home fires."[1]

The physical and emotional illnesses La Follette suffered during World War II undoubtedly contributed to his extreme political lassitude in 1945–1946. A major streptococcal infection and, possibly, the effects of rheumatic fever contracted as a child seriously affected his health. He suffered from depression and, some thought, from an overindulgence in alcohol. His declining health did not impair his performance in the Senate, but it gave him another reason for not devoting more time to Wisconsin matters. At one point, La Follette decided not to run for reelection in 1946.[2] At a meeting in Washington in late April 1945, an unhappy and weary La Follette said that he was seriously considering retiring after his current term. He complained of constant pressure and criticism. Glenn Roberts, one of his closest political advisers, was shocked and pleaded with him to persevere: "We must believe there is a lot to be done and . . . better days ahead." La Follette reconsidered and decided to run again, but without

55

enthusiasm. Patrick Maney, La Follette's biographer, summarized the senator's thoughts: "If the people wanted him back in the Senate, he would serve. If they did not want him, that was all right too."[3] La Follette apparently never recovered from his melancholy. Whatever caused his suicide in 1953 probably also caused his lethargic concern for his own political welfare in his last campaign. While his personal world disintegrated, so did his political party.

After Phil's defeat for reelection as governor in the 1932 Republican primary, the disgruntled La Follettes maintained their organization and supported Franklin D. Roosevelt in the general election. Phil's defeat and the brothers' public support of the new Democratic president broke the family's traditional hold on the state Republican party. The thought of joining with the decrepit Wisconsin Democrats was distasteful. It seemed impossible at the time that either the Democratic or Republican party in Wisconsin could ever become an adequate vehicle for liberal or radical change or for the La Follettes' ambitions. Thus, in 1934, the La Follettes broke with the Republicans and formed the Progressive party as a third party in Wisconsin.[4]

The Progressive organization was loose, informal, and personal from the beginning. Local Progressive clubs existed primarily to get the vote out on election day, and the party depended on dedicated volunteer workers. Progressives saw politics as a constant struggle between progressive and reactionary forces, between right and wrong, good and evil. There always had to be an antagonist or foil—privilege, greed, big business, special interests—as a target for Progessive indignation. Virtue lay with the Progressives.[5]

At first, the new party did well. In 1934, Phil was the voters' choice for governor. In alliance with Roosevelt, the Progressives won a resounding triumph in 1936. But thereafter, the party began to decline. After a series of squabbles and a conflict of egos, Phil broke with Roosevelt and formed a national third party, the National Progressives of America (NPA), in April 1938. The party was stillborn. Organizing efforts failed. Roosevelt's liberal followers rejected any action that might split the liberal coalition and open the way to a conservative takeover. The Nuremberg trappings of the NPA, plus its stress on nationalism and strong executive leadership, convinced many people that Phil was a fascist.[6]

In the 1938 election, the NPA fared poorly in other states and met shattering defeat in Wisconsin. Wisconsin Democrats, reflecting the conservative temper of their party, agreed to a coalition with Republicans to defeat the Progressives. When the principal Democratic candidate for governor withdrew after the primary in favor of the Republican Julius Heil, Heil's triumph was assured. Besides Phil's defeat, Progressives lost every state office, five of seven congressional seats, and saw their numbers reduced in the state senate and assembly. Democrats also lost ground as Republicans recaptured their historic dominance in the state. Two years later, Bob had considerable difficulty winning reelection to the Senate.

As World War II approached, foreign policy divided Progressives into two opposing groups. Some Progressives favored the president's policies, but Phil and Bob, as their father had done with Woodrow Wilson before World War I, opposed them. Phil resisted every move Roosevelt made to give more aid to Great Britain and France and addressed America First gatherings. Most of the isolationists began to drift into the Republican party; interventionists joined the Democrats.[7]

The Progressives lost the services of their most able leader when Phil La Follette entered the armed forces during the war. Bob La Follette, more than anyone else, kept the party alive during the last six years of its existence. More local leaders might have returned to the GOP if Bob had not declared his intention to stick with the third party regardless of what others did. A Progressive won the governorship in 1942, but it was a personal victory for Orland Loomis, who died before he could assume office, and did little to strengthen the party.[8]

By 1946, the terms of political debate had changed greatly from a decade earlier. In 1936, the Progressives rode to their greatest victory in close alliance with the leader of the liberal forces. In 1946, however, the two major parties increasingly presented adequate alternatives to voters, and Progressives found themselves becoming a minority party. In the late 1930s, large numbers of urban liberals, labor leaders, and rank-and-file union members began joining the Democratic party. Their choice was made almost by default: the Progressives were isolationist, the Socialists weak, and the Republicans conservative. In Wisconsin in 1946, however, conservative Republicans dominated the state. The GOP was entering its eighth year of uninterrupted political control, measured by its dominance of the executive and legislative branches of government and of the majority of municipal and congressional offices.[9]

A major reason for the Republicans' success was Thomas Coleman, the undisputed leader of Wisconsin Republicans throughout most of the 1940s and early 1950s. From 1943 to 1947, he served as state chairman of the Republican Voluntary Committee (RVC). Coleman was a handsome, white-haired industrialist from Madison whose soft-spoken manner disguised an inner drive and intense feelings. Liberal critics called him the Republican "Boss" of Wisconsin. Coleman liked the job, but deplored the title. Unlike the stereotyped machine boss whose power rested on patronage, Coleman's power derived from his organizing talent, pioneering use of public-opinion polls, and ability to get money from rich industrialists to build his organization and to elect his candidates. His dominating personality, capacity for decisive action, and reputation for political wisdom also contributed to his commanding position in the party. He sought no reward in politics except the ideological one of creating a political climate conducive to the growth and progress of American business. Coleman's greatest weakness was the bitter anger he directed toward Republicans who disagreed with him on important tactics or issues. He hated the La Follette family. He later recalled fondly that the greatest moment in his life was the night in 1946 when he learned that Bob La Follette had lost the primary election.[10]

Coleman believed that the best way to defeat Bob La Follette in 1946 was to force him to run as a Progressive. If the general election became a three-way battle, the Republican candidate would easily win. However, La Follette had shown ominous signs of rejoining the GOP. Fearing that La Follette and his Progressive supporters might win the 1946 Republican primary and take over the party, Coleman urged the Republican state legislature to pass a "fence" bill—a barrier to prevent Progressive candidates from running on the Republican ticket. A compromise bill would have allowed a candidate to change parties only by filing an affidavit with the party committee more than a year before the 1946 primary. Progressives vigorously opposed the measure. The bill passed, but, to Coleman's chagrin, it was vetoed by Republican Gov. Walter Goodland.[11]

The Progressives agreed to meet at Portage, Wisconsin, on 17 March 1946 to decide the fate of their party. They had three alternatives. Maintaining their third party was one possibility, but few desired to continue with an organization that had deteriorated so badly in the past eight years and offered so little hope for the future. They could accept the pleas of many Wisconsin Democrats to join their organization. Senator La Follette, a legendary vote-getter, and his Progressive supporters could make the Democrats a real force in state politics. But La Follette, convinced that urban machines and conservative southerners dominated the Democratic party, found its national leadership repellent. More important, the state Democratic party was a perennial loser, and realistic Progressive politicians liked to play on the winning team. Roberts advised La Follette that in Wisconsin the "Democrats are absolutely done."[12]

The winning team in Wisconsin was the Republican party. The overriding factor in La Follette's decision to rejoin the GOP was his appraisal of political realities. Wisconsin was a Republican state in 1946 and probably would remain so for many years. Progressive principles were only one side of the coin; the other side was to get elected. Most observers agreed that he could win as a Republican but not as a Democrat or a Progressive.[13]

Phil La Follette, who wanted to retain the Progressive party, vigorously opposed his brother's decision. Bob sent intermediaries to urge Phil not to appear at the Portage gathering for fear he might cause trouble. Phil consented and did not attend. He took no part in Bob's campaign, either, because it was obvious that Bob's advisers did not want him to.[14]

As the Portage convention approached, no one doubted what the Progressives would do. The press spoke in terms of *when*, not *if*, the Progressives would return to the GOP. Most county caucuses methodically, if unenthusiastically, voted to join the Republican party. A reporter described the delegates at one caucus as having an attitude of "indifference, lack of spirit, pessimism, acceptance of defeat and humiliation." On the urging of

Senator La Follette, who described his decision as "practical idealism," the delegates at Portage completed the formalities and voted to return to the Republican party.[15]

La Follette's decision angered three powerful groups in Wisconsin: conservative Republicans, Democrats, and organized labor. Bob was personally popular with his Republican colleagues in Washington. Politically, they liked him for turning against President Roosevelt on the war issue and for the assistance he would bring in electing a Republican president in 1948. Conservative Republicans in Wisconsin, however, had fought the La Follette family for too many years to welcome Bob's return to their party. They loathed his liberal ideology and vigorous support of the New Deal. Angered by Goodland's veto of the fence bill, they girded themselves to defeat La Follette in the Republican primary.[16]

Although many state Democrats had urged La Follette to join their organization before the Portage convention, they were prepared to oppose him if he ran as a Republican. Daniel Hoan, who became the Democratic candidate for governor in 1946, explained this position clearly: "If Bob runs on the Republican ticket, . . . I will campaign against him as a deserter of the principles of his father. On the other hand, if he runs on the Democratic ticket for the U.S. Senate and I become a candidate for governor, nothing can beat us." The Portage decision left the Democrats frustrated and angry. Only political expediency, they thought, could explain Bob's decision. In a letter to La Follette, Democratic assemblyman Henry Berquist wrote that "I cannot concede that the election of any one man, even yourself, should demand that all things be subordinated to it. In the end, we would find we have perpetuated in office labor-hating reactionaries."[17]

During his twenty years in the Senate, La Follette had done much for organized labor and, during his early career, labor rewarded him with their support at the polls. But in 1946, most of organized labor allied closely with Democrats, and union leaders wanted La Follette to join the Democratic party. His decision to bring his forces into the "party of reaction"—the party of the "labor hater," Sen. Robert Taft—angered union leaders and the labor press.[18]

*   *   *   *

A fluid political situation obviously existed in Wisconsin in 1946, and out of the confusion and turmoil emerged Joe McCarthy. After he left the service, McCarthy toured the state, and his energetic campaign for the Republican Senate nomination made steady progress. He said little to relieve Republican anxieties about the judge-in-politics issue or his 1944 financial support, but these were only minor causes of concern. To overcome the Republican establishment's major worry, McCarthy made a critical shift in strategy: he decided to convince skeptical Republicans of his sincere conversion to conservative principles. The enthusiastic Democrat–New Dealer of 1936 became its caustic critic in 1946. At Republican gatherings throughout the state, he repeatedly attacked the New Deal's bureaucracy, the day-to-day foreign policy of the Truman administration, the inadequate handling of labor–management disputes, and the Democratic farm policy that threatened to "kill off the farmer."[19]

As he prepared for the RVC convention in the spring of 1946, McCarthy had two interrelated objectives: he wanted the convention to endorse candidates, and he wanted its senatorial endorsement. Every election year, the RVC decided whether or not to endorse candidates. The question had provoked controversy at the 1942 and 1944 conventions, and the issue sparked debate again in 1946. Part of the opposition stemmed from the feeling among many Republicans that endorsement would be politically unwise because La Follette would probably win the primary anyway. McCarthy and his supporters had opposed endorsement in 1944 because most of the delegates favored Alexander Wiley. But the circumstances in 1946 differed since McCarthy was the only regular Republican to announce his candidacy. If the RVC convention endorsed him, he would have its financial assistance and unified backing. However, in his tours of the state, to avoid appearing too self-interested, he urged party members to vote for endorsement because it was good for the party. Over the signature of district chairman Robert Watson, McCarthy surreptitiously wrote to all the prospective delegates to the Oshkosh gathering, stressing the need for endorsement to combat the influx of Progressives and to preserve the purity of the Republican political bloodstream. The letter emphasized McCarthy's devotion to conservative Republican principles or, as one columnist put it, his "political Aryanism."[20]

McCarthy journeyed to Washington to seek the support of Wisconsin's Republican congressional delegation. When someone asked him why he did not take his time in politics and run for the state legislature first, McCarthy responded that he was too old to climb the political ladder. He said his Senate campaign would cost less than those conducted by conventional politicians because he planned to do more legwork than the average candidate. The congressmen were impressed with his grit and enthusiasm.[21]

McCarthy captured important backing from the Young Republicans. In late 1945, he helped to reorganize the dormant Young Republican organization in Milwaukee and secured its leadership for a trusted follower, Loyal Eddy. The revived group became the youth auxiliary of the Wisconsin RVC and received financial assistance from the state organization. McCarthy cultivated friendships and secured speaking engagements at many local chapters. By early 1946, the Young Republicans had thoroughly embraced him. He struck them as warm and appreciative. Like them, he was young and dynamic and could lead the charge against the old guard of the GOP and make their group a force to be reckoned with in state politics.[22]

At the Young Republican convention in late April 1946, McCarthy gave the keynote address, and his backers ballyhooed his candidacy. Convention delegates accepted his ideas on military reform, which called for a professional volunteer army rather than universal military training. In the evening, McCarthy sponsored a beer party and solicited support in his drive for endorsement at the RVC convention.[23]

Occurring a few weeks before the RVC convention, McCarthy's enthusiastic reception at the Young Republican convention was crucial. Senior Republicans were impressed and became convinced that they had no other choice. Coleman was one of the converts. He had watched McCarthy's rise to prominence with suspicion and doubt. He worried about McCarthy's independent financial backing and deplored his unsophisticated style. To Coleman (and other urban party leaders), McCarthy seemed a roughneck and a country bumpkin. Once, early in 1946, McCarthy asked Coleman for an interview to discuss his candidacy. Coleman agreed and arranged to meet McCarthy at the prestigious Madison Club in the capital city. The club required patrons to wear a coat and tie, but McCarthy showed up in a soiled marine shirt and was denied admittance. Embarrassed, Coleman found his guest a coat and tie, and the meeting commenced. In March, Coleman complained that Republicans did not need an ex-Democrat on their ticket, but, by April, he had changed his mind. He had grown to appreciate McCarthy's personality, and he judged him an excellent campaigner and potentially a good senator. The party needed a youthful candidate to offset the aging Republicans who would probably make up the rest of the state ticket. Above all, Coleman recognized that McCarthy was the only hope for conservative Republicans and that he was clearly preferable to that "hypocrite" La Follette.[24]

As it turned out, McCarthy had no serious rivals at the RVC convention held in Oshkosh on 4 and 5 May. He had intimidated some delegates by threatening to run as a Republican whether or not he received the backing of the convention. The delegates realized that endorsing someone other than McCarthy would create a three-man race and almost assure La Follette's nomination.

Some opposition did surface. After his well-received keynote address, a few Republicans pressured Rep. Frank Keefe to seek the endorsement. But Keefe refused to give up his favorable position in the House to do battle with the powerful La Follette.[25]

Another potential candidate was Walter Kohler, Jr., a forty-two-year-old war veteran and member of a prominent Wisconsin family. Coleman and other GOP leaders had met with him to discuss his possible candidacy, but Kohler's fear of splitting the anti–La Follette vote apparently convinced him not to seek the nomination.[26]

Only former Gov. Julius Heil showed overt interest in challenging McCarthy. Heil had arrived at the convention hoping for a draft from the delegates. In his hotel suite on the night before the balloting, McCarthy engineered a scheme to deal with this threat. He found ten loyal Young

Republicans who belonged to different county delegations and instructed them on exactly what to say as they casually approached Heil in the hotel lobby. Thus, when the former governor asked what the sentiment was for drafting him, each young delegate responded similarly: "God, Julius, I'm all for you. I have been ever since the first time you were governor. But among my delegation, I can't make any headway. I don't know what it is; they're all going for that damn fool McCarthy." After hearing variations on this theme from other well-briefed Young Republicans, Heil, fearing an embarrassing defeat, bowed out of the contest the next day.[27] With strong urging from Coleman and the McCarthy forces, the convention voted to endorse candidates. McCarthy easily won the senatorial contest with 2,328 votes to 298 for Perry Stearns, the Milwaukee lawyer.

Another important race was for governor. Endorsing the elderly incumbent, Walter Goodland, was a logical political move since he was honest, tremendously popular, and could undercut a Goodland–La Follette alliance. But Coleman opposed Goodland's endorsement because of his progressive views, veto of the fence bill, and senility (a fact not publicly known). On the second ballot, Coleman triumphed, and the delegates chose the colorless Delbert Kenny, whose only distinction was his devoted service to the party.[28]

McCarthy's success at Oshkosh stemmed from his vigorous preconvention campaign, his devious schemes, the influence of Young Republicans at the convention, and the desire of some GOP leaders to have a young combat veteran on their ticket. Most important, however, was the other potential candidates' fear of La Follette's strength; McCarthy essentially won the endorsement by default. Liberal critics charged that Boss Coleman had handpicked McCarthy, but actually McCarthy had literally pushed himself on the RVC with such skill and determination that the Republicans had to endorse him.

Republicans left the Oshkosh convention in low spirits. Everyone agreed that Kenny's candidacy was hopeless. McCarthy's nomination aroused no spontaneous feeling of exultation; most Republicans accepted his candidacy with indifference. Delegates had greeted his nominating speech with embarrassing silence, and McCarthy had made enemies by the bulldozing tactics he used to get the endorsement. Rumor circulated that Republican leaders met secretly two weeks later to consider a new ticket. One writer concluded that the "Republican convention laid a couple of eggs at Oshkosh."[29]

\*    \*    \*    \*

Now that McCarthy had the endorsement, however, Republican party leaders and workers had to put aside their doubts and resentments and rally behind him to crush the Progressive onslaught. As the campaign opened, La Follette seemed to hold an insurmountable lead. Public-opinion surveys showed him far ahead. McCarthy did not have "a ghost of a chance," commentators noted, and would take "the soundest drubbing any candidate for high office ever received in decades." Most La Follette campaign workers agreed. They underestimated McCarthy's candidacy and misjudged his prospects.[30]

The candidates took positions on national and international questions, but these issues did not excite the electorate. La Follette said little on foreign policy. Although he had an isolationist background and had opposed the loan to Great Britain, he had voted for the United Nations, the Bretton Woods financial agreements, the reciprocal tariff program, and funds for the import-export bank. He attacked the Soviet Union and discussed the struggle between democratic government in the United States and totalitarianism in Communist Russia. On domestic policy, he called for the destruction of monopolies, anti-inflation measures, preservation of labor's bargaining rights, federal aid to education, liberalization of social security, expansion of rural electrification, measures to increase employment, a voluntary military force, and a seventy-five-cent minimum wage. Although he supported the policies of the Office of Price Administration in principle, he opposed some of its discriminatory amendments.[31]

La Follette's statements in 1946 were often vague and platitudinous. He contributed nothing to public enlightenment by such remarks as "I am running on my record. . . . My single yardstick has been the welfare of the people. . . . The way to save the world is to make democracy work in America."[32] He refused to answer questions on his isolationist record or on his controversial endorsement by conservative Sen. Robert Taft.

McCarthy was equally vague on most issues. He lashed out broadly at unspecified evils and spoke for and against some measures. Surprisingly, he seldom attacked La Follette's vulnerable isolationist background. He did charge that La Follette had played into the hands of the Communists by opposing world cooperation. Although he supported the United Nations, McCarthy hoped to preserve America's strength and freedom of action. With some reservations, he favored the loan to Great Britain. The country should maintain a strong army, he argued, but with volunteers and not conscription. He was not very critical of Soviet Russia, but he did promise to oppose world communism. He offered few specifics and basically designed his nebulous program to not offend anyone. Few could argue with his plea for more "fresh thinking" and "courage" in handling foreign affairs. In one unenlightening yet typical statement, McCarthy announced, "Today, with our international affairs handled by mental fuzzy-wuzzies, America commands little respect from other great powers."[33]

As a self-conscious new Republican, McCarthy hammered hard on the New Deal's domestic record, particularly its stifling bureaucracy and centralization of power. He charged that "Senator La Follette and the New Dealers believe that for every problem that confronts us there should be federal legislation or a federal bureau, while I believe that the less federal legislation, the less centralization of power, the more that is left to the individual state, the better off we will be." The New Deal had ignored the farmer, he said, and its programs would kill off farmers or communize the farm. But he presented no specific program for agricultural improvement. He courted the returning serviceman with a veterans' pension plan drawn up by veterans. He favored restrictions on organized labor. Labor deserved all its present rights but now must accept its responsibilities. Yet he repeatedly assured workers that he was not antilabor, since he had been a union member for a short time and his two brothers belonged to unions. With flagrant disregard for judicial ethics, he appealed for the support of organized labor in Milwaukee by citing four of his court decisions that allegedly favored labor unions. He titled his newspaper advertisement the "Labor Record of Judge Joe McCarthy." Conservative newspapers, which dominated the news media in Wisconsin, advanced McCarthy's candidacy by their frequent attacks on La Follette's "provincialism" and "isolationism" in foreign affairs and his allegiance to the devilish programs of the New Deal.[34]

But, in general, discussions of foreign and domestic policy evoked little interest or response. The bitter personal accusations traded by both camps were more significant. In this battle, McCarthy was clearly victorious. *The Capital Times* spearheaded the assault on McCarthy. He was called a puppet of Boss Coleman and an inordinately ambitious politician. Moreover, critics again claimed that it was improper and illegal for a circuit judge to run for another political office during his term. McCarthy replied that state law could not restrict a candidate running for a federal office. "The constitution of the United States, not the constitution of Wisconsin," he contended, "establishes the qualification of members of the U.S. Senate." But the *Milwaukee Journal* found more than cold legal arguments at stake; the issue involved moral principle. Judicial elections were supposed to be nonpartisan, and every effort had been made in the past to keep them that way. "The people of Wisconsin, for a hundred years, have surely meant that neither Judge McCarthy nor any other constitutional jurist should be free to enter a political race." For the most part, however, the judge-in-politics issue had little impact. Columnist John Wyngaard observed accurately in this case that "arguments about political ethics are too fine and too subtle to make much impression upon the mind of the rank and file elector."[35]

The McCarthy camp's personal attacks on La Follette were more effective. Capitalizing on the widespread feeling that La Follette had neglected his constituents, McCarthy forces labeled him the "gentleman from Virginia" because he allegedly owned a pre–Revolutionary War home in that state. Actually, La Follette had once owned a run-down house in Virginia, but he never lived in it and, in fact, had sold it before 1946. He owned and lived in a modest home in the District of Columbia, but the truth remained unknown to most Wisconsin voters. The allegation was made forcefully and often, and the denials never caught up with the original charge. The resourceful McCarthy also extracted a clause from the La Follette bill to reorganize Congress to charge that the senator's real intention was to increase senatorial income by raising the legislators' pensions and salaries.[36]

Coleman and McCarthy also successfully attacked the profit La Follette had accumulated from a Milwaukee radio station during the war. In 1935, a group of Milwaukee businessmen including one of La Follette's close political advisers, Glenn Roberts, organized a radio station, WEMP, and applied to the Federal Communications Commission for a license. As a favor to Roberts, La Follette apparently recommended the station to Eugene Sykes, the FCC commissioner. The FCC granted the license, and La Follette later became part-owner of WEMP.[37] In 1944–1945, his one-fourth ownership of the radio station resulted in a profit of $47,339.78. According to McCarthy, La Follette made a 314 percent profit because a federal agency that depended on his vote for its appropriation had granted the station its license. La Follette had fought "long and hard for a larger appropriation for FCC than anyone else thought it should have." The issue became incredibly distorted when the McCarthy camp portrayed La Follette as a war profiteer who was guilty of fraud and corruption and paid extremely low wages to his station employees.[38]

La Follette did make a handsome profit from his ownership of the radio station, but the other allegations misrepresented the evidence. Congress routinely appropriated money for the FCC. McCarthy supporters would have had difficulty finding any outside business interest that did not come under the jurisdiction of some government agency. No evidence existed that La Follette engaged in fraud or corruption, and employees of the station received standard wages. La Follette's biographer concluded that he was "not guilty of wrongdoing" but was guilty of "poor political judgment."[39]

Illustrations of the surprising impact of the radio-station issue can, nevertheless, be found in the private views of two quite different Wisconsin politicians. In the mind of Sen. Alexander Wiley, the La Follettes unquestionably "used their position to benefit themselves in getting those radio outlets."[40] For Thomas Amlie, a radical Democrat and former Progressive congressman, La Follette "had no business with that ownership in WEMP." "Coleman was right," Amlie insisted. "Bob and his friends made almost $200,000 a year on that station. . . . No man can get involved in that way and still be with the common man."[41] La Follette ignored the controversy, which gave McCarthy the chance to drum into the mind of the public the idea that silence meant assent. The constant review of this scandal in newspapers and campaign advertisements seriously damaged La Follette.

Besides these personal attacks, La Follette had to contend with the organized opposition of the RVC, the Democratic party, and portions of organized labor. Conservative Republicans depended on Coleman's leadership to preserve the purity and prestige of their organization. Although a boring speaker who ordinarily never took to the stump, Coleman made an exception in 1946 and toured the state to rally the party faithful behind McCarthy. The RVC flooded the state with literature that promoted the entire endorsed slate but emphasized McCarthy's candidacy.[42]

Wisconsin Democrats had tried to lure La Follette into their party before the Portage gathering, but after the convention they bombarded him with criticism in speeches and newspaper advertisements. They condemned his isolationism and opposition to the Office of Price Adminstration. They criticized him for selling out President Roosevelt and for allying with the reactionary Robert Taft. The charges were only outward manifestations of a more substantial grievance. In their attempt to become the instrument of liberal action in the state, the Democrats saw the Progressive–Republican La Follette as their major threat. His popularity would help to elect conservative and antilabor Republican candidates. Near the end of the primary campaign, the Democratic senatorial candidate, Howard McMurray, bitterly charged that "Bob La Follette can skip nimbly from party to party whenever he feels the ground slipping beneath him, but in one respect he never shifts. He never changes his lifelong slogan, 'I am for me.' "[43]

Beyond their public denunciations, Democratic leaders tried to arrange hot nomination contests in Milwaukee and southeastern Wisconsin, the second district (including Madison), the lakeshore counties, and the Fox River valley. By inducing former Progressives to seek nomination on the Democratic ticket, they hoped to wreck La Follette's campaign and to build up their own organization by luring Progressive voters and labor into the Democratic fold.[44]

Organized labor in Wisconsin had divided loyalties in the 1930s. Nationally, they supported President Roosevelt and the New Deal; on the state level, they backed the La Follette Progressives. La Follette's strong prolabor record gave labor ample reason to support him. He had unmasked many brutal and unlawful techniques employed by management, pressed for investigation of labor disturbances in New Jersey and Pennsylvania, lobbied for the extension of the collective-bargaining principle throughout the defense industry, and condemned the Smith–Connolly Act. But, unfortunately for La Follette, many Democrats had similar prolabor records. The force pulling labor to the Democratic party gradually strengthened, which withdrew support from the Progressives. This process had almost been completed by 1944.[45]

Even after he rejoined the GOP, La Follette retained some labor support. William Green, president of the American Federation of Labor (AFL), endorsed his candidacy, as did five railroad brotherhoods in the state. Some prominent state AFL leaders also endorsed La Follette. Twenty-nine of them—led by William Cooper, president of the Building Service Employees; William Nagorsne, secretary of the Wisconsin Federation of

Labor; and Frank Ranney, secretary of the Milwaukee Federated Trades Council—formed the Milwaukee AFL Committee for the Reelection of Robert M. La Follette. Their efforts failed miserably; they were only able to raise $175 for La Follete's campaign. Green's endorsement also proved insubstantial. The national AFL office did little more than suggest that La Follette's candidacy be given close consideration.[46]

Although a few made sniping remarks, the majority of state Federationists greeted La Follette's candidacy on the Republican ticket with silence and neutrality. One reason for labor's anger was Robert Taft's endorsement of La Follette. The labor press constantly reminded its readers that the Ohio Republican had "adopted" La Follette and that La Follette had not repudiated the endorsement. La Follette's lack of concern for labor's needs also rankled some labor leaders. Pleas for action on Federation projects were answered with form letters on several occasions. "Here we were, an organization with more than a hundred thousand members," recalled George Haberman, president of the Wisconsin Federation of Labor, "and all we got from La Follette was a stock reply from one of his secretaries." What labor feared most, however, was that, as a Republican, La Follette would draw antilabor Republicans into office.[47]

Peter Schoeman, president of the Milwaukee Building and Construction Trades Council and the most influential moderate labor leader in the state, urged labor to remain neutral until after the primary election. Schoeman conceded that La Follette's labor record was spotless but was opposed to his views on foreign policy. Besides, prolabor Democrats deserved support. Schoeman's influence partly explained the decision of the United Labor Committee, comprised of AFL and CIO unions and the railroad brotherhoods, to refuse to assist or endorse La Follette's candidacy.[48]

The Wisconsin CIO, bitterly divided into pro- and anti-Communist factions, also viewed the Portage decision with grave apprehension. The vast majority of anti-Communist CIO leaders placed their allegiance to the Democratic party above any moral commitment to perpetuate La Follette's political career. The pro-Communist faction vigorously opposed La Follette's election. Particularly in Milwaukee, Communists dominated the CIO, and its official organ, The Wisconsin CIO News, followed the party line. The Communist leaders were Melvin Heinritz, state secretary-treasurer of the CIO; Harold Christoffel, head of Local No. 248 of the United Auto Workers at the Allis Chalmers plant near Milwaukee; and Meyer Adelman, a member of the state CIO executive board.[49]

Before the Portage convention, the Communists mainly confined their criticism to La Follette's foreign-policy views. Angered at his opposition to aid for the Russians in 1941 and at his sharp criticism of the Soviet Union near the end of the war, The Wisconsin CIO News charged that he wanted to destroy friendly relations between the USSR and the United States. After the Progressive convention, they broadened their attack to include La Follette's domestic policy. By misrepresenting his voting record and statements, they portrayed him as antilabor, anti-Negro, a tool of the National Association of Manufacturers, an opponent of the Office of Price Administration, and in favor of lowering the minimum wage. After one such distortion, however, Nathan Cowan, national legislative representative of the CIO, publicly came to La Follette's defense and set the record straight.[50]

The defection of labor was a major blow to La Follette. Its support had made his 1934 victory impressive; in 1940 it alone had made victory possible. In 1946, with his Republican candidacy greeted with silence, neutrality, and some disparaging remarks by moderate labor and with vituperation by the Communist-dominated CIO, it contributed to his defeat.[51]

Instead of answering the vicious attacks of his critics, La Follette concentrated his energies on getting his reorganization bill through the Congress. His supporters remained confident but, nevertheless, continually urged La Follette to come home and campaign. In May, Roberts, La Follette's campaign director, pleaded with him: "Frankly, Bob, our leaders have a feeling that perhaps you do not care too much for them." But La Follette kept making excuses.[52] When he finally returned from Washington, only a week remained in the campaign—time enough for him to commit a major political blunder.

During the campaign, Governor Goodland had done nothing to antagonize the Progressives. In 1944, he had incurred the wrath of Republican stalwarts by inviting Progressives to rejoin the GOP. Goodland disliked Coleman and McCarthy, although he knew of nothing specifically wrong with the latter. La Follette was friendly with the aged governor and even praised him at the Portage convention. Political lines appeared drawn between the endorsed conservative Republican candidates, McCarthy and Kenny, and the liberal Republicans, La Follette and Goodland. Or so it seemed. After the Republican convention in May, Ralph Immell also entered the race for governor. A vigorous campaigner with popular appeal and close ties to the La Follettes, Immell was expected to provide the major challenge to Goodland in the primary. Progressives had lined up behind Goodland but, after Immell's candidacy, they divided their support between the two men. La Follette's best course lay in benevolent neutrality, and he remained silent on the gubernatorial contest until the end of the campaign; Goodland and Immell did the same on the Senate race.[53]

The Immell forces, however, pressured La Follette to endorse his loyal friend. The Progressive–Republican Association of Milwaukee and Madison campaigned jointly for La Follette and Immell. Some Progressives in the Milwaukee County Progressive Organization embarrassed La Follette by endorsing Immell. Other Progressives worried about antagonizing Goodland. Stanley Jarz, south-side Milwaukee Republican leader and executive director of the Milwaukee La Follette for Senator Club, threatened to cancel La Follette's speaking engagement at a Republican

Women's Forum in Milwaukee if Immell appeared on the same program. But the Immell forces assured La Follette that he was in no danger and could safely assist them. Finally, five days before the primary, La Follette endorsed Immell, who then returned the endorsement. The action shocked supporters of both La Follette and Goodland and shattered the neutrality they had expected. Coleman's private polls showed Kenny far behind and McCarthy close to La Follette, so Coleman shrewdly switched the support of his organization to Goodland to prevent Immell from winning. An Immell victory would represent a La Follette victory. Coleman's action brought many Goodland supporters, who would otherwise have voted for La Follette, into McCarthy's camp.[54]

     *     *     *     *

While La Follette's brief campaign floundered, McCarthy's lengthy one flourished. McCarthy's campaign was managed by two different groups. One, centered at headquarters in an Appleton hotel, comprised his most intimate associates: Urban Van Susteren, his campaign manager; Olive Kornelly, his sensible and efficient sister; and Ray Kiermas, his dependable and loyal friend from Stephensville and the owner of several small businesses. Coleman hired Kiermas to work full-time and provided him with two paid assistants. The Appleton headquarters recruited hundreds of volunteers and organized a massive direct-mail campaign.[55]

After the Oshkosh convention, a second and more powerful organization was established with headquarters in Milwaukee. Probably with Coleman's urging, a group of prominent corporate executives—Walter Harnishfeger, Frank J. Sensenbrenner, D. C. Everest, and Harold Falk, Sr.—established the McCarthy Club. These veteran Republicans had a common animosity toward the New Deal's bureaucracy, minimum wages, controls, and labor unions. To chair the club, they secured the voluntary services of Harold Townsend, a Wauwatosa floor-covering contractor and veteran political organizer. Townsend worked full-time with a committee of sixty. The club concentrated on Milwaukee, where Townsend had excellent contacts among Polish voters, but organized statewide as well. It arranged speaking engagements, distributed literature, bought radio time, coordinated efforts with the RVC, and, most important, raised $50,000–$100,000.[56]

McCarthy assumed that voters were not interested in traditional domestic and foreign-policy issues. He spoke on them because he was expected to and because they gave him publicity. He believed that people voted with their emotions, not with their minds. Basing his campaign on this premise, McCarthy had an advertising firm in Oshkosh print a booklet, "The Newspapers Say." Each page had a picture of McCarthy and a short, commendable newspaper quotation about him. No lengthy policy statement appeared. The issues covered were his Marine Corps record, Horatio Alger qualities, efficient judicial career, and capacity for hard work. "Show them a picture," he told Van Susteren, "and they'll never read." To confirm his suspicions, volunteers surveyed three towns to test the booklet's effectiveness. A poll taken before its distribution in West De Pere showed a commanding two-to-one margin for La Follette. The results depressed Van Susteren; surely this was too great a lead to overcome. But another survey, taken after they flooded the town with the new literature, placed McCarthy even with La Follette. Improvement was shown again after voters received the booklet in Two Rivers. In the final test in Nekoosa, Van Susteren recalled, La Follette's three-to-one advantage dropped to three-to-two after they deluged the community with the literature. Delighted with the outcome, the excited Van Susteren wangled $30,000 from Coleman to underwrite the expense of sending out 700,000 copies.[57]

Another imaginative technique was the penny-postcard campaign. McCarthy had used postcards in 1939 during his campaign for circuit judge, but their effectiveness had never been tested. The opportunity arose in March 1946 while Henry Hughes campaigned for the Wisconsin Supreme Court. McCarthy asked Hughes what cities he would not be visiting during his campaign. Just before the judicial election, McCarthy's headquarters deluged one of them, Beloit, with penny postcards. On one side was a picture of Hughes and on the other was the handwritten note: "Dear Mr. and Mrs. Smith, Your vote Tuesday will be greatly appreciated by Henry Hughes." The McCarthy forces found that Hughes received proportionately three or four times more votes in Beloit than in other cities where he did not campaign and where postcards were not sent. Convinced of their effectiveness, McCarthy's Appleton headquarters sent out 750,000 "personal" postcards—actually written mostly by retired Appleton residents and Lawrence College students—on the eve of the primary election. "We felt that that bundle of postcards," Van Susteren recalled, "meant the election to the United States Senate."[58] A rural letter carrier in a remote section of the state confirmed their value.

> When Joe McCarthy sends postal cards with his photo on one side addressed in a very neat handwriting, "Dear Mr. and Mrs. John Doe, Your vote will be appreciated by Joe McCarthy," don't kid yourself that the rural patrol [sic] or small businessman is going to vote for La Follette when all he could do was chuck their box full of boxholder papers.
>
> I personally interviewed 20 farmers in a 60 mile area and seven out of ten said that Joe had personally written to them.[59]

While La Follette remained in Washington, McCarthy crisscrossed the state. As if he were running for a county office, he marched up and down the main street of town, into the bank, the hotel, the barber shop, and lawyers' offices. He made sure he was introduced to everyone. He told a war veteran in an Evansville factory that he, too, had been in the service with the marines in the Pacific. In Edgerton, McCarthy walked in and out of the stores along the street, shaking hands with the women and the aged men sitting on the shaded bench in front of the tavern. "I don't want to lose your vote, sir," he said, stepping foward with outstretched hand. "My name's McCarthy, I'm running for the United States Senate—against Bob La Follette, you know."[60]

McCarthy also used his uncanny ability to remember names to flatter people, motivate his volunteers, and win votes. He had perfected this technique by 1946. When introduced to someone, McCarthy looked at the individual as he repeated the name aloud, and when they met again— sometimes many years later—McCarthy could not only remember the person's name but often the details of their first meeting.[61]

His vitality and endurance were astonishing. On one especially strenuous day, he awoke at 5:00 A.M. in Marinette in northeastern Wisconsin. He started for Superior, 250 miles to the northwest, where he was to make a radio address at 5:00 P.M. and a public appearance a few hours later. On the way, he gave numerous street-corner speeches. His car had four blowouts over the first 100 miles of rough road. After ditching it at Rhinelander, he boarded a small plane and continued his journey. Over Butternut, the plane developed an oil leak and landed in an oat field. He found a taxicab, but its engine coughed out at Ashland. In a small plane borrowed from a lawyer friend, he flew himself to Superior. He missed the radio date, but he spoke at the public meeting.[62]

A large group of Young Republicans executed a sensational campaign maneuver three days before the primary. Led by Eddy, the "Flying Badgers" gathered at a designated spot to receive instructions. Traveling in three airplanes and 208 automobiles, they scattered throughout the state distributing campaign literature to every city of over three thousand people (excluding a few of the largest cities) and to every fair in the state.[63]

McCarthy also gained more than La Follette did from newspaper endorsements. La Follette received the enthusiastic support of only one major newspaper (*The Capital Times*) and the mild backing of two others.[64] Six important papers endorsed McCarthy, though their stance was more anti–La Follette than pro-McCarthy.[65] Most newspapers remained neutral, including the two large Milwaukee papers, but most neutral publications took a conservative Republican editorial position that helped McCarthy.[66]

Generally, news coverage of the campaign was deficient and biased. The press allowed the candidates to campaign on nebulous issues. *The Capital Times* repeatedly criticized McCarthy for his vagueness but rarely discussed La Follette's isolationist background or demanded firm policy positions from him. Few publications printed anything on La Follette's voting record. Liberals charged that Boss Coleman had handpicked McCarthy to run against La Follette, but only the *Wisconsin State Journal* published the story of Coleman's opposition when McCarthy first announced his candidacy. News coverage mostly assisted McCarthy: no newspaper investigated his exaggerated military-service record or his war injury; none questioned his past judicial conduct, and few questioned his current ethics. Only *The Capital Times* debunked the story of La Follette's "lavish" Virginia estate. Labor papers in Racine, Kenosha, and Milwaukee refused to print La Follette's speeches and press releases.[67]

Early in the evening of election night, 13 August 1946, La Follette led slightly in rural counties. But, as later returns came in, his lead dwindled and then disappeared. In 1940, La Follette had won in Milwaukee by 54,820 votes; in 1946, 48,614 people voted for McCarthy, 38,437 for La Follette, and 31,816 for McMurray. The final count was McCarthy 207,935 (41 percent); La Follette 202,557 (40 percent); and McMurray 62,361 (12 percent).

One reason for McCarthy's stunning upset was the exceptionally low voter turnout, a situation that usually hurts an incumbent. It had been a nonpresidential election year, the primary was held unusually early, and the campaign had been rather dull. As a result, two-thirds of the eligible voters simply stayed home. La Follette's reputation as an isolationist hurt him in some parts of the state since 1946 was a bad year for isolationists. Burton Wheeler of Montana and Henrik Shipstead of Minnesota also lost renomination bids. In his attempt at a political comeback, former Sen. Gerald Nye was denied the Senate nomination in North Dakota.[68] La Follette's personal problems and remoteness, his overconfident and ineffective organization, his endorsement of Immell, the radio-station issue, and newspaper opposition contributed substantially to his defeat. Campaign financing was also a factor: McCarthy's campaign spent ten times more than La Follette's.

Of the many reasons for McCarthy's triumph, however, three stand out. First, La Follette's campaign was lackluster and ineffective, while McCarthy's was vigorous, organized, and imaginative. Second, La Follette's campaign suffered withering attacks from the RVC, the Democratic party, and radical segments of organized labor. Finally, by 1946, the Progressive coalition, which had elected La Follette earlier, had collapsed. The urban liberal wing, attracted to the program of the Democratic New Deal, entered the Democratic primary to support McMurray and other Democrats. McMurray's labor support in the primary was limited almost exclusively to Milwaukee, Racine, and Kenosha, where the political influence of labor unions was coupled with the growing power of the Democratic party. David Oshinsky has demonstrated the magnitude of labor's political realignment. In 1940, La Follette had received 49.4 percent of the Milwaukee County vote and 58.4 percent in sample labor wards, as opposed to 17.3 and 24 percent, respectively, for his Democratic opponent. In 1946, La Follette captured 32.3 percent of the Milwaukee County total and only 26.5 percent in working-class wards. McMurray, on the other hand, won 26.8 percent of the county total and an impressive 44.1 percent in labor districts. The conservative–rural faction of the Progressive coalition, composed predominantly of German-Americans, had begun defecting to the Republicans as early as 1938. Originally, German-Americans had been attracted to the isolationism of the La Follette Progressives, but the isolationism of the state GOP, plus its economic conservatism, inclined them toward the Republican standard. Only the liberal, largely Scandinavian, rural counties remained loyal to La Follette.[69]

Because of McCarthy's later fame as an anti-Communist crusader, the impact of the Communist-dominated Milwaukee CIO on the 1946 primary has aroused much controversy. By their constant attacks and statements urging CIO members to vote in the Democratic column, the Communists unquestionably took votes away from La Follette. Later, however, during McCarthy's anti-Communist crusade in the 1950s, his opponents distorted the role of Communists in the 1946 primary to discredit and embarrass him. With their eye on the 1952 election, McCarthy's critics claimed that he could not have defeated La Follette without the Milwaukee Communists' support. Noting the irony, William T. Evjue, the editor of *The Capital Times*, caustically wrote in 1952 that McCarthy's "self-proclaimed one-man crusade against communism is the creation of Communists themselves." Pressing this theory to ludicrous extremes, a labor newspaper charged in 1954 that Communist leaders assisted McCarthy "because Joe favored doing business with Russia." Miles McMillin, the indefatiguable political reporter for *The Capital Times*, maintained that McCarthy made "pro-Communist speeches" that were "just appalling" in their nature. McCarthy's opponents also gleefully quoted a remark he had allegedly made after his primary victory. When a reporter asked him what he thought of the assistance he had received from Communists, he was said to have replied that "Communists have the same right to vote as anyone else, don't they?" This supposedly proved his joyful acceptance of their support.[70]

The truth is quite different. No evidence exists in general-circulation newspapers or in the labor press that Communist labor leaders instructed their members to enter the Republican primary or to give McCarthy any assistance whatsoever. On the contrary, the CIO press ignored him and concentrated on electing Edmund Bobrowicz, the Democratic nominee in the Fourth Congressional District. (Bobrowicz won the primary but lost the general election after the *Milwaukee Journal* criticized his Communist sympathies.) The CIO endorsed almost the entire Democratic ticket in the primary and promoted McMurray's candidacy.[71]

McCarthy attacked communism on a few occasions during the primary. Only one moderate and offhand statement—that Stalin's plan for disarmament should be credited as sincere—could in any way be described as following the Communist party line. He never made pro-Communist speeches that were appalling in nature. His statement that Communists had the same right to vote as anyone else is probably fiction.[72]

One national labor leader, who had tried to link McCarthy's victory to the Communists, had to admit privately that, "while there can be no question that the Communists did carry on a vigorous campaign against Bob La Follette and thereby helped elect McCarthy, we have not been able to find any concrete evidence of their open support of McCarthy." In their efforts to explain the five-thousand-vote margin by pointing to the Milwaukee Communists, anti-McCarthyites ignored 202,000 other people who voted for him. An observer noted sarcastically and correctly that the five thousand votes could just as easily be accounted for by "red-headed women or men with fallen arches."[73]

\*　　\*　　\*　　\*

After McCarthy's startling primary upset, the general election was anticlimactic. Privately, McCarthy derisively referred to McMurray as a "nobody." For a few pessimistic supporters, he confidently predicted a 250,000-vote victory margin.[74] His optimism was well founded. Republican senatorial candidates received seven times more votes in the primary than McMurray, who ran unopposed. Democrats in Wisconsin had few solid leaders and an ineffective organization. Reflecting on the 1946 campaign, one Democratic leader sadly observed: "The present state central committee is a joke as far as any real organization is concerned. Outside of writing a few letters they did not function at all, and as a campaign organization must be disregarded." As a liberal, McMurray represented a new breed that, with the influx of former Progressives, would soon liberalize and revitalize the dormant Democratic party in Wisconsin. But this process had only begun in 1946. Much of the leadership still emphasized party labels and patronage rather than principles and philosophy. The few principles they did have were conservative, often dating to the coalition formed by Catholics and "wets" during the 1920s.[75]

McMurray was a professor of political science at the University of Wisconsin, Madison. He had served one term in Congress, and in 1944 Alexander Wiley had defeated him in the contest for the Senate. Urbane, poised, and egotistical, McMurray waged a vigorous but hopeless campaign against his younger opponent. Neither candidate stressed traditional national issues. McCarthy continued to attack the New Deal while McMurray supported it. For the most part, the candidates ignored specific foreign-policy issues.[76]

The dramatic highlights of the campaign occurred when both camps traded bitter personal accusations. *The Capital Times* and the urban labor press helped the Democratic candidate to portray McCarthy as a reactionary politician and an unethical judge. Again they fictionalized McCarthy's subservience to conservative Boss Coleman. In addition, they discovered that after the primary McCarthy had huddled with ultraconservative publisher Robert McCormick of the *Chicago Tribune*. Later, when McCarthy received the endorsement of American Action Inc., a remnant of the prewar America First organization that had formed to defeat all radical and Communist candidates, McMurray supporters used this evidence to prove McCarthy's close alliance with reactionaries.[77]

McCarthy's opponents directed their heaviest barrages at his judicial conduct. Would a judge with integrity, they asked, appoint Van Susteren, his divorce counsel (a nonpartisan position), to be his campaign manager in a race for a partisan political office? McMillin dug up and publicized Judge McCarthy's improper handling of the Quaker Dairy case.[78]

Liberals endorsed the move by Fred F. Wettengel of Appleton, who started an action in the state supreme court after the primary to enjoin the secretary of state and the board of canvassers from certifying McCarthy's primary victory. Wettengel had made a career out of challenging elections, having contested three others, including McCarthy's 1939 election to the circuit court. He charged that McCarthy had violated the state constitution by running for another political office while still retaining his judgeship. In late September 1946, the court ruled in McCarthy's favor. He could run for senator, the court argued, because state law did not apply to a candidate for a federal office. Despite the decision, McMurray made the issue a major campaign slogan. Advertisements proclaimed: "No, Not on *Our Money*, Two-Job Joe." McCarthy retorted that he could not resign his judgeship because he needed the salary. The court's ruling and the failure of most newspapers to pursue the matter doomed McMurray's attempt to successfully exploit the issue.[79]

In September, McMillin journeyed to Appleton to trace rumors that McCarthy had failed to pay state taxes on his 1943 income. Instead, he discovered something meatier. On his arrival, he visited a Democratic lawyer friend who told him that many lawyers and judges in the Appleton area were laughing at McCarthy's weird judicial ethics. He had recently granted quick divorces to political friends. McMillin investigated and published the following story during the campaign.[80]

After a long delay in Milwaukee court, with no immediate prospect of settlement, the uncontested divorce case of *Kordas* v. *Kordas* was filed in McCarthy's court on 3 September 1946. McCarthy granted the divorce two days later. The plaintiff, Mrs. Verna Kordas, was represented by the law firm of Kersten and McKinnon, which in 1944 had represented the Committee to Elect Joseph R. McCarthy and, by rebating its legal fees, had given $500 to that campaign. Arlo McKinnon, a member of the firm, gave $50 to McCarthy's 1946 campaign and, with his partner, Charles Kersten, worked for McCarthy's election. The parties in the divorce had wanted to avoid scandalous publicity and had searched for a judge outside Milwaukee to grant the divorce. McKinnon found McCarthy willing. It is unlikely that McCarthy would have been as accommodating for an outside party who had no political connection with him. Van Susteren, the divorce counsel for Outagamie County, was responsible for investigating all divorce cases that occurred in the county. "Can a divorce counsel," McMillin asked, "make such an investigation in a 'quickie' divorce that is granted in two days?" Similar action took place in the divorce granted to Mrs. Chester J. Roberts, whose husband chaired the Milwaukee Young Republican Club and strongly backed Judge McCarthy. Max Litow, his attorney, donated nearly $50 to McCarthy's 1946 campaign. McCarthy had granted hundreds of quick divorces, but these two smacked of judicial favoritism to political supporters.[81]

McMurray quickly sought to exploit the issue: "If you belong to the right political party and make contributions to the right candidates and remove your case to the right court you can get a divorce in three days." The *Milwaukee Journal* provided the best insight into the controversy: "If Wisconsin needed an example of why the state founding fathers insisted that the judiciary had no place in politics," McCarthy "has now provided one." The divorce actions were probably legal, the newspaper concluded, but raised ethical questions. "Is Wisconsin justice to be used to accommodate political supporters of a presiding judge? Are Wisconsin courts the place in which to settle political debts?"[82]

McCarthy and the few conservative newspapers that discussed the issue replied that he merely followed the law. He had no discretion in the cases, and, since they had been pending in Milwaukee courts for many months, they were not quick divorces. Usually, McCarthy's defenders ended discussion quickly by calling the charges "trumped up political propaganda."[83] Because most newspapers ignored it, the quickie-divorce scandal was an ineffective campaign issue in 1946, though it later became an important weapon in the anti-McCarthy arsenal.

Another exposé by McMillin revealed that of the 1944 campaign contributions to McCarthy's campaign, $17,600 came from his father, brother, and brother-in-law whose poor financial conditions precluded them from giving such large contributions. But in 1946 McMillin could offer no explanation for this strange development.[84]

Goodland's antipathy toward his senatorial running mate somewhat assisted McMurray. Goodland thought McCarthy was a weak candidate. He declined to be seen on the same platform or to pose for campaign pictures with him, and he refused to endorse him.[85]

On the whole, however, McCarthy had all the advantages in the campaign, including the most important ones of better organization, plentiful financial backing, favorable newspaper publicity and endorsements, a glamorous image, and a Republican electorate.[86] McMurray suffered for his extreme criticism of La Follette in the primary. Despite his appeals to Progressives to join his cause, many refused. The Milwaukee County Progressive Organization and numerous Progressive leaders threw their support to McCarthy. Glenn Roberts, the last state chairman of the Progressive party, noted that most Progressives were "very bitter" toward McMurray. "Whatever they may feel about McCarthy, they will always remember that it was McMurray who knifed Bob in the back."[87]

Although communism played an important role in the general election in Wisconsin in 1946, McCarthy himself did not emphasize the issue. The CIO's political arm, the Political Action Committee (PAC), mainly supported Democratic candidates, including McMurray, in the state election. Primarily, it sought to elect Democrat Edmund Bobrowicz in the Fourth

Congressional District. After the primary, the *Milwaukee Journal* charged Bobrowicz with Communist sympathies. After studying the evidence, state Democratic leaders, including McMurray, agreed and repudiated his candidacy. Republicans would not allow the controversy to die so easily, however, and charged that Wisconsin Democrats had allied with the Communist-dominated CIO–PAC. Their red-baiting apparently achieved some success. In heavily Catholic Green Bay, for example, one Democratic leader bemoaned the fact that the Communist issue had aroused Catholic antipathy toward the Democrats.[88]

Conservative newspapers dwelt on McMurray's alleged connection with Milwaukee Communists. They publicized Socialist Norman Thomas's charge that McMurray had been called a "fellow traveler" by the Communist *Daily Worker*, and they demanded to know if he accepted that endorsement. They continued to harp at this theme and to associate him with left-wingers even after McMurray categorically repudiated communism and Communists.[89]

Some state Republican congressional candidates emphasized the Communist issue in their campaigns. In his speeches, Frank Keefe, incumbent Republican congressman from the Sixth District, stressed the insidious Communist infiltration of the United States. Charles Kersten, who would soon make a congressional career out of red-baiting, urged Milwaukee voters to "Put Kersten in Congress and Keep Communism Out." Tenth District Rep. Alvin O'Konski alleged that the campaign assistant of his liberal opponent was "a CIO–PAC Communist fieldman sent here by Moscow to purge O'Konski."[90]

In contrast, the Communist issue received only moderate attention from McCarthy. Never one to avoid a good issue, McCarthy described McMurray as "communistically inclined" and a "little megaphone" of the "Communist controlled PAC." He warned that Communists had bored deep into the Democratic party and had sufficient power to influence legislation. But these statements were not a preview of charges to come or a "nightmare in Red." Rather, assured of election, McCarthy was content to exploit his glamorous image and to make general attacks on the New Deal and the Truman administration.[91]

For both the primary and the general elections, McCarthy worked obsessively to create an attractive image. His campaign advertisements—and those of the RVC—and Republican newspapers portrayed him as a marine hero, a contemporary Horatio Alger, and a dynamic, hard-hitting man.[92]

McCarthy's service record was neither more nor less heroic than that of countless other soldiers. But, in 1946, partially because of McCarthy's campaign literature and statements, which fooled even such a subsequent critic as the *Milwaukee Journal*, and partially because of partisan Republican newspapers, his campaign grossly distorted his war service. Thousands of Wisconsinites were told that he had displayed patriotism and sacrifice by resigning his $8,000, draft-deferred position as circuit judge to enlist in the marines. They were told that he had spurned a deferment because "you can't let the neighbors fight a war" and had enlisted as a buck private, rising through the ranks to the level of captain. Then he "qualified as a rear seat gunner in a marine dive bomber squadron and took part in 14 raids against Jap installations in the South Pacific." He participated in bloody strikes over Rabaul, Kahili, Buka, Kara, Munda, and Balalac and sustained a serious leg wound during one combat mission. While in the combat zone, he experienced many weary months in some of the most "foul and stinking spots on earth carrying out bloody and desperate missions." For this he deserved the "respect of every person who has any admiration for manhood."[93] The same devotion to his country that he displayed in fighting the Japanese now inspired his race for the Senate. McCarthy went to war because there was a job to be done. "There's nothing forcing him to run for the United States Senate either," a friendly columnist wrote; "Joe just feels that 'there's a job to be done' in Washington."[94]

In the primary, when La Follette's supporters criticized McCarthy for not resigning his circuit judgeship before running for the Senate, the RVC countered vigorously that McCarthy's critics had not sacrificed for the war effort.

> Did the newspaper publishers who suggest that Joseph R. McCarthy resign his judgeship while being a candidate for office give up their $30,000 to $50,000 incomes per year? Did the Progressive senator who returns to the state only intermittently from his estate in Virginia, chiefly for campaign purposes, make any sacrifice at all?

McCarthy's supporters accepted his explanation that his financial situation prevented him from resigning his judgeship. "He has never had the commodious salary of an editor nor grossed during the war a hundred thousand dollars a year out of radio on the side," a pro-McCarthy newspaper argued, referring to Evjue and La Follette. While others made fortunes out of the war, McCarthy "lived on hope and courage and a few shillings a day."[95]

Newspapers supporting McCarthy, more than McCarthy himself, insinuated that McMurray was a coward for preferring ivy-covered halls to front-line trenches. Unlike McCarthy, Professor McMurray had neglected to stand with the common man during the war. "It would have been a high example of ethics had he, of very suitable fighting age, given a demonstration of his faith by joining the army."[96]

Even McCarthy's critics portrayed him as a personification of the Horatio Alger success story. McCarthy came from a background of toil and hard knocks. He quit grade school as a young farm boy and set out, in accordance with the Alger scripts, to conquer the world. Touched "by the torch of ambition," he began running a chicken farm and then a grocery store. At the age of twenty he discovered his need for an education. He enrolled at Manawa High School and completed the four-year program in only one year, thanks largely to Mrs. Frank Osterloth, the elderly widow who took care of him and "kept the coffee pot boiling for him while he burned the midnight oil."[97]

As an undergraduate he struggled through Marquette University working at a variety of part-time jobs. Having surmounted impossible odds by becoming a lawyer, he repeated the process in 1939 by being elected the youngest circuit judge in the state's history. He did so without the benefit of a well-heeled organization; rather, he accomplished it on his own by writing letters and by arduous campaigning. When the war came, he dropped "his safety, his salary, and his security." His impossible victory over La Follette and his subsequent defeat of McMurray added more testimony to an already well-established image.[98]

For some, McCarthy's background exemplified a distinctive American character and past imperiled by modern society. An editorial in the *Berlin* (Wis.) *Journal,* reprinted in "The Newspapers Say," expressed this sentiment.

> Joe McCarthy is largely a self-made man who had to come up the hard way, but it made him strong of mind and body and he will make a fine campaign, winning voters away from the false Gods of bureaucracy, socialism, communism and back to the American way of life.

The McCarthy story was the true "American type"; he is "where he is today largely because of the efforts of Joe McCarthy and should be beholden to no man."[99]

McCarthy's supporters viewed his capacity for hard work as largely responsible for his success as a chicken farmer, grocery-store manager, lawyer, judge, soldier, and politician. Even McMillin credited McCarthy's upset of La Follette to "his ability and willingness to just plain WORK." The columnist doubted whether Wisconsin had "ever seen a politician who is more ambitious politically or more untiring and unremitting in his campaigning."[100]

Because of his perseverance and determination, McCarthy was a man to be reckoned with whatever he engaged in. He was a young Irishman "who dares to do that which all orthodox opinion customarily regards as impossible." Nobody thought he could win the judicial election in 1939, but he did. No other Republican was willing to take on La Follette, but McCarthy did. Nobody thought he could defeat the venerable senator, but he did. "Against the disadvantage of a hostile press," John Wyngaard observed admiringly,

> with the handicap of an organization which was something less than enthusiastic . . . against the habitual belief that Sen. La Follette was too big to topple, against the opinion of practically every professional political observer who publicly recorded his estimates of the situation, McCarthy plowed ahead.[101]

The young Republican aspirant was also lauded as a down-to-earth, intelligently practical man with horse sense and native intelligence.

McCarthy's speeches and statements encouraged suspicion of intellectuals in the federal bureaucracy and on college campuses. During a discussion of farm problems, he lashed out at experts in Washington who sought to "communize or sovietize our farms." In the general-election campaign, observers noted the differences between "chicken farmer" McCarthy and "Professor" Howard McMurray. During a debate between the two antagonists, McCarthy received rousing applause for his response to a question "What are your backgrounds for office?"

> McMurray: I am a university professor, with a doctor of philosophy degree from our state university, the highest degree the university can give.
>
> McCarthy: I'm no professor—just a farm boy.

A McCarthy advertisement urged voters to elect him because "we need practical, farm-born men at Washington. There are too many professors there now."[102]

The belief that McCarthy was an especially virile man was also an important part of his appeal in 1946 and became vastly more significant after 1949. His difficult and strenuous life on the farm, his amateur boxing career at Marquette University, his war record, and his barrel-chested appearance led publicists to portray him as rugged and manly. McCarthy's vague foreign-policy pronouncements during the campaign persistently demanded that America not "kowtow" to other nations. He said that sometimes a little "fist-banging clears the atmosphere and leads to understanding and respect." After his opening speech of the general-election campaign, a friendly newspaper described how he came out of "his corner with both fists swinging. . . . There wasn't a tender touch, a pussyfoot step, a trim, or a duck in one line of his comprehensive speech."[103] Belief in McCarthy's virility became so pervasive that even the most absurd stories about him were accepted as fact. A *Milwaukee Journal* column reported seriously that, instead of using a hone, he sharpened his double-edged razor on the palm of his hand.[104]

Wisconsin Republicans swept the election, and McCarthy won 620,430 to 378,777 votes. After many years of national Democratic dominance, Republicans throughout the nation received a favorable response to their question, "Had Enough?" As a Republican candidate in a Republican state in a Republican year, McCarthy coasted to an easy victory. Nevertheless, he was a weaker candidate than other Republicans. He received 62,000 fewer votes than Secretary of State Fred Zimmerman, who led the GOP ticket, and he trailed the general Republican congressional slate by an average of 4.2 percentage points.[105] This weakness would become even more apparent in the next three years.

# Chapter 5

# Decline and Comeback: 1947–1949

Joe McCarthy journeyed to Washington amid much fanfare from friendly Wisconsin newspapers. They dramatized his initiation into the complex world of national politics and the even more complicated one of international affairs. They speculated on how the handsome bachelor would adjust to Washington's social world.[1] But the honeymoon soon ended, and the writers turned to other duties, leaving McCarthy with the problem of building a record or at least making an impression. From Wisconsin's perspective, he succeeded in doing neither during the next three years. His political fortunes in the state deteriorated badly. Most newspapers ignored him. No powerful interest groups consistently praised his work. Only his enemies followed his career attentively, and they found much to criticize. By the fall of 1949, his political future looked bleak. At that point he began his political comeback by exploiting the issue of communism.

During his early years in the Senate, McCarthy jumped from issue to issue—from championing veterans to opposing public housing; from ending sugar controls to defending German soldiers accused of the Malmedy massacre; and from seeking the impeachment of the secretary of the navy to befriending Wisconsin fur farmers. After the election, he indicated that he would follow the liberal Republican policy of former Gov. Harold Stassen of Minnesota rather than the conservative one of Sen. Robert Taft of Ohio. Actually, from 1947 to 1949, McCarthy supported Sen. Arthur Vandenberg and Republican internationalists on foreign affairs, but on domestic issues he more closely followed Taft's conservative policy. McCarthy owed his election partly to the financial and organizational support of conservative Republicans in Wisconsin. Key McCarthy staff members during these years—Victor Johnston, Thomas Korb, and George Greeley—had close ties with the conservative Coleman organization, and McCarthy's voting record on domestic legislation was strictly conservative. He consistently voted for restrictive labor legislation, the lifting of controls on consumer goods, tax cuts for higher-income groups, and smaller federal budgets. He voted against federal aid to education, public housing, and public-power appropriations. His accomplishments were inauspicious and aroused no interest in his home state.[2]

McCarthy did make an impression in Washington. Historian Robert Griffith has pointed out that McCarthy's early Senate career was remarkable not for his policy positions—liberal or conservative, internationalist or isolationist—but rather for his "continual violation of the rules, customs, and procedures" under which the Senate operated. During the debate on sugar decontrol in 1947, for example, he was rude and provocative. He refused to yield the floor for unfriendly questions and responded to interrogation with personal charges or accusations.[3] But his constituents knew little about these activities because few newspapers covered his record closely, much less his high-handed methods on the Senate floor.

His early Senate career evoked only occasional praise in Wisconsin. Some applause greeted his efforts to remove excise taxes from furs and to solve the housing shortage. His "far-sighted" opposition to organized labor and his investigation of the high costs of building materials also received positive comments.[4] Columnist John Wyngaard detected a favorable change in McCarthy's personality. McCarthy had lost his "natural brashness," Wyngaard wrote in 1947; his "contact with the deep concerns of the Congress and the historic problems of international relations appear to have had a sobering effect upon him, to have cooled his impetuousness and the formerly cock-sure attitude that the world was his oyster."[5]

As a major Republican officeholder, McCarthy sought to influence Wisconsin politics. Shortly after his election, he disclosed his endorsement of Harold Stassen as the Republican nominee for president. Thomas Dewey had not yet declared his candidacy, and Stassen was the early favorite to capture the Wisconsin presidential primary on 6 April 1948. The Stassen forces warmly welcomed McCarthy into their camp because of his stature as a senator and his close ties to the dynamic Young Republican organization. At a Milwaukee meeting in May 1947, McCarthy was elected temporary chairman of the Stassen for President Club.[6]

Stassen's strength in Wisconsin derived from that state's proximity to Minnesota, where he had served as governor, and from Wisconsin's large Scandinavian population. Although the Republican Voluntary Committee (RVC) took no official position during the primary, many prominent committee members, led by Thomas Coleman, declared themselves for Stassen. It is likely that Coleman influenced others to support Stassen in order to control the situation and to head off dissension within the party. Stassen posed the fewest difficulties in terms of party control.[7]

As the primary approached, Gen. Douglas MacArthur loomed as Stassen's major opposition. Coleman and the party leadership did not care for MacArthur's candidacy because of the people who supported him in Wisconsin. The MacArthur organization included an odd combination of Republicans: older, conservative party leaders, such as William Campbell, founder of the RVC; Philip La Follette, the former Progressive governor, who was anathema to the Coleman organization; and Lansing Hoyt, an anti-Coleman conservative Republican. The Coleman organization feared the alliance arrayed against them under the MacArthur banner and raised an issue that ultimately overshadowed all others: La Follette, the Progressives, and the dissident Republicans were using MacArthur as a popular vehicle to take over the Republican party.[8]

In a letter to thousands of Wisconsin voters, McCarthy attempted to shatter MacArthur's hopes by portraying the general as too old for the office and out of touch with civilian life. McCarthy's letter is most memorable for the insidious remarks he directed at MacArthur's personal life. A common misconception among state residents, McCarthy noted, was that MacArthur was a Wisconsin native. Actually, he continued,

> the general was born in Little Rock, Arkansas, on January 26, 1880, and not in Wisconsin. He is not listed on any poll list as a voter of Wisconsin. Neither his first nor his second marriage, or his divorce, took place in Wisconsin. He first married in Florida to Mrs. Walter Brooks of Baltimore, who now lives in Washington D.C. After she divorced him in Reno, Nevada, he was remarried in New York City. Neither wife ever resided or voted in Wisconsin. In a sworn marriage application for his second marriage he did not claim Wisconsin as his residence and Baltimore, Maryland, as the domicile of his former marriage.[9]

McCarthy obviously aimed his parade of MacArthur's marriage difficulties at the Catholics and Lutherans in Wisconsin, who were opposed to divorce.

McCarthy may have attacked MacArthur in order to cement his relationship with the Coleman organization and to strike another blow at former Progressives. In any case, he pursued his attack without consulting the Wisconsin leaders of the Stassen campaign. His extreme action embarrassed Johnston and Coleman. If also infuriated MacArthur's conservative Republican backers. Campbell was indignant. George Gilkey, another former chairman of the RVC, chastised McCarthy for his "dirty politics."[10]

Stassen won the primary, but McCarthy had no reason to rejoice. Despite being listed first on the Stassen delegate slate, he received fewer votes than another Stassen delegate, Walter Kohler, Jr. Kohler's surprising showing stemmed partly from his distinguished family background—his father had been governor from 1929 to 1931—but young Kohler had held no political office, and his showing embarrassed McCarthy.

Traditionally, the delegate with the most votes in the presidential primary led the Wisconsin delegation to the national Republican convention. But in May 1948, when the Stassen delegates met in Milwaukee to plan their convention strategy, some party leaders, led by Johnston, suggested McCarthy for chairman. McCarthy sat silent while his supporters insisted that not being selected to lead the delegation was an insult to his dignity as a senator. But Kohler's friends were adamant. Led by Mrs. Melvin Laird, Sr., and Wilbur Renk, they successfully elected Kohler. Because of his connections with national party leaders, however, McCarthy unofficially directed the delegation at the Republican convention at Philadelphia. Feelings were hurt. Some Wisconsin Republicans blamed McCarthy for what they thought was his attempt to deny Kohler the delegation chairmanship and for the way Kohler was cast aside at the Philadelphia convention.[11]

At the end of the national convention in Philadelphia, after Dewey's nomination, McCarthy sought to mend his fences in Wisconsin by introducing a resolution praising MacArthur. The convention did not act on the resolution, and McCarthy's transparent attempt at flattery did not appease MacArthur forces in Wisconsin. Campbell fumed that McCarthy was a "blatherskite." He had introduced the resolution to "save his own face." "He is going to hear from this when he comes up for reelection in 1952 and no one knows it better than he does."[12]

McCarthy's efforts in the Stassen campaign had alienated prominent Republicans in both the Stassen and MacArthur camps without making any noticeable contribution. Moreover, the political significance of a U.S. senator's being outdistanced by a comparative unknown was obvious— McCarthy had slipped. The presidential primary was the first statistical evidence of his declining popularity, which had been somewhat apparent even before the primary and became glaringly obvious by the fall of 1949. In retrospect, a remarkable aspect of McCarthy's early years in the Senate was his decline in popularity in his home state.

From 1947 to 1949, expression of support for McCarthy was sporadic. Major newspapers ignored him for months at a time. His name appeared so infrequently in letters to newspapers that one wonders if any constituents cared about him or his senatorial career.

No Wisconsin interest groups publicly supported his activities. No business interests applauded him. He was anathema to organized labor even before he favored the Taft–Hartley Act. Of the two major farm organizations, the conservative Farm Bureau Federation said nothing publicly about his record on agriculture, and the liberal Farmer's Union listed him among those most unfavorable to their program.[13]

Having been a war veteran, a Legion member, and a sponsor of some veterans' measures, McCarthy should logically have been praised by the Wisconsin American Legion, but the group's only public statement criticized his opposition to universal military training, one of the Legion's major goals. *The Badger Legionnaire* warned him that he was "very definitely letting them down," and Legion officials informed delegates of McCarthy's own Legion district of his disappointing stand and urged them to bombard the senator with letters.[14] When pressure for Legion measures became too intense, he finally pleaded with a state official to "turn off the heat."[15]

While McCarthy's friends criticized part of his Senate record, his enemies investigated and criticized every facet of his life. Spearheaded by two prominent newspapers, *The Capital Times* and the *Milwaukee Journal*, they repeatedly criticized his record and challenged his probity. As an influential member of the Joint Housing Committee that toured the country in 1947–1948 investigating postwar housing shortages, McCarthy insisted that "private enterprise must be our chief reliance." He opposed all public-housing measures.[16] To some, he was a tool of the real-estate interests. Mayor Francis Wendt of Racine, a former Progressive, was "ashamed of the low grade antics" of the senator. He "appears to be the 'water boy' for the real estate lobby." The Wisconsin League of Women Voters and several liberal newspapers made similar accusations.[17]

McCarthy became known as the "Pepsi-Cola Kid" after his legislative efforts on behalf of the Pepsi-Cola Company were disclosed by columnist Drew Pearson. Russell Arundel, a Pepsi-Cola lobbyist who wanted to end wartime controls on sugar for the soft-drink company, befriended McCarthy in 1947. Subsequently, McCarthy worked to end the controls and succeeded in lifting them six months earlier than scheduled. McCarthy claimed that he wanted to help consumers, but, after 1950, investigators uncovered another motive. In 1947, when McCarthy's credit with the Appleton State Bank was being stretched to the breaking point, Arundel had endorsed a $20,000 note that took the pressure off for a while. Bank examiners later rejected the note because Arundel showed no liquid assets. For all his efforts, McCarthy only acquired another derisive nickname in his home state.[18]

McCarthy's critics in Wisconsin concentrated on his lack of ethics. *The Capital Times* repeatedly attacked and reviewed his quickie divorces, the judge-in-politics issue, and his censure by the state supreme court in 1941. Shortly after McCarthy left for Washington, revelations that he failed to pay taxes became a new and potent issue. On 13 February 1947, the *Milwaukee Journal* and *The Capital Times* published front-page stories on the Internal Revenue Service's decision to assess McCarthy $3,500 on the $42,353.92 in profits he made on the stock market in 1943.[19] State tax authorities also turned the screws and levied an assessment of $2,459.54 in state taxes plus $218.32 in interest. McCarthy's opponents now linked his stock-market bonanza with his mysterious 1944 campaign contributions and concluded that he had probably channeled his own money through his relatives to avoid the statute limiting the amount a candidate could contribute to his own campaign. Reports also revealed that he had paid no state income tax on his 1946 and 1947 incomes.[20]

McCarthy responded that his problems with federal tax authorities were merely a difference of opinion between California tax officials who allowed certain deductions for his 1943 tax return and Wisconsin officials who did not. He agreed to pay the levy.[21] His defenders castigated the partisan motives of his critics, charging that the public was "smart enough to recognize newspaper hysterics, persecution, and political brickbats when they see them."[22] Of the state tax assessment, McCarthy claimed: "I spent no time in the state in 1943. I had no property in the state. I received no income from within the state, so I assumed it was unnecessary for me to file a return."[23] Others thought this an inadequate defense. How could McCarthy decide not to regard himself as a Wisconsin resident in 1943 after he spent his entire life there, voted there, attended schools and entered military service from there, held his judgeship there, paid state taxes there in 1942 and 1944, and planned to run for the Senate from there in 1944? "It all adds up to a very great disappointment," the *Milwaukee Journal* concluded, "over a young man whom the people elected to office with high hopes."[24] William T. Evjue's newspaper, *The Capital Times*, was more severe. "How long," it asked, "is this fellow McCarthy going to be permitted to toy with and make a mockery of the prestige and majesty of the great state of Wisconsin?" On the day McCarthy was to address a Madison audience, Miles McMillin sarcastically suggested that he probably would speak on "Why You Must Pay Taxes—And I Do Mean YOU."[25]

McCarthy was struck another blow by a state supreme court decision in July 1949. Predictably, the case originated in the offices of *The Capital Times*. McMillin had repeatedly urged his boss to initiate disbarment proceedings against McCarthy, but Evjue hesitated because his attorney, W. Wade Boardman of Madison, was a member of the Wisconsin Board of Bar Commissioners, the official state body governing the conduct of lawyers. Boardman insisted that Evjue's public denunciations of McCarthy made it unethical for him to get involved. Evjue finally allowed McMillin, who was a lawyer as well as a political reporter, to file a complaint on 7 July 1948.[26] In his letter to the bar commissioners, McMillin reviewed McCarthy's campaigns for the Senate in 1944 and 1946 and his refusal to resign his judgeship. McMillin then noted that the canons of judicial ethics of the American Bar Association contained the following provision: "While holding a judicial position he [a judge] shall not become an active candidate either at a party primary or at a general election for any office other than a judicial one."[27] McMillin urged the board to investigate McCarthy's ethics and to start proceedings against him. The five commissioners promptly began their inquiry but so quietly that McMillin assumed that they had ignored his complaint.[28]

McCarthy's response to the accusation revealed his complete misunderstanding of the charge against him: he replied that the state supreme court had already decided the case in *State* ex rel. *Wettengel* v. *McCarthy,* when it ruled that state constitutional barriers could not prevent a judge from seeking a federal political office. The bar commissioners quickly advised him that the issue was not his legal right to run for the U.S. Senate but his qualifications and fitness to practice law within the state of Wisconsin.[29]

The commissioners were disturbed by political advertisements used by McCarthy and his supporters in 1946 that solicited votes on the basis of decisions he had rendered as a judge. "It is bad enough for a judge while holding a judicial office to run for a political office," a disgusted member pointed out, "but it is even worse for one who while holding a judicial office seeks preferment on the basis of judicial decisions rendered by him which are favorable to some particular group, faction, or class." Whether or not it was true that McCarthy granted quick divorces to political friends in 1946, the same board member insisted, "by retaining his judicial office while running for a political office, the Judge left himself wide open to such criticism."[30] The commissioners were so disgusted with McCarthy's unethical conduct that they referred to him in private correspondence as "demagogue" and "Slippery Joe."[31]

The commission's complaint urged the state supreme court to discipline McCarthy for violating "the public policy of the State of Wisconsin, the Code of Judicial Ethics, his Oath of Office as Judge, and his Oath of Office as a Member of the Bar." On 12 July 1949, the court ruled that he had indeed violated his oaths as a circuit judge and as an attorney and had committed "an infraction of the moral code" that deserved "just censure." Yet the court dismissed the case against him because his action "is in a class by itself which is not likely to be repeated" and because he had never previously been "derelict in the discharge of his duties and obligations as a lawyer."[32] (The latter rationale overlooked McCarthy's censure by the same court in 1941.) Justice Marvin Rosenberry, who wrote the decision, subsequently stated that the court had reasoned that "the only thing to do was to censure him since it didn't seem a matter worth disbarring him over."[33]

Assuming a posture of injured innocence, McCarthy claimed vindication and demanded that the bar commissioners resign their posts. "In view of the unanimous decision of the court in dismissing the case as having no merit," he charged, "it must be assumed that the bar commissioners knew that their case had no merit and were playing politics or that they are completely incompetent as lawyers."[34] Some observers thought the court had made a hairline decision that only the professional eye could discern.[35]

The decision perplexed the *Milwaukee Journal.* "How," it asked, "can the high court even surmise that this betrayal of a public trust . . . will not be repeated? What is there in this wishy-washy decision to deter other judges, although sworn not to do so, from running for federal political office?"[36]

On the whole, the reaction to the decision injured McCarthy. Liberals pointed to the court's language as proof of the fledgling senator's lack of integrity. They noted correctly that, although the court had dismissed the case, it had issued an extraordinary condemnation. Three Republican newspapers rebuked McCarthy for his failure to follow the moral code.[37] Most significant were the observations of Wyngaard, whose columns usually ignored charges against McCarthy. Although McMillin had initiated the action for partisan motives, Wyngaard conceded that the bar commissioners "had good cases." The court's censorious language might ruin McCarthy's political future because his enemies "will not let the public forget." It may be "hazarded with complete confidence," he observed ominously, "that the opinion will be the chief campaign document of the opposition when McCarthy next runs for office . . . in 1952."[38]

The income-tax revelations and the court decision were serious blows to McCarthy, but their impacts were lessened considerably because most newspapers refused to publish unfavorable material about him. Aside from those that had publicized the charges against him during the 1946 campaign, no additional ones reported his questionable handling of divorce cases, his censure by the state supreme court in 1941, and other revelations. Except for McCarthy's rebuttal, almost every Wisconsin newspaper ignored his failure to pay income taxes. Only ten newspapers discussed the extraordinary case of a U.S. senator's having been censured by the state's highest court.[39] Three of the five newspapers that defended him did not even mention the censorious language of the court's decision.[40]

Unlike his first Senate campaign when he waltzed to victory over an unorganized and dispirited Democratic party, McCarthy could expect vigorous opposition in his 1952 reelection bid. In 1948–1949, liberals in Wisconsin had constructed a more effective political vehicle, the Democratic Organizing Committee of Wisconsin (DOC). The immediate reason for the creation of the DOC was the personal and political feud between two Democratic leaders, Robert Tehan and Charles Greene, for control of the party. After Tehan defeated Greene for the post of national committeeman, Tehan's supporters laid down a plan for a new organization that resembled the RVC. Greene, the chairman of the statutory party, thought he would have no place in the new structure and refused to resign his position. Under state statues there was no way to remove him. State delegates to the 1948 national Democratic convention attempted to circumvent Greene by creating a voluntary organization headed by Tehan and Jerome Fox. The Wisconsin DOC met in Fond du Lac on 19 May 1948 and proclaimed itself the leader of the liberal wing of the party. The group's first statewide conference in July drew up an aggressive liberal platform.[41]

Although it was only a paper organization during the 1948 campaign, election results encouraged the DOC. Democrats carried the state for Truman, elected young Thomas Fairchild attorney general, increased their membership in the state legislature, elected two new congressmen, and ran a strong race for governor. DOC leaders boasted that their organization was now solidly established as the only liberal–progressive vehicle in Wisconsin.[42]

Able young liberals helped to form or soon joined the DOC. Among them were McMillin, Fairchild, Carl Thompson, James Doyle, Gaylord Nelson, Patrick Lucey, William Proxmire, and Horace Wilkie. Most were ex-servicemen, former La Follette Progressives, university graduates, and lawyers.[43] They organized county DOC units and worked to weld urban New Deal Democrats with former Socialists and dissident Progressives.[44] McCarthy probably worried about his prospects against the revitalized Democrats. He was particularly nervous about running against Fairchild.[45]

McCarthy's position within the Republican party remained tenuous. Being an Irish Catholic in a Protestant-dominated organization was no asset. He had been endorsed in 1946 because no one else would challenge La Follette, not because he was so desirable. Despite his intensive campaign, he was still new to Republican circles and almost unknown in some counties. His swift climb to the top of the Wisconsin political scene had not given him time to build one of those networks that most politicians carefully tend for years.[46]

McCarthy's Senate career aroused little enthusiasm among Wisconsin Republicans. Some were upset by his failure to pay his income taxes and his censorship by the state supreme court in 1949. McCarthy's committee assignments caused him anguish. After assignments were announced for 1949, he complained angrily to Senator Taft of the "awful foul deal" that was "extremely embarrassing" back in Wisconsin. Some constituents and Republican leaders were disturbed by McCarthy's inadequate handling of his constitutents' needs. He did not answer his mail or leap to satisfy constituents' demands in the way that Senator Wiley did. Although his staff's efficiency improved considerably after 1949, earlier it sometimes took his office a month to answer mail. The problem had been acute in 1947 when Johnston was his administrative assistant. Johnston had little interest in such details. On one occasion, after a Milwaukee constituent complained that he had written many letters to McCarthy and had received no acknowledgment, Ray Kiermas, McCarthy's office manager, found a hundred similar unacknowledged letters on Johnston's desk.[47]

After three years in the Senate, McCarthy was in serious political trouble. Gov. Oscar Rennebohm and fast-rising Walter Kohler, Jr., received warm receptions at the 1949 Republican state convention, but the applause for McCarthy was only polite and perfunctory.[48] "I think I could take Wiley [in 1950]," a Republican senatorial aspirant allegedly remarked, "but I'll wait for the easy one in 1952."[49] "Sometimes I am frightened at the fury with which some of his old champions denounce him," McMillin sardonically noted. "Things have come to such a pass that I have found myself, on rare occasions, uttering a word in his defense."[50]

Liberals such as McMillin who predicted McCarthy's downfall could be accused of wishful thinking, but no such accusation could be made against Wyngaard. In 1950, after McCarthy's anti-Communist crusade had made him the hero of Wisconsin Republicans, Wyngaard reflected on McCarthy's predicament only a year earlier. "It has been no secret that McCarthy slipped badly in political support at home since his spectacular and original campaign in 1946," Wyngaard noted. "Always a plunger and rarely discreet, McCarthy had been marked off by some of those politicans in the Republican organization who were thinking about the 1952 elections."[51]

McCarthy's political future looked dismal by the fall of 1949. Fortunately for him, he discovered the Communist issue that, in less than a year, propelled him into the national spotlight and into the hearts of Wisconsin

Republicans. He learned, firsthand, the political potential of the issue when he attacked an obscure reporter for *The Capital Times*.

\* \* \* \*

In the late 1940s, amid the growing tensions of the cold war, Democratic and Republican politicians increasingly seized on the Communist issue as a means of advancing their political fortunes. Democrats such as George Smathers and Willis Smith and Republicans such as Richard Nixon and Karl Mundt found it advantageous to accuse their opponents of pro-Communist sympathies. The manner in which McCarthy came to select the Communist issue as his own is important because of its typicality and because of McCarthy's later notoriety. It is also important to clear away the considerable confusion that surrounds his initial use of the Communist issue.

Like many other Republican campaigners, McCarthy had first used the Communist issue in 1946, when he accused his Democratic senatorial opponent, Howard McMurray, of being "communistically inclined" and a "little megaphone for the Communist-controlled PAC." In April 1947, he appeared in a radio debate on "Town Meeting of the Air" to argue that the Communist party should be outlawed, and in May of that same year he unsuccessfully sought to add an amendment to the Taft–Hartley bill that would allow employers to dismiss workers previously expelled from unions because of membership in the Communist party or Communist sympathies.[52]

But these were relatively isolated incidents, and most commentators have stressed other factors in attempting to explain the immediate circumstances that led McCarthy to adopt anticommunism as a political issue. The most recent and least reliable account has been suggested by Roy Cohn who, as a brash young man, served as McCarthy's chief assistant in 1953–1954.[53] According to Cohn's account, a G-2 officer took an FBI report on subversion and passed it around to various people. A small group became concerned and sought out a senator who would awaken the public to the danger. Just before Thanksgiving in 1949, three men approached McCarthy and asked him to publicize the report. "Literally overnight," Cohn insisted, "the senator decided to make the battle against communism his issue." He did so because he was patriotic and worried about Communist subversion, and because the issue presented a dramatic political opportunity.[54] Although there may be some truth to Cohn's account, his close association with McCarthy and his book's obvious bias make one hesitant to accept it. His story is hopelessly vague; the G-2 officer, the small group that became interested in the report, and the three men who approached McCarthy remain unidentified. No one, moreover, has substantiated his account.

According to a second and more widely accepted view, McCarthy adopted the Communists-in-government issue because of a suggestion made during a dinner at the Colony Restaurant in Washington, D.C., on 7 January 1950. The dinner was arranged by Charles Kraus, a member of McCarthy's staff and an instructor of political science at Washington's Georgetown University. Those invited included McCarthy; Father Edmund A. Walsh, the scholarly dean of Georgetown University's foreign-service school; and the noted Washington attorney William A. Roberts. After-dinner conversation focused on McCarthy's political future. He confessed to his three fellow Catholics that he desperately needed an issue with which to build a record for his 1952 reelection bid. "How about pushing harder for the St. Lawrence Seaway?" suggested Roberts. McCarthy was not impressed. He then suggested a Townsend-type pension plan for the elderly, but his friends rejected that idea. The conversation drifted on until Walsh remarked, "How about communism as an issue?" McCarthy allegedly pounced on the suggestion. "The government is full of Communists," he declared; "the thing to do is hammer at them." Supporters of this interpretation believe that the priest's suggestion inspired McCarthy to seek information on subversives in government and that, as a result, he publicly initiated his anti-Communist crusade a month later at Wheeling, West Virginia.[55]

The dinner did take place, and communism was no doubt discussed. Perhaps Walsh's remarks did inspire McCarthy to some degree; possibly there is some truth in Cohn's account as well. But McCarthy needed little encouragement to take up the Communist issue, for he had used it very effectively three months earlier in a successful, if little noticed, attack on *The Capital Times* and its city editor Cedric Parker.

William T. Evjue, editor of *The Capital Times*, liked tough, independent reporters. Reckless, hard-drinking Cedric Parker admirably measured up to this criterion. In his twenty-one years on Evjue's staff, Parker had earned his reputation as a crack reporter by performing such stunts as storming into gambling joints just ahead of raiding policemen. Evjue rewarded Parker by promoting him to city editor in 1948. Parker's renown as a reporter was equaled by his reputation as a left-wing CIO official who had allegedly followed the Communist party line before World War II. It was that aspect of his career that attracted McCarthy.

From 1947 to 1949, *The Capital Times* had repeatedly attacked and exposed McCarthy's record. Its reporters had revealed the quick-divorce scandal, investigated his financial affairs, publicized his censure by the state supreme court in 1941, and initiated the proceedings that led to his censure by the same court in 1949. A few other major newspapers publicized these devastating stories and criticized his Senate record. This publicity would not have endangered his political career so much if the dominant conservative press had found something good to say about his three years in the Senate. Republican papers did sometimes defend him from critics, but they rarely praised him. By the fall of 1949, all the evidence indicated that McCarthy was in serious political trouble. He could partially blame the liberal Madison daily for this frightful predicament.

McCarthy had been scheduled to address the Madison Shrine Club on 11 November 1949. Two days before the speech, he mailed out a nine-page mimeographed document to four hundred daily and weekly newspapers, all the radio stations in Wisconsin, and the school clerks of Dane County (which included Madison). Attached to each copy was a note from McCarthy that read: "Enclosed is a document which I thought you might be interested in. I intend to discuss this matter in some detail while back in Wisconsin."[56]

In this press release, he charged that Cedric Parker was a Communist and that *The Capital Times* followed the Communist party line. He leveled seven specific accusations at Parker. First, he charged that Evjue had once called Parker "the Communist leader in Madison." Second, he declared that Farrell Schnering, a former Communist party member from Milwaukee, had testified under oath that "the president of the Dane County [Communist] Council is Cedric Parker, a reporter of *The Capital Times,* who has been a sympathizer with the party and a fellow traveler since early in 1935. He joined the party toward the end of 1935." According to McCarthy, Parker had also been identified as a Communist by Kenneth Goff of Delavan, a Young Communist party member from 1936 through 1939. Parker was also listed as a sponsor of a mass meeting held in June 1938 by the American League for Peace and Democracy, which, McCarthy pointed out, had been labeled an "advocate of treason" by the House Un-American Activities Committee (HUAC). McCarthy charged that Parker and Eugene Dennis, a Communist leader, had organized and sponsored a statewide conference on farm and labor legislation in April 1934. HUAC, he declared, listed this organization as "Communist controlled." Parker had also attended a meeting of the Wisconsin Conference on Social Legislation, a group listed by the U.S. attorney general as a Communist organization. Finally, McCarthy charged that HUAC had named Parker as "being affiliated" with the Communist-inspired Citizens Committee to Free Earl Browder. The evidence indicated, McCarthy concluded, that Parker was "at one time a member of the party and was closely affiliated with a number of Communist-front organizations." Nothing in his subsequent writings "would indicate he has in any way changed his attitude toward the Communist party."[57]

The rest of the press release attempted to prove that *The Capital Times* was the "red mouthpiece" for the Communist party in Wisconsin and that it never attacked Communists. This was accomplished mainly by noting the "similar" views of Evjue's newspaper and the Communist *Daily Worker.* McCarthy concluded:

1. Has the Communist party with the cooperation of the Capital Times Corp. won a major victory in Wisconsin?

2. Is Cedric Parker, city editor of *The Capital Times*, a Communist?
3. Is the Capital Times Corp. the red mouthpiece for the Communist party in Wisconsin?
4. What can be done about this situation?[58]

At his 11 November speaking engagement before three hundred Madison Shriners and their guests from the Knights of Columbus, McCarthy repeated his charges and added some new twists. He taunted Evjue on his employment of Parker. "I sent Mr. Evjue a wire yesterday," he informed his audience, "and told him 'I have a question to ask you. Were you lying [on 14 March 1941] when you said Parker was Madison's leading Communist? If so, tell us when he changed.' " He urged Evjue to start a libel suit "if a single word of what I say is not the truth." His audience should seriously consider whether they desired to support a newspaper with Communist sympathies. "When you can expose a Communist paper," he said, "no businessman should write a check for advertising in it. And anyone who spends a nickel to buy that paper should remember he is helping the Communist cause." Quoting J. Edgar Hoover, McCarthy claimed that the Communist party's primary aim in the United States was to plant party members in important newspapers and radio stations, especially in college towns. Evjue owned a newspaper and a radio station, and the University of Wisconsin was located in Madison; the implication was clear. Adopting the posture of a fearless, principled public servant willing to court political danger by attacking a powerful newspaper, McCarthy revealed a soon-to-be characteristic retort: "When the time comes that I quit exposing things because I might bleed a little in return, I promise you, gentlemen, I will resign from the U.S. Senate." Then he lectured his audience on the immorality of communism, the danger of Communists in college towns, the need for government officials to expose them, and the possibility of a final showdown between the Soviet Union and the Western world.[59]

To this barrage, Parker responded: "I am not a member of the Communist party." He admitted having been a sponsor of the American League for Peace and Democracy but declared that he did not consider it subversive since "many good Americans were members." He denied any connection with the Browder committee; doubted that he had sponsored the Farm and Labor Legislation Conference; and disclaimed any acquaintance with Goff and Schnering. If he had attended the Conference on Social Legislation, he did so as a reporter. Evjue defended his newspaper's anti-Communist credentials, noting correctly the many occasions on which it exposed or criticized Communist activities. According to the angry editor, McCarthy's charges were a defense mechanism. Like other reactionary Republican leaders, McCarthy was striking back at people who opposed him by labeling them as Communists.[60]

Despite these disclaimers, for the first time in his career, McCarthy had maneuvered his major media nemesis into a defensive position. According to news accounts, Parker refused to answer a direct question about whether he had ever been a member of the Communist party. Evjue issued the embarrassing statement that Parker "has repeatedly assured the management of *The Capital Times* that he is not a member of the Communist party." Initially, Evjue was certain that he had the effective answer to McCarthy's barrage: in 1948, the last time Parker was elected president of the Madison Newspaper Guild, Evjue confidently asserted, he had signed a non-Communist affidavit and filed it with the National Labor Relations Board. But McCarthy was prepared with a devastating reply. During his Madison speech, taking note of Evjue's rebuttal, he pulled from his briefcase a letter from Claude Calkin, affidavit compliance officer for the National Labor Relations Board. "This office has no record of a non-Communist affidavit having been filed by Cedric Milford Parker," the letter stated.[61]

In an elaborate but awkward attempt to defend his fellow worker, Aldric Revell, a reporter for *The Capital Times*, tried to rationalize Evjue's remarks of 1941. Parker had made a speech at the University of Wisconsin in which he called Evjue a "war monger" and a "red baiter." At that time, Revell said, Parker was a reporter for *The Capital Times* and an influential leader in the Dane County CIO. Evjue called Parker a Communist because Parker's "view that the coming war was imperialistic happened to be the view held by Communists at the time."[62].

When first confronted by McCarthy's allegations, Evjue claimed that he could not recall when or if he had called Parker a Communist. During his Madison speech, McCarthy enlightened Evjue by waving aloft a photostatic copy of his 14 March 1941 editorial. Evjue refused to comment.[63] He was obviously embarrassed because he had indeed made the charge. In early 1941, the fiery editor had become embroiled in an argument with the CIO leadership at the Gisholt Machine Company in Madison. He demanded that the union members at Gisholt categorically repudiate communism. The union leaders objected to his attempt to dictate union policy. When the local union passed an innocuous resolution opposing "Communism, Nazism, and Fascism," Evjue blasted the leaders in a public letter to Clifford H. Johnson, secretary of the Steel Workers Organizing Committee of Madison. "I am wondering, Mr. Johnson," Evjue angrily asserted, "why are you so fearful of dictation at the hands of the editor of *The Capital Times* and why you accept so easily dictation at the hands of Mr. Cedric Parker, the Communist leader in Madison. . . . Let's get down to cases. Mr. Parker is a Communist and I defy him to publicly deny that statement."[64]

Perhaps Parker was a Communist party member before the war, or at least a fellow traveler. Certainly Evjue thought so in 1941, despite his subsequent rationalization for his editorial.[65] On 9 November, the day of McCarthy's initial assault, Evjue called Parker into his office and asked him if he belonged to the Communist party. Parker said, "No." "Were you ever a member of the Communist party?" Evjue persisted. "Yes," Parker responded, "I was a member . . . for a few weeks many years ago." McMillin later recalled: "I think that he [Parker] was certainly going along a Communist line. . . . I know that, because I talked to him in those days."[66]

It was difficult to trace many of McCarthy's undocumented charges; some of them were exaggerated, and others were distorted. Parker did associate with Wisconsin Communists and did join organizations in which Communists played prominent roles. Neither Parker nor Evjue attempted to deny that.[67] The important point, however, is not that Parker was or was not a Communist before World War II, but that in November 1949 McCarthy was successful in making Parker *appear* to have been a Communist. As for McCarthy's attack on *The Capital Times*, this aspect of his allegations severely misrepresented and distorted the Madison newspaper's persistent anti-Communist stance. Articles and exposés by *The Capital Times* were partly responsible for ousting Communists from the state CIO in 1946–1947. Indeed, Evjue's consistent and vigorous anti-Communist stance partly explains his discomfiture over McCarthy's charges. Evjue, who had made Parker the target of his red-baiting in 1941, now ironically became the target of McCarthy's red-baiting because of his employment of Cedric Parker.

Neither *The Capital Times* nor any of the state's other journals were willing to challenge the assumptions behind McCarthy's attack. They apparently shared his belief in the damaging nature of Communist associations. Indeed McCarthy's charges were potent precisely because they drew on an emerging anti-Communist consensus. In the absence of a challenge to this consensus, Evjue and *The Capital Times* were left with only lame excuses and rationalizations.

Republican leaders attending the address at the Shrine Club were delighted with McCarthy's speech. Governor Rennebohm, a frequent target of the Madison newspaper, sat beaming with satisfaction.[68] Besides embarrassing the staff of *The Capital Times* and throwing them on the defensive, McCarthy's assault gave him much-needed publicity. After his Senate victory in 1946, for example, McCarthy received very little news coverage in the *Wisconsin State Journal* (Madison). His initial attack on Parker, however, resulted in the largest single article printed about him from 1947 to 1949 by the conservative newspaper. In all, it carried about four thousand words on the incident. *The Capital Times* printed eight thousand words on the controversy. The *Milwaukee Journal*, which had been very critical of McCarthy's Senate record, wrote five lengthy articles and an editorial, totaling about seventy-five hundred words. McCarthy must have been especially pleased with the coverage the controversy received in the Fox River valley. The two largest circulation newspapers in the area prominently displayed his entire six-thousand-word press release, along with the numerous articles on the resulting feud. Smaller newspapers printed at least one or two long reviews of the incident. Even *Time* magazine covered the story.[69] McCarthy received as much or more publicity during this controversy than for any other action or policy statement during his first three years in the Senate.

More important, the publicity was favorable for a change. Newspapers printed the most dramatic captions: "McCarthy Quotes Record to Show How Capital Times Follows Reds," "McCarthy to Welcome Libel Suit on Red Charge," "Sen. McCarthy Points Red Finger at Capital Times," "McCarthy Dares Editors to Debate Red Charges," "Evjue Called Parker a Red, Senator Recalls Date."[70] The contents of the articles undoubtedly pleased McCarthy. Twice the *Milwaukee Journal* printed Evjue's entire 1941 editorial in which he labeled Parker a Communist.[71] Most articles described McCarthy's charges as "documented" or "from the record." His accusations usually appeared first and took up the initial three-quarters of the article. *Time*, which slanted its story in McCarthy's favor, described his opening salvo as a "blistering letter." It noted that Parker "had faithfully followed the Communist line" and that, although Evjue had called him a Communist in 1941, he promoted him to city editor seven years later.[72] While newspaper accounts made McCarthy appear as the defender of "Christian democracy," the rebuttals of Parker and Evjue seemed vague and evasive.

Wisconsin journalists recognized the publicity value of McCarthy's attack and its connection with his 1952 reelection bid. McCarthy "has decided to start his campaign early," one columnist wrote, "judging by the newspaper headlines he's trying to create." Another described his offensive as the "opening shot of his campaign for reelection in 1952." Evjue called the charges "the first note to be sounded in his campaign for reelection." Another anti-McCarthy editor thought his aim was to get "a lot of publicity . . . in preparation for his 1952 campaign. And here we are suckers enough to give it to him." Revell urged Evjue not to sue his antagonist because this would only give McCarthy more publicity. "The Republican newspapers in Wisconsin," he noted prophetically on 15 November 1949, "would love to conduct McCarthy's [1952] campaign for him on the Communist issue and forget all about his voting record."[73]

Thus, McCarthy actually began his anti-Communist crusade on 9 November 1949, when he distributed his document on Parker and *The Capital Times*. Two days later, when he repeated and extended his allegations before the Madison Shrine Club, the title of his speech was "Communism as a Threat to World Peace." At that time he told reporters that his tour of the state was a "personal campaign against communism."[74] Throughout November and December he kept the controversy alive and received more publicity as he constantly repeated his charges, challenged Evjue and Parker to start a libel action, and urged Evjue to debate him.[75]

By the late autumn of 1949, McCarthy had discovered the political value of red-baiting. More important, he extended his anti-Communist attacks to new and more dramatic targets. At a Young Republican gathering in Kenosha on 15 November, his major theme was Communist infiltration of the State Department. He specifically attacked John Stewart Service and castigated the State Department which, he charged, had a "red tint" and was "honeycombed and run by Communists."[76] On 3 December, at a gathering of realtors in Philadelphia, McCarthy devoted half of his speech to blaming the State Department's "bumbling foreign policy" for America's precarious position in the cold war.[77] On 5 December, he again assailed the State Department during an address to the Marquette University chapter of Alpha Kappa Psi. "The picture of the current 'war' between the Communist atheistic world and the Christian nations is becoming more and more dangerous," he said, "not every month or year but every minute. We are losing at a tremendous pace." But this was not surprising, "when we look [at] the personnel of the State Department."[78]

On the Senate floor on 5 January 1950—two days before he allegedly discovered the Communist issue at the Washington dinner—McCarthy again attacked Service. Why was he "still in charge of personnel and placement in the State Department," he demanded, after he was picked up by the FBI for espionage and was "accused of having had a sizable number of secret documents in his possession which he was handing over to the Communists?"[79] On 21 January, he indicted Secretary of State Dean Acheson for supporting Alger Hiss and alleged:

> There are lots of borers from within—left behind in the State Department, and they are under Acheson's nose every day [sic].
> It is these men who are largely responsible for Acheson's defeatist policy in the Far East.
> It is time Acheson either clean the Communists out of the State Department or resign and let President Truman appoint someone who will.[80]

Four days later, he reiterated his remarks on Acheson in a brief statement to the Senate.[81]

Scholars have overlooked the Cedric Parker incident as the origin and stimulant to McCarthy's campaign against communism.[82] His offensive was a sharp reversal from his previous neglect of the issue. Perhaps the substantial evidence he discovered on Parker convinced him that Communists were a real danger. More likely, however, the publicity and success he amassed made him aware of the issue's political potential. In any case, communism was the major theme of his speeches for three months before his historic Wheeling address. After his successful attack on Parker and The Capital Times, it was no wonder—if Cohn's account is correct—that McCarthy was so receptive to the small group with the intelligence report on subversion, or that he accepted Father Walsh's suggestion so readily.

By early 1950, then, McCarthy had hitched his career to the rising issue of anticommunism. He could hardly have foreseen the consequences of that commitment, though they were surely foreshadowed by the growing intensity of public concern over spies and subversives. In part this growing concern was the product of the cold war and the militantly anti-Communist rhetoric that the Truman administration used to justify its foreign policies. It was also the result of increasingly bitter attacks on the Truman administration by Republican partisans who believed that the Communist issue was a means to unseat the Democrats. The explosion of a nuclear bomb by the USSR, the takeover of China by Mao Tse-tung, and the conviction of Alger Hiss all served to catalyze popular fears that had already been excited by partisan appeals from both Democrats and Republicans.

McCarthy, fresh from his triumph in Wisconsin, intersected this growing national concern on 9 February 1950 in Wheeling, West Virginia. His speech, a logical if extreme outgrowth of his mounting interest in anti-Communist politics, touched a popular nerve with its apparent revelations about Communist infiltration in the State Department. The subsequent reaction made McCarthy a national figure and marked the beginning of his turbulent five years at the center of American politics.

# Chapter 6

# The Issue, Politics, and Debate: 1950–1952

"The way to get to be a political leader and the way to get the support of your party," McCarthy told his friend Urban Van Susteren on many occasions, "is to just lambast the hell out of the Democrats—in every way."[1] This approach paid big dividends for McCarthy after his famous address at Wheeling, West Virginia, on 9 February 1950. He charged that 205 people, known to the secretary of state to be members of the Communist party, were still working in the State Department and shaping American foreign policy. In subsequent speeches during February at Salt Lake City and Reno, the budding red-hunter repeated his accusations but changed the number of alleged Communists in the government agency.

McCarthy's charges were mostly fantasy, but the political byplay that surrounded them was real. After bitter Senate sessions on 20 and 22 February, during which he argued his case, the Senate resolved to investigate his charges. Millard Tydings, a Democrat from Maryland, chaired the subcommittee of the Senate Committee on Foreign Relations that conducted the inquiry. After flailing about ineffectively in the early weeks of the investigation, McCarthy began to make progress. By holding open hearings, the committee afforded him unlimited publicity. On 15 March 1950, when President Truman ordered government files to be withheld from investigation, McCarthy's supporters made it appear that the president was covering his tracks. McCarthy dramatically announced on 21 March that he was about to name the top Russian spy still at large. In executive session, he named Prof. Owen Lattimore as the culprit; columnist Drew Pearson broke the story. On 30 March, McCarthy pleaded his case against Lattimore. Although the Tydings committee report would eventually denounce McCarthy, he emerged from the hearings politically stronger and with growing support from the Republican party. His charges had become caught up in the furious partisan debate over the failure of American policy in China, and hardly a day passed without an attack on the State Department.[2]

The Truman administration's foreign policy, loyalty program, and strident anti-Communist rhetoric bear some of the blame for the rise of McCarthyism. McCarthy's unique personal qualities—his exaggerated sense of drama, willingness to gamble, and talent for political invective and press-agentry—also contributed, but McCarthyism was preeminently a partisan weapon used by Republicans against Democrats. The Senate's acceptance of the Tydings committee report, which branded McCarthy's charges a "fraud and a hoax," on 20 July 1950 did not allay partisan division on the McCarthy issue. On a critical vote on a Republican point of order aimed at rejection of the report, forty-five senators—all Democrats—voted against the measure, while thirty-seven Republican senators voted for it.[3]

National opposition to McCarthy was improvised, unsustained, and ineffective. Truman and his staff disliked McCarthy, but their attitude, when translated into action, produced policies of halting uncertainty. Dean Acheson, Truman's secretary of state, was vulnerable because of his abrasive personality, few friends in Congress, and public defense of Alger Hiss. In the Senate, Democratic leaders were unassertive and possessed modest ability and initiative. Few powerful senators were willing to take on McCarthy. Fear goes far to explain the dearth of volunteers. This was particularly true after the 1950 election when many observers credited McCarthy's campaign efforts with the defeat of Senator Tydings and other Democratic senators hostile to him.[4]

The Korean War, which broke out on 25 June 1950, accentuated the pressures and anxieties that perpetuated McCarthy. Although the war momentarily removed him from the headlines, by the end of summer a full-scale Red Scare had come into being. Julius and Ethel Rosenberg, Morton Sobell, and others were arrested on spy charges. The firing of Gen. Douglas MacArthur in April 1951 focused attention on the president's foreign and military policies and allowed Republicans to keep charging that Truman had been duped into playing the Kremlin's game. For the last year and a half of his administration, Republicans continued to harass Truman for his alleged softness toward communism.[5]

McCarthy remained in the limelight in 1951 and 1952 for several reasons. After adopting tougher standards, the federal Loyalty Review Board reopened hundreds of loyalty cases. Despite six prior clearances, John Stewart Service was judged a loyalty risk by the board in December 1951. Service had been a prominent McCarthy target, and his dismissal was a major victory for McCarthy. Each time the State Department dismissed or suspended someone, McCarthy's stature increased. The McCarran Internal Security Subcommittee harassed people previously attacked by McCarthy including John Carter Vincent, John Paton Davies, Lattimore, and Service. Overall, however, McCarthy's gains were modest in 1951–1952. "Every story of a dismissal, resignation, or reinstatement carried an acknowledgment of his initial charges," historian Richard Fried has noted, "but these ricochets seldom scored the bullseye of publicity which McCarthy had enjoyed in 1950."[6]

\*   \*   \*   \*

In Wisconsin, McCarthy's vilification of the Truman administration transformed his status from a bumbling senator doomed to political oblivion into the idol of Wisconsin Republicans. When he first made his unsupported accusations and carried them on clumsily for several weeks, Wisconsin Republicans were conspicuously silent and uneasy. Aware that some national GOP congressional leaders were reluctant to associate with his cause, and that much of the national press was against him, they wondered if he possessed more evidence or would fail miserably. At the end of March 1950, party officials became convinced that he had thrown the Truman administration on the defensive, and, as letters to newspapers showed, had aroused grass-roots voter support in Wisconsin. On 28 March, Sixth District Rep. Frank Keefe backed up McCarthy's blast against Philip Jessup. The following day, Second District Rep. Glenn Davis reiterated McCarthy's attack on Lattimore. The flood had started. In late March, Wayne Hood, chairman of the Republican Voluntary Committee (RVC) and his executive secretary, Jack Rouse, consulted the state GOP congressional delegation in Washington about the McCarthy furor. McCarthy assured them that he possessed more evidence.[7]

After Hood and Rouse returned from Washington, state party leaders convened a top-level meeting during which they decided to support McCarthy. Surprisingly, most of them seemed more concerned about McCarthy's charges that "sex perverts" were employed in important government agencies than they were about Communists in the State Department.[8]

On 11 April, in a speech to Dane County Republicans, Hood warned that Democratic propaganda had sought to try McCarthy instead of the Communists. McCarthy had made some "poor" statements, Hood conceded; nevertheless, he must be supported in his lone fight against the unfair Tydings committee. Hood's address was the first public indication that GOP leaders had rallied behind McCarthy.[9] During the next two months, resolutions and statements of praise poured in from party officials and from county and district GOP meetings.

Privately, Republican leaders delighted in the political potential of McCarthy's crusade. Hood wrote to McCarthy on 13 April that the Communist issue was "getting hotter all the time," and it would be "almost impossible for the Democrats to sit on the lid much longer."[10] More than anyone else in Wisconsin, Thomas Coleman, then an influential adviser to the RVC, rallied the party faithful to McCarthy's banner and sought to exploit the issue that McCarthy had created. Throughout the spring of 1950, Coleman worked feverishly to convince national GOP leaders to pursue the same course. Coleman deplored the Democrats' control of everything from federal judgeships to the chairmanships of congressional committees. The Democrats had vilified Republicans for seventeen years, "branding every businessman an enemy of the Republic." The best thing for the country, he argued, was a Republican president in 1952 and a Republican Congress in 1950.[11]

Throughout the spring, Coleman helped to orchestrate Republican senatorial attacks on Tydings. He and Arthur Summerfield, in cooperation with Republican Senate and House committees, also organized a national fund-raising campaign to provide McCarthy with investigators, special counsel, and publicity. By the end of June 1950, Coleman had personally raised about $6,500.[12]

On 20 April, Coleman urged the National Republican Strategy Committee to embrace McCarthy's crusade. The Tydings committee's investigation had raised an important question of party strategy. "There has not been such a hot political fight for years, and the New Dealers have been out-maneuvered." Tydings was obviously partisan. He intended to try McCarthy instead of performing his duty. The Maryland Democrat hoped to control procedure completely and to clear every government employee as he appeared. Tydings would have succeeded, Coleman argued, if Republican senators had not resisted and if McCarthy had not "put up a grand battle against all of the artillery of the opposition." Republicans had thrown Tydings on the defensive, Coleman summarized, the Hiss case had been "thoroughly re-publicized," and the nearly "4,000 homosexuals" employed in the government had been exposed. "Our party is finally on the attack and should stay there," he concluded enthusiastically. "And, best of all, we may get rid of many Communist sympathizers and queers who now control policy."[13]

Coleman reported to the Wisconsin Republican Finance Committee on 6 May that Democratic senators were so worried by McCarthy's onslaught that Tydings intended to hold closed committee meetings, take over the Communist issue, and make the Democrats the great heroes in fighting communism. "The Republican job," Coleman warned, "is to prevent any such result. I think that we can keep the people believing, as they should, that through McCarthy this is a Republican exposé."[14]

In April, Hood had asked McCarthy to keynote the Wisconsin Republican convention, to be held on 9 and 10 June. McCarthy's presence would assure good attendance, Hood noted in his invitation, and would "help us set a crusading tone for the balance of the convention."[15] McCarthy was apprehensive about this reception at the convention, but he need not have worried; it was tumultuous. Before his keynote speech, he distributed two thousand packets of mimeographed and photostatic documents, each containing forty-two sheets of copy that supposedly proved his charges that there were Communists in the government. In his aggressive, unabashed style, he lashed out at President Truman, Dean Acheson, Jessup, and Lattimore. The twenty-five hundred delegates responded enthusiastically to his assertion that the time had come to "pin-point individually" dangerous Communists and then if "lumberjack tactics are the only kind they understand then we shall use lumberjack tactics on them." The howling, cheering crowd interrupted his speech nineteen times. Many streamed to the rostrum at its conclusion. Surrounded by well-wishers and autograph seekers for a half-hour, McCarthy finally had to make his escape by ducking down the side stairs. Even then it took an hour for him to walk through the hotel lobby, so eager were fans to shake his hand and to talk with him. A long, fulsome, and adulatory resolution praised his "courage, patriotism and loyalty."[16]

With the outbreak of the Korean War in late June, Coleman assumed McCarthy would reassess and temper his campaign. He expected McCarthy to lose financial backing and publicity. "I think it would be well to make a complete recast of the situation before making any important moves," Coleman urged McCarthy. But McCarthy strongly disagreed. "As the casualty lists mount and the attention of the people is focused upon what actually happened in the Far East," he responded confidently on 15 July, "people can't help but realize there was something rotten in the State Department." He predicted that the war would be "the major campaign issue this fall." Coleman was convinced. Coleman wrote to the senator on 17 July that the public would not have been prepared for war if it had not been for McCarthy. Republicans had to "keep the public realizing" that Democratic blunders and treachery had caused the country's current problems.[17]

In the 1950 campaign, McCarthy made thirty addresses in fifteen states. Nationally, his main influence was on tactics. The campaign witnessed an unusual amount of scurrility, distortion, and red-baiting. All over the nation, candidates denounced their opponents for being soft on communism, for permitting Communists in government, and for being "dupes, fellow travellers and pinks." A character in one of Herbert Block's editorial cartoons asked, "Is Joe Stalin running in all these elections?"[18]

As the election approached in Wisconsin, state GOP leaders felt that McCarthy had the goods on the State Department and the support of the voters. Coleman and Cyrus Philipp, Republican national committeeman, successfully urged party strategists to stress McCarthy's crusade in the campaign and to deemphasize traditional state issues. Although state Republicans constantly boasted of their accomplishments in providing good government in Wisconsin, they concentrated on more dramatic national and international issues. The party's major campaign tabloid proclaimed, "Korea: An American Victory. A Democratic Blunder." Campaign propaganda stressed the themes of Yalta, appeasement, the abandonment of Nationalist China, Alger Hiss, and, particularly, McCarthy's allegations of pro-Soviet influences in the making of American foreign policy. One campaign sheet, "Voter's Digest," used most of McCarthy's arguments in a prominent display entitled "Ask Your Democratic Friends These Questions."[19]

Because his presence was in great demand nationally, McCarthy curtailed his state appearances during the campaign. In Wisconsin speeches, he devoted himself exclusively to the same theme: the contest with the Soviets in international affairs and the failure of American diplomacy under Truman and Acheson. On one occasion, he soberly labeled the Truman administration as "puppets of the Politburo." He drew large crowds. In the small town of Beaver Dam, McCarthy captivated eight hundred people, including many Democrats. His listeners were quiet and attentive, and their applause was long. After his speech, in what was becoming a customary response, scores of people crowded the rostrum to shake his hand and give encouragement. McCarthy drew two thousand people to a Kenosha speech on two days' notice, while, in Milwaukee, Vice-President Alben Barkley only attracted half as many to a well-publicized speech in a major auditorium.[20]

Rallies of other state Republican candidates were well attended only when McCarthy was on the program. Walter Kohler and Vernon Thomson, the GOP candidates for governor and lieutenant governor, discovered that they received a more enthusiastic response when they joined McCarthy in his denunciation of Communists and Democratic foreign policy than when they spoke on the mundane details of state government. Liberals accused Kohler of adding a new twist to the anti-Communist lexicon—"guilt by multiplication"—when he declared that he had not "the slightest doubt that there are thousands of Communists in key places of the government. The case of Alger Hiss proves that." Critics blasted the Republican campaign strategy for its reliance on deception, emotion, and McCarthyism. The *Milwaukee Journal* blamed Coleman for the tactics. "Mr. Coleman apparently thinks it is a sure way to victory, and that seems to be about all that has ever interested Thomas E. Coleman politically. The means he employs and the damage he causes do not seem to concern Mr. Coleman."[21]

Early in the campaign, Thomas Fairchild, the Democrat running against Sen. Alexander Wiley, accused his opponent of identifying with McCarthy and the "standards of public morality he represents." But, on the whole, Democratic strategists decided not to meet McCarthy head-on because they feared that fighting on his issues would be dangerous.[22]

Republican campaign techniques appeared to pay off as the GOP swept to victory in Wisconsin. Most state Republicans attributed their success to McCarthy's influence, but many factors probably accounted for the results, including traditional Democratic weakness in the state, the declining popularity of President Truman, corruption in his administration, and accumulated anti-Democratic grievances throughout the nation. Still, Wisconsin Republicans pointed to the large crowds McCarthy attracted and the emotional response to his speeches. "I can't tell you how much we appreciated your efforts during the campaign," Hood told McCarthy after the election, "or how much we feel the results are due to those efforts and the issues that you raised." The Korean situation and the Communist issue had put the Democrats on the defensive early in the campaign, Hood observed. His only regret was that more states had not followed the example of Wisconsin's Republicans.[23]

Some liberals would not concede that McCarthy had been an asset to the Republicans. Wisconsin Democrats had done better than usual. Their gubernatorial candidate made a 2-percent gain over his showing in 1948 when Truman won the state. Fairchild captured 46 percent of the vote—a sharp challenge to Wiley. Although the Democrats lost ground in Milwaukee (where the Polish population may have responded to the Communist issue), they improved on their 1948 performance in twenty-three other counties. The Democratic vote declined in forty-three counties, but the Republican vote declined in sixty. With a few exceptions, wherever McCarthy appeared in the state—Madison, Eau Claire, La Crosse, Marathon County, and Columbia County—Democrats increased their percentage of the vote. Whether this trend was caused by McCarthy or other factors cannot be known for certain.[24]

On the other hand, some Democratic candidates strongly felt the influence of McCarthy's presence. Patrick Lucey, unsuccessful candidate for Congress in the Third District, thought that McCarthy was an important factor in his defeat: McCarthy had brought out a thousand people in the small town of Prairie du Chien and had branded Lucey a "Commiecrat." McCarthy's crusade was a potent force for Carl Thompson, Democratic candidate for governor. To prove his Americanism, Thompson played a corny record at many campaign stops:

> The only Red we want
> is the Red we got
> in the old Red, White, and Blue.[25]

The effects of the Communist issue in other states ranged from considerable to marginal. In the Maryland election, the McCarthy issue was a primary cause of Senator Tydings's defeat. That election demonstrated that McCarthy did exercise some influence on voting results. For most observers, both in Wisconsin and in the country at large, the belief in McCarthy's political invincibility continued to grow, only to be dispelled by the 1952 election.[26]

McCarthyism had a major impact on the Republican presidential primary in Wisconsin in the spring of 1952 as the candidates—Earl Warren, Harold Stassen, and Robert Taft—confronted the issue. Warren's delegate list was made up of liberal and moderate Republicans, most of whom (including Philip La Follette and Ralph Immell) were former La Follette Progressives. Warren opposed McCarthy but successfully avoided questions about him during the campaign. Stassen strongly endorsed the Communists-in-government issue without committing himself to McCarthy.[27]

Senator Taft, however, had major difficulty with the touchy McCarthy issue. Taft had paid little attention to McCarthy until 1950. When McCarthy launched his anti-Communist crusade, Taft was as surprised as anyone. McCarthy had not asked for advice from Taft or any other top

Republican. Ordinarily Taft could be expected to oppose McCarthy because of Taft's strong defense of civil liberties, reverence for law, and painstaking respect for facts. He also felt personally uncomfortable with his crude and undisciplined colleague. Initially, he criticized McCarthy in private for his reckless performance and for overstating a good case.[28]

But Taft did not attempt to restrain McCarthy and even publicly defended him. Taft shared many of McCarthy's views and had damned communism in American life long before McCarthy entered the scene. Above all, Taft was intensely partisan and was ambitious for the Republican presidential nomination in 1952. Taft had long known that the Wisconsin primary on 2 April 1952 would be a crucial test for his candidacy. Wisconsin had been the graveyard of presidential hopes for many candidates. In 1940 Thomas Dewey knocked Arthur Vandenberg out of the race in Wisconsin and in 1944 destroyed the candidacy of Wendell Willkie. In 1948 Stassen deflated the boom for MacArthur. In 1952 Taft would campaign in Wisconsin for twenty-two days, give 250 speeches, travel three thousand miles throughout the state, and spend $100,000.[29]

Taft won the support of 80 percent of the state Republican county chairmen and nearly all the state party officials. His leading Wisconsin backers were also McCarthy intimates. Walter Harnischfeger, Thomas Korb, and Hood played major roles in Taft's campaign. Victor Johnston directed Taft's national headquarters in 1952. Coleman was Taft's Midwest manager and floor manager at the Republican national convention.[30]

On 10 June 1951, at the urging of Coleman, Korb, and Hood, Taft commended McCarthy, who shared the rostrum with him at a $100-a-plate Republican dinner in Milwaukee. When the two stood up together, the crowd shouted: "There's the '52 ticket; Taft and McCarthy." On this and other occasions, Taft could not have failed to note McCarthy's popularity among Wisconsin Republicans. However, after McCarthy's attack on Gen. George Marshall on 14 June 1951, Taft openly demurred and refused to acknowledge a special relationship with McCarthy.[31]

At Des Moines, Iowa, on 22 October 1951, Taft came as close to publicly denouncing McCarthy as he would ever get. He conceded that McCarthy had "overstated his charges in some cases," and that he disagreed with McCarthy's "extreme attack" on Marshall. McCarthy was piqued. He said he hoped that Taft had not joined the "left wing camp followers in opposing my Communist fight." Although he had earlier been thought to be a Taft supporter, McCarthy now stressed the great popularity of Gen. Douglas MacArthur. In early November, McCarthy said on television that, before he would endorse Taft, the Ohio senator had to prove he could win in the primaries. Historian John Ricks concluded that "McCarthy was giving Taft a dose of his own medicine—less than full endorsement, but not a disavowal either." A successful testimonial dinner in December and the dismissal of John Stewart Service increased McCarthy's confidence and his unwillingness to compromise.[32]

Some McCarthy supporters in Wisconsin were also irritated with the Ohio senator. "If Bob Taft thinks he can win friends by being mealy-mouthed," one declared, "he's dead wrong." A McCarthy campaign manager argued:

> McCarthy doesn't need Taft to win in Wisconsin, but the reverse is not true. Taft is putting all his eggs in one basket here—he's made Wisconsin the one state where he hopes to prove that he can carry other states as he did Ohio in his 1950 campaign. He can't do that with just the anti-McCarthy votes.

On the other hand, some Republicans were disappointed at McCarthy for insisting that Taft categorically endorse him.[33]

Throughout November and December 1951, the McCarthy problem worried Taft and his aides. Taft asked Coleman to find out McCarthy's attitude. Coleman replied on 26 December that McCarthy was "way up in the clouds and expect[ed] . . . complete support of himself on all things. I do not see just what he is after, but you may be sure that he feels that he has the upper hand. I cannot feel that any sense of loyalty to any of us or to anyone at all has any part in the picture." Coleman told another campaign official that McCarthy had developed a "Christ-like complex."[34]

As it would also do for Governor Kohler, the dismissal of Service prompted Taft to embrace McCarthy more closely. In a Beloit speech in January 1952, Taft described McCarthy's investigation as "fully justified by repeated dismissals of employees of doubtful loyalty" and cited the example of Service.[35]

As the primary approached, Taft received pressure to disavow McCarthy. The editor of the Milwaukee Journal told a Taft campaign aide that his paper would not endorse Taft if he continued to support McCarthy. But during the spring, Taft again sounded friendly to McCarthy. "Senator McCarthy has dramatized the fight to exclude Communists from the State Department. I think he did a great job in undertaking that goal." Taft also worked quietly with Coleman to get McCarthy's endorsement. "I have talked over the matter at length with Tom Coleman," Taft wrote Herbert Hoover, "and he feels that he can bring McCarthy around." Taft won the primary, capturing 46 percent of the vote and twenty-four of the thirty delegates. But neither Coleman nor anyone else brought McCarthy around. McCarthy's only blessing for Taft was silence.[36]

Most Wisconsin Republicans remained enthusiastic about McCarthy until 1954. As one columnist observed in 1951: "whatever 'McCarthyism' may be, the working Republicans want it and will continue to support it." Yet, beneath the surface, there was some apprehension and disagreement. McCarthy's crude methods, impulsiveness, and instinct for political gambles disturbed some Republicans, as did his legal troubles, tax difficulties, and personal finances. As his attitude toward Taft showed, he appeared hardened and embittered by constant criticism and seemed unable to compromise with politicians who had been neutral or lukewarm toward him in the past.[37] However, these sentiments were not expressed openly until 1954.

The most vocal opposition to McCarthy within his own party came from those on the fringe of the organization or those without influence. Former Progressive Leonard Schmitt, only a nominal Republican, regularly castigated him. Assemblyman Arthur Peterson and State Sen. Harry Franke incurred the wrath of party leaders by their outspoken criticism in the state legislature. Anti-McCarthy sentiment was strong in the Young Republican chapters in Manitowoc County and at the University of Wisconsin.

McCarthy's crusade and character aroused some disapproval from leading Republican politicians. Oscar Rennebohm, who retired from the governorship in 1950, disliked McCarthy and never publicly endorsed him or his anti-Communist campaign. Secretary of State Fred Zimmerman, perennially his party's leading vote-getter, never disguised his contempt for his Republican colleague. Asked in August 1951 if he opposed McCarthy, Zimmerman responded, "You're damned right." Queried on why he did not attend a speech by McCarthy in Madison, he replied bluntly: "I don't want to go anywhere where McCarthy is."[38] Zimmerman predicted that Wisconsin voters would repudiate McCarthy in 1952. His record as a prophet had been blemished, however, because of an earlier prediction: he had told fellow Republicans that La Follette would beat McCarthy two-to-one in 1946.

Kohler, elected governor in 1950 to succeed Rennebohm, vacillated on McCarthy. Kohler's upper-class background predisposed him against that "rascal." He told friends of his disgust with McCarthy's personal ethics and of his disagreement with McCarthy's tactics and some of his charges. He was particularly irritated by McCarthy's blasts at Marshall, whom Kohler deeply respected.[39] On occasion, this led him to make anti-McCarthy statements and to contemplate running against him in the 1952 Republican primary. On the other hand, Kohler was a loyal Republican. The thought of disrupting party unity over the McCarthy issue and losing the 1952 presidential election horrified him. Kohler's conviction that Communist sympathizers were in the federal government and that McCarthy had succeeded in rooting some out usually led him to endorse McCarthy's campaign and to associate with him at party gatherings.[40]

Sen. Alexander Wiley's reactions to the McCarthy controversy illustrate how long a politician can successfully maintain a precarious perch atop the political fence. Vain and pompous, Wiley was nevertheless an accomplished politician and an effective campaigner. He irritated fervent ideological conservatives with his platitudinous and pious speeches. He waxed eloquent on God and patriotism. After a typical Wiley speech in 1950, one frustrated Republican leader observed: "He talks about God, and as far as I know, God isn't an issue in Wisconsin." Privately, Coleman described Wiley as a "stupid son-of-a-bitch."[41]

Wiley never publicly criticized McCarthy until after 1955. His initial reaction to McCarthy's Communists-in-government charges typified his response to most controversial issues: he would suspend judgment pending further evidence. The issue was not McCarthy or Acheson, he insisted, but "whether or not there are any disloyal people in government."[42] During his 1950 campaign, Wiley suppressed much of his ambivalence about his Senate colleague. He welcomed McCarthy's support, mentioned him favorably in a few speeches, echoed his attacks on Communists in government, and, after his victory, thanked McCarthy for his support.[43] The relations between the two senators remained formally cordial and polite until 1956.

Privately, however, Wiley and McCarthy did not get along. Like Rennebohm and Kohler, Wiley apparently told friends of his personal antipathy for McCarthy. McCarthy had disparaged Wiley in their primary battle in 1944, and Wiley did not forget.[44] Understandably, Wiley was jealous and resentful of his previously inconspicuous colleague's notoriety. Wiley's speech to the state Republican convention of 1950 was only briefly mentioned in state newspapers while McCarthy's address received prominent display.[45] Wiley deplored the vicious name-calling that passed between McCarthy and his opponents. As he told his brother: "name-calling—you know my philosophy—never gets anyone anywhere." During the Tydings hearings in April 1950, Wiley was surprisingly sympathetic to Lattimore who had done a "tremendous job" of defending himself against McCarthy's allegations.[46]

A change in Wiley's ideological views got him into serious trouble with the dominant wing of the state GOP and partially explained his poorly disguised opposition to McCarthy. Wiley had been a prewar isolationist and had not been conspicuously bipartisan. After the war, having been influenced by Sen. Arthur Vandenberg and, perhaps, by his membership on the Senate Foreign Relations Commitee, he began to expound an internationalist and bipartisan foreign policy. By 1950, he regularly complimented General Marshall and Secretary of State Acheson. The following year, he called President Truman's State of the Union address the "greatest speech of Truman's career."[47] In April 1952, he called for nonpartisan cooperation between the legislative and executive branches of government. He praised the Marshall Plan and opposed as a matter of principle those in his own party who had "the mistaken idea that simply because 'the other fellow' [that is, the Democrats] recommended a policy, it is necessarily wrong." He urged Republicans to look to the future instead of the past (for example, to Yalta and the fall of China), to offer a positive program, and to support the anti-Communist foreign policies of the Truman administration. Although praised in liberal circles, Wiley's new posture found little support within Wisconsin's isolationist and partisan Republican organization. His stance also seemed to be a direct slap at

McCarthy. Wiley's cordiality to Acheson impugned the whole basis of McCarthy's reelection campaign at a crucial point in his career.[48]

In public, McCarthy maintained cordial relations with Wiley for the sake of party unity. In private, however, he expressed "gigantic, superb contempt" for him, often referring to him as a "bag of wind," or a "blatherskite." McCarthy hoped that Wiley would remain neutral on his anti-Communist campaign because he was afraid that Wiley would embarrass him if he spoke on his behalf.[49]

\*  \*  \*  \*

McCarthy's anti-Communist crusade was publicly supported by most conservative Republicans and most Wisconsin newspapers as well as by major state GOP leaders. They argued their case forcefully in speeches, testimonials, editorials, and hundreds of letters to newspapers. They believed that a serious danger existed; that an international Communist conspiracy, aided and abetted by Communist agents and sympathizers within the federal government, planned to take over the United States. The most extreme wing of the pro-McCarthy camp, a vocal minority, held that America's recognition of the Soviet Union in 1933 was the first step in this evil design. This allowed Russian agents, spies, and sympathizers to enter the United States with the encouragement and connivance of the Democratic party. Communists and crackpots filled the White House during Roosevelt's administration and continued to do so under Truman's tenure. Meanwhile, Democratic foreign policy, influenced by these Communists, furthered the designs of the Soviet Union at Yalta, Tehran, and Potsdam, resulting in the Communist takeover of much of Europe and Asia. Alger Hiss was a perfect example of the workings of this "invisible government."[50]

Most McCarthy enthusiasts held less extreme views. They argued that Roosevelt's naive, optimistic belief in the Soviet Union's postwar intentions and the influence of Russian spies and sympathizers on Democratic foreign policy had allowed Communists to take over much of Europe and Asia. The spy problem centered in the State Department where strategically placed individuals such as Alger Hiss had damaged American foreign policy. Thanks to the weakness and stupidity of Roosevelt and Truman, Communist sympathizers had convinced the State Department to abandon Chiang Kai-shek's government in China.[51]

Especially disconcerting to McCarthy backers was their belief that Democratic administrations—either because of embarrassment or softness toward communism—had done nothing about internal subversion. They had ignored investigations and exposés by congressional committees and the FBI. McCarthy supporters repeatedly cited the Hiss case as an example. Whittaker Chambers had taken his case against Hiss to the State Department in 1939, yet nothing had been done until nine years later when the House Un-American Activities Committee took up the issue and exposed him. Truman's description of the case as a red herring indicated his lack of concern for its implications, and Secretary of State Acheson continued to support Hiss even after his conviction. The Democratically controlled Tydings committee was another attempt to cover up internal subversion. Instead of investigating the extent of Communist influence in the government, as Senate Resolution 231 had called for, the Democratic majority had concentrated on discrediting McCarthy.[52] Under the circumstances, McCarthy supporters argued, McCarthy had no alternative but to take his case to the American people and to demand action. He might defy tradition, make some mistakes, and occasionally use questionable methods, but all this was understandable considering the scope of the problem and the obstacles placed in his path.[53]

His partisans insisted that McCarthy's crusade had been partly successful. His persistent charges had probably reversed the administration's "idiotic" Asian policy so that it immediately confronted the Communist invasion in South Korea. Many people exposed by McCarthy had lost their government jobs. The dismissals of Stephan and Esther Brunauer, William Remington, John Paton Davies, Lattimore, Service, and others proved that McCarthy's accusations had substance. Without his vigilance, these individuals would still be influencing government policy.[54] Every time McCarthy's supporters read about someone leaving the government, whether McCarthy had a hand in it or not, they assumed that the person was a Communist sympathizer who had been scared out by McCarthy.

McCarthy's assault on George Marshall, however, received very little support. Marshall was a man of great dignity and prestige who had served with distinction in the highest military and civilian posts; even McCarthy conceded that the general was regarded by many people as the "greatest living American." McCarthy had criticized Marshall on numerous occasions, but, in a lengthy indictment on 14 June 1951, he accused Marshall of participating in "a conspiracy so immense and an infamy so black as to dwarf any previous such venture in the history of man."[55] Most of McCarthy's backers remained silent on his Marshall speech, and some eventually defended the general from the implication of treason.[56]

A negative source of McCarthy's strength was his admirers' indifference to the moral implications of his personal and legislative record. Anti-McCarthyites could not drum up debate on his ethics and integrity because his supporters would not discuss those aspects of his career. Questions involving his failure to pay taxes, his military record, the two censures by the state supreme court, his acceptance of a highly questionable $10,000 from the Lustron Corporation, the Tydings election scandal, and many others elicited little comment from the pro-McCarthy camp. His admirers sometimes dismissed these charges as smear tactics or mere politics. William J. Campbell (who had denounced McCarthy in 1949 but now defended his every action) declared flatly: "I care nothing about Joe McCarthy's personal affairs."[57] In all his dealings with him, Coleman argued, McCarthy

> never asked me to do anything unethical, so why should I believe the smears that people try to pin on him? Take the Maryland campaign: Joe never used any composite pictures in Wisconsin, so why should I believe that he had a hand in the composite picture in Maryland?[58]

In another rationalization, McCarthy's practices were justified because the Democrats did even worse. Bradley Taylor, influential Tenth District Republican and prominent member of the Wisconsin American Legion, argued that both political parties "have bad apples." When people criticized his friend McCarthy for accepting $10,000 from the Lustron Corporation, Taylor noted, the obvious rebuttal was that Lustron "run by Democrats got 37 million [dollars in loans from the Reconstruction Finance Corporation] and perhaps Joe should have charged them 25 grand."[59]

Another approach minimized the extent of McCarthy's unethical conduct. During a debate with Rep. Richard Bolling, a Democrat from Missouri, Charles Kersten was asked to comment on the many charges leveled against McCarthy. The Milwaukee congressman replied sharply: "Now there isn't any one of us concerning whom some peccadillo may not have been uncovered with regard to his past life." When Bolling asked Kersten if he considered the destruction of court records, perversion of the court process, and attempts to evade taxation as "peccadillos," Kersten muttered that Bolling should get the facts.[60] Usually, though, McCarthy's admirers responded to attacks on his integrity with silence.

For the most part, then, Republicans enthusiastically endorsed McCarthy and his cause. They did so, however, only so long as McCarthy attacked and embarrassed the Democratic Truman administration. Only later, when McCarthy's target changed, did it become apparent that most Wisconsin Republicans had a higher regard for their own and their party's interests than they had for McCarthy.

*　　*　　*　　*

Opposition to McCarthy within Wisconsin stemmed from a mixture of ideological, moral, and partisan motives. The movement was spearheaded by three newspapers, labor-union journals, leaders of the Democratic Organizing Committee (DOC), a few independent liberals and moderates, and some dissident Republicans. His opponents were equally as critical of the methods and validity of his anti-Communist crusade as they were of his unethical personal and legislative conduct. Critics virtually ignored his voting record until the 1952 general election.

Although consistent anti-Communists, McCarthy's opponents were generally less worried about communism than the senator's supporters were. McCarthy was wrong to insist that the Truman administration was soft on communism. Its many effective anti-Communist measures included assistance to Greece and Turkey, the Berlin airlift, the Marshall

Plan, the organization of NATO, and military aid to South Korea. China fell to the Communists in 1949 because Chiang Kai-shek's government was reactionary and corrupt, not because the president was negligent or there were Communist sympathizers in the State Department. "In their desperation," *The Capital Times* theorized, "the people of China turned to the Communists, as they will in any country where misery and suffering are allowed to go unchecked."[61]

Under President Truman, McCarthy's critics contended, appropriations for the FBI had increased, and the bureau worked as part of a team with the attorney general and the president. Because of this cooperation, many Communist leaders and agents had been caught and prosecuted. The anti-McCarthy camp uncritically accepted the work of the Tydings committee. The investigation had been thorough and its report devastating. The committee's facts were matters of record and had nothing to do with political partisanship. McCarthy's opponents argued that, if there were some Communists in the government, the problem should be dealt with by loyalty boards and the FBI, not by public exposure and "scattergun" charges.[62]

McCarthy's methods aroused bitter criticism. They were terrifying and debased. He used clever distortions, twisted historical facts, quotations out of context, guilt by association, vilification, multiple untruths, half-truths, and the threat of boycott. He employed these tactics to impugn the reputation and distinguished careers of many innocent people who had no legal recourse against him because of the immunity from libel enjoyed by members of Congress. "The man who isn't willing to say OFF the Senate floor the things he says about people ON the Senate floor is 'hitting below the belt.' " In this way, he soiled the reputations of such outstanding individuals as Jessup, Dorothy Kenyon, and Marshall.[63]

Opponents charged that, for all the fuss McCarthy had created, he had not proven the existence of even one Communist. The government did dismiss some of McCarthy's targets, but only because reasonable doubt existed about their loyalty and not, as McCarthyites claimed, because they were proven Communists.[64] McCarthy's irresponsible campaign ruined the morale of government employees and threatened traditional American liberties. A witch-hunt climate existed. Hysteria had engulfed the nation, and this atmosphere endangered freedom of speech and the press.[65]

McCarthy's critics also doubted his sincerity. They felt that McCarthy had adopted the Communist issue solely for its political mileage and publicity. He had been a "dead duck" politically in Wisconsin by late 1949 mainly because of the adverse publicity concerning his unethical conduct. George Haberman, president of the Wisconsin Federation of Labor, charged that McCarthy was so opportunistic that he "would sell his country down the river for 30 headlines a month."[66]

Opponents leveled an enormous amount of criticism at McCarthy's personal and legislative ethics. Again and again, they reviewed previous investigations and scandals to emphasize his dreadful personal traits. They reveled in the new disclosure that involved McCarthy in a scandalous relationship with the Lustron Corporation, a builder of prefabricated homes. In 1948, Lustron's president, Carl Strandlund, paid McCarthy a fee for publication rights to an article on housing that had been compiled by McCarthy's staff. At a press conference on 28 February 1949, McCarthy declined to give the exact amount of this fee but stated that it was "embarrassingly small. Besides I have to split it with 10 people." Nothing more was said of the incident at the time. But after Lustron went into receivership in 1950, costing the federal government about $30,000,000 in loans, a Senate committee investigated the company and discovered a $10,000 payment to McCarthy. Considering that the article was only seven thousand words, this amount hardly seemed "embarrassingly small." Moreover, according to McCarthy's tax return, he had kept the entire amount. At the time he accepted the Lustron check, McCarthy was a member of the Banking and Currency Committee, which had jurisdiction over the Reconstruction Finance Corporation (RFC), which in turn had loaned Lustron over $37,000,000. McCarthy wrote part of the Housing Act of 1948, one provision of which authorized the RFC to make loans of $50,000,000 to manufacturers of prefabricated housing. This allowed Lustron to receive its third RFC loan of $7,000,000. Although all the details of McCarthy's relationship with Lustron did not surface until 1953, his critics had enough evidence to ask insistently if, under the circumstances, it was ethical for him to accept the money.[67]

In 1950, John Marshall Butler defeated the incumbent, Millard Tydings, in the Senate race in Maryland. McCarthy had campaigned vigorously against Tydings. Because so many irregularities occurred during the campaign, the Senate appointed a committee to investigate the election. The Monroney committee described the Maryland affair as a "despicable, back street" type of campaign. The committee found that Butler's campaign propaganda, prepared partly by McCarthy's staff, included a fake photograph depicting the conservative Tydings in friendly conversation with Communist party leader Earl Browder. The committee's findings gave McCarthy's Wisconsin opponents more evidence about their resident ogre.[68]

In February 1951, Miles McMillin and Morris Rubin, editor of *The Progressive* magazine (Madison), spearheaded the drive to establish The Wisconsin Citizens' Committee on McCarthy's Record. A small group, consisting mostly of former La Follette Progressives and liberal newspapermen, held research and editorial sessions throughout the year and began compiling a comprehensive and critical booklet on McCarthy's career. Rubin, the editor, insisted on "impeccable accuracy and factual reporting." He intended to "dump everything and anything that isn't absolutely provable." The group hoped that *The McCarthy Record* would win over intelligent conservative Republicans, moderates, and independents to the anti-McCarthy camp. The results were impressive. The Citizens' Committee consisted of prominent Wisconsin bankers, industrialists, clergymen, educators, doctors, and lawyers. Although the booklet contained no original exposés, the editors had systematically compiled one of the first anti-McCarthy tracts. Published in the summer of 1952, the *Record* circulated widely, was serialized in anti-McCarthy newspapers, and served as major campaign material for McCarthy's opponents in the 1952 election.[69]

By 1951, McCarthy's adversaries had found much to criticize in his background, but his military-service record during World War II withstood numerous muckraking attempts and remained a laudatory interlude in an otherwise iniquitous career. As late as 1950, McCarthy's opponents still accepted his version of his war exploits. Noting McCarthy's combat missions and his tail-gunner adventures, John Hoving of the *Milwaukee Journal* concluded that "McCarthy's enemies have tried to slur over those bids for glory, but I would say that he has a good deal of personal courage."[70]

But in 1952, Robert Fleming of the *Journal* uncovered many of the facts behind McCarthy's mythical marine record. The evolution of the Fleming story and its aftermath illustrate the determination and perseverance, the satisfactions and disappointments of anti-McCarthy journalism. In 1950, Fleming was a bright but undistinguished young reporter for the *Journal*. Two years later, as a consequence of his investigation of McCarthy, he had become famous in newspaper circles, and McCarthy's critics throughout the nation consulted him on all aspects of the senator's career.

Fleming began working for the *Journal* in the late 1940s. After a year's leave of absence as a Nieman Fellow at Harvard University, Fleming was assigned to uncover what was expected to be damaging material on the increasingly controversial Wisconsin senator. *Journal* executives were bothered by more than McCarthy's methods and unethical conduct in his anti-Communist crusade. In the summer of 1950, McCarthy directly attacked the *Journal*. He had sought to intimidate the newspaper by calling it the Milwaukee version of the Washington *Daily Worker* and by urging advertisers to boycott it.

"As I understand my assignment now," Fleming wrote his superiors in the fall of 1950, "it's this":

> Collect all available information on McCarthy for a file in Wally's [probably Wallace Lomoe of the *Journal*] office, reporting anything that I can't substantiate as only rumor, and documenting all that I can. I'm to share information with public officials. It appears that there may not be much in news stories unless officials act, but this is not [to be] a controlling factor in what leads we follow.[71]

Besides covering Wisconsin politics and McCarthy's public appearances in the state, Fleming probed every aspect of the senator's career from his mysterious 1944 campaign contributions and income-tax payments to his specific charges of Communists in government. For a while, Fleming thought he had uncovered a major scandal in McCarthy's "obvious falsification" of his income from speaking fees on his 1950 tax return. McCarthy reported only a half-dozen engagement fees despite having made many more appearances. Fleming did extensive research but, for unknown reasons, published nothing.[72] Nevertheless, he appeared to revel in the assignment. It was a "fine project," he wrote a friend enthusiastically in July 1950. "My earlier conviction is unchanged: McCarthy is either very stupid or crooked, and no one has convinced me that he's stupid."[73]

During a research trip to Washington in April 1951, Fleming discovered that some leading McCarthy opponents desired a cooperative effort against the elusive senator. The major aspect of this plan involved hiring an investigator, paid for by funds provided by leading McCarthy antagonists, to thoroughly probe the senator's career. Among those interested in this approach were Tydings; the Democratic National Committee; Philip Graham, publisher of the *Washington Post*; and Joseph Pulitzer of the *St. Louis Post-Dispatch*. They agreed that it was too expensive for each anti-McCarthy group or individual to hire its own investigator and that the "flow of news caused frequent interruptions in efforts to keep someone on Joe."[74] The proposal excited neither Fleming nor the management of the *Journal*. They objected to the participation of the Democratic National Committee, which, if exposed, would be the kiss of death for politically independent newspaper efforts like those of the *Journal*.[75] Although opposed to any plan of formal cooperation, Fleming and the *Journal* subsequently exchanged information with such noted critics as Drew Pearson (especially with his lawyers Warren Woods and William Roberts), Jack Anderson and Ronald May, Hornell Hart, Oliver Pilat and William Shannon, Sen. William Benton, Tydings, and the Democratic National Committee.

Fleming's initial research uncovered no significant material about McCarthy's military career. "I doubt that there's any story in McCarthy's alleged war record," he noted in the fall of 1950.[76] But one aspect of McCarthy's war exploits continued to perplex Fleming and inspired him to further investigation. For many years, newspapers friendly to McCarthy had reported dramatically that he had been wounded in the Pacific theater. But, according to Fleming's sources, McCarthy himself had spoken only of being injured. Furthermore, Fleming perceptively noted, McCarthy had only received a citation for his wound or injury and not the Purple Heart, a symbolically more prestigious award. Fleming speculated that McCarthy might not have requested that medal because it required more investigation by military officials to establish that the proposed recipient had actually been wounded in action and not simply injured while in the service. As Fleming facetiously observed: "Maybe he fell off a jeep or a bar stool, for all I know."[77]

The breakthrough for Fleming apparently stemmed from the research of *Time* magazine, particularly that of Robert Sherrod. In the fall of 1951, *Time* editors dispatched reporters throughout the nation to gather material for the magazine's critical cover story on McCarthy published on 22 October 1951. One important fact, mysteriously uncovered and documented by Sherrod from classified navy records, placed McCarthy aboard the seaplane tender *Chandeleur* on 22 June 1943, the day he was allegedly wounded.[78] Eyewitness accounts established that McCarthy was injured, not wounded, in a hazing incident aboard the ship. Sherrod repeatedly warned his superior not to disclose the source of his information. After describing his findings in a memorandum on 15 October 1951, he concluded:

> This is the record (which was obtained only with greatest difficulty). Again, let us caution you not to mention any official documents. Suggest you put it all on a *Time* correspondent who was on board *Chandeleur* with McCarthy at the time.[79]

Either because of fear of using classified documents, or because Sherrod's account appeared too late for the magazine's deadline, *Time* did not use his material. Under the informal policy of sharing information, Sherrod's memo found its way to Fleming, who by this time had dug deeply into McCarthy's war record. Besides Sherrod's study, Fleming contacted people who had known McCarthy personally during the war. Fleming also received assistance from national Democratic leaders and the Truman administration. The repercussions of using classified information worried Fleming as it had Sherrod. He persuaded Secretary of the Navy Dan Kimball (who apparently needed little persuading) to inspect the same records and tell Fleming their contents.[80] Then, in preparing his article, Fleming quoted Kimball's description of McCarthy's injury on the *Chandeleur*, most of which, of course, the *Journal* reporter already knew from Sherrod's memorandum.

As he readied his article for publication, Fleming feared that McCarthy would counter with a libel suit. He recalled years later:

> Sure enough, when we talked with the lawyers the next day, the *Journal* lawyer said: "He'll sue you, sure as the devil, and he'll sue you for a million dollars on this one." And Ferguson [John Donald Ferguson, then editor of the *Journal*] slapped his hand down on his desk and said: "Fine! I've been trying to get him into court, and if this one will do it, fine. Let's have at it."[81]

In his devastating account published on 8 June 1952, Fleming stated that McCarthy had not been injured in an airplane accident but in a "shellback" initiation aboard the seaplane tender *Chandeleur*. McCarthy's stories about participating in combat missions were also shot down as Fleming told how, after the fighting ended on Guadalcanal in 1943, bored pilots tried to see who could set the record for flights in one day, and McCarthy joined in the fun. When news of the record reached Wisconsin, Fleming pointed out, its publicity value delighted McCarthy. He told friends the story was worth "50,000 votes for me." Fleming's account also showed that McCarthy had applied for a commission before enlisting in the marines and had misled reporters at the time when he implied that he had entered the service as a buck private. Last, Fleming's article pointed out that McCarthy had left the service before the major Pacific battles of Iwo Jima and Okinawa.[82]

Fleming's story appeared in anti-McCarthy newspapers throughout the nation and served as further evidence of McCarthy's propensity to exaggerate and distort. For unknown reasons (although general fear of McCarthy was a possibility), the wire services neglected to pick up the story, and, consequently, many people continued to regard McCarthy as a war hero. The anticipated libel suit never materialized. In subsequent conversations with Fleming, McCarthy merely joked about the story and never argued with its contents.[83] In fact, McCarthy had always been friendly to Fleming despite the latter's employment by the *Journal* and his critical reporting.

The timing of the story's publication was not accidental. Fleming had accumulated all the information he needed by the end of 1951, yet the *Journal* delayed publication until 8 June 1952. On 18 September 1951, Fleming noted that material on McCarthy in his own and in the *Journal*'s files was "being withheld for considerations of political timing."[84] The article appeared only three months before the 1952 Wisconsin primary election and five months before the general election. Schmitt, in particular, and Fairchild both used Fleming's story in their campaigns against McCarthy. After the appearance of the article, Patrick Lucey, organization director for the Wisconsin DOC, expressed elation with Fleming's findings and was "simply delighted with the reaction."[85]

Although Fleming was now a leading newspaper critic of McCarthy, he became at least temporarily disillusioned with the effectiveness of journalistic exposés of his nemesis. After McCarthy defeated Fairchild in the 1952 general election, Fleming complained about the difficulty "of getting people to trust dependable sources of information."[86]

Fleming's story was one of the most successful investigations of McCarthy, but there were many others. McCarthy's enemies in Wisconsin never tired of exposés, evidence, proofs, charges, rumors, investigations, and scandals—as long as they served to undermine McCarthy's character and political base. Some of these produced substantial information and good publicity. A few extensive investigations proved unfruitful. One sought to establish that Ralph Capone, brother of the infamous Al, had made a deal with McCarthy in 1945; McCarthy would allegedly receive $80,000–$100,000 to prevent the revocation of a lease to a hotel operated by Capone in Mercer, Wisconsin. Another explored his hunting trips to the Gateway Resort, supposedly a haven for crime-syndicate leaders. State investigators also tried to establish that George Greeley, a Wisconsin native and McCarthy's former administrative assistant, had kicked back part of his salary to McCarthy in return for his inside tips on the stock market.[87]

One of the sadder aspects of the McCarthy controversy in Wisconsin was the tendency of some of his opponents to ape his worst techniques and personal traits. Perhaps this was inevitable in any intense political confrontation. In any case, McCarthy and his followers had no monopoly on emotionalism, pettiness, smearing, name-calling, guilt by association, vilification, and distortion.

McCarthy was repeatedly labeled a Fascist, a Nazi, and even a Communist. Critics compared him to Joseph Stalin and Adolf Hitler.[88] The McCarthy–Hitler comparison occurred most frequently. "He resembles Hitler in his actions more than anyone else," observed a labor journal, because "Hitler . . . maintained that if you tell a big enough lie often enough, people will believe it."[89] The editor of one labor journal insisted on spelling the senator's name "joe mccarthy" in keeping with his lowercase stature.[90] In May 1950, a Milwaukee labor union seriously proposed that the U.S. Senate impeach him because his actions were "at variance with the liberal principles" of Wisconsin citizens.[91] George Haberman, president of the state AFL, described McCarthy as "a liar, cheat and fraud who even goes against his God—he's a hypocrite of the first order."[92] When writing about his favorite subject, Miles McMillin displayed a peculiarly schizophrenic journalistic style. *The Capital Times* reporter wrote numerous articles on McCarthy that were dispassionate, devastatingly revealing, and based on extensive research, but at other times he abandoned this approach and lashed out at McCarthy in vindictive, hate-filled articles. During McCarthy's Senate career, McMillin used more than twenty different caustic adjectives—ranging from "Hitlerite" and "Fascist" to "Jumping Joe"—to describe his enemy.

Subtle attempts were made to smear McCarthy with Hitlerian characteristics by connecting him with anti-Semitism. This mushroomed out of a minor incident in which McCarthy placed an article by Upton Close into the *Congressional Record*. Close was allegedly anti-Semitic, and his article criticized two prominent Jews, Felix Frankfurter and Harold Laski, for their influence on State Department personnel. Angry protests erupted from the *Wisconsin Jewish Chronicle* and David Rabinowitz, a Sheboygan lawyer, county Democratic leader, and cochairman of the Federalist Jewish Charities.[93] McCarthy, who probably did not know of Close's reputation, responded by expunging the articles from the *Record* because, as he stated, "I have so many friends who are Jewish." He refused to concede, however, that the article was anti-Semitic. Some of McCarthy's opponents would not allow the incident to die. He had allied with "race haters." "Many leading citizens," so the argument proclaimed, were now convinced that McCarthyism was a "real threat to minority groups—especially Jews."[94] Fortified by the additional charge that many anti-Semites strongly backed his anti-Communist movement, they continued to imply that McCarthy was anti-Jewish.[95] Never during McCarthy's career did any of his critics in Wisconsin comment on the fact that the chairman of the McCarthy Club in 1952 (Steve Miller) and McCarthy's close advisers in 1953–1954 (Roy Cohn and David Schine) were Jewish, or that McCarthy had circulated an article on anti-Semitism in the Soviet Union, or that, during his investigation of the Voice of America, he had claimed to be disturbed by the elimination of the Hebrew language desk.[96]

Thus, McCarthy's opponents tried many approaches to discredit him, from reasoned critiques of his Communists-in-government issue to unsubstantiated charges of anti-Semitism. Oddly enough, they seldom used a technique that on one occasion seriously rattled their elusive foe— ridicule. On 13 May 1951, McCarthy delivered an address to seven hundred faculty members, students, and townspeople at the University of Wisconsin in Madison. His audience, to say the least, was not awed by his presentation. When McCarthy opened his talk by calling Gen. Douglas MacArthur the "greatest military leader since Genghis Khan," the audience broke into laughter. Surprised, McCarthy responded angrily that he would "like to put you in the army." When he referred to *The Capital Times* as the "Madison edition of the *Daily Worker*," the audience booed. Later, when one of his statements met with derision, he called his audience "braying jackasses." The spectators could not keep a straight face as McCarthy stumbled, fumbled, and finally reached into his briefcase for "proof, not just names," when asked to name one Communist then employed by the State Department. Finally, he gave up his search and shouted to the crowd: "Naming them won't convince you—I don't go to Communist party meetings—I can't tell you which of them has paid a $2 fee." The question period was cut short after he told the gathering that he had to catch a plane back to Washington "for an important committee meeting." Again the audience broke into laughter. He never appeared on the Madison campus again.[97]

By 1952, the issue of Joe McCarthy had been hotly debated in Wisconsin for two years. Now both sides assessed their strategy and readied their resources for the senator's bid for reelection. It promised to be interesting.

# Chapter 7

# The 1952 Election

After McCarthy began his national crusade against communism, political speculation increasingly focused on his bid for reelection in 1952. National news magazines and major newspapers sent reporters to Wisconsin to cover the dramatic developments. McCarthy had aroused more extreme feelings of admiration and loathing than any contemporary politician, and Wisconsin voters had the unique opportunity to decide if he would continue his career. Within national Democratic ranks, the 1952 election produced unusual resolve to meet the McCarthy challenge boldly. During the campaign, historian Richard Fried has noted, Democrats were "willing to speak out against McCarthy, the 'ism' named after him, and the Republicans' refusal to repudiate him."[1]

Although McCarthy won in 1952, the election yielded long-range benefits for his opponents, particularly for the Wisconsin Democratic party. McCarthy's position at the tail end of the entire Republican ticket contributed to the growing awareness that his political power had been exaggerated, and this knowledge apparently led some previously fearful senators to vote for his censure in 1954. Moreover, the frustrating years of failure for Wisconsin Democrats ended in 1957 as the party experienced a period of unparalleled success. According to party leaders, the McCarthy controversy assisted this revitalization. The Democratic organization attracted some Republicans and independents who found McCarthy repugnant. McCarthy also drove young, idealistic, and hardworking individuals into the Democratic fold because of their revulsion for him and their attraction to the character and integrity of Thomas Fairchild and Adlai Stevenson. Last, McCarthy's activities presented Democrats with an issue on which they could all agree. Without him to zero in on, Democratic and Republican party leaders have insisted, the Democrats could never have pulled all their people together and kept them together through the middle 1950s when Democrats were coming close to winning but not quite succeeding.[2]

Anti-McCarthyites failed, nonetheless, in their immediate goal of unseating McCarthy and encountered a frustrating series of disagreements, problems, and setbacks. They could do little to overcome his numerous advantages: substantial financial backing, strong party organization, overwhelming newspaper support and publicity, and, in the general election, the coattails of Dwight Eisenhower.

*   *   *   *

As the 1952 Wisconsin senatorial campaign approached, political commentators speculated endlessly on a variety of questions. Who would oppose McCarthy? Would any Republican challenge him? Which techniques and issues were most effective against him? How much support did he have from the people and his party? Most political observers agreed on only one point: the campaign would be one of the toughest, dirtiest slugfests in Wisconsin political history.

Anti-McCarthyites had two chances to defeat McCarthy: in the Republican primary election in September 1952, and in the general election two months later. Wisconsin's open primary law, which permitted Democrats to vote in the Republican primary, aroused speculation about potential Republican challengers. Secretary of State Fred Zimmerman, the only prominent Republican to speak out against McCarthy, was considered too old to wage an effective campaign. Former Gov. Oscar Rennebohm disliked McCarthy and desired a Senate seat but was in poor health. Because of his famous name and earlier popularity, observers scrutinized the attitude of Robert M. La Follette, Jr. For reasons known only to himself, however, Young Bob never indicated interest in a political comeback. Rumor circulated that Wisconsin Supreme Court Justice Henry Hughes would resign his seat to challenge McCarthy. With his handsome appearance, vigorous campaign style, and popularity in the Fox River valley, Hughes held impressive credentials, but he never entered the race and eventually worked for McCarthy's reelection. Walter Kohler, Jr., the young and increasingly popular governor, was a formidable prospect, but few expected him to enter the contest. Merrill attorney Leonard Schmitt was the most likely Republican aspirant. A former Progressive and a maverick Republican, constantly at odds with the conservative GOP organization, Schmitt was conceded little chance of defeating McCarthy because of the trouncing he took from Kohler in the 1950 gubernatorial primary.

Madison attorney James Doyle and State Sen. Gaylord Nelson were often mentioned as likely choices for the Democratic nomination. Both were dynamic leaders who were well respected within the party but virtually unknown throughout much of the state. Because of his leadership in the anti-McCarthy movement, a labor journal urged William T. Evjue to enter the race, but the editor of *The Capital Times* was too old and too controversial to be seriously considered amd declined the offer. Henry Reuss, a little-known Milwaukee lawyer, desired the nomination, but his candidacy aroused little excitement. On the other hand, many Democrats were excited about Thomas Fairchild. With his victory in the 1948 race for attorney general, Fairchild, the first Democrat since 1932 to win statewide office, had established himself as a proven vote-getter. His reputation did not diminish when he ran a strong but unsuccessful race against incumbent Sen. Alexander Wiley two years later.

By the end of 1951, some anti-McCarthyites optimistically predicted McCarthy's defeat. *The Capital Times* used a variety of evidence—from the addition of another newspaper to the anti-McCarthy camp to a disappointing turnout for a McCarthy testimonial dinner—to document his waning popularity.[3] Evjue was "confident that a big reaction is setting in against McCarthy here in Wisconsin. People are now getting wise to his record, his tactics, his demagoguery and his unscrupulous action." Evjue would be disappointed "if we don't have this bird on the run before the next election."[4]

Conflicting pressures, campaign tactics, and personal ambitions seriously handicapped Democratic preparations for the anti-McCarthy drive. Only a few party leaders were as confident of defeating McCarthy as they publicly pretended to be. One was James Doyle, the spark plug and leader of the Democratic Organizing Committee (DOC) for the 1952 campaign. Doyle was a soft-spoken and shrewd political leader noted for his toughness and endless diligence. After establishing a brilliant record at Columbia Law School, he became a clerk for U.S. Supreme Court Justice James F. Byrnes. Returning to Wisconsin in 1946, he practiced law and helped to rejuvenate the state's weak Democratic party.

Doyle's distaste for McCarthyism and for McCarthy was unequivocal. However, Doyle was opposed to making McCarthy's defeat the DOC's major goal. Doyle observed in the fall of 1951 that the DOC had made great progress since its inception three years earlier, and "in long range terms, the paramount need is to develop in Wisconsin a broad, enduring and successful alternative to conservative Republicanism."[5] Doyle was referring to the conflicting pressures on the DOC leadership over the emphasis to place on ousting McCarthy. On one hand, a small but troublesome minority of Democrats wanted to ignore McCarthy. Some were state legislators who felt strongly that traditional Democratic issues would be most effective for their reelection bids. In pro-McCarthy areas such as the Fox River valley, some party leaders were understandably reluctant to base their campaign on the issue of McCarthyism.[6] More powerful pressure came from lower-echelon party officials, independent liberals, and anti-McCarthy newspapers who wanted to wage a "moral crusade" against the monstrous evils of McCarthyism. They were willing to support any candidate, including a Republican, to defeat McCarthy. State Democratic leaders, CIO officials, and some labor publications warned of the dangers of supporting a Republican. The *Wisconsin Democrat*, the party's official organ, attempted to discredit "visionaries" who thought that any Republican could be a good alternative to McCarthy. "We will gain little," observed one labor journal, "if we replace McCarthy with a man who will vote the same line McCarthy has followed, even though the man may be respectable enough to get us out of the political garbage can."[7]

The problem of tactics also had to be resolved. Since the beginning of McCarthy's anti-Communist campaign, most of his opponents reasoned that a two-pronged counterattack was the most effective: refute McCarthy's Communists-in-government charges and attack his methods, and document his immoral and unethical conduct. McCarthy's critics assumed that Wisconsinites would act rationally and not vote for a man whose attack on Communists was a political gimmick and whose personal behavior was objectionable. This view received articulate and comprehensive expression by The Wisconsin Citizens' Committee on McCarthy's Record. During the summer of 1951, leading Democrats used the same approach. Partly to give exposure to potential Democratic senatorial aspirants and partly to articulate an anti-McCarthy position, they organized a speaking campaign against McCarthy. Their tour, called Operation Truth, consisted of Democratic party leaders journeying throughout Wisconsin, giving street-corner speeches that exposed McCarthy's ethics and the motives behind his Communist charges.[8]

Even at this early stage in the campaign, some people questioned the wisdom of repeatedly attacking McCarthy's issue of Communists in government. Shrill cries against McCarthyism merely gave McCarthy more publicity. Labor journals suggested that his voting record be scrutinized more carefully.[9] Before Democratic Sen. William Benton spoke in Wisconsin, Doyle advised him to attack McCarthy only by "indirection."[10]

Aldric Revell, the Socialist columnist for The Capital Times, most eloquently challenged the established view. Revell had no quarrel with publicizing McCarthy's unethical conduct, but he disagreed with efforts to discredit McCarthy's anti-Communist crusade. If McCarthy was to be defeated, Revell argued in August 1951, the average voter had to stop identifying McCarthyism with anticommunism. McCarthyism had different meanings for different people. For The Capital Times, the Democratic party, and intellectuals, it meant "the big lie, the Un American [sic] tactic of guilt by association, and the negation of fair play." Rank-and-file Republicans in Wisconsin, however, especially those in rural areas, associated McCarthyism with "two-fisted fighting against odds" and with the battle to save the country from subversive Communists in the State Department. This being the case, "to wage a campaign on the issue of McCarthyism is to strengthen the McCarthy forces, since reiteration of this word rings a Liberty Bell in the minds of the uninformed." This situation had arisen because McCarthy had effectively diverted attention from his voting record, which opposed public housing and equitable taxation and favored restrictive labor legislation and big business. Revell also criticized Operation Truth. It had "not convinced a single person that McCarthy's anti-Communist crusade is a joke. It has been a flop because it has sought to fight emotionalism with rationalism." Revell hoped that new tactics would be devised before the 1952 election.[11]

The immediate problem facing Democrats was agreement on a strong candidate to oppose McCarthy. Unlike the Republicans, who had a policy of endorsing candidates, the DOC had no machinery to narrow the field of primary aspirants. A minority of party leaders, including Doyle, unsuccessfully urged revision of the DOC's constitution to allow endorsement. Most party officials agreed that the next best approach was to concentrate early on one candidate. Despite the strong open primary tradition in Wisconsin, they reasoned that, in view of the late primary date (9 September), a bitter internal contest might leave the winner too spent and the party's resources too depleted to conduct an effective campaign. Democrats were wary of repeating the disastrous primary battle of 1950. As Daniel Hoan reflected on that campaign: "Most of the money [was] spent in the primary and the rank and file of each group and many of the leaders [were] either sore, depressed [or] at least lacking all enthusiasm after their favorite candidate lost out in the primary."[12]

While the party pondered procedures for selecting a candidate, an incident occurred that nearly sent long-time Democrats into cardiac arrest. Apparently at the urging of the Truman administration or national Democratic officials through their intermediary, Averell Harriman, some DOC members asked La Follette whether, given adequate support by leading Democrats, he would run as a Democrat against McCarthy. Liberal Democrats who had fought La Follette for many years because he endangered their organization as a Progressive and liberal Republican breathed a sigh of relief when, for "compelling personal reasons," La Follette refused the offer. "What a hell of an insurrection would have taken place," Hoan told a friend, "if some small group would plan to promote him in our primary!"[13]

State unions and wealthy Democrats from outside the state pressured the DOC to agree on one candidate so that funds could be raised and work started on the anti-McCarthy drive. The Democrats were in a dilemma. They desperately sought to avoid a primary fight, but a candidate selected by a small clique might prove unsuitable to other party members. They finally agreed to poll DOC members. More delay resulted from the difficulty of agreeing on a survey format.[14] Meanwhile, three of the four leading contenders—Doyle, Nelson, and Reuss—began negotiations to determine who was the strongest candidate. Nelson and Doyle, who were close friends and had no desire to compete with each other, agreed that Nelson was the stronger of the two. Doyle thereupon took himself out of consideration, and the Democrats selected him to head the DOC.[15] As the U.S. attorney for western Wisconsin, Fairchild was in no position to be active in politics and did not participate in the negotiating process. Thus the field narrowed to Nelson and Reuss.

By November 1951, it appeared that either the DOC survey or informal negotiations would unite the party behind one candidate. Then the whole process collapsed. Reuss and his supporters claimed that the agreed-upon procedure would break the tradition of an open primary and would prove unproductive. They saw no real indication that the factions would be able to decide on one candidate or that the decision would be binding. Some of Reuss's Milwaukee partisans also charged that the Madison wing of the party was conspiring to deprive Reuss of the nomination. Consequently, Reuss broke off negotiations on 6 November 1951, and on 8 November declared his candidacy for the Democratic senatorial nomination. Two days later, the results of the DOC poll showed Nelson the winner, followed by Fairchild, Reuss, and Doyle, but Reuss's decision had already ruined its value.[16]

Reuss was a young, wealthy, and successful Milwaukee attorney whose Cornell and Harvard Law School polish contrasted sharply with McCarthy's crudeness. In 1948, Reuss had finished second in a field of eighteen candidates for mayor of Milwaukee. Two years later, he was the unsuccessful Democratic candidate for attorney general. As the 1952 primary approached, Reuss worked vigorously to build committees of supporters and succeeded in getting the backing of some labor leaders, state legislators, and county and district Democratic chairmen. He traveled to New York, Washington, and other cities to raise funds from wealthy liberals and national union officials.[17]

But Reuss's candidacy disappointed many anti-McCarthyites. His unexpected decision surprised and angered some Democratic leaders for its effect on their attempts to agree on a single strong candidate. Reuss had angered Democrats by pulling out of the race for lieutenant governor in 1948 after committing himself to run, and he was virtually unknown outside Milwaukee. In January 1952, a University of Wisconsin journalism class, surveying the coming state election, asked a hundred Madisonians to identify Governor Kohler, McCarthy, and Reuss. The results showed that 89 percent could identify the governor, and 87 percent knew Senator McCarthy, but only 7 percent could identify Reuss.[18] His campaign never caught fire. One observer noted privately that "Reuss's campaign seems to be getting nowhere."[19]

Despite its inadequacies, Reuss's candidacy temporarily outmaneuvered those who had agreed against a primary contest, since they now faced the alternative of supporting him or precipitating the very contest they had tried to avoid. Soon after Reuss announced his candidacy, Nelson took himself out of consideration. On 19 May 1952, Fairchild declared that he would not become a candidate. With no other Democratic challenger in sight, the state AFL and CIO gave Reuss their official endorsement.[20] Reuss had apparently preempted the Democratic field. Even before he declared his candidacy, however, attention had turned to the Republican primary and a more serious threat to McCarthy.

*    *    *    *

Governor Kohler was an urbane man with a roundish photogenic face, natural warmth, and charm. There were striking differences between McCarthy and the popular forty-seven-year-old chief executive. McCarthy was boisterous, impetuous, and cynical; Kohler was quiet, thoughtful, and cordial without being effusive. McCarthy was a mediocre lawyer, an erratic judge, and an indifferent legislator who had recently displayed isolationist leanings; Kohler was a successful business executive, a student of legislation, and an internationalist who admired General Eisenhower.

The first indication that Kohler might challenge McCarthy in the Republican primary came in July 1951, after an uproar at the Republican state convention. The eighteen hundred delegates hysterically cheered, yelled, and whistled as McCarthy struck out at alleged Communists and fellow travelers in the Truman administration. When two young Republicans, Arthur Peterson of Prescott and the Reverend Al Eliason of Oconto, rose to speak against a resolution praising McCarthy, they were booed, heckled, and physically threatened by the predominantly pro-McCarthy delegates. The convention proceeded to pass the resolution overwhelmingly. A few days later, Kohler, who was not at the convention during the turmoil, criticized the delegates for their "disgraceful" and "unruly procedure" in not allowing Peterson and Eliason to express their views.[21] Attempting to capitalize on this apparent breach in Republican ranks, Democratic party leaders invited Kohler to publicly declare his attitude toward McCarthy. Kohler shocked Republicans by inviting the Democrats to discuss the matter privately.[22] Wayne Hood, chairman of the Republican Voluntary Committee (RVC), warned him that liberal newspapers and Democrats were trying to create strife over McCarthy for two reasons: "one is to beat McCarthy, and the second is to drive wedges into the Republican party which would allow the Democrats to make a better showing."[23] Other Republicans moved quickly to convince Kohler to reverse himself. They succeeded. State Sens. Warren Knowles and Melvin Laird met with Kohler staff members and wrote a public statement for the governor. Before the Democratic representatives could meet with him, therefore, Kohler blasted them as "publicity seekers." He emphatically opposed the "infiltration of Communists into our government," he said, and urged a "full and fair hearing" of McCarthy's charges.[24] Democratic officials immediately accused Kohler of succumbing to pressure from pro-McCarthy forces within the Republican party. GOP unity behind McCarthy was apparently restored. Yet a Republican columnist questioned the extent to which Kohler had bowed to Republican influence: "Certainly if he'd [Kohler] been guided by state party leaders he would have backed McCarthy completely instead of suggesting that the senator's charges need a full and fair hearing."[25]

Many factors apparently led Kohler to consider challenging his famous Republican colleague. He had always hoped to be a senator, and his wife wanted to live in Washington, D.C. Even McCarthy's supporters conceded that Kohler disliked McCarthy. The governor thought that McCarthy's Communist hunt was designed to get votes and headlines, which Kohler hardly considered commendable goals.[26] In reviewing McCarthy's career as a lawyer and jurist, the governor told a *Time* magazine correspondent confidentially in the fall of 1951: "He strikes me as a mediocre lawyer with an easy conscience."[27] Kohler deplored the methods and some of the targets—especially Gen. George Marshall—of McCarthy's anti-Communist campaign.[28] While Mrs. Charlotte Kohler had little enthusiasm for politics, politicians, and public life, she had even less enthusiasm for Joe McCarthy.

Kohler's flirtation with the anti-McCarthy camp continued. According to a rumor in early September 1951, Kohler had met secretly with state labor leaders to discuss his possible senatorial candidacy. Despite the rumor, the governor's statement on 25 September took observers by surprise. On Kohler's return from a European vacation, a reporter asked him if it were true that he would not run against McCarthy. Kohler responded: "I never have said I will not run against McCarthy for senator."[29] He promised a decision in three or four months. A few days later, in what was interpreted as a slap at McCarthy, Kohler condemned "irresponsible attacks" on individuals. But Kohler was vague and cagey in answering all questions about McCarthy and never directly attacked him.[30]

Some people in the anti-McCarthy camp were skeptical of Kohler's announcement. He could increase McCarthy's chances for reelection if he decided to run again for governor because no outstanding Democrat would come forward while anti-McCarthy sentiment rested with Kohler. Most DOC leaders feared the alignment of anti-McCarthy energy behind the Republican governor. They realized that they needed support from independents, ex-Progressives, and anti-McCarthy Republicans if their candidate were to win. Much of this support would not commit itself to any Democrat as long as there was any possibility that Kohler would oppose McCarthy in the Republican primary. Funds that would normally go to Democrats for important early campaigning would be withheld if Kohler remained undecided.[31] Carl Thompson observed that the long-range effect of Kohler's statements could be to "confuse and divide the anti-McCarthy forces in Wisconsin until such a late date that irreparable damage will be done their campaign."[32]

Kohler's potential candidacy, however, received enthusiastic support. "This newcomer Kohler," Evjue noted, "is probably the only man in the state who could beat McCarthy."[33] A few staunch Republican weekly newspapers cast McCarthy aside and endorsed Kohler for senator although they had never previously found serious fault with McCarthy. Delegates to the state Democratic convention in October 1951 admitted privately that Kohler could count on the support of organized labor and many Democrats. Even outgoing DOC chairman Jerome Fox, in a discussion with President Truman on 24 October 1951, suggested Democratic cooperation with a Kohler candidacy in the Republican primary as the best means of defeating McCarthy. An extensive statewide survey of farmers by the respected *Wisconsin Agriculturist and Farmer* disclosed that Republicans favored Kohler over McCarthy in a Republican primary race by a margin of 41 to 40 percent. The margin was two-to-one for Democratic farmers. The formation of a Kohler for Senator Club on the University of Wisconsin campus drew two hundred members in the first two days. Various citizens' committess also endorsed the governor.[34]

McCarthy's persistent critic, *Milwaukee Journal* reporter Robert Fleming, was Kohler's friend and tried to persuade him to enter the race. He sent inquiries to Sen. Estes Kefauver, requesting more information about his recent election victory over the opposition of his state party organization. Kohler was very interested in Kefauver's published account of his tactics, Fleming wrote. "We both saw the importance of your decision to disregard working politicians in building your organization." Fleming was one of the many Wisconsinites willing to support any strong and competent challenger to McCarthy, regardless of party affiliation. In justifying his backing of the Republican Kohler, he told the Democratic Kefauver: "it seems to me so important that we change that I'm not interested in the party label."[35]

Officials of the Wisconsin Federation of Labor, who were usually at odds with Republican officeholders, actively urged Kohler to enter the primary and promised him money and support. After a meeting with the governor in October 1951, state chairman George Haberman found him noncommittal. Haberman promised to "get sufficient pressure exerted in order to convince him he should change his mind and get into this campaign."[36]

While most anti-McCarthyites praised Kohler and urged him to enter the race, Republican leaders were upset that he would even consider such a move. As a GOP official explained:

> As things stand now, they [Democrats] have little chance of beating McCarthy, and almost no chance of unseating Kohler. But, if Kohler opposes McCarthy, the Democrats have already won half of the battle. They will have got rid of one of our two top men.[37]

Virtually the entire state, district, and county leadership of the GOP vigorously opposed Kohler's candidacy. No state party official talked with him about his possible bid or directly put pressure on him, but lower-echelon party leaders did. Dodge County GOP officials informed Kohler that all the Republican leaders in the county supported McCarthy. Kohler's friends, such as Knowles and Republican assemblyman Charles Peterson, advised him not to enter the race. McCarthy was too popular, Peterson told him, and "it would be terrible if you should run and be beaten." To offset the support for Kohler among rank-and-file Republicans, Wayne Hood urged McCarthy to make more appearances in the state.[38]

Conservative Republicans had their way. On 30 January 1952, Kohler announced that he would seek reelection as governor. Frustrated and bitter, anti-McCarthy forces blasted him for placing party above principle. Kohler angered them further when he enthusiastically supported McCarthy and even campaigned for him during the primary and general elections.

Perhaps McCarthy's opponents were correct in assuming that Kohler lacked the courage to risk his career by challenging his powerful colleague, but other factors may have been involved. In Wisconsin, a governor's term of office was only two years, and Kohler felt obligated to run at least once for reelection. Virtually unbeatable in a reelection bid, he probably wanted to complete his legislative program. If he were to enter the primary, he thought, the Republican party in Wisconsin would be "split to a degree which would take years—perhaps a generation—to repair."[39]

McCarthy's apparent success with his anti-Communist campaign also influenced Kohler. The governor had long been troubled by the Communists-in-government issue, especially by the exposures of Alger Hiss, John Abt, Nathan Witt, and others. Yet McCarthy's methods, particularly his attack on General Marshall, disturbed Kohler. On 12 July 1951, one month after McCarthy's famous blast at Marshall, Kohler denounced the pro-McCarthy delegates at the Republican state convention for harassing the two McCarthy critics. The next day, headlines in state newspapers reported that John Paton Davies, Jr., and Oliver Edmund Clubb—both targets of McCarthy—had been suspended from their State Department jobs pending the outcome of loyalty investigations. A few days later, Kohler criticized the Democrats and urged a fair hearing for McCarthy's charges. Similarly, a month before Kohler's decision not to oppose McCarthy, the State Department discharged John Stewart Service, whom McCarthy had called a Communist. The Service case had an important impact on Kohler and partially explained his decision not to run. During the primary campaign, Kohler cited the dismissals of Clubb, Service, and others and claimed that the "factual foundation" of McCarthy's crusade had "already been demonstrated."[40] It made little difference for the 1952 elections that Davies, Clubb, and Service were later cleared of any disloyalty. Anti-McCarthyites were once again stuck with the largely unknown Reuss.

* * * *

Reuss's supporters were jubilant when Fairchild withdrew from the race in May 1952. But, just as most Democrats had settled on Reuss, Fairchild changed his mind. Many Wisconsin liberals still considered Fairchild the strongest candidate against McCarthy because of his proven vote-getting ability and his appeal to independent Republicans. At the state Democratic convention in June, he was the center of attention, receiving a spontaneous public ovation and private expressions of confidence from many local leaders. Believing himself still the strongest available candidate, he entered the race at the last moment, on 8 July, one day before the filing deadline.

The Reuss forces were angry and bitter. Reuss functionaries Herman Jessen, Gerald Flynn, and Leland McParland criticized Fairchild's candidacy for creating an irreparable division among the anti-McCarthy forces that had united behind Reuss. Fairchild had double-crossed their candidate. As they saw it, earlier party talks had determined that there would be agreement on a single candidate to avoid a primary contest. The Democrats were severely divided. Doyle conceded that Fairchild's candidacy would make it more difficult to acquire funds for the general-election campaign.[41]

Moreover, while Reuss remained the only Democratic aspirant, his friends on the *Milwaukee Journal* staff had tried to arrange for him to address the national Democratic convention in Chicago in July. McCarthy's appearance before the Republican convention received much publicity—an asset Reuss badly needed. Sen. William Benton, Connecticut Democrat and prominent McCarthy critic, had considered the idea, but Fairchild's candidacy ruined any such prospects. As Benton noted, Fairchild's surprise decision "means we can't do anything for Reuss at the convention in Chicago. The Democrats [in Wisconsin] now have a primary fight on."[42]

For many opponents of McCarthy, however, Fairchild's entry had the most immediately damaging effect on Schmitt's candidacy. A Catholic of German descent, Schmitt was the third important candidate to enter the race and the only formidable one to challenge McCarthy in the Republican primary. The dynamic, vigorous, but humorless former Progressive announced his candidacy in June under the assumption that anti-McCarthy efforts would concentrate on his primary battle. His most important backing came from Evjue and *The Capital Times*. Schmitt had known Evjue since childhood and had briefly worked for the newspaper while attending the University of Wisconsin. The two had similar ideological views; both were militant fighters for the "little fellow" against the "millionaire bosses" who ran the Republican party. Against the wishes of most of his staff, who thought Schmitt's candidacy a hopeless cause, Evjue coaxed Schmitt into entering the primary contest and then, with single-minded devotion, supported him during his campaign.[43] Fairchild's candidacy hurt Schmitt. With a tough Democratic primary, he could not expect a large Democratic crossover vote. Republican strategists estimated that Fairchild's entry would cost Schmitt at least fifty thousand votes.

As the September primary approached, anti-McCarthy forces were severely divided. *The Capital Times* and a few independent groups urged voters to support Schmitt. Every opportunity, they reasoned, must be taken to defeat McCarthy. If Schmitt lost in the primary, McCarthy's opponents could try again in the general election. Evjue blasted Democratic leaders for putting "party and political expediency above a great moral crusade." Fairchild's candidacy was purely a partisan decision, dictated by the fears of a few party leaders that the party might lose prestige if Democrats voted for Schmitt.[44] On the other hand, most labor leaders and journals advised workers to stay in the Democratic primary and for the most part ignored Schmitt's candidacy. Doyle insisted that Democrats remain in their own primary. Only with the strongest Democratic candidate, he argued, could they defeat McCarthy in November.[45]

Besides, Democrats had many important local elections to decide. In Milwaukee County, many Democrats sought the party's nomination for sheriff.

As the primary approached, most attention focused on the Schmitt–McCarthy race. Schmitt followed essentially the same strategy used by McCarthy's opponents since he began his crusade: publicize his unethical conduct and refute his charges of Communists in government while criticizing his methods. McCarthy's red-hunt was a "gigantic hoax," Schmitt asserted; McCarthy had done "absolutely nothing to chase Communists out of the government."[46]

Schmitt began with a traditional stump campaign, delivering street-corner speeches from a sound truck, but this was a failure. Crowds seemed resentful and, according to Schmitt, stared at him "like dumb animals." He needed public exposure. When he heard about the amazing success of the talkathon as a campaign device in Arkansas, he decided to base his entire effort on that format.[47] The talkathon was a marathon radio talk in which the candidate answered questions from all comers. In some large cities, Schmitt remained on the air for as long as twenty-five continuous hours, answering questions about himself and McCarthy. With his physical stamina, calm manner, and keen knowledge of the issues, Schmitt seemed ideally suited for this technique. The publicity it received and the interest it aroused seemed to confirm its success.

But talkathons were not nearly enough to give Schmitt the victory. Aside from *The Capital Times*, a few citizens' groups, and some segments of the state AFL, his candidacy received little support. As a whole, organized labor ignored his campaign and urged its members to vote in the Democratic primary. R. Merrill Rhey, secretary of the Kenosha Trades and Labor Council, argued that Republicans should "put their own house in order."[48] While ignoring Schmitt's press releases, conservative Republican newspapers withheld no editorial criticism. They reminded their readers that Schmitt had refused to support Kohler after Kohler defeated him in the 1950 gubernatorial primary and that he had been an outspoken critic of the RVC.[49]

Schmitt's vigor and dedication could not compensate for his lack of financial support, party endorsement, and statewide organization—assets that McCarthy possessed. Financial problems frustrated Schmitt. His plan to raise money from the "little people" through a "Dollars for Decency" campaign was a complete failure. Fairchild's candidacy destroyed his hope of acquiring funds outside the state. Meyer Cohen, a lawyer and Democratic party leader from Green Bay, tried to collect money for Schmitt among contacts in New York and had expected to raise $50,000. About the time Cohen arrived in New York to close the deal, however, Fairchild entered the Democratic primary. Since most of Cohen's contacts were labor officials and Democrats, they immediately changed their minds, and he returned to Wisconsin with only about $5,000.[50]

\*     \*     \*     \*

By 3 May 1952, when McCarthy formally announced for reelection, he was so confident of victory that he decided not to wage an active, personal campaign. "Look," he told Ray Kiermas, "I can't see where putting on a campaign would help me any. I'm certain I'll win without a campaign." McCarthy knew about state GOP polls that showed him far ahead of any rival and reasoned that he had made enough speeches in Wisconsin and had received plenty of national publicity.[51]

McCarthy chose Steve Miller, a wealthy cheesebroker from Marshfield, to direct his campaign organization, the McCarthy Club. Miller was a determined, uncompromising person with ultraconservative political views but no experience in political campaigns. He may have been selected partly because he was Jewish. A McCarthy intimate had suggested to the senator that he choose Miller "to eliminate any question of McCarthy being anti-Semitic."[52]

Republican leaders in Wisconsin shared McCarthy's optimism about his reelection. After a tour of the state in November 1951, Hood had predicted that "McCarthy would be re-elected by the largest majority in the history of the state of Wisconsin."[53] As the campaign approached, the number of requests for McCarthy to speak became staggering; he declined most of them. A persistent civic official from Hartland, Wisconsin, declared that

> we are arranging our affair complete in every form except as to date. Joe McCarthy is going to decide the date. It has been said in our local group that we are going to arrange this meeting when Joe McCarthy can speak to us even if it must be at midnight.[54]

McCarthy was a symbol for conservative Republicans in Wisconsin. He had defeated their hated enemy, La Follette. Then, as a slugging fighter against Communists in government, he had wounded the Democratic Truman administration. The enthusiasm that McCarthy aroused among Wisconsin Republicans even led them to repudiate their party's leading vote-getter, Secretary of State Fred Zimmerman. In July 1952, Republicans refused to endorse Zimmerman for his tenth term partly because of his outspoken opposition to McCarthy. Leading Republicans who disliked McCarthy would say nothing bad about him publicly because he had damaged the Democrats. "I am not a great admirer of McCarthy," Knowles wrote before the primary, "but I do feel that it is more important to our Republican cause to see him reelected." In the fall of 1951, a prominent Republican district chairman noted that "a Republican Congress would throw McCarthy out in a minute, and I'd love to see them do it. But not now!"[55]

The only mention of McCarthy's voting record during the campaign occurred in the back pages of one campaign brochure. Aside from charges of smear tactics, his campaign rarely discussed accusations against his personal conduct. State Republicans "don't defend McCarthy," a columnist observed, "they just swear by him."[56] There was one issue and one issue only: communism.

Pro-McCarthy forces continued to press the same four-point argument on behalf of his Communist campaign: an international Communist conspiracy endangered the United States; the Democrats did nothing to solve the problem; McCarthy, against difficult obstacles and baseless smears, attempted to solve it; and he had succeeded in exposing some hidden Communists. His campaign emphasized the last two arguments.

According to McCarthy, a million-dollar smear campaign had mobilized against him. Campaign literature charged that opponents had subjected him to the "worst attack of jeers, sneers, and smears in American political history." They sought to "destroy him" personally in order "to hide the issue as to whether there are Communists in YOUR government."[57]

McCarthy's propaganda repeatedly asserted that he was responsible for the dismissal or conviction of eleven government employees with Communist leanings.[58] Two hundred Appleton residents promised to reelect him because they knew

> that 11 people have been removed from government since you exposed their records. We know these facts were available to congressional committees but only you, Joe, had the courage to bring the facts to public attention.[59]

McCarthy's speech to the national Republican convention on 9 July 1952 was a publicity triumph. Headlined articles in state newspapers told how the crowd roared when the convention chairman introduced "that fighting marine from Wisconsin." At his side was his ever-present satchel from which he again hauled out the dog-eared, much-thumbed documents and photostats. Holding them high with one hand in a posture that had become his trademark, he slapped them with the other for emphasis. As one pro-McCarthy writer observed:

> This was the peak effort of McCarthy's life, and something about which he probably dreamed when he was planning his political career in those days long ago when he worked as a barefoot boy in his father's Outagamie County cornfields.[60]

For months, Wisconsin had seen little of McCarthy. Then, in July 1952, he underwent an operation to repair a hernia in the large muscle separating his chest and abdominal cavities. He recuperated in northern Wisconsin and was not expected to campaign at all in the primary. Medical reports indicated that surgery was unnecessary at that time, that he might have waited until after the general election. Perhaps he wanted to avoid the continual dates with attorneys and judges over libel suits, which would have handicapped his Wisconsin campaign. In any event, he became a martyr, and his incapacity hardly affected fund raising.[61]

In McCarthy's absence, a host of speakers canvassed the state in his behalf. Governor Kohler and Harvey Matusow, a former Communist undercover agent for the FBI, campaigned for him. Arthur Bliss Lane, former ambassador to Poland, drummed up support for McCarthy among Wisconsin's Polish communities. Lane's tour was sponsored by the McCarthy Club and a committee of prominent Polish-Americans. He spoke of the importance of McCarthy's crusade and of his own experience as witness to the fall of Poland to the Russian Communists.[62]

Schmitt's talkathons apparently scared McCarthy enough to rouse him from his sick bed a few days before the election. "Joe McCarthy Talks! America's most fearless fighter against Communism and Corruption brings his story directly to you." So read the campaign advertisement for McCarthy's statewide radio address from Shorewood on 3 September 1952. After appealing for votes, McCarthy delivered his customary barrage against Truman, Acheson, Marshall, American foreign-policy failures, and some specific alleged Communists. He capped it off with snide remarks about the *Milwaukee Journal* and *The Capital Times*. His only new idea was to associate Democratic presidential aspirant Adlai Stevenson with Alger Hiss.[63]

McCarthy had some last-minute assistance from Washington. On the evening before the primary, Jack Poorbaugh, investigator for the subcommittee reviewing Sen. William Benton's resolution to investigate McCarthy, resigned from the subcommittee staff. He charged the subcommittee with conducting a biased inquiry of McCarthy and with supplying information to newspapers for the purpose of smearing him. The timing of the resignation was not coincidental. Poorbaugh, who had assisted McCarthy before, had consulted with McCarthy's friends before releasing his resignation to the press. The same evening, Sen. Herman Welker, a staunch McCarthy supporter, resigned from the subcommittee in a telegram given to newspapers in time to make the election morning editions. Both incidents made front-page news in Wisconsin and enhanced McCarthy's image as a martyr.[64]

Despite many problems, cautious optimism pervaded the Schmitt camp on the eve of the primary. Some believed that McCarthy's fanatically vocal supporters might have created the impression that his backing among Republicans was greater than it was. Notwithstanding the urging of their leaders, Schmitt's partisans felt that many rank-and-file Democrats and working men would vote for Schmitt.

Anti-McCarthy forces were stunned, therefore, when McCarthy trounced Schmitt by a two-and-a-half-to-one margin (515, 481 to 213, 701), winning all but two of Wisconsin's seventy-one counties. Fairchild narrowly defeated Reuss in the Democratic race (97,321 to 94,379), but the two candidates received only 17 percent of the total vote, compared to the Democrats' 30 percent in the 1950 senatorial primary. McCarthy received 100,000 more votes than the combined total of all his opponents (five Republicans and two Democrats). He won the labor strongholds of Milwaukee, Kenosha, and Racine. The farm vote, the labor vote, the white-collar vote, and some Democratic votes, observers believed, went to the incumbent. Now convinced of his vote-getting power, many of McCarthy's critics sought explanations for the debacle in the strength of isolationism in the state, McCarthy's overwhelming Catholic support, his concentration on a single issue, his underdog image, and especially the effective issue of Communists in government. "I think," a shaken Schmitt observed, "that Wisconsin people are voting against Stalin."[65] McCarthy partisans were jubilant; to them the results were clear. As one postelection headline read: "Joe Landslide Shows Faith in War on Reds."[66]

McCarthy appeared politically invincible, but actually this was not the case. Anti-McCarthy prospects for the general election were not as gloomy as most observers believed. Democrats traditionally did poorly in primarys. This was particularly true in 1952 when the party would triple its primary vote in the general election while McCarthy's would increase only fractionally. With few exceptions, Democrats either abstained from voting in the primary, voted in the Democratic column, or voted for Schmitt. McCarthy did best in those counties with the fewest Democrats and did worst in traditional Democratic strongholds.[67] But only a few Democratic strategists perceived this pattern. The primary tabulations demoralized many party workers and supporters, which handicapped Democratic efforts during the general-election campaign.

\* \* \* \*

After the primary, the Republican National Committee and the Republican Senatorial Campaign Committee demanded that McCarthy assist them in electing a Republican Congress. The state GOP realized the risk but, expecting an easy victory, canceled many of McCarthy's Wisconsin appearances.[68] During the campaign, McCarthy spoke in thirteen states. His decision not to campaign in Wisconsin amazed and frustrated his opponents. After reviewing McCarthy's sordid record, Revell threw up his hands in dismay: "Here's this guy, as phoney as a three-dollar bill, and now he's so confident he don't even think he has to campaign in Wisconsin."[69]

McCarthy's campaign used the same strategy as in the primary. Hundreds of campaign advertisements described McCarthy as a fearless fighter who pulled no punches in combating communism. "America loves him for the enemies he has made," meaning Stalin, "the pinks," and "the reds."[70] Some Republican congressional candidates, capitalizing on McCarthy's apparent success in the primary, stressed the Communist issue in their campaigns, often using McCarthy's terminology.[71]

McCarthy blasted Adlai Stevenson in a nationally televised speech in Chicago on 27 October 1952. He claimed to have carefully documented the background of the Democratic standard-bearer. He blamed Stevenson for the U.S. policy during World War II that, McCarthy said, had sought to force the Italians to accept Communists in a coalition government. He stressed Stevenson's well-known character reference for Alger Hiss and referred to "Alger—I mean Adlai." An historian has described the speech as a "gaggle of falsehoods, half-truths, and harmless truisms," but many Wisconsin newspapers published favorable reviews.[72]

The tension between McCarthy and Republican presidential candidate Dwight Eisenhower and the papering over of their disagreement provided the dramatic highlight of the 1952 campaign. Apart from his personal distaste for McCarthy, of which he left no doubt in private conversations, Eisenhower had an almost obsessive hatred for McCarthy's smearing of the Roosevelt and Truman administrations. His blood boiled at the mention of McCarthy's assault on his friend General Marshall.[73] On the other hand, Eisenhower had to appease the strong pro-McCarthy faction in his party. Particularly in Wisconsin, where Robert Taft's supporters controlled the state organization, he had to soothe disgruntled conservatives, who were bitter over Taft's defeat at the 1952 Republican national convention.[74]

At first, Eisenhower attempted to avoid the problem by taking an ambiguous stand. At a news conference in Denver, Colorado, on 22 August 1952, he distinguished between a general, party-line endorsement for an entire Republican slate and a specific declaration of personal support for a particular candidate. He would not support anything that smacked of "un-Americanism" such as "the unjust damaging of reputation." He could not give a "blanket endorsement" to anyone who held such views. When a reporter mentioned General Marshall, Ike jumped to his feet and said with obvious feeling, "George Marshall is one of the patriots in this country. . . . I have no patience with anyone who can find in his record of service for this country anything to criticize." He promised, however, to support any candidate as a "member of the Republican organization."[75]

Ike's coolness bothered some McCarthy supporters, but, after McCarthy's overwhelming primary victory, Eisenhower had no alternative but to endorse him. Eisenhower could not win the state, one Republican official insisted, "unless Mr. Joe can carry the ticket."[76] Neither would win if they continued to feud.

Ike might have avoided taking a position on McCarthy—other than the hopelessly ambiguous one between blanket endorsement and support—if he had not campaigned in Wisconsin. State Republican leaders had difficulty convincing him to come to the state. Hood, a member of the Republican National Committee, was instrumental in convincing Sherman Adams to urge Eisenhower to make the trip. If the general avoided Wisconsin, Hood urged, more attention would be focused on his differences with McCarthy.[77]

When Eisenhower learned of the trip, he suggested to his speechwriter, Emmett John Hughes, that they make the Wisconsin tour an occasion for a personal tribute to Marshall. Ike was to declare that the "right to question a

man's judgment carries with it no automatic right to question his honor."
With respect to Marshall, he planned to say:

> I know that charges of disloyalty have in the past been levelled against
> General George C. Marshall. Any of his alleged errors in judgment while
> serving in capacities other than military, I am not here discussing. But I was
> privileged throughout the years of World War II to know General Marshall
> personally as Chief of Staff of the Army. I know him, as a man and a soldier,
> to be dedicated with singular selflessness and the profoundest patriotism to
> the service of America. Here we have a sobering lesson of the way freedom
> must *not* defend itself.[78]

Ike's proposed address was a direct challenge to McCarthy and a threat
to the delicate balance of national and statewide party unity. As the
campaign train traveled through Illinois, a heated argument broke out
among Eisenhower's advisers. Those opposed to his defense of Marshall
argued that the passage was alien to the context of the speech, that it was
an obvious affront to McCarthy, and that it might bring the entire Republican ticket in Wisconsin to defeat.[79]

That was the scene on 2 October 1952 as the Eisenhower train lay at a
siding in Peoria, Illinois, ready to roll into Wisconsin. That afternoon,
Henry Ringling, Republican national committeeman; Kohler; and McCarthy flew from Madison to Peoria. That evening, Kohler and McCarthy
talked with Eisenhower, but their discussion did not turn to the Marshall
speech.[80]

Early the next day, the train moved into Wisconsin, picking up party
dignitaries along the way. The smiling senator entered the general's private car with Kohler before appearing on the same platform with
Eisenhower at his first scheduled speech at Green Bay. As Ike greeted
McCarthy he said, "I'm going to say that I disagree with you." "If you say
that, you'll be booed," McCarthy shot back. "I've been booed before and
being booed doesn't bother me," Ike retorted.[81]

At Green Bay, McCarthy and a dozen other Republican bigwigs looked
on nervously as the general began to speak. But McCarthy, Kohler, and
most of Ike's top staff members broke into big smiles as the general called
for the election of the entire Republican slate. "I want to make one thing
very clear," he said, referring to McCarthy; "the purpose that he and I have
of ridding this government of incompetents, and dishonest and above all
the subversive and disloyal are one and the same. Our differences apply
not to the end result but to method." McCarthy shook his head in disagreement and disapproval, however, as Eisenhower went on to say that
the primary responsibility for dealing with loyalty and subversion questions rested with the president and not with Congress. Wisconsin Republicans were satisfied. As one party official noted of the Green Bay speech:
"I guess we can say he's for—but. And who's going to remember the
'but.' "[82]

At Appleton, Eisenhower again called for the election of the entire

Republican ticket. As the train headed toward Milwaukee, Kohler asked Sherman Adams if he could see the speech planned for that evening. Disturbed by the paragraph on Marshall, Kohler urged its deletion. He reminded Adams of the political background of Wisconsin, of Thomas Coleman's close association with Taft, of the disappointment of the Republican organization at Taft's defeat at the Chicago convention, of the importance of the state's twelve electoral votes in view of the apparent closeness of the contest, of the fact that Eisenhower had earlier made his position clear on Marshall, and of the undeniable fact of Communists in the government. Wisconsin was politically unpredictable, he argued. It voted for Dewey in 1944 against Roosevelt and for Truman in 1948 against Dewey. The inclusion of a paragraph that would "gratuitously alienate many ardent McCarthy supporters could well lose the state and conceivably also the election to Stevenson."[83]

In Kohler's view, Eisenhower was going out of his way to open up a can of worms that did not need to be set free in Milwaukee. Adams agreed. Adams, Kohler, and Ike's trusted aide Jerry Persons went to see Eisenhower and started to review Kohler's arguments. Adams had only begun when Eisenhower interrupted impatiently to ask if Adams were suggesting that the reference to Marshall be deleted. "That's what I'm going to recommend," Adams responded. "Take it out," Eisenhower snapped. Kohler was amazed at the remarkable ease with which Eisenhower agreed: "There was no lengthy discussion, no debate, no urging, no wavering, no indecision, no argument, no pressure."[84]

The deletion of the Marshall paragraph became an open secret among reporters on Eisenhower's train and, despite denials by embarrassed Republican leaders, was flashed across the country. Without the balancing effect of the Marshall passage, the speech attacking communism was interpreted as an endorsement of McCarthy and his anti-Communist fight.[85]

*   *   *   *

To McCarthy's critics, the meaning of the 1952 primary election was clear: it was suicidal to fight the senator on his Communist issue. A minority of his opponents had held this position all along, but it became the dominant view after the Schmitt debacle. After the primary, Revell again reminded anti-McCarthyites that "it does no good to quote reams of statistics attempting to prove that McCarthy has failed to expose Communists in Washington. The people believe that he has."[86]

Leading DOC strategists, who now assumed leadership of the anti-McCarthy drive, adopted this view. McCarthy won the primary, they reasoned, because he had convinced voters that there were Communists in government and that he had tossed them out. The Truman administration had been ineffective in meeting McCarthy's onslaught. Wisconsin Democrats should no longer "slug out the campaign on the issue of McCarthyism." Instead, while continuing to publicize his unethical conduct, they should concentrate on his neglect of farmers, labor, and small businessmen and point out the economic progress of the past twenty years under national Democratic control.[87]

With such slim prospects of defeating McCarthy, it was more difficult to raise money for Fairchild's campaign. Liberal publications began to pay less attention to defeating McCarthy and concentrated on more promising contests. Morris Rubin, editor of *The McCarthy Record*, was bitter and angry about the pessimism that pervaded the anti-McCarthy camp. He blamed the national news media for inaccurately reporting the significance of McCarthy's primary victory. "I am greatly disturbed about how some of the columnists and commentators have gone off slightly cockeyed on the McCarthy story," he wrote columnist Marquis Childs, one of the culprits. "I think it is a serious mistake to regard the decision of the general election in November as a leadpipe cinch for McCarthy."[88]

Rubin and DOC leaders such as Doyle and Patrick Lucey, Fairchild's campaign manager, were notable exceptions to the prevailing mood. They sincerely believed that the primary results had been misinterpreted and that Fairchild still had a chance to upset McCarthy. Since Democrats traditionally did better in presidential election years and in the general election, Fairchild's candidacy was by no means a hopeless cause. According to their reasoning, Fairchild would receive two-thirds of the votes cast for Schmitt in the primary, one-half of the fifty thousand votes for minor Republican candidates, and all the votes for Reuss. Democratic strategists instructed party workers to flush out the stay-at-home vote in Madison and other large eastern cities. The Farmer's Union territory in the northwestern part of the state, where Fairchild had led Senator Wiley in 1950, was another DOC target. Democrats ignored the rural areas that went heavily for McCarthy in the primary.[89] The DOC underestimated Eisenhower's strength. Lucey, for example, assumed that Fairchild would run better than Stevenson but that Stevenson would also poll well. Being governor of the neighboring state of Illinois and having what sounded like a Norwegian name (Wisconsin had a high percentage of persons of Norwegian ancestry), Stevenson was expected to run a close race with Eisenhower.[90]

Anti-McCarthyites in Wisconsin repeatedly taunted Eisenhower about his tolerance of McCarthy after the senator had maligned Marshall. Part of the Democrats' strategy was to "make the most of his ambiguous statement of support of McCarthy to show that he really repudiates him."[91] But Democrats found it difficult to attack Ike. They had planned to run against Taft. At their state convention in 1948, the Democrats had witnessed an uncontrollable and spontaneous demonstration on behalf of drafting Eisenhower for the Democratic nomination for president. Richard Haney, historian of the Wisconsin Democratic party, has observed that Democrats "found it hard to denounce, as a McCarthyite, that same Eisenhower, even if the general was the Republican presidential nominee."[92]

Fairchild was a former La Follette Progressive who moved into the Democratic party after La Follette's defeat in 1946. Soft-spoken and dignified, Fairchild had aroused more genuine respect than any man who had risen to prominence in the reorganized Democratic party and was the most formidable candidate the Democrats could put forward. But he was almost too modest and retiring for politics, and his dull manner of speaking was a handicap for a claimant for high office. Even his gestures on the speaking platform were restrained. His waving from an open car was jerky and cautious, as if he feared that bystanders really did not want him to wave. He inspired respect but little enthusiasm.

The styles of Fairchild and McCarthy were in striking contrast. McCarthy, the conservative-backed incumbent, campaigned with the free-wheeling intransigence once associated with Old Bob La Follette, while Fairchild, the New Dealer, exhibited the sober moderation and restrained dignity suitable to a starch-stiff conservative. "At times," a student of the campaign has observed, "Fairchild seemed like a staid minister scolding the town rowdy, and McCarthy resembled a Populist fire-eater threatening to impale the plutocrats on a pitchfork."[93]

If the Fairchild campaign had a single thread of strategy, it was to divert the preoccupation of various groups with McCarthy's Communist hunt to issues that normally tied them to the Democratic party. In Milwaukee, for example, Democrats sought to capture the Polish–Catholic–labor vote that McCarthy had attracted because of his Roman Catholicism and his anticommunism. Democrats placed advertisements in Polish newspapers, depicting Fairchild with popular Milwaukee Democratic Rep. Clement Zablocki and stressing the gains of labor under the Democratic party.[94]

Fairchild seldom questioned the veracity of McCarthy's charges of Communists in government. On one occasion, Fairchild alleged that McCarthy had not exposed any Communists, that the only ones "who have been convicted have been rooted out by the FBI, the justice department and the courts of the United States." Usually, when he discussed the issue at all, he attacked McCarthy's methods, which had destroyed "the rights of free speech and free thought."[95]

On the whole, Fairchild's campaign stressed those aspects of McCarthy's career that seemed most vulnerable. Fairchild reviewed the great variety of controversial activities that made up McCarthy's personal record. Campaign advertisements asked Wisconsinites to vote for "honorable representation" and "the man Wisconsin can be proud of."[96]

For the first time, the major thrust of the anti-McCarthy movement, spearheaded by Fairchild, aimed at criticizing McCarthy's conservative voting record. Fairchild repeatedly attacked his opponent's neglect of farm issues, votes for tidelands oil (which benefited states with offshore oil rather than Wisconsin), and opposition to social security and federal aid to education. Fairchild tried unsuccessfully to goad McCarthy into discussing something other than communism. "With the election day less than a month away," Fairchild charged, "people of Wisconsin have yet to hear him talk about the problems of agriculture, labor–management relations, social security, housing, inflation." The major theme of Fairchild's newspaper advertisements urged voters to elect him "for continued prosperity." "It remains to be seen," a pro-McCarthy columnist observed of Fairchild's strategy, "whether soft-pedaling the Communist issue and hitting at McCarthy's first-term voting record can produce any real effect in the few short weeks left."[97]

Ironically, the Fairchild campaign's attacks on McCarthy's voting record and unethical personal conduct were less successful than its frontal assault on the validity of his anti-Communist crusade. McCarthy ignored Fairchild's campaign until the day before the election, when he was forced to recognize the gravity of a charge brought against him by Edward P. Morgan, former administrative assistant to FBI director J. Edgar Hoover and a specialist on Communist activities. Coaxed into coming to Wisconsin by Rubin, Morgan appeared on Milwaukee television with Fairchild on 2 November and made a fervent appeal for McCarthy's defeat. Morgan revealed a personal—and until then confidential—incident in which McCarthy used a forged civil service commission report on security studies in a Senate speech attacking Communists in government. He also charged that, after McCarthy's Wheeling, West Virginia, speech, McCarthy's desperate aides came to Morgan to ask for assistance in identifying just one Communist to build into another Hiss case. McCarthy was obviously stung by the charges. On election eve, he responded that Morgan had posed as an FBI agent when actually he had left the bureau in 1947 (which Morgan had stipulated) and called Morgan's attack a "new low in campaign degeneracy." But the use of an ex-FBI agent was apparently magic in combating McCarthy. Scores of people from Milwaukee and surrounding areas enthusiastically responded to the program. Democrats quickly realized its importance and rushed tape recordings of the show to radio stations throughout the state. Democrats considered Morgan's television appearance the most effective tactic of their campaign.[98]

Despite his vigorous efforts, Fairchild could not offset McCarthy's major advantages: better financial backing, stronger party organization, and overwhelming newspaper support and publicity. Fairchild raised more funds than Schmitt, but he did not match McCarthy's financial support. A major portion of the contributions to Fairchild's campaign came from eastern states. The National Committee for an Effective Congress, based in Washington, D.C., raised from $20,000 to $30,000 for the Democratic aspirant.[99] While the exact amount of labor's financial involvement remains a mystery, national, state, and local union groups constituted the largest single source of monetary support for Fairchild.[100] It remains un-known exactly how much McCarthy's campaign raised or spent. As of 1 November 1952, the RVC had collected over $400,000 for all its candidates. The McCarthy Club raised between $150,000 and $200,000. Much of the club's funds came from corporations. Llewellyn Morack, McCarthy's stockbroker and friend, collected about $75,000 for the club from corporate treasuries around the country. Executives of the Miller Brewing Company (Milwaukee) picked up checks from other industrialists. McCarthy had so much money that he gave a substantial portion back to the RVC to use for other state candidates.[101]

Unlike their Republican counterparts, the Democrats lacked adequate organizational strength. Although the formation of the DOC in 1948 had improved their organization, Democrats had won few state and local offices. They had to operate without the county offices that provided the basic strength of most successful state party organizations.

In the 1952 general election, an overwhelming majority of state news-papers endorsed the entire Republican ticket, including McCarthy. Those papers editorially favoring McCarthy supported him consistently in their news columns as well. McCarthy's name appeared in three-and-one-half times more news items than his opponent's. An analysis of front-page attention revealed that McCarthy appeared four times more often than Fairchild. In front-page headlines, the ratio was almost five to one.[102] These handicaps proved too much for Fairchild.

    \*    \*    \*    \*

With party unity assured, Wisconsin Republicans rolled to a landslide victory in the November election. McCarthy won with relative ease, cap-turing 54 percent of the vote. The final tabulation gave him 870,444 votes, compared to Fairchild's 731,402. But McCarthy trailed the entire ticket. He received 169,000 or 12 percent fewer votes than Zimmerman, the leading GOP vote-getter; 139,000 or 9 percent fewer votes than Kohler; and 110,000 or 7 percent fewer votes than Eisenhower. McCarthy ran behind his own total in 1946 and 7.3 percent behind the state Republican congressional ticket.

Besides shattering the myth of McCarthy's political invincibility, the 1952 election provided social scientists with important data to explain the nature of McCarthy's support and, by implication, the nature of McCar-thyism. McCarthy's vote was concentrated primarily in areas of Republi-can strength and was not distributed in a pattern unique to him. For example, his strongest showing took place in those counties that gave Kohler overwhelming support.[103] Like other Republicans, McCarthy ran strongest in predominantly rural, economically backward counties with a lower level of education.[104] He ran well ahead of his state average in townships heavily populated with people of German extraction. This was also true of other Republicans, including Taft in the 1952 primary and Republican presidential candidates in 1944, 1948, and 1952. McCarthy capitalized on the large Republican following among German-Americans who were already disturbed about communism and American foreign policy. Although the Germans were "the backbone of McCarthy's support," Michael Rogin has shown, "they were not a group attracted by his unique appeals."[105]

McCarthy did slightly better (2.2 percent) than the state GOP average in nine counties surrounding his hometown of Appleton. He had a 3.3 percent edge over the average of his party colleagues in seven nonindustrial Catholic counties. He also had unique appeal in eight nonurban Polish counties and five Czechoslovakian counties—2.4 and 6.7 percent, respectively, above the state Republican average. Poles and Czechs were probably disturbed about the recent Communist takeovers of their native countries.[106]

In Wisconsin's fourteen most rural counties, McCarthy's vote was 3.1 percent higher than the average Republican total. Both McCarthy and Midwestern Republicans in general benefited from rural suspicions of the values, groups, and power centers of urban, industrial society. Perhaps McCarthy had been particularly attractive because his attacks were more virulent. McCarthy's appeal did not seem to rest on economic discontent because he did as well in prosperous rural sectors as in those with economic grievances. McCarthy's 1952 vote showed that he shared a common agrarian appeal with the Progressive Robert M. La Follette, Jr. McCarthy did 1.4 percent better than the regular Republican vote in twenty-six Progressive counties. Yet these counties were the least important source of McCarthy's support. While McCarthy won backing from rural areas generally throughout the state, La Follette had been consistently rejected in the rich, southern countryside. In addition, the characteristic of Catholicism, the friends-and-neighbors effect, and Czechoslovakian background apparently reinforced the tendency of rural areas to support McCarthy.[107]

McCarthy was considerably weaker than other Republicans in the eleven most industrial counties in the state, falling 6.2 percent below the regular Republican vote. He received only 39 percent of the vote in Milwaukee County (compared with 49 percent for Kohler and 52 percent for Eisenhower) and 38 percent in Dane County (compared with 51 percent for Kohler and 50 percent for Eisenhower). Milwaukee's two congressional districts were drawn roughly along class lines with the Fourth District heavily Polish working class and the Fifth more middle class. The Fourth gave Eisenhower 10 percent more votes than McCarthy, and the Fifth gave him 12 percent more.[108]

The Milwaukee labor districts had been the target of intense campaign efforts by the DOC and organized labor. In the city of Milwaukee, Fairchild captured 63.4 percent of the vote, but his percentage increased to 75.3 percent in blue-collar areas. David Oshinsky has shown that occupation was the single variable most clearly associated with the McCarthy vote in Milwaukee. The six most pro-McCarthy wards had relatively low percentages of employed male blue-collar workers. Five of the six most anti-McCarthy wards ranked at the top of Milwaukee's twenty-six wards in percentage of employed male blue-collar workers. A similar pattern emerged in the city of Madison. Stevenson's city total of 48.2 percent jumped to 61.2 percent in Madison's labor wards, while Fairchild's percentage rose from 62.0 to 71.4 percent.[109]

Political scientist Martin Trow has theorized that membership in a labor union was a major factor in shaping a worker's attitude toward McCarthy. A union channeled free-floating frustrations and anxieties about the social and political order into an institutional framework, thus making these emotions unavailable for exploitation by McCarthy. Moreover, Fairchild's campaign had successfully portrayed McCarthy as an anti–new deal conservative whose shortcomings on domestic policy outweighed his value as an anti-Communist. The election results demonstrated not only that workers had unions through which to express their grievances, but that McCarthy could not mobilize their voting support by attacking Roosevelt, the New Deal, and the Democratic party.[110]

Two additional factors, often overlooked by analysts, help to account for McCarthy's pattern of voter support. Most of the state Democratic candidates in 1952 were unknown and poorly financed. For example, William Proxmire, Kohler's opponent, had only recently moved into the state, had served only one term in the assembly, and had little financial backing. Fairchild, on the other hand, was a well-known, formidable challenger with major financial support, and McCarthy campaigned little against him. This partly explains why McCarthy trailed other state Republican candidates. The pattern of news coverage was also important. McCarthy did well in all areas of the state where Republican newspapers publicized and endorsed his anti-Communist crusade and refused to print critical accounts about him. On the other hand, his poor showing in Milwaukee and Dane counties can be accounted for partly by the severe criticism of him by the *Milwaukee Journal* and *The Capital Times*. The same influence appeared important in Eau Claire and Sheboygan counties where the two Eau Claire newspapers and *The Sheboygan Press* opposed his reelection. McCarthy lost both counties.

McCarthy's adversaries were proud of the moral victory they achieved. They had not won the election, but McCarthy's position at the bottom of the state ticket showed that he was politically vulnerable. Nevertheless, he had won another six-year term in the Senate. His reelection was a "black day in the history of Wisconsin," *The Capital Times* noted sadly, a day on which the people "with full knowledge of the record—endorsed the cult of McCarthyism."[111] The sentiments of his opponents and an accurate prediction of the events of the next five years were best expressed by James Doyle's statement following the election:

To President Eisenhower: Our full and fervent support in the task of building the peace.

To Gov. Stevenson: Our eternal admiration for the most gallant and eloquent campaign in American history.

To Gov. Kohler: Our congratulations on your decisive victory.

To Senator McCarthy: War unto the death.[112]

And so it would be.

# Chapter 8

# Doubt and Criticism: 1953

Now that the GOP controlled the federal government, most Republican leaders in the country expected McCarthy to cease his hunt for Communists. The Eisenhower administration and the Republican majority in Congress would toss out a few thousand Truman appointees and keep an eye on their replacements. The new president assured the country that he regarded this housecleaning task as an executive responsibility that he would perform with dispatch. The House Committee on Un-American Activities and the Senate Committee on Internal Security would expose the incompetence of the Truman administration, but this would not take long.[1]

Wisconsin Republicans agreed with this forecast.[2] McCarthy and other red-hunters had "held the fort" while Truman "flirted dangerously with 'red herrings.' " Now, with a Republican president, McCarthy could devote his energy to a wider variety of problems.[3] John Wyngaard speculated that sooner or later McCarthy would have to "get used to the idea that there are agricultural and labor and tax and military issues before the government and the Congress."[4] Wisconsin Republicans did not warn McCarthy directly about embarrassing the new administration by continuing his anti-Communist fight; apparently they sincerely believed that he naturally would not consider such a course.

On the other end of the political spectrum, Miles McMillin advanced another scenario. McCarthy would play around under Republican team rules for a while but not for long. "His eyes have seen the glory of too many front page headlines and his ears have heard the roar of those in the cult of the club." McCarthy had taken on bigger men than Eisenhower, McMillin warned. "The Republicans should remember, as they so often told us during the recent campaign, 'Joe ain't afraid of nothing.' "[5]

At first, McCarthy appeared content to accept a smaller role. The day after the election, he told the Scripps-Howard newspapers that he planned "an entirely different role" for himself. "The picture has so infinitely changed," he said. "Now it will be unnecessary for me to conduct a one-man campaign to expose Communists in government. We have a new president who doesn't want party-line thinkers or fellow travelers. He will conduct the fight."[6]

A month later, he talked differently. "We've only scratched the surface on communism," he said, and he promised to continue his crusade. Re-

publican strategists had hoped to control him by assigning him to a seemingly dull and impotent position on the government operations committee
instead of the red-hunting internal security committee, but McCarthy
outsmarted them. As the aggressive chairman of the committee's permanent subcommittee on investigations, he found an instrument for continuing his anti-Communist activities. Before the Eisenhower administration
and the new Congress were a month old, McCarthy was again creating
turmoil in the State Department. He found two file clerks who testified that
department records had been rifled of damning evidence of communism
and homosexuality.[7] McMillin was right—the crusade had resumed.

Back in Wisconsin, the McCarthy furor declined in the wake of the
dramatic 1952 election. Although anti-McCarthy newspapers continued to
criticize his every action, on the whole, little discussion of McCarthy took
place in 1953. Democrats were particularly apathetic. Only a month after
the November election in 1952, James Doyle asked Democrats: "What has
become of the righteous indignation against McCarthy that drew so many
of us into common cause this year?"[8]

Nevertheless, the year witnessed three significant developments in the
McCarthy controversy, each of which eroded his support in Wisconsin.
Some of his supporters began to have serious misgivings about his character and judgment as a result of the Hennings report and the Nathan Pusey
incident. More important, the feud between McCarthy and President
Eisenhower led some staunch Republican newspapers and party leaders to
blame McCarthy for the resulting damage to party unity. Last, late in the
year, the special election in the Ninth Congressional District perked up the
Democrats and revealed declining concern for McCarthy's anti-Communist campaign.

On 2 January 1953, as the Eighty-second Congress came to a close, the
Senate Subcommittee on Privileges and Elections, then under the direc-
tion of Missouri Democrat Thomas Hennings, reported on the charges
made by Sen. William Benton a year-and-a-half earlier. The substantive
part of the report dealt almost exclusively with McCarthy's financial tan-
gles. It described the Lustron fee as "highly improper" and questioned
whether McCarthy had "collected funds for his anti-Communist fight
which he had possibly diverted to his own use." (McCarthy had channeled
one contribution into soybean futures.) The report suggested that McCarthy had used his family and friends to obscure the sources of funds
diverted to campaign expenses and noted that his dealings with the Appleton State Bank had caused that institution to violate federal and state laws.
The report offered no conclusion but contained enough evidence to
strongly suggest that McCarthy had engaged in illegal and unethical practices. The subcommittee explained that definite answers were impossible
because McCarthy had refused six invitations to testify and had "deliber-
ately set out to block any investigation."[9]

For the most part, reaction to the report in Wisconsin was predictable.

Democrats and anti-McCarthy newspapers found in it further evidence of McCarthy's wickedness and urged more investigation of the unanswered questions. Some Republican newspapers labeled the report "smear tactics," without addressing themselves to its contents, the morality of McCarthy's actions, or his failure to appear before the subcommittee. Most Republican newspapers, columnists, and politicians had no comment whatsoever. However, the revelations disgusted a few newspapers that had ignored such charges earlier. The subcommittee had raised "grave questions of moral turpitude," one editorial stated, "which go beyond ordinary political considerations."[10] McCarthy should answer the "grave questions" raised, the *Wausau Daily Record-Herald* asserted. To call them "smear tactics," as McCarthy had done, "no more suffices as an answer than does similar outbursts from some of those the senator has accused of following the red line."[11] Considering the Republican credentials of the newspapers and their former devotion to McCarthy, their observations were significant and ominous.

Later in the year, some Republicans in the Fox River valley questioned McCarthy's judgment after his slashing assault on Nathan Pusey, the distinguished and popular president of Lawrence College in Appleton. In the summer of 1952, Pusey had joined the group of prominent Wisconsin residents in sponsoring *The McCarthy Record*. During the 1952 campaign, McCarthy had refused to comment on the book or its sponsors. In the late spring of 1953, Harvard selected Pusey to head its institution. Wisconsin newspapers congratulated Pusey and commended Harvard for its wise choice.

After Pusey's appointment, Neal O'Hara, columnist for the *Boston Traveler*, asked McCarthy for his estimate of his fellow townsman. McCarthy replied that "Harvard's loss is Wisconsin's gain." Pusey was " a man who has considerable intellectual possibilities but who has neither learned nor forgotten anything since he was a freshman in college." Pusey, McCarthy continued, "appears to hide a combination of bigotry and intolerance behind a cloak of phony, hypocritical liberalism." McCarthy concluded cynically: "I do not think Pusey is or has been a member of the Communist party," but he was a "rabid anti, anti-Communist."[12]

In Appleton, Pusey responded: "When McCarthy's remarks about me are translated it means only—I didn't vote for him." The Lawrence College Board of Trustees indignantly rejected McCarthy's criticism. Elmer Jennings, a prominent Republican and a board member, found it difficult to argue with a man "who seemingly has such a meager conception of what are the basic concepts of education." The incident considerably embarrassed Republicans in the Appleton area. Some hoped that McCarthy had been misquoted; others rebuked him. Charles R. Seaborn, executive vice-president of the Thilmany Paper and Pulp Company in Appleton and a major supporter and fund raiser for McCarthy in 1952, telegraphed him that his attack on Pusey was "uninformed and unadvised" and expressed sorrow that McCarthy was "letting down so many old friends." The next day, McCarthy countered sharply: "curious to know what old friends are being let down by the exposure of bigoted intolerant mudslinging enemy of mine?"[13]

McCarthy's broadside also angered Republican newspapers that had seldom, if ever, criticized him. "A new low," "ridiculous," lacking in "courtesy and propriety," three of them editorialized.[14] The *Appleton Post-Crescent* assumed that McCarthy's attack stemmed from Pusey's opposition to him in the 1952 campaign in which case McCarthy was "way out of bounds." Pusey had "a perfect right to take whatever stand he pleased in a political campaign, and should not be subjected to personal slaps for so doing." The paper continued:

> In stating that "I do not think Dr. Pusey is or has been a member of the Communist party," McCarthy used a gutter-type approach. He could have referred as correctly to Pope or President.[15]

For many McCarthy partisans, the Pusey incident was important because it raised serious doubts about the senator's credibility. Pusey was known and admired throughout the state, and his integrity was beyond question. McCarthy's misdirected attack on him seemed to indicate that, if McCarthy were that far off base about Pusey, who lived in his own hometown, he was off base on other charges as well.

A more important source of consternation for the state GOP was the running feud between McCarthy and President Eisenhower. In March 1953, McCarthy fought the confirmation of Eisenhower's nominee Charles Bohlen as ambassador to the Soviet Union. During his maneuvering to defeat the nomination, McCarthy implied that Secretary of State John Foster Dulles had lied in endorsing Bohlen and implicitly challenged the president's judgment and honesty. With Sen. Robert Taft's assistance, however, the administration won its battle to secure Bohlen's appointment.

State GOP leaders did not comment publicly on the incident, but Republican newspapers did. Some tried to smooth over the differences between the two men and praised McCarthy for not becoming a rubber stamp for the new president.[16] Others rebuked McCarthy and praised Bohlen and Eisenhower. The *Wisconsin State Journal* found McCarthy's case against Bohlen weak, his overall antics silly, and concluded that the incident had "hurt him immensely."[17] The *Waukesha Daily Freeman* praised the confirmation and expressed pleasure that Eisenhower and not McCarthy was boss in Washington.[18]

While observers were still buzzing over the Bohlen incident, McCarthy announced that, in his capacity as chairman of the permanent subcommittee, he had negotiated an agreement with Greek shipowners that would "have some of the effects of a naval blockade." He hoped to deprive Communist nations of goods that had until then been delivered to their ports by 242 ships. He said that he had made the agreement without consulting personnel in the State Department because "I don't want interference by anyone." Harold Stassen, head of the Foreign Operations Administration, angrily charged that McCarthy had undermined the authority of the secretary of state and other officials, but Eisenhower refused to support Stassen's remarks. The administration even seemed to accept the senator's personal diplomacy when Dulles and McCarthy issued a joint statement that the agreement was "in the national interest."[19]

In Wisconsin, some Republican newspapers endorsed McCarthy's diplomacy. "If his committee's actions have the practical result of cutting off goods to the men who are killing Americans in Korea," a typical view held, "we aren't going to bother much about protocol."[20] Others thought he "went too far" into the powers reserved to the State Department.[21]

In July 1953, the J. B. Matthews incident aroused louder protest against McCarthy's investigative committee. Matthews, staff director of the McCarthy committee, wrote in the July issue of the *American Mercury* that "at least seven thousand" Protestant ministers supported the Communist conspiracy, making up the "largest single group supporting the Communist apparatus in the United States today." Although he tempered his attack somewhat by asserting that the majority of the clergy were loyal Americans, his charges brought indignant protests from clergymen of all faiths. Prompted by his staff, Eisenhower criticized "generalized and irresponsible attacks" that brought "contempt for the principles of freedom and decency." As a result, McCarthy backed down and severed his connection with Matthews. Wisconsin Republican newspapers that commented on the incident sided with Eisenhower and condemned hysterical generalizations, reckless accusations, and disregard for truth and fair play.[22]

Meanwhile, the smoldering feud within the Wisconsin Republican party exploded in the summer of 1953. The dominant wing of the GOP, informally led by Thomas Coleman, was conservative and isolationist and idolized Gen. Douglas MacArthur, Taft, and McCarthy. Still bitter that Taft had lost the Republican nomination in 1952, they were unhappy with the Eisenhower administration. As Coleman put it, they did not respect Secretary of State Dulles and did not believe that the United States had "taken its proper place in world affairs" under the new administration.[23] The moderate internationalist faction, including Sen. Alexander Wiley and Gov. Walter Kohler, looked to Eisenhower for leadership. Kohler and Coleman had not been on speaking terms since the 1952 presidential primary in Wisconsin when Kohler refused Coleman's invitation to become a Taft delegate.[24] Their feud illustrated the degree of animosity between the two factions.

But Eisenhower was too popular and too essential for GOP strength and unity to be attacked directly. As an alternative, conservative Republicans turned their wrath on Senator Wiley. Conservatives had never forgiven

Wiley for his conversion to internationalism and bipartisanship, friendship with Dean Acheson, and failure to campaign for or endorse McCarthy
against Leonard Schmitt and Thomas Fairchild. In 1953, party workers
often said of Wiley:

> He's an internationalist. He wants to give this country away.
> He played ball with Truman.
> It's that British wife of his. He's soft on England.[25]

With the election of Eisenhower and a Republican Congress, Wiley
became chairman of the powerful Senate Foreign Relations Committee. In
1953, a major issue in Congress was the so-called Bricker amendment to
the Constitution, which aimed to limit the independence of the president
in making treaties and executive agreements. Wiley and Eisenhower opposed the amendment, but the entire Wisconsin GOP leadership and most
lower-echelon party officials endorsed it. Republicans who supported the
Bricker amendment usually supported McCarthy; those who opposed the
amendment often privately criticized him. Wiley remained loyal to the
president on the issue, despite protests from his state party organization.
"It seems to me," Wayne Hood wrote in urging Wiley to support the
amendment, "that your responsibility is to the people of the United States
and not to the administration."[26]

There were other reasons for dissatisfaction with Wiley. As Coleman
advised Leonard Hall, chairman of the Republican National Committee,
part of the objection "was just because he was Wiley," by which Coleman
presumably meant vain, pompous, and platitudinous.[27] Wiley was also
independent in a way that outraged organization people. He never asked
for help or advice from state GOP leaders and never took orders from
them.

The frustrations and bitterness burst into embarrassing public view at
the GOP state convention in June. With his appearance staged for its most
dramatic impact, McCarthy was to deliver the main address on 12 June.
When the time came for his speech, the master of ceremonies, Frank
Panzer, called for him, but he was nowhere to be seen. The crowd stood up
expecting him to come down the main aisle as the other dignitaries had.
When he finally appeared from in back of the stage, the delegates went
wild. As one delegate described the scene, "it was like the 'French perfume
that rocks the room' only this was the 'perfect entrance that rocked the
rafters!' " The microphone, which had been out of kilter all afternoon,
worked perfectly, and McCarthy "filled the room with the power of his
voice."[28]

Although he castigated Truman and Acheson and generally praised
Eisenhower, McCarthy also expressed disappointment that the housecleaning of Communists in government had "not progressed as rapidly as
many of us would desire." After tumultuous applause, the delegates

expressed their appreciation "in the extreme" for McCarthy's investigations during which he displayed "courage . . . patience . . . and intelligence."[29]

In contrast, party leaders ignored Wiley from the moment he arrived in Madison for the convention. Hood's address to the delegates praised McCarthy profusely but carried only passing references to Eisenhower and Wiley. No outstanding Republican would even accompany Wiley to the speaker's platform. Half the audience applauded politely when he was introduced; the other half howled a lusty chorus of boos. His address, a straightforward delineation of Eisenhower's foreign policy, went uninterrupted by applause. When he finished, the crowd again booed and heckled.[30]

The convention proceeded to censure Wiley and passed other resolutions that seemed to strike at Eisenhower. The delegates endorsed the Bricker amendment but included a peculiar provision making it appear that Eisenhower did also. The delegates opposed radical proposals to amend the McCarran–Walter Immigration Act, which the president had asked Congress to revise significantly. Finally, the delegates gave only a terse, perfunctory commendation of the president. No responsible party official publicly defended Wiley or Eisenhower. Their friends were neither bold nor organized. Kohler responded timidly that the resolution to censure Wiley was "ill advised."[31]

When most newspapers interpreted what happened at the convention as a slap at Eisenhower, responsible party leaders became frightened. They disclaimed any part in the affair, and the instigators—mainly younger Republicans—insisted that they had meant only to chastise Wiley. But Wiley belabored the point that they had opposed the president. In fact, Wiley surprised observers by the belligerence of his counterattack. The amiable back-slapping senator, expected to look for a way to crawl back into favor with his state organization, turned into a warrior and redoubled his efforts to convince people that he and Eisenhower were correct. Even before the convention, when it appeared he would not be invited to speak, Wiley sensed the mounting hostility and urged friends in Wisconsin to get word to his enemies in the GOP leadership that such an insult would result in Wiley's failure to cooperate with patronage appointments.[32] In a revengeful mood after his censure, he sought to identify Republicans with the "jackass attitude" toward him.[33] He was also angry about the Eisenhower administration's failure to come to his defense. "A month has gone by and it [the administration] has been utterly silent," he wrote Atty. Gen. Herbert Brownell. "Am I to understand that the White House does not care whether its supporters are attacked, but it only cares to give split-second attention to its enemies who might make more trouble for it?"[34]

McCarthy made more trouble for the president in November. Brownell had accused the late Harry Dexter White of Communist subversion while employed as a Democratic Treasury Department official. When former President Truman called Brownell's remarks an example of McCarthyism, McCarthy obtained equal television time. Although he attacked Truman, McCarthy jolted many Republicans by also turning his guns on the Eisenhower administration. McCarthy charged that, in some cases, the administration "has batted zero—struck out" in not firing individuals that McCarthy had accused. American fliers remained in captivity, and the "blood trade" continued between American allies and Red China. McCarthy demanded the termination of mutual security assistance to Great Britain if that country continued to trade with Communist China. Communists in government would be an issue in the 1954 election, McCarthy warned, despite Eisenhower's wish that it not be.[35]

On 1 December, Secretary of State Dulles, without mentioning McCarthy, stressed that the United States had no intention of turning loyal allies into satellites. The following day, also without mentioning McCarthy, Eisenhower defended the effectiveness of his loyalty program and promised to "protect the basic rights of loyal American citizens."[36]

Some Republican newspapers praised McCarthy's speech, but their remarks referred only to his scathing assault on the Truman administration and came prior to the rebuttals by Dulles and Eisenhower. Other newspapers were angered by McCarthy's attack on Eisenhower. One thought that McCarthy planned to challenge Eisenhower for the presidency in 1956.[37] Another observed that "Republicans now have a clear choice between the president's moderate position and the self-serving radicalism of the Wisconsin senator."[38] The most common concern was for the future of the Republican party. A conservative newspaper hoped that the "sharp exchange of words will not serve to split the Republican party and that the difference can be adjusted amicably."[39]

Despite provocation throughout 1953, Eisenhower failed to move boldly against McCarthy for several reasons. His administration wanted to avoid a confrontation with all nettlesome Republican senators because Republicans controlled the Senate by only a forty-eight to forty-seven margin. Ike also believed that McCarthy was primarily the Senate's responsibility. And last, Ike opposed a pugnacious policy for strategic reasons: "I will not get into the gutter with that guy," he exclaimed to an adviser.[40]

In any case, as Wyngaard found in December, the year-long feud was "discouraging and debilitating, from the standpoint of local GOP morale."[41] It is impossible to determine the loyalties of the mass of Wisconsin Republican voters at the end of 1953. The same is true of most GOP leaders who, afraid of aggravating party tension, said nothing publicly. Probably most Republicans supported both McCarthy and Eisenhower. Increasingly, however, they were being forced to make a choice. During the year, some Republican newspapers joined Senator Wiley and Governor Kohler in the Eisenhower camp. In the Fox River valley, a strong minority of Republicans began to criticize McCarthy at party gatherings and party donations began to slacken.[42] Some moderates complained bitterly that Eisenhower had not done enough to curb the demagogic senator. Ellis Dana, vice-chairman of the Wisconsin Citizens for Eisenhower in 1952, demanded the president's answer to some pointed questions: How long was McCarthy going to "tell Ike what to do?" "When is Ike going to take over?" "How long are you—Ike—going to say 'sweet nothings' to McCarthy?"[43] Others blamed conservative party leaders for their inability to acquire patronage. James LaChance, chairman of the RVC in the Second Congressional District, complained: "To get patronage you must have a record of loyalty to Tom Coleman et al., you must have supported Taft, and you must be a member of the anti-Wiley group. Since I can lay claim to none of these qualities, I may as well give up."[44]

The McCarthy–Taft Wing of the party included Coleman, Henry Ringling, John Rouse, Hood, and most lower-echelon party officials as well as some newspapers. Their displeasure with Wiley continued and led them to endorse Rep. Glenn Davis to oppose him in the Republican senatorial primary in 1956. But McCarthy's excesses and the death of Robert Taft in July 1953 forced them on the defensive. Throughout 1953, Coleman, Ringling, Hood, Rep. Melvin Laird (an Eisenhower Republican), and others met with McCarthy and with representatives of Eisenhower in an unsuccessful effort to cool off their feud.[45]

While Republicans experienced growing party division during 1953, Democrats suffered from lethargy. But at the end of the year, they discovered the traditional cure for that particular political disease—victory. Following the Republican sweep of Wisconsin in 1952, Wisconsin Democrats' organization and enthusiasm both went into a slump. The party publication, the Wisconsin Democrat, was reduced in size and appeal. The paper concentrated on watching President Eisenhower and discussing reapportionment but performed both of those tasks with little fervor. In May 1953, James Doyle called for Wisconsin Democrats to cease the mourning begun on election day the previous November, but his statement did nothing to relieve the doldrums.[46]

Although the anti-McCarthy crusade waned, McCarthy's most vociferous opponents persevered. They returned to their earlier policies of exposing his lack of character and criticizing his anti-Communist campaign. They publicized the Hennings report, refuted McCarthy's attack on the Voice of America, decried the book-burning madness, and worried about the fear and the hysteria unleashed by his investigations. Above all, they dwelt on the McCarthy–Eisenhower feud and predicted that the senator would challenge the president's renomination in 1956, or head a supernationalistic third party.

Then on 13 October 1953, voters of the Ninth Congressional District went to the polls to fill a vacancy created by the death of Republican Rep. Merlin Hull. The district comprised eleven counties in the west-central part of the state. Although traditionally Progressive, the district was Republican in recent voting habits and had voted for McCarthy in 1952 by a three-to-two margin. The region had never gone Democratic, and the Republican aspirant Lester Padrutt was expected to win easily. To everyone's surprise, Democrat Lester Johnson won by a comfortable margin.

The election provided no direct evidence of the district's current feelings about McCarthy. He was seldom mentioned during the campaign, even by Democrats, and he took no personal part in it. The campaign rarely discussed communism either. Johnson's victory stemmed from farmers' anger at the Eisenhower administration's conservative farm program. Farming accounted for approximately 80 percent of the district's income, and farmers blamed falling farm prices on the administration in general and on Secretary of Agriculture Ezra Taft Benson in particular. "Issues of the pocketbook," Richard Haney observed, "replaced the emotional issue of Joseph McCarthy overnight." Within a month of the victory, Democrats convened a state convention with "a new-found spirit of optimism."[47]

Johnson's election shocked Wisconsin Republicans. "You can see that we are on the defensive," Coleman reflected; "rather, you might put it that the Democrats are on the offensive and doing a pretty good job of it." Coleman used the defeat to vent his anger at Eisenhower and his cabinet for not being political enough. "They do not realize that our whole problem from this time until next fall is almost exclusively politics."[48] For most GOP leaders, the election meant that Republicans should concentrate more on agricultural problems. The Johnson upset even momentarily affected McCarthy's priorities. Two months after the election, he declared that the major issues in the 1954 congressional elections would be low farm prices, *followed* by the Communist issue.[49] Later, he advocated 100 percent fixed parity payments for farmers.

The Democratic victory again focused attention on McCarthy's vulnerable voting record and his apparent lack of concern for mundane legislative issues. In Wyngaard's view, McCarthy had given "less than ordinary congressional service to the state that he represents . . . with the result that if his sedition-in-government issue ever subsides—as it must ultimately under a government of his own party—he will have a thinner record than most to show to the people of his own constituency." Wyngaard noted that McCarthy's worldwide stature would not mean much "if the Wisconsin farmer . . . gets the notion that he is indifferent to his economic interests."[50]

McCarthy's critics, who had ignored his voting record throughout 1953, also learned from Johnson's upset. Anti-McCarthyites, particularly McMillin, now devoted much of their energy to updating their information about McCarthy's voting record. The fruits of their labor, widely publicized in the spring and summer of 1954, attempted to show that McCarthy had voted against the interests of most of his constituents.

McCarthy's strength in Wisconsin had been seriously undermined during 1953. He had made no new converts, and his feud with Eisenhower displeased many Wisconsin Republicans. A few former supporters now suspected his character, methods, and targets, and Johnson's victory indicated that voters were more interested in bread-and-butter issues than in chasing Communists. According to a national Gallup poll, favorable opinion of McCarthy had dropped from 35 percent in June to 34 percent in August, while unfavorable responses rose from 30 to 42 percent.

Yet there was no large-scale defection from the McCarthy camp. No state Republican leader publicly criticized him. Only a few small newspapers left the McCarthy bandwagon during the year; one that did was *The Sauk-Prairie Star*, edited by Leroy Gore, who would shortly launch a recall drive. In fact, as the year closed, McCarthy appeared stronger than ever. His comeback was sparked by his investigation of the Army Signal Corps Center at Fort Monmouth, New Jersey. In October 1953, McCarthy had begun hearings on alleged Communist infiltration and espionage at the center. He would interrogate witnesses in executive session and then emerge with dramatic accounts for waiting newsmen. He claimed to have found traces of "extremely dangerous espionage" that struck at "our entire defense against atomic attack." Gullible newspapers wrote lurid accounts of the investigation and led many people to believe that he had actually uncovered a major spy network.[51] This explains a Gallup poll in January 1954 that found that 50 percent of Americans had a favorable opinion of him, 29 percent opposed him, and 21 percent had no opinion.

Time would show, however, that McCarthy could not substantiate his exaggerated claims. While thirty-three scientists were suspended during McCarthy's inquiry, the majority were exonerated and reinstated, and no spy was discovered. In Wisconsin, the seeds of doubt and criticism sown in 1953 were more substantial than the fleeting notoriety he received from the probe. The following year would bring renewed controversy with the popular Eisenhower that, along with other factors, worked to further undermine McCarthy's influence and popularity.

# Chapter 9

# The Senator Becomes a Liability: 1954

Because of the tumultuous events of 1954, McCarthy's popularity declined substantially in Wisconsin during the year but did not disappear completely. The acrimonious debate about his character and crusade continued much as it had in the past. Democrats and other critics opposed everything he did. Wisconsin opponents updated *The McCarthy Record* in the April 1954 special edition of *The Progressive* magazine, and the ninety-six-page indictment sold 185,000 copies. On the other side, some Republican newspapers, many GOP party members, and thousands of ordinary citizens continued to prefer him over Eisenhower, endorsed his position in the Army–McCarthy hearings, and bitterly opposed his censure. Nonetheless, the most significant development during the year was his political decline. Major defections from the McCarthy camp occurred among a large number of conservative newspapers, farmers, and Republicans, so that, by the end of the year, the tone of Wisconsin opinion was irrevocably anti-McCarthy. As an outgrowth of this change in sentiment, opponents organized the Joe Must Go recall movement, the largest grass-roots protest in Wisconsin history.

"There arrives a point in the political process when no leader or group of leaders can any longer determine the course of events," historian Robert Griffith has observed of the celebrated Army–McCarthy hearings. With Eisenhower's weak leadership and a divided Republican party, this point arrived quickly. Neither the president nor the Republican leadership welcomed the display of party disunity, but neither was able to prevent it. The controversy unfolded by a dynamic of its own.[1]

During his investigation of alleged Communists at Fort Monmouth, New Jersey, McCarthy discovered that the army had promoted Dr. Irving Peress, a New York dentist, to the rank of major and granted him an honorable discharge despite his refusal to answer questions about his Communist activities. In early February, McCarthy demanded to know the names of all individuals connected with the Peress case, and, after Secretary of the Army Robert Stevens declined his request, McCarthy turned on Gen. Ralph Zwicker, commandant at Camp Kilmer, New Jersey, where Peress had been discharged. When Zwicker refused to criticize his superiors for granting the discharge or to talk about security coverage in the service, he incurred McCarthy's wrath. "You are a disgrace to the uniform," McCarthy raged. "You're shielding Communist conspirators.

You're not fit to be an officer. You're ignorant. You are going to be put on public display next Tuesday." McCarthy implied that Zwicker did not have the "brains of a five-year-old child."[2]

On 3 March Eisenhower called for fair play in congressional investigations. McCarthy replied the same day with a crackling statement, interpreted as defiance of the president. He had "no fight with Eisenhower," McCarthy said, but, referring to Zwicker, "if a stupid, arrogant, witless man in a position of power" was found "aiding the Communists," McCarthy would expose him.[3] These remarks offended some Republican friends in Wisconsin, and, led by state party treasurer Claude Jasper, they took the unprecedented step of asking McCarthy in writing to repudiate his statements.[4]

Other developments underscored McCarthy's increasing vulnerability. When he demanded equal time on radio and television to reply to criticism by Adlai Stevenson, Republican National Chairman Leonard Hall maneuvered artfully to have Vice-President Richard Nixon give the Republican rebuttal. Republican Sen. Ralph Flanders of Vermont excoriated McCarthy in a Senate speech on 9 March, charging that he was "doing his best to wreck the party." The same evening, CBS television commentator Edward R. Murrow devoted his thirty-minute program "See It Now" to a powerful documentation of McCarthy's lies and distortions. The network was swamped with calls and telegrams sympathetic to Murrow's position.[5]

McCarthy's attack on General Zwicker was particularly resented in Wisconsin because Zwicker had grown up in Stoughton, a small community southeast of Madison. Stoughton residents reacted to the attack on their native son the same way Appleton did to McCarthy's attack on Nathan Pusey. In a widely publicized affair, reenacted for CBS television, the previously apolitical Stoughton chapter of the Veterans of Foreign Wars unanimously passed a resolution on 2 March that condemned McCarthy's "abusive and insulting treatment" of Zwicker and expressed confidence in Zwicker's patriotism and gratitude for his valiant service on the battlefield.[6]

As expected, anti-McCarthyites condemned McCarthy's treatment of Zwicker, reviewed the general's long and distinguished military career, and dwelt on the renewed conflict between McCarthy and Eisenhower.[7] More noteworthy, long-time pro-McCarthy newspapers joined the chorus of denunciations. An "insult," a "vicious attack," "browbeating," three of them charged.[8] A Republican paper found Nixon's rebuttal to Stevenson refreshing compared to McCarthy's antics because Nixon had not used "loud boisterous charges and insinuations."[9]

In Washington, there were conferences, more charges and countercharges, and then, finally, on 11 March, the army officially filed twenty-nine charges against McCarthy, his subcommittee counsel Roy Cohn, and its staff director Francis Carr. The army accused McCarthy and Cohn of seeking preferential military treatment for G. David Schine, a member of

McCarthy's staff who had been drafted by the army. The following day, McCarthy countered that the army had tried to divert his investigation to other branches of the service and that Schine had been held hostage to compel McCarthy to stop his investigation.

The Senate established an investigative committee to weigh the charges, and the Army–McCarthy hearings began on 22 April 1954. Nothing remotely like these hearings had ever occurred in American history. The television audience alone numbered about 20 million at times; hundreds of thousands watched every hour. With the lax and permissive atmosphere of the Senate caucus room and the weak chairmanship of Karl Mundt, McCarthy quickly began to dominate the hearings. There were typical McCarthy gambits—a cropped photograph of Schine and Secretary of the Army Stevens and a phony letter from J. Edgar Hoover. McCarthy also made violent personal attacks on participants and repeatedly interrupted proceedings. As most of the nation watched, McCarthy showed himself to be an enemy of the established order. In Wisconsin, newspapers received hundreds of letters from previously neutral or pro-McCarthy people who now found him demanding, humorless, obstructive, and dictatorial.[10]

The hearings sprawled out through two months of confusion and turmoil, developing through a series of episodes rather than by any logical exploration of the issues. The most dramatic incident, and the most damaging to McCarthy, occurred on 9 June, the thirtieth day of the hearings. After a heated exchange between Cohn and army counsel Joseph Welch, McCarthy interrupted with a point of order to charge that a young member of Welch's law firm, Fred Fisher, "has been for a number of years a member of an organization which was named, oh, years ago, as the legal bulwark of the Communist party." In a low and deadly calm voice, Welch replied that "until this moment, Senator, I think I never really gauged your cruelty or recklessness. . . . Have you no sense of decency, sir, at long last? Have you left no sense of decency?"[11]

The Fred Fisher incident disgusted many people in Wisconsin, including Republican newspapers that had seldom, if ever, found fault with McCarthy. The senator had shown "his colors" in a "brutal, needless 'smear,' " the *Racine Journal Times* noted; another found his attack "inexcusable" and urged that he "save such below the belt blows for the Communists" and not "his fellow Americans."[12] The most weighty reaction came from the *Wisconsin State Journal* which, with few exceptions, had supported McCarthy since 1946. McCarthy had held his own in the hearings, the *Journal* sadly observed, until his attack on Fisher:

> Then, in one black second, McCarthy—in, let us face it, too typical McCarthy fashion—wrecked it all. He blew his angry head of steam and cast out an ugly, unsupportable, non-sensical smear on a young man who had absolutely no connection with the case.
> It was worse then reckless. It was worse than cruel. It was reprehensible.[13]

The events surrounding the hearings and their effect on the Republican party, more than anything else, precipitated McCarthy's fall. Furthermore, during the hearings, thousands of Wisconsinites, who had come to regard McCarthy as reckless, cruel, and reprehensible, released their frustrated moral outrage and subjected him to a massive recall movement.

\*    \*    \*    \*

Until he inspired the recall effort against McCarthy in the spring of 1954, Leroy Gore was an undistinguished newspaper editor in Wisconsin. An Iowa native and a graduate of the University of Nebraska's School of Journalism, Gore had spent twenty years in advertising and had assisted the publishers of three Midwestern weeklies. In 1947, he began publishing the *Spring Valley Sun* and in 1952 moved to Sauk City, Wisconsin, where he took over management of *The Sauk-Prairie Star*.

Gore usually voted Republican and supported McCarthy and Eisenhower in 1952. But he became increasingly disillusioned with McCarthy because of his sniping at Eisenhower, disruption of the Republican party, and attacks on General Zwicker and George Marshall. As a spokesman for Wisconsin's beleaguered dairy farmers, Gore watched the steady growth of dairy surpluses after World War II with mounting concern and urged increased federal subsidies for farmers. McCarthy's lack of concern for the problem irritated Gore, and after some soul-searching, he decided to act.[14]

Gore's headline editorial for *The Sauk-Prairie Star* of 18 March 1954 proclaimed that Wisconsin did not have to wait four more years to remove McCarthy. Gore had discovered that the state's infrequently used recall law could be used to oust McCarthy from office. The Wisconsin constitution provided that an elected officeholder must stand for reelection if, within a sixty-day period, recall petitions were signed by at least 25 percent of the people who had voted for governor in the previous election. This meant that Gore's recall petitions would need 403,000 signatures, seemingly an impossible number. In 1950, a similar movement by Students for Democratic Action at the University of Wisconsin had gotten nowhere.

But Gore had sensed the depth of anti-McCarthy sentiment in 1954, and his editorial struck a nerve. Still, he could not have predicted the uproar his call would arouse. He immediately found himself in the state and national spotlight. His phone rang constantly, and reporters hounded him for interviews. Eight thousand letters poured into his office within a few days. Overwhelmed by the response, Gore accepted advice to form a statewide recall organization. On 28 March, delegates from throughout the state assembled for an organizational meeting at the Riverside Ballroom in Sauk City. Newspapers, radio, and television covered the event. As the delegates entered the hall, they were met with large signs proclaiming "Joe Must Go," a slogan born in the confusion of the first days of the recall. The crowd, while enthusiastic, was not the hysterical throng that often attended political rallies, and the delegates conducted business in an orderly manner. Ivan Nestingen, a lawyer and alderman from Madison, Morris Rubin, and Gore gave rousing speeches.

The delegates established a statewide steering committee and elected Harold Michael president. The twenty-eight-year-old Michael, who first suggested a statewide organization, was a Korean War veteran from Amery, Wisconsin. His position as temporary chairman of the Polk County Republicans was an important reason for his selection. To offset the inevitable accusation that their drive would be branded Communistic, recall supporters sought leadership primarily from Republicans and businessmen rather than from Democrats and labor, McCarthy's traditional enemies.[15] Michael was a good choice, Gore thought, because "he was politically 'untouchable' and no one could find a single hole in his armor of political virtue."[16] The original steering committee consisted of ten Republicans, five Democrats, and five independents.

The moral issue of McCarthyism energized the movement. David Thelen and Esther Thelen, in their excellent study of the recall, observed that this factor "exerted a strong appeal" on men and women susceptible to this sort of direct confrontation and "accounted in part for the astonishingly broad spectrum of people who participated."[17] With no professional politicians in the movement, McCarthyites could not condemn partisan politicians for stirring up trouble.[18] Furthermore, the Army–McCarthy hearings, which appeared on television during the drive, provided free publicity. "After every session," observed two Dane County organizers, "we would receive calls asking for a chance to sign, many specifically mentioning the hearings."[19]

McCarthy pretended to ignore the drive. "You can make the headlines every day of the week if you want to call McCarthy an S.O.B." But he apparently did fear its success or at least its harmful publicity; he spent every weekend speaking in Wisconsin as if he were up for reelection.[20]

After initially waiting for petitions to come to Sauk City, the Joe Must Go leaders sought out signatures by advertising in newspapers, printing brochures and bumper stickers, and passing out leaflets. Organizers mailed petitions to Eisenhower supporters and Democrats. The movement was desperate for money. Gore appealed for funds during trips to New York, Washington, Buffalo, Chicago, and Los Angeles. The Los Angeles Daily News raised $8,000 in small donations. The anti-Semitic hate mail that deluged Sauk City headquarters convinced recall leaders to exploit the material to open the wallets of wealthy Jews in the eastern United States. They invited Jewish leaders to send a representative to read some of the mail, but this approach to fund raising proved as unfruitful as most of the others. When the recall drive ended, it had taken in only $32,454 and spent $26,572, not nearly enough for the kind of publicity it needed.[21]

Near the end of the sixty-day period, recall organizers extended the time limit for three weeks because the first three had been so poorly organized.

This led to some dissatisfaction in Madison, Sheboygan, and Milwaukee where early efforts had been extensive. As the drive approached the new deadline, the pace quickened. "Our two needs at this date," Nestingen noted on 18 May, "are one—more circulators, two—more money." But on 5 June, the last day, the drive had failed.[22] No exact tabulation of signatures was ever made because of the threat of subpoena from the Sauk City district attorney's office. Reporters viewed 335,000 signatures at the Conrad Hilton in Chicago. Another 50,000 were reported in Minneapolis. "Probably the best estimate of the total," according to Thelen and Thelen, "is that a third of a million Wisconsin voters signed properly legal petitions in the sixty days ending on June 5, 1954."[23]

Inefficient organization, poor leadership, inadequate finances, and internal dissension seriously handicapped the movement. Gore was not primarily an organizer, and he was out of the state too often to provide strong leadership or to prevent dissension in Sauk City headquarters.[24] Even many of McCarthy's opponents considered the recall unconstitutional. Some refused to sign a petition for fear of losing their jobs, or because of a vague apprehension that someday someone might hold them accountable for it.

McCarthy's supporters accused Gore of organizing the recall to promote his political ambitions and to stimulate his newspaper's circulation. Roman Reuter, a Sauk City restaurant owner, started a Door for Gore Club with the intention of driving Gore from the city. Darrell MacIntyre, the attorney for Reuter's organization, persuaded Harlan Kelley, Sauk County district attorney and McCarthy supporter, to subpoena Gore; Carl Lachmund, the organization's treasurer; and all the records of the Joe Must Go organization. They argued that the recall leaders had unlawfully engaged in political activity by operating as a corporation in violation of Wisconsin's corrupt practices act. Gore found his recall efforts continually interrupted by frequent trips to the Sauk County courthouse to answer subpoenas. In 1955, the state supreme court ruled that the organization had not violated state law.

The recall drive's most serious handicap was its lack of endorsement by professional organizations. The Republican party and Republican newspapers naturally opposed it. Farmers' organizations did not support it, nor did any organized group of Catholics, Protestants, or Jews. More surprising was the limited backing the recall received from anti-McCarthy newspapers, the Democratic party, and organized labor. While the "little people" were breaking their backs trying to curb McCarthy, Gore complained bitterly, the "big people" were thinking thoughts about the "psychological, political and moral effects of failure."[25]

Neither the *Milwaukee Journal* nor *The Capital Times* endorsed the recall, although they publicized and praised some of its activities and defended recall leaders from detractors. Soon after Gore's editorial, Miles McMillin warned that "The Wrong Ox May Be Gored." McMillin argued that, if the recall failed, McCarthy would grab hold of this fact as definitive proof that the people of Wisconsin were behind him.[26]

Gore's Republican party affiliation and the preponderance of Republicans in the recall's leadership had made Democratic party leaders suspicious. To them, Gore was an adventurer who sought only to promote himself. Some Democrats also believed that McCarthy had aided the Democrats by splitting the Republican party, that the recall movement had serious constitutional barriers and was so amateurish that it would probably fail, and that McCarthy would win reelection even if it succeeded. Four days after Gore's editorial, therefore, state Democratic chairman Elliot Walstead announced that the drive would not become a party project.[27]

Three weeks later, Democrats had to modify their position after Henry Reuss introduced a resolution to endorse the movement at the party convention in La Crosse. Reuss initially opposed party endorsement because of the "unknown elements" in the campaign, but he changed his mind when he learned that recall leaders were people of good will from both political parties.[28] Reuss's resolution embarrassed the state administrative committee. They had no alternative to backing Reuss;[29] doing otherwise at a public gathering would have left the impression that they supported McCarthy. But the party only gave token support. They allowed Gore to use their mailing list but rejected his requests for funds and would not enlist party workers to assist the drive.

Organized labor reacted similarly. For many years, Wisconsin labor leaders and journals had criticized McCarthy's voting record on labor issues and condemned his campaign against Communists. Although individuals and union locals participated in the recall drive, state labor leaders refused to swing their powerful organizations behind it. They suspected the Republican Gore, expected the drive to fail, and doubted its constitutionality. Furthermore, they argued, participation would violate prohibitions against political activity stipulated by the Taft–Hartley Act. Gore and other recall leaders deserved much of the blame for failing to capture labor's support because they were so slow in approaching labor leaders. The executive committee finally told Gore to contact state labor officials, but only after the recall was three weeks old.[30]

Pressure from rank-and-file labor forced labor leaders to modify their position. The *A.F. of L. Milwaukee Labor Press*, official organ of the Milwaukee Federated Trades Council (FTC), the *Kenosha Labor*, and the Madison *Union Labor News* were unenthusiastic at first but eventually supported the recall movement. On 5 May, the Milwaukee FTC went on record urging members of affiliated unions "to circulate and sign such petitions as individual citizens." Such mild action, however, was a far cry from official endorsement.[31]

The recall won some backing within the state American Federation of Labor. After union leaders in Madison and Milwaukee pressured the AFL, its president, George Haberman, modified his earlier opposition and encouraged individual locals to assist the drive. Haberman himself served the Milwaukee area Citizens Voluntary Committee on the McCarthy Recall in an advisory capacity.[32]

Although local union pressure impelled state labor toward a more friendly position on the recall, organized labor as a whole refused to identify with it or to grant financial assistance. The Wisconsin State Industrial Union Council never mentioned the recall in its *Actiongrams*.[33] The *Wisconsin CIO News*, official organ of the State Industrial Union Council, ignored it, and the *Racine Labor* gave the drive only scattered publicity.

Gore planned another recall for after the 1954 election when the vote for governor would be smaller than in 1952. Volunteers transferred the names of signers to addressograph plates, and Gore wrote the book *Joe Must Go* to publicize it. In mid-October 1954, Gore predicted a successful new effort. He naively assumed that anti-McCarthyites could rally behind one of three possible candidates: Democrat Thomas Fairchild, Republican Wilbur Renk, or independent J. Martin Klotsche (president of Wisconsin State College, Milwaukee). But the second recall never materialized for several reasons. Recall leaders argued among themselves and worried about legal harassment. Democrats and labor again withheld support, and the Democrats vowed to run a Democratic candidate if a recall succeeded. Moreover, after his censure, McCarthy dropped out of the news, and Wisconsinites lost interest in him and a new recall campaign.[34]

Thelen and Thelen have concluded that the Joe Must Go movement was a truly spectacular grass-roots action:

> Farmers participated, though their spokesmen opposed it; union members participated, though their leaders failed to endorse it; Democrats and Republicans participated, though their party managers shied away from it; Protestants, Catholics and Jews participated, though their pulpits were silent.[35]

But the movement's failure provided a sobering lesson. Recall leaders discovered that every institution or pressure group had a vested interest in perpetuating its own existence, and "when public endorsement of an unorthodox social or political movement might threaten that existence, the institution inevitably balks, hesitates, and in the end does nothing at all."[36]

\*     \*     \*     \*

During his Senate career, McCarthy had only haphazardly concerned himself with Wisconsin farm problems, especially after 1949 when he concentrated on his anti-Communist campaign. By the same token, farm leaders seldom sought his assistance on agricultural matters particularly after he began his red-hunting activities. As a farm observer noted in 1954: "it isn't that they dislike him so much as that they feel that any discussion with him would be of no avail, or they are just afraid or lack the persistence to see him."[37] McCarthy's incidental attention to their concerns and his failure to meaningfully communicate with farm officials did not lead farmers to oppose him. On the contrary, as the 1952 election showed, his charismatic personality and his war on Communists attracted farmers to him.

By 1954, the situation had changed as agricultural problems in Wisconsin became acute and politically volatile. The Commodity Credit Corporation revealed that in 1952 and 1953 a butter surplus of 42 million pounds had increased eight times to 321 million pounds. Dairy farmers who sought to ameliorate the problem through increased federal subsidies were alarmed when Secretary of Agriculture Ezra Taft Benson announced on 15 February 1954 that he would lower dairy price supports from 90 to 75 percent of parity beginning on 1 April. The Wisconsin Farm Bureau Federation and the Republican party supported Benson's proposal, but the GOP congressional delegation demurred. Sensitive to the anger of many of their rural constituents, they denounced the program in Congress and worked for a compromise. The Farmer's Union, most dairy farmers, and the Democratic party castigated Benson and endorsed supports at 90 percent of parity.[38]

"I'd like to know what McCarthy has ever done for the farmer while he has been a senator in Washington," a Dane County dairy farmer asked in March 1954.[39] Few farmers had cared to ask this question earlier, but in 1954, as the farm depression worsened, many did so for the first time. In an effort to answer the question and to discredit McCarthy, his critics investigated his voting record on agricultural issues and publicized their findings in the spring of 1954. With the exception of the more wealthy and conservative farmers, represented by the Wisconsin Farm Bureau Federation, McCarthy had not voted for programs supported by most state farmers. He had opposed fixed price-support programs and had favored reducing the support level to 75 percent. He had voted against increased appropriations for the soil-conservation program and against increased storage facilities and borrowing authority for the Commodity Credit Corporation.[40]

In February and March 1954, while farmers gathered to denounce the Benson program, McCarthy raged against the U.S. Army and, consequently, remained oblivious to the plight of his rural constituents. In February, 150 members of the Wisconsin Farmer's Union journeyed to Washington to discuss the farm depression and Benson's plan with the state's congressional delegation. The group reported that all the legislators had sympathized with their plight except Rep. Glenn Davis and Senator McCarthy. A leader of the delegation complained that McCarthy was too preoccupied with chasing Communists and that his secretary "didn't seem to know anything had happened to farm prices." Throughout March, state Republican congressmen conferred with Benson to seek an accommodation. On 3 March all the state's Republicans in Washington, except McCarthy, met to plan their strategy. On 9 March, Governor Kohler discussed the problem with the same group, but McCarthy sent only an aide to represent him.[41]

Then, in May, with the recall campaign reaching its climax, McCarthy suddenly discovered the crisis and offered an extreme solution. He urged that farm prices be supported at 100 percent of parity.[42] At the state Republican convention on 12 June, he suggested that, if the nation could "spend 200 billion dollars and hundreds of thousands of lives for wartime prosperity, perhaps it is not too much to ask that we spend a few billion dollars to make sure we have farm prosperity."[43]

Clearly McCarthy had lost the pulse of the state dairy farmer. His belated and preposterous suggestions were denounced throughout Wisconsin. As Thelen and Thelen have pointed out: "At a time when Republican leaders were seeking a compromise with Benson—Congressman Melvin Laird was willing to settle for 82½ percent—McCarthy's blatantly political gesture hurt their efforts and annoyed them with its irrelevance."[44] Liberal critics and some farm journals castigated his demagoguery. They assumed that he championed 100 percent of parity as a slap at Eisenhower and as a reserve issue in case his anti-Communist crusade lost popularity.[45]

Leaders of the Farm Bureau Federation were also displeased with McCarthy's new farm posture and with his quarrel with Eisenhower. By December 1954, James C. Green, executive treasurer of the Wisconsin organization, complained "that only a psychiatrist has any chance of talking this confused man out of his chaotic dilemma." Green and other bureau officials disapproved of McCarthy's receiving farm advice from his long-time friend Steve Miller, the cheesebroker from Marshfield. "Brokers and their kindred in the dairy business," Green argued, "are not as interested in the welfare of agriculture as in the best price that they can pay, because a good price enhances their position."

Farm Bureau leaders lined up with Eisenhower in his feud with McCarthy, especially after the senator's criticism of the president in December. They thought McCarthy wanted to split the Republican party. Thomas Coleman had not altered his animosity toward Eisenhower and had teamed with McCarthy to spite the president. No one in Wisconsin could curb McCarthy. "Where this adventurer will go now I cannot tell you. If I could think of ways to restrain him, I would so advise you," Green told a friend.[46]

McCarthy had angered important segments of Wisconsin's agricultural community, and his popularity with state farmers plummeted during the first half of 1954. Since 1950, public-opinion surveys conducted by the *Wisconsin Agriculturist and Farmer* had shown consistent and overwhelming approval for McCarthy's hunt for Communists. But, because of the excesses of that campaign during the first five months of 1954, that support dropped dramatically. In January and again in June 1954, the journal asked farmers if they felt that McCarthy's anti-Communist charges did more good or harm. The precentage of those who felt that McCarthy did more harm than good increased from 25 percent in January to 32 percent in June. Sixty percent of the farmers surveyed in January supported McCarthy's crusade against Communists in government, but by June that figure had dropped to 44 percent. The decline probably would have been more precipitous if the second poll had been taken at the end of the year.[47]

Leroy Gore noticed that the revolt of dairy farmers against McCarthy grew in direct proportion to the increasing severity of the dairy crisis.

> Back in 1952, when dairy prices were good, and things were booming in America's Dairyland—when Joe was picking on the Democrats—the farmers approved of keeping Joe in the Senate. But in early 1954 dairy surpluses were piling up, dairy prices were skidding, and Joe was picking on Republicans. The dairy farmers were in no mood for gags, especially if their industry and their political party were the victims.[48]

Consequently, farmers supported the recall. In rural Lincoln County, far more people signed recall petitions than had voted for Fairchild in 1952. Of the seventeen thousand Wisconsin residents who wrote to Sauk City for petitions, 26.4 percent were farmers. Farmers also took an active role in leading the drive. Joe Must Go clubs in Kenosha and Superior had farmers as officers. The Polk County Club had farmers in all its executive positions. Thelen and Thelen observed that "it was this revolt on the farm, as much as anything else, that gave the recall movement its grassroots character."[49]

\*    \*    \*    \*

Throughout 1954, particularly in the first half of the year, McCarthy retained a hard core of Republican support. Young Republicans and delegates to the state convention maintained an intense, emotional attachment to him. More than a thousand Republicans gave him a standing ovation on 7 February for his Lincoln Day speech in Madison. Organizers decorated the hall with a huge white banner, trimmed in red, with a portrait of McCarthy in the center and the words, "For America, For Wisconsin, Welcome Sen. Joe McCarthy." Claude Jasper told reporters at the gathering that McCarthy was "gaining in stature and respect everyday in Washington."[50] On 1 May, during the Army–McCarthy hearings, a convention of the Wisconsin Young Republicans passed a pro-McCarthy resolution by a margin of over four to one, and, during the recall movement, the executive committee of the Republican party formally commended McCarthy's "courage and fortitude."

At the state GOP convention in June, McCarthy's appearance galvanized the rally, drew the only enthusiasm shown for any of the principal party spokesmen, and inspired a convention-hall parade. Perhaps drawing confidence from the attitude of the delegates, McCarthy defiantly attacked the Eisenhower administration. He refused to become a "rubber stamp even to protect a party I regard as the greatest party in the country" and rejected the notion that "party loyalty is a game of following the leader." The convention praised his "accomplishments in his crusade against subversives." McCarthy's opponents were disappointed. "There is no question that the anti-McCarthy sentiment among the delegates is more solid and widespread than it was at convention time last year," McMillin noted, "but it is still only a shadow of what the pro-McCarthy sentiment is."[51]

Pro-McCarthy sentiment often meant virulent anti-Eisenhower sentiment. Republican delegates told stories about the president that, for sheer malice, rivaled any they had ever told about Roosevelt. Eisenhower had ignored "old-time Republicans," Coleman scornfully told Arthur Summerfield. Coleman doubted whether the administration had a "feeling of loyalty" to the party or even a feeling that the "party amounts to a great deal."[52]

Eisenhower Republicans such as Wilbur Renk of Sun Prairie were amazed at the fanatical support McCarthy still generated among regular Republicans. "They seem to have rallied to his dwindling cause and anyone who talks out against him or even looks a little cross-eyed at him is a complete jacksnipe." Renk continued:

> Being an Eisenhower supporter I don't know when I have taken so much abuse from Republicans who should be honored that we have a great Republican in the White House. Mature women who move in good circles just are unreasonable! It is not doing the Republican party in Wisconsin one bit of good, because obviously, if they determine a good Republican in Wisconsin by the fact that he is for McCarthy, many of us will be found wanting.

Renk resented the fact that Taft supporters such as Coleman still had not accepted Eisenhower's popular leadership. "Yes, we Wisconsin Republicans are like elephants," Renk observed, "dumb and many seem to never forget."[53]

As the turmoil continued, more and more Republicans came to agree with Renk's assessment and to question McCarthy's value to their party. This was particularly true of elected Republican officeholders and state and local party officials. Some party leaders blamed McCarthy and Wiley for the long delay in naming a new federal judge for Wisconsin. McCarthy's preoccupation with his anti-Communist campaign had caused him to neglect the mundane problems of his constituents. "People at home are beginning to notice," Wyngaard pointed out on 15 March, "and local politicians are beginning to talk." McCarthy's belated and extreme solution to the state dairy crisis prompted Governor Kohler to declare in May that "any politician who seeks votes and tells dairy farmers that price supports of 90 to 100 percent of parity is the answer to their problem is lying to the dairy farmer."[54]

McCarthy's excessive drinking began to cause concern. Knowledge of his serious problem with alcohol did not become widespread in Wisconsin until later, but state party officials and some members of the Republican congressional delegation knew about it in 1954 and blamed the problem for his reckless performance and rash statements.[55] McCarthy's arrogance and rudeness were also irritating. In March, a group of Young Republicans led by Richard Cecil arranged a celebration in Milwaukee to mark the centennial of the Republican party and invited all leading Wisconsin Republicans. To the dismay of the organizers, McCarthy ruined the festive atmosphere by taking over the entire event to level an irrelevant blast at Adlai Stevenson.[56]

The foremost source of dissatisfaction stemmed from McCarthy's divisive feud with Eisenhower. While he was attacking Democrats and was the butt of liberals, most Wisconsin Republicans supported him, although even then some had reservations about his roughneck approach. But the situation had obviously changed. McCarthy raising the red issue against Democrats was one thing; McCarthy pinning the issue on the Republican administration was highly dangerous.

Even Republicans ideologically and personally close to McCarthy realized the predicament. "I don't think there is any question but what the Democrats have 'mouse-trapped' us on the Communist issue," Wayne Hood complained in March; "I only hope that we are smart enough to get it straightened out in the very near future." In April, Coleman blamed "left wingers" and "New Dealers" for attempting to crush McCarthy as they had done other Communist-hunters. "The unfortunate thing is that Joe receives no support from places [that is, the Eisenhower administration] that should be giving it to him."[57]

After the confrontation with General Zwicker and the verbal duel between McCarthy and Eisenhower, the attitude of Wisconsin Republicans ranged from disquiet to annoyance. State Republicans were depressed about the Army–McCarthy hearings because, no matter what their outcome, the party could not win. If McCarthy won his case, the administration would lose; if the administration won its case, McCarthy would lose. The Wisconsin organization remained so close to him— as shown by the steady flow of resolutions supporting him—that either result could only benefit the Democratic opposition.[58]

Although McCarthy supporters were clearly on the defensive and many refused newspaper interviews on the subject, few party leaders publicly criticized him until the end of the year. The reason for this was obvious: he was still a Republican officeholder with four more years to serve. "In a primary," Wyngaard observed ominously in May, "with a reasonably acceptable and apt challenger, such reservations would be expressed quickly enough."[59]

Some Republicans did express resentment. Rep. Melvin Laird publicly branded the Army–McCarthy hearings a "circus" and privately described McCarthy's speech at the state GOP convention as "exceedingly poor."[60] Governor Kohler was moved to make jokes at McCarthy's expense at, of all places, a conference of state CIO officials. He also branded the Army–McCarthy hearings a "great-to-do about nothing and a waste of time."[61] Compared with earlier years, active opposition to McCarthy increased among regular Republicans. About 25 percent of the delegates to the Young Republican convention in May voted against a pro-McCarthy resolution; about 10 to 20 percent of the delegates opposed a similar one at the state Republican convention. In May, Republican caucuses in the Second and Tenth Congressional districts refused to endorse McCarthy, and the Tenth warmly commended Wiley for cooperating with Eisenhower.

Hundreds of Republicans took part in the Joe Must Go recall campaign, and thousands signed petitions. Secretary of State Fred Zimmerman endorsed it and signed a petition. State Sen. Harry Franke, a conservative Republican, served as finance director of the Milwaukee County recall organization. Former Gov. Oscar Rennebohm called recall headquarters and offered to run against McCarthy. Other Republicans who accepted leading roles included Harold Michael; Chester Roberts, secretary of the Milwaukee Eisenhower–Nixon Club in 1952; and William G. Connor, former vice-chairman of the Milwaukee County Young Republicans. The Young Republican Club of Wisconsin State College, Milwaukee, actively supported the recall.[62]

Republican leaders tried desperately to preserve party solidarity in preparation for the congressional elections in November, but their efforts failed. Party officials stressed unity at the state convention in June, and speakers mentioned McCarthy infrequently and made no reference to his conflict with Eisenhower. To the frustration of Wisconsin Republicans, neither McCarthy nor Eisenhower would cooperate. McCarthy adopted a callous attitude. Before the convention, when asked about the importance of party unity, he argued that a divided Democratic party had defeated a united Republican party in 1948, and that one reason the Democrats lost in 1952 was their "unreasonable demand for unity." The following day, he promised never to be a rubber stamp for the administration.[63]

Nor did Eisenhower contribute to party harmony. On 26 June, Vice-President Nixon spoke to three thousand people at a GOP fund-raising dinner in Milwaukee. Nixon urged party members to minimize the differences among Republicans and to emphasize those between Republicans and Democrats. He warned that, if the Republican party were to stay in power, the voters must become convinced that it is "capable of leading." A party "torn by dissension and strife" inevitably loses the confidence of the people. "If the Republican party is to continue to be a great party, its members must be united on fundamental principles which transcend the differences we have." According to Nixon, the damage caused by the Army–McCarthy hearings was not fatal. Moreover, if Republicans failed to unite and lost the elections of 1954 and 1956, "A.D.A. left wingers," who dominated the Democratic party, would take over.[64] Wisconsin Republicans enthusiastically received Nixon's address, particularly his call for party solidarity. Rep. John Byrnes thought it had brought "unity of purpose" among Wisconsin Republicans. Both those who favored McCarthy and those who opposed him sang Nixon's praises.[65]

At a news conference a few days later, President Eisenhower dampened their spirits as he dissociated himself from Nixon's statements. The president said that he might not have said what Nixon said, that the vice-president was speaking on his own responsibility and was entitled to his own opinions. Eisenhower's remarks infuriated Wisconsin Republicans. "The wishy-washy, non-committal attitude of the president in his press-conference," Laird wrote disgustedly, "was indeed deplorable in not whole-heartedly supporting the vice president."[66]

By the summer of 1954, both parties still expected McCarthy to be a major factor in the fall elections. James Doyle predicted that McCarthy would tour the country and that his efforts would be "ludicrous" and "loud" but "sometimes effective." In August, Robert Pierce, the new chairman of the RVC, hoped that McCarthy would be available to campaign in the state. "We plan to use the issue of Communists in government," he said, "and no one is better qualified to help than Joe."[67]

But as the campaign progressed, McCarthy made no appearances in the state, and, because of his increasingly defensive position in Washington, his decision did not displease Wisconsin Republicans. Even while the Mundt committee worked on what turned out to be inconclusive reports on the Army–McCarthy hearings, three senators brought charges of misconduct against McCarthy. On 3 August, the Senate authorized a bipartisan select committee to consider McCarthy's censure, and, during the fall campaign, the committee, headed by Republican Sen. Arthur Watkins, conducted its investigation.

As the primary election approached, the only candidates who mentioned McCarthy criticized him. John Shafer, Republican hopeful for the Fourth-District nomination for Congress, outspokenly opposed him. James Doyle, candidate for the Democratic nomination for governor, stressed farm and labor issues during his campaign but also linked McCarthyism to Governor Kohler. Kohler was a "sly conspirator, a stealthy operator" who worked for McCarthy behind the scenes.[68]

Democrats made substantial progress in the primary election. Voters cast more ballots in the Democratic column than ever before in the history of the state, and a higher percentage of the electorate voted Democratic than in any year since 1912. Insofar as McCarthy was an issue, he took a beating. Shafer won his bid for nomination by a six-to-five margin over his closest opponent. In Sauk City, Republican D. A. Harlan Kelley, who had openly harassed the Joe Must Go organization, lost to a political novice, James Seering, a young attorney backed by the McCarthy recall organization. Kelley failed to win a single precinct.[69]

After the primary, McCarthy canceled his scheduled appearances for the duration of the campaign. Speculation abounded that he intended to boycott it in the expectation that Republicans would lose; the responsibility would then have to rest exclusively with Eisenhower. Wisconsin Republican officials and party candidates shed few tears over McCarthy's decision and willingly got along without him. They knew that he had been hurt badly. The details of the incessant McCarthy controversies were not as important as the total impression. The excessively long dispatches about the Washington hearings on censure probably did not interest the average voter, but the majesty of the U.S. Senate seemed inordinately occupied in investigating him. "The voter knows that McCarthy has been on the defensive for months," Wyngaard noted, "and the rank and file politician wonders whether he is against the ropes."[70]

The only general-election race in which McCarthyism remained a major issue was the contest in the Fifth District between incumbent Republican Rep. Charles Kersten and Reuss. Although the Reuss campaign emphasized Kersten's poor attendance record in Congress, his votes in favor of Texas oil interests, and extreme foreign-policy position in favor of liberating iron-curtain countries, it also pointed to Kersten's "slavish" devotion to McCarthy. Kersten, who had staunchly supported McCarthy earlier, dissociated himself from the beleaguered senator during the campaign. During a debate on 28 October, when Reuss demanded that Kersten take a stand for or against McCarthy, Kersten replied: "I don't think anyone should stand or fall on someone else's record. I'll stand or fall on my own." Kersten fell as Reuss captured the congressional seat by a six-thousand-vote margin.[71] Democrats made gains elsewhere in the state, increasing their representation in the state senate by two seats and in the assembly by twelve. Although they failed to win any major state offices, the large vote for Democratic candidates signaled that Democrats would be serious contenders in the future.

Nationally, the 1954 election reinforced the belief that McCarthy's star had fallen. His predicament embarrassed the whole Republican party. Almost all liberal Democratic incumbents won reelection. Democrats defeated three of McCarthy's most vociferous supporters in the House and captured control of both the House and the Senate.

\*     \*     \*     \*

After the November election, political attention focused on the Watkins committee and its censure resolution. The committee had insisted that the rules of the Senate be applied in the committee room and that no television cameras be allowed. In short, the committee denied McCarthy all his familiar props. Robert Griffith has noted that "there was no audience to play to, and no antagonists to harass and intimidate. . . . No drama, no hovering specter of a foreign conspiracy."[72] The committee recommended that McCarthy be censured on two counts: for his contempt of the Subcommittee on Privileges and Elections in 1951–1952 (the Hennings committee), and for his abuse of Gen. Ralph Zwicker. On 2 December 1954, the Senate censured him on an amended version of the committee's resolution. They dropped the Zwicker charge and added a new one—abuse of the Watkins committee.

The McCarthy-censure issue placed Sen. Alexander Wiley in a delicate political position. He was no admirer of McCarthy, and his natural inclination was to favor censure. The Eisenhower wing of the party to which he belonged generally took this position. If he voted against censure, he risked losing his independent support in Wisconsin. On the other hand, if he voted for it, he would inflame McCarthy supporters in the state and reopen the smoldering war between himself and the state GOP.

He decided not to vote at all. This decision displeased both sides, but probably not as intensely as if he had taken a definite stand. For his constituents, Wiley rationalized that the rules of "fairness" and "judicial conduct" influenced his decision because he was "personally" and "directly" involved. "I, alone, of all 94 other senators, am from the same state and responsible to the same sovereign constituency as our junior senator."[73] In mid-November, Wiley took off for a junket to South America where he remained until after the censure vote.

McCarthy's Wisconsin supporters put forth several arguments against censure: the Watkins Committee had persecuted McCarthy because he had the courage to fight Communists, General Zwicker deserved criticism, censure jeapordized freedom of speech in the Senate and set a dangerous precedent, and the Hennings committee was politically partisan.[74] They repeatedly harped on the theme that McCarthy was a Wisconsin problem who should be dealt with only by Wisconsin voters. "The voters of this state need no help in making up their minds about him," the *Wisconsin State Journal* noted; "Joe McCarthy is our business."[75]

McCarthy's opponents pushed for censure, but their arguments for it were vague and general. They seldom confined themselves to the Watkins committee's specific charges. McCarthy had disrupted the Senate by being "arrogant," "boisterous," and a "bully." *The Capital Times* wanted him expelled from the Senate so that Wisconsin voters could pass judgment on him.[76] All agreed that censure would not deter McCarthy's aggressiveness.

Much of McCarthy's support defected when he lashed out at President Eisenhower after the censure vote. After the president publicly commended Senator Watkins for his investigation, McCarthy angrily responded on 7 December that Eisenhower had displayed a "shrinking show of weakness" toward the Red Chinese, and McCarthy apologized for telling voters in 1952 that Ike would lead a vigorous assault on communism. The horrified reaction among even McCarthy's stalwart supporters in the Senate showed that he had gone over the edge.[77] In Wisconsin, only a fraction of Republican newspapers sided with him. Some papers worried about the effect of this open break on the future of the GOP. *The Oshkosh Daily Northwestern* hoped that the "house divided" would not be permanent and that "repairs can be made to the advantage of the 'Grand Old Party.' "[78]

McCarthy's traditional opponents cited his blast at the president as typical of his demagoguery. More noteworthy, much of the Republican press agreed and sided with Eisenhower. They found McCarthy's remarks "arrogant," "intemperate," "ill advised," "insolent," and "indecent." The most obvious reason for their backing of Eisenhower was that few wished to cast into oblivion a president who had broken all voting records in 1952 and had maintained almost undiminished popularity.[79]

Most state Republican leaders were embarrassed and refused comment or issued vague statements supporting both McCarthy and Eisenhower. In an example of semantic virtuosity, the state RVC unanimously passed a resolution on 10 December that praised both McCarthy and Eisenhower for combating communism.[80] Some prominent GOP officials publicly rebuked McCarthy. Robert Pierce stated that "McCarthy's judgment on the loyalty of others to their country seems sometimes out of perspective." "Somewhere along the line," Pierce continued, McCarthy had "lost his ability to make friends and influence people." Without mentioning McCarthy, Senator Wiley praised Eisenhower for "relentlessly" battling communism. Governor Kohler thought McCarthy's statement was "senseless." H. J. Fiefarek, chairman of the Dane County Republican Club, condemned McCarthy's "irresponsible" remarks as "another example of McCarthy lashing out at things without being able to back them up." Near the end of December, Wyngaard, addressing himself to those out-of-state observers who still thought McCarthy dominated the state Republican party, observed: "If that ever was true, it is true no longer." McCarthy's organizational backing had cooled fast.[81]

As the year closed, McCarthy's influence and popularity had declined drastically in the state and the nation. The end of the Korean War had defused the Communist controversy. The issue of McCarthy and McCarthyism had been debated for so long that the average person could no longer maintain interest in either subject, and the senator had nothing new to offer.

# Chapter 10

# Profiles: Catholics, Charisma, and "McCarthyism"

The McCarthy controversy in Wisconsin aggravated religious tension, aroused intense emotional support for McCarthy's leadership, and endangered civil liberties. The strength of this controversy testified to the unique power of McCarthy and the movement he symbolized. His followers were not the least bit reticent about proclaiming the virtues of the anti-Communist champion. The USSR's call for Communist world domination following World War II had produced a near tidal wave of fear and anxiety in the United States. Serious assaults on civil liberties took place almost everywhere. These same forces also emerged in Wisconsin, but, unlike other states, in most cases Wisconsin's institutions defeated action that threatened civil liberties.

Although the subject was seldom discussed openly, a strong undercurrent of Protestant–Catholic tension marked the years of McCarthy's prominence. In 1950, 46.4 percent of all church members in Wisconsin were Roman Catholics. From the moment McCarthy burst on the Wisconsin political scene in the mid-1940s, his Catholicism was a source of religious tension in the state. The tension abated during McCarthy's early years of Senate obscurity but increased dramatically during the years of his anti-Communist crusade. McCarthy's opponents felt uncomfortably vulnerable to the charge of religious bigotry because Catholics seemed to make up the hard core of McCarthy's support. Only in 1954 were they able to neutralize the tension and feel confident that Catholicism and McCarthyism did not necessarily go hand in hand.

McCarthy's religious life seems to have been regular, strict, unquestioning, and nontheological. He would no more question his religion than miss Sunday mass. His Wisconsin friends had seen him leave fishing camps, stop auto trips, and otherwise make great efforts to get to church. He tried to win the Catholic vote in all his campaigns but, for the most part, did not parade his religion. In 1946, observers closely scrutinized the political effect of his Catholicism. Before the primary, a columnist speculated that McCarthy's religion would handicap him because the strength of the state GOP rested on Protestant voters. Others thought that, because he was a Catholic, church members in the Fox River valley worked hard for him. McCarthy may have had his eye on the Catholic vote and the Catholic church's hostility to communism when he linked Howard McMurray with the "Communist controlled" Political Action Committee of the CIO. To rebut the charge, Outagamie County Democrats countered with an advertisement that quoted liberal Catholic Bishop Bernard Sheil, who argued that when pro-business candidates could not meet the issues they dragged in the "Communist smear" campaign.[1]

After 1949, McCarthy's reputed widespread backing from Catholics substantially aggravated religious strain in Wisconsin and elsewhere. Supersensitive to the charge of disloyalty, Catholics prided themselves on being among the most loyal of American minorities. Their sensitivity stemmed from their troubled relationship with non-Catholics. For years, Catholics had suffered second-class status because they spoke foreign languages; pursued strange, alien customs; owed allegiance to a foreign ruler; and practiced a religion Protestants had come to America to escape. Historian Donald Crosby found that McCarthy's anti-Communist campaign intensified Protestant–Catholic tension in several ways. Many Catholics believed that Protestants opposed McCarthy solely on the basis of his Catholicism. Many Protestants believed that Catholics defended McCarthy simply because of his religion. In addition, some Protestants believed that McCarthy was a threat to the American democratic process because as a Catholic he believed in a religion that was conformist, authoritarian, and undemocratic.[2]

Although the Catholic population was profoundly concerned about the Communist problem, their concern did not express itself in a drive for a massive red-hunt. Nor did they overwhelmingly back McCarthy. A national opinion poll in January 1954 showed that Catholics favored McCarthy more than Protestants by only nine percentage points (58 to 49 percent).[3] In his 1952 reelection campaign, McCarthy received only fractionally more Catholic support than the average for the state Republican ticket.

Anti-McCarthyites in Wisconsin, however, viewed the situation differently. Catholics as a group may not have supported McCarthy and his crusade, but it seemed that way. McCarthy often spoke to Catholic groups and received enthusiastic receptions. In 1953, the pope gave his blessing to McCarthy's marriage to his secretary, Jean Kerr. Nationally, the Catholic hierarchy divided on McCarthy's merits, but the belief persisted, as Crosby has noted, "that the bishops had taken to McCarthyism like the Communists to the Revolution." Cardinal Spellman, who many non-Catholics and Catholics thought spoke for the Catholic church in America, was one of his admirers and declared in August 1953: "McCarthy is against communism and he has been doing something about it. He is making America aware of the dangers of communism." A few months later, the cardinal argued that the "loss of American prestige in Europe and Asia because of McCarthyism is a reflection not upon America, but upon European standards of honor and patriotism."[4]

Many people believed that the highly visible Catholic press was the Catholic community and that what the newspapers and magazines wrote was what Catholics believed. The Catholic press seemed overwhelmingly pro-McCarthy. Only a handful of Catholic newspapers spoke out against him, most notably the liberal publications *America*, a Jesuit weekly, and *Commonweal*, a weekly published by Catholic laymen. But as an anti-McCarthy Catholic from Wausau perceived: "How many Catholics read *Commonweal*? An infantismal [sic] fraction of those I know have even heard of it." People in her area regarded Cardinal Spellman as the official spokesman of the church.[5]

Catholics in Wisconsin did not organize for or against McCarthy. The Wisconsin hierarchy was neutral, as were most diocesan newspapers. Catholic fraternal organizations—the Wisconsin Knights of Columbus and Catholic War Veterans—did not make McCarthyism an issue. On the other hand, no Catholic clergymen, periodical, and few laymen publicly criticized McCarthy. *The Catholic Herald Citizen*, the most widely circulated Catholic weekly in the state, combined nationally syndicated and local editorials, articles, and columns in its various diocesan editions and in general—especially in the syndicated column of Rev. Jerome Gillis—strongly attacked communism and backed McCarthy. After McCarthy's initial charges against the State Department, the Madison edition told readers not to dismiss them lightly because "ever since Roosevelt and Truman traded bread and promises with Stalin, the State Department has functioned as an alien agency, not as part of the United States government." Someone had to kick "the lid off the kettle even though he'll probably be kicked in the face for doing it." The Milwaukee edition expressed a similar sentiment. Americans wanted a cleanup and wanted it fast and cared little about McCarthy's manners.[6]

Rev. Andrew Breines, editor of the Madison edition, defended McCarthy during the first two years of his crusade, after which Breines had no comment at all. The priest observed in May 1950 that the burden of proof that Communists had infiltrated the government did not lie with McCarthy, but with Sen. Millard Tydings and his subcommittee. After returning from the national convention of the Catholic Press Association, at which McCarthy spoke, Breines told his readers that McCarthy "impressed the Catholic editors by [his] dispassionate presentation of new facts" in the Owen Lattimore case. His "unaffected sincerity and humility" won admiration. He "stooped neither to invective nor name calling" despite the smear campaign against him.[7]

In contrast, Protestant and Jewish leaders almost unanimously disapproved of McCarthy. The *Wisconsin Jewish Chronicle* and prominent Jewish spokesmen such as Rabbis Herbert Friedman of Milwaukee and Manfred Swarsensky of Madison publicly reproached him. According to Madison recall organizers, Jews were "almost entirely with us."[8]

Almost all the Protestant clergymen in Wisconsin who expressed an opinion were anti-McCarthy. Each of the sixteen Protestant ministers who wrote Sen. Alexander Wiley on the 1954 censure issue favored McCarthy's censure. Methodists were the most outspokenly critical. In October 1952, 135 Wisconsin Methodist pastors affirmed their opposition to McCarthy's "irresponsible accusations, assertions of guilt by association, and reckless demagoguery." Rebecca Barton, director of the Governor's Commission on Human Rights, probably had McCarthy in mind when she stated in November 1950 that antagonism was growing between Protestants and Catholics in Wisconsin, a situation she partly attributed to partisan politics.[9]

Anti-McCarthy strategy on this delicate subject was aimed at undermining the widespread assumption that most Catholics stood in McCarthy's corner by publicizing the anti-McCarthy views of prominent American Catholics. The mimeographed material distributed by the Joe Must Go organization included critical comments by prominent religious spokesmen. Of the officials quoted, two were priests and one was a Catholic layman. The Capital Times regularly reprinted anti-McCarthy editorials and articles from Commonweal, especially those that refuted the notion that McCarthy spoke for the Catholic church. When James Eldridge of Chicago berated McCarthy in May 1950, the front-page caption in the Madison daily proclaimed: "High Catholic Layman Assails Sen. McCarthy's 'Shotgun' Probe Methods." Both editions of The McCarthy Record used the same approach. In preparing the 1954 edition, Morris Rubin sought contributions from anti-McCarthy Catholics. "The more conservative the source, the better," Rubin wrote one contact; "certainly a quote or two from Catholic individuals, publications, or organizations would mean most."[10]

McCarthy's critics were delighted when, in April 1954, Bernard Sheil, then auxiliary bishop of Chicago, denounced the "immorality" of McCarthyism during an address before the International Education Conference of the United Automobile Workers in Chicago. Bishop Sheil argued that communism was evil and had to be controlled but stated that an "immoral" anti-Communist crusade would be ineffective. He reproached McCarthy for "playing-for-the-grandstand" and for falsely accusing innocent people of communism. He reminded his listeners that he spoke only for himself and not for the church, but that the church

> does take a position on lies, calumny, the absence of charity, and calculated deceit. These things are wrong. . . . They are morally evil. . . . They are not justified by any cause—least of all by the cause of anti-Communism, which should unite rather than divide all of us in these difficult times.[11]

Bishop Sheil's speech made front-page news throughout the country and helped to dispel the impression that belief in Catholicism and support for McCarthy were inseparable. "After Bishop Sheil's address," Vincent De Santis has pointed out, "no one could reasonably say that Catholicism and McCarthyism necessarily went hand in hand, or that one was somehow less a Catholic for being anti-McCarthy."[12]

Anti-McCarthyites in Wisconsin quickly exploited Bishop Sheil's attack.

To counteract McCarthy support in heavily Catholic Green Bay, the Brown County Joe Must Go group reprinted the bishop's remarks in a full-page advertisement in the local newspaper.[13] The anti-McCarthy press reprinted the entire speech. *The Capital Times* seemed relieved and promoted Bishop Sheil's condemnation as an "answer to those who charge that the hard core of . . . McCarthy's support in this country comes from the Catholic church." Religious tension had grown out of the McCarthyism controversy, it noted. "It is tragic to see these tensions develop at a time when unity is necessary to meet the challenge of communism."[14] Bishop Sheil's attack on McCarthy had helped to neutralize religious tension in Wisconsin, but the strain did not disappear entirely until McCarthy's political demise.

\*    \*    \*    \*

In 1946, McCarthy himself, his campaign organizations, the Republican Voluntary Committee, and the Republican press had portrayed McCarthy as a combination of Horatio Alger and John Wayne. The glamorous image that they succeeded in creating substantially assisted McCarthy's election to the Senate. After 1949, when the anti-Communist issue propelled him to national prominence, the nature of his appeal changed. From 1950 to 1954, McCarthy's supporters described him as authentic, as a defender of Christian morality, as a patriot, and, most notably, as courageous and virile. McCarthyites not only regarded McCarthy's traits as unique, they admired them so intensely that one must rank McCarthy alongside that small fraternity of charismatic leaders. "We have been places where throngs waited for presidents, potentates and princes of this and that," a reporter observed of a McCarthy appearance in 1953, "but for McCarthy the waiting throng is charged with something extra. An electric thing, a mighty thing, it is."[15]

For his admirers, McCarthy's ability to convey an impression of authenticity gave validity to his anti-Communist charges. His promise to name names, his knowledge of a specific number of Communists, his document-filled briefcase, and the reports, affidavits, and photostats he brought to public gatherings played on his constituents' desire for concrete detail. According to Rubin, what most impressed any audience that responded favorably to McCarthy "was that briefcase with the documents and the nature of the charges."[16] McCarthy's book, *McCarthyism: The Fight for America*, came replete with 314 footnotes; this spray of citations conveyed the image of a man who had great scruples with the facts.[17]

After a McCarthy speech in the state, friendly newspapers often informed readers that he had "thumbed documents and photostats," or that he had "significantly remarked that he has friendly informants" in the State Department. The "photostatic documents of government records and reports which he brings with him to his meetings in huge mail sacks" impressed Wyngaard. After a "well documented" address in Green Bay that left McCarthy's "conclusions almost inescapable," the local newspaper editorialized on his "earnestness and sincerity."[18]

The reaction of Republicans to the techniques that McCarthy used to attack Adlai Stevenson over national television and radio in October 1952 was typical. It was a "smashing fact-filled" address, during which he uncovered "meaty propositions" established from "written texts." McCarthy campaign workers were jubilant over his successful use of "blowup photographs and photostatic copies of documents and other published material."[19] Few of those who were so impressed by his documents, photostats, reports, and so forth, ever went beneath the surface to analyze their pertinence, content, or accuracy.

An intense sentiment among a relatively small group of McCarthy enthusiasts held that he was a gallant defender of Christianity and morality from the menacing onslaught of atheistic communism. This theme continually recurred in McCarthy's speeches during his red-hunting days. The more religiously inclined of McCarthy's admirers visualized him as a God-fearing man, "zealous in fighting for his idea of Christian civilization and institutions." His anti-Communist fight was a "contribution to national morality."[20] The most consistent spokesman for this view was John Chapple, the eccentric editor of the *Ashland Daily Press*. Chapple defined communism as a worldwide anti-Christian conspiracy. For him, McCarthy was attempting to save America, "the one remaining bulwark of a civilization based on the high moral code outlined by Jesus."[21]

McCarthy's crusade also automatically clothed him in the aura of patriotism. He made the most of it with speeches calling for patriotic citizens to save their country from Communist domination. His partisans hailed his efforts to preserve American liberties and compared him favorably with such earlier American patriots as George Washington, Abraham Lincoln, and Paul Revere.[22] He was a "proven, loyal American," *The Shawano Evening Leader* observed, and his anti-Communist crusade had "sprung from a sense of loyalty that obviously motivated the famous Minutemen of 1776."[23] Richard Walsh, Dodge County GOP chairman, argued that those who "have been against Senator McCarthy" were also those who were "against the American flag."[24] As McCarthy was about to address the state Republican convention on 7 July 1951, some Young Republicans broke into song:

> Fighting Joe McCarthy
> We're one and all for you
> Our land you'll save
> The flag will wave
> The true red, white and blue.[25]

In November 1954, an exuberant housewife from Plymouth, Wisconsin, summed up one of McCarthy's two major attractions. She urged the indecisive Senator Wiley to risk criticism and vote against McCarthy's censure. "It will require courage, I suppose, but it is what is so badly needed in the world today—COURAGE! McCarthy has it."[26] In the view of his supporters, McCarthy possessed extraordinary courage. They recalled his unremitting and successful struggle to overcome the handicaps and hardships of his early life. After 1949, resolutions from hundreds of GOP gatherings in Wisconsin praised him with variations on the theme that he had shown "unremitting courage . . . in the face of severe criticism and seemingly overwhelming odds."[27]

Admiration for McCarthy's courage crystallized around two themes. The first, most prominent from 1950 to 1952 during the Truman administration, held that McCarthy was one of the few important public officials to wage war relentlessly on Communist subversives and sympathizers. As a consequence, he suffered persecution at the hands of Communists, leftists, liberals, and Democrats. McCarthy himself conveyed the impression that he was a martyr, a lone embattled figure standing with his back to the wall, with most of the world arrayed against him. It was not easy, he said on one occasion, "for a man to assert that he is the symbol of resistance to Communist subversion—that the nation's fate is in some respects tied to his own fate."[28]

His supporters agreed. Until McCarthy undertook to do so, no one had effectively ferreted out dangerous Communists. McCarthy had the temerity to wade into those who, through tactics of "fear, smear, and propaganda," had stifled "less timid men."[29] Wyngaard observed in 1950 that, while others might have been "cowed and detoured" by the "unparalleled violence" and the "concentrated ordeal of attack and invective," McCarthy remained the same flamboyant and cheerful extrovert.[30] His partisans characterized every criticism—whether directed toward his methods, ideology, or acceptance of $10,000 from the Lustron Corporation—as a left-wing or Communist-inspired smear. A major slogan for the McCarthy campaign in 1952 was "America loves him for the enemies he has made," meaning "Joseph Stalin, the pinks, and the reds." After the primary debacle, a disappointed campaign worker for Leonard Schmitt observed that many people thought McCarthy must be a "brave man to stand up against all that criticism."[31]

McCarthyites praised the senator for never substituting politics for principle. His attack on Gen. George Marshall received no enthusiastic reception in Wisconsin, but the philosophy behind it did. At the 1951 state Republican convention, McCarthy explained that friends had warned him not to attack Marshall because it was poor politics and would cost him votes. But he promised never to let such unworthy concerns stop him. The delegates cheered his conclusion that the country needed fewer "two bit" politicians who tempered their words and their actions to the number of votes affected.[32]

Although he lost the allegiance of many Wisconsin Republicans after 1952 because of his divisive feud with President Eisenhower, McCarthy retained an intense and loyal following partly because of his courageous stand for principle. He promised never to be a rubber stamp for his party's president.[33] "Whenever I intimate that I think we Republicans are doing anything wrong," McCarthy said on many occasions in 1954, "I always hear the hue and cry that 'McCarthy is attacking Eisenhower.' " He would not swerve from his course. "I cannot conscientiously live up to my oath of office if I do not state my views."[34] Many people in Wisconsin admired this stand and praised him for his "defiance of tradition," "unwillingness to call a hornswaggler a gentleman," having the "courage of his convictions," and willingness "to stand against a majority."[35]

Another appealing McCarthy trait was his virility. His vulgarity, ruggedness, and fighting nature were especially attractive. A speaker at the testimonial dinner in McCarthy's honor in Milwaukee on 13 November 1954 explained this view.

> You have sent to the Senate a virile man. He is not afraid to stand up and fight. Most of these critics, these slanderous opponents, are men who have passed the age where they can fight—or do anything else.[36]

Because of his struggle against "ruthless" communism, McCarthy's spartan background, commencing with his childhood life on the farm, assumed more importance. His boxing career at Marquette and alleged heroism in World War II were widely heralded. "I will have to blame some of the roughness in fighting the enemy to my training in the Marine Corps," McCarthy told his audience on many occasions. "We weren't taught to wear lace panties and fight with lace hankies in the Marine Corps."[37]

During McCarthy's red-hunting days, his appearance, statements, and constant wranglings with alleged Communists and critics further substantiated his manliness. "McCarthyism is Americanism with its sleeves rolled up," he often said, and, sure enough, there he was with his hairy arms bare to the biceps. He seemed to enjoy his reputation as a vulgarian who swore and belched in public. He did not want the world to think of him as respectable. Instead, as Richard Rovere noted, he encouraged photographers to take pictures of him

> sleeping, disheveled, on an office couch, like a bum on a park bench, coming out of a shower with a towel wrapped around his torso like Rocky Marciano, or sprawled on the floor in his shirt sleeves with a hooker of bourbon close at hand.

Other politicians sought to conceal a weakness for liquor, gambling, and wenching, but McCarthy tended to exaggerate those tastes.[38]

McCarthy valued his reputation for toughness. He seemed undisturbed by the uproar created during the 1952 campaign after he threatened to go aboard Adlai Stevenson's campaign train "with a slippery elm club" in order to make a good American of him. He taught audiences his Indian Charlie technique of overpowering assailants: if one were ever approached by another person in a not completely friendly fashion, one should start kicking at the other person as fast as possible below the belt until the assailant was rendered helpless.[39] When forced to perform the disagreeable task of exposing prominent people who would surely retaliate—such as Drew Pearson—McCarthy recalled how back on the farm his mother used to ask him to clean out a nest of skunks, and how he and his brother had to do the smelly job because the skunks were killing chickens.[40]

A convention of Young Republicans in Janesville in 1950 smirked, guffawed, and cheered as their idol expounded on alleged perverts in the State Department.

> Individuals with peculiar mental aberrations as far as sex is concerned. . . .
> He hangs around the men's room in Lafayette Park. . . .
> One of the secretaries said that this man was "a pretty nice fellow." He apparently meant pretty nice if you like this type.[41]

But his admirers found McCarthy's "fighting" qualities most appealing. McCarthy often alluded to his fight against communism and defined McCarthyism as the "fight for America." His campaign literature and advertisements in the 1952 campaign stressed this theme. In one advertisement layout, the word "FIGHT" was printed twice as large as any other word including the senator's name. In another major ad, derivatives of the word "fight" appeared seven times in a brief "Open Letter from Senator Joe."[42]

On thousands of occasions, when describing their hero and his battles with Communists and critics, McCarthyites used terminology normally applied to boxing contests or barroom brawls. McCarthy was a "red-blooded fighter," "rough and tumble fighter," "rugged fighter," "champion," "scrapper," "brawler," "slugger," "battler," and "pug." His accusations against opponents were "savage uppercuts," "spectacular rushings," and "blows." An address was "hard hitting," a "fighting report," or a "bare knuckle job," during which he "clenched his fists" and aroused his audience to a "fighting mad mood." Verbal exchanges with critics were "tilts," "rounds," and "brawls." In dealing with his enemies, supporters observed admiringly that he never used "kid gloves," or "pulled punches," nor was he afraid to get "hurt."[43]

McCarthy's most vociferous critics in Wisconsin often deferred to his fighting image and judged themselves and prospective candidates by how well they would stand up to him in the political "ring." After pointing out that anti-McCarthy newspapers, labor, and the Democratic party failed to endorse his recall movement, Leroy Gore speculated on their reasons: "Obviously, this anaemic, spindle-legged, sunken-chested challenger [that is, Gore himself] wouldn't last more than a round against Joe's bulging muscles of deceit and slander."[44] Some of McCarthy's antagonists predicted that the 1952 senatorial contest would be one of the "dirtiest slugfests" in the state's history, one in which the leading Democratic challengers had a serious liability. Democrats needed a candidate who would "roll up his sleeves" and "slug it out toe to toe with McCarthy." The Democratic candidates were woefully inadequate in this regard. With his dignified, soft-spoken, and reasonable approach to politics, it was difficult to imagine Reuss unseating McCarthy. Fairchild needed to convince the voters that "he is a fighter too," but this appeared an impossible task. Leonard Schmitt, on the other hand, was the ideal candidate from this perspective. Schmitt was a "slugger," a "militant, two-fisted man," made to order for the job of meeting McCarthy in the political arena.[45]

McCarthy partisans believed that the Communist danger was so imminent and Communists so ruthless that they had to be dealt with on their own terms—by a fighter—rather than by reason or general condemnation. "Joe treats the Communist party member as someone to be dealt with via the fist," a high-ranking Wisconsin politician observed approvingly; "he's a slugger."[46] McCarthy alluded to this necessity in his speeches. A person could condemn communism in general terms, he explained, "in the Acheson manner with a lace hankerchief, a silk glove, and with a Harvard accent, if you please. But you can't fight Communists in that fashion."[47] There was "a common-sense limit to gentleness and delicacy. That limit is where disloyalty and treason begin."[48] His supporters agreed. Moreover, his roughneck approach had succeeded in rooting Communists out of government agencies.

McCarthyites used numerous metaphors to justify his techniques and to illustrate the nature of the conflict between the American way of life and the Communist system. The struggle was like a "barroom brawl" in which one could not always "fight square." As one enthusiast expressed it: "You've got to kick and maybe kick hard. Joe's fighting a barroom brawl against a crowd that sure has messed things up for this country."[49] Communists were like rats in the American household. Sometimes you could catch them by using strong cheese; at other times, as McCarthy found necessary, "you have to hit them over the head with a shovel."[50]

McCarthy enthusiasts felt that McCarthy's fighting qualities were the same as those that had made the United States a great country, and that the nation was somehow losing those admirable traits. During the 1952 campaign, the McCarthy Club reprinted and widely distributed an editorial that argued this point.

> Sen. Joe McCarthy fights like a real American. He fights like a truck-driver who faces wind and snow and slippery roads night after night. He fights like a man who goes down into the mines where there's a cave-in to rescue those he can. . . . He fights like a Marine walking forward steadily to an island shore as his buddies drop around him. . . .
> These are the kind of fighters we most highly respect, for these are the fighters who made America mighty. We hope Sen. McCarthy continues to be one of those rough, tough, and gallant fighters. We never want to see him

lounging on the end of his spine, gesturing in "lah-de-dah" style, talking about "beauty" and smelling a rose, as if the odor of the world was a bit too much for him.[51]

McCarthy, the rugged fighter, was too harsh and barbarian an image for some of his followers. They searched for insights into the soft side of his character. Friendly publicists occasionally discoursed on his personal kindness, warmth, and love for children. McCarthy's appearance at a dinner in his honor in 1951 emotionally aroused twenty-two hundred admirers. After receiving plaudits from long-time friends and colleagues, McCarthy arose and said:

> I used to pride myself on being tough, especially in the last 18 months, when we've been kicked around and damned. I didn't think I could be touched very deeply. But tonight, frankly, my cup and my heart are so full I can't talk to you.[52]

The audience remained hushed during his speech, after which McCarthy broke down and cried.[53]

On the whole, however, it was the tough, virile, fighting McCarthy who attracted Wisconsin residents to his standard. In December 1951, McCarthy fought with columnist Drew Pearson in the washroom of a private club in Washington. The incident disgusted anti-McCarthyites who believed Pearson's charge—which was never proven—that McCarthy kicked him in the groin. Possibly because publicity focused on McCarthy's subsequent attempt to "expose" Pearson's Communist connections, the fight aroused little comment by McCarthy supporters in the state. Nevertheless, judging by the powerful appeal of his fighting image, one can reasonably assume that thousands of Wisconsinites also believed Pearson's account and thanked God for McCarthy.

\*　　\*　　\*　　\*

The United States has endured numerous waves of intolerance throughout its history, with the focus of attention on suspicious groups ranging from anarchists to trade unions, from Catholics to Communists. The Kremlin's call for Communist domination following World War II caused a panic reaction in America. Actions against alleged Communists took place not only in government but in labor unions, schools, mass media, churches, and libraries. Searches for Communists relied on witch-hunt tactics. Wisconsin experienced no witch-hunt and defeated legislative assaults on basic freedoms, but anti-Communist zealots backed by the activities of Senator McCarthy did leave their marks.

Before examining Wisconsin's experiences, an overview of the pervasiveness of the Red Scare nationally will provide a clear perspective on the political and cultural atmosphere. At the federal level, executive orders and legislative requirements extended loyalty-security processes to passport applicants, port employees, industrial workers, American officials at the United Nations, recipients of government research grants, and scientists engaged in official research-development programs. The military and the Atomic Energy Commission conducted their own clearance procedures. In 1948, the federal Loyalty Review Board had 150 loyalty boards in operation. Although the boards operated under some procedural safeguards, they still embraced the popular doctrines of guilt by intention and association, uncovered no cases of espionage, and wrecked the careers of many government officials accused without proof. Regional boards in particular were staffed by conservatives of narrow vision who frequently treated any deviation from the status quo as an indication of disloyal tendencies. In one district in Indiana, 128 of 139 postal employees questioned by loyalty investigators were Jews and Negroes. From about the end of World War II to 1956, about thirty-nine hundred federal employees were dismissed from their jobs; another fifty-four hundred in private employment on federal programs were also dismissed.[54]

Even liberal congressmen and senators, who traditionally had defended civil liberties, buckled under the pressure. In 1954, Congress debated the Communist Control Act which aimed to deny the Communist party the rights, privileges, and immunities of a legal body and to deprive party members of certain citizenship rights. The act offered its most blatant threat to civil liberties by establishing the legal means to regulate and limit political expression to what the legislators thought acceptable and safe to the current majority. Despite an American Civil Liberties Union declaration that the bill made a "mockery . . . of our most basic Constitutional guarantees," liberals supported it. The Senate approved the bill unanimously, and the House concurred 265 to 2.[55]

State and local actions to test loyalty were also extreme. Maryland's Ober Act deprived "subversives" of political rights and imposed $20,000 fines and maximum prison sentences of twenty years. Tennessee proclaimed the death penalty for treason. Almost everywhere, state and local legislative committees and police officials utilized and expanded the U.S. attorney general's list of subversive organizations at their pleasure. By 1956, forty-two states and more than two thousand county and municipal subdivisions and state and local administrative commissions required loyalty oaths from teachers, voters, lawyers, union officials, residents in public housing, welfare recipients, and, in Indiana, wrestlers. By 1950, localities scattered throughout the country—Birmingham, Alabama; Jersey City, New Jersey; McKeesport, Pennsylvania; Miami, Florida; Los Angeles, California; Cumberland, Maryland; New Rochelle, New York—had ordinances requiring Communists and others to register with the police or, in some cases, to leave town entirely. The laws often failed to maintain a constant focus on subversive activities. They created uneasiness about dissent, advocacy, and ideas in general.[56]

In many instances, legislators faced formidable political pressure to vote against communism. Once the issue was cast in the black-and-white terms of voting for or against the so-called Communist conspiracy, even extreme programs passed easily. Only the most courageous legislator ran the risk of casting a negative vote that could be interpreted as sympathy for communism. In Maryland, the wide-ranging Ober Act required little debate once the choice presented was one between Americanism and communism. The Maryland senate passed the proposal unanimously, and the house agreed by a vote of 115 to 1. The lone dissenter lost in the next election.[57]

States bordering Wisconsin were enveloped in this wave of general hysteria and, in taking the offensive against subversion, also struck at basic freedoms. Both Illinois and Michigan had major investigations to identify Communists or dissidents. In 1950, the Michigan legislature, ignoring the recommendations of Gov. G. Mennen Williams, passed a law authorizing the commissioner of the state police to create a subversive activities division in his department. The bill granted extraordinary power to the commissioner, including the power to maintain confidential files. Governor Williams signed the law. The same year, Michigan provided the penalty of life imprisonment for writing or speaking subversion. In 1949, the city of Detroit established a commission to rid the city of disloyal employees. Newspapers, the mayor, and other public officials supported the proposal; voters endorsed it by a three-to-one majority. Detroit thus became the first municipality in the United States to launch a full-scale program to test the beliefs and associations of public servants.[58]

During the McCarthy era and often since, McCarthy's critics have contended that McCarthyism triggered the same flood of fear, hysteria, and anti-civil-liberties actions in Wisconsin. A witch-hunt atmosphere pervaded the state, they said. Americans "are permitted to speak and read only as McCarthyism dictates we read and speak," said Leroy Gore. "We live today in an environment of fear—fear of engaging in controversy, of expressing one's thoughts and the fear of new ideas," Wisconsin Democrats proclaimed in 1954. The *Milwaukee Journal* thought the situation at one point resembled "Russia under communism, Germany under the Nazis, Italy under fascism—or terror under any tyranny."[59]

These alarmist reports were more often a political strategy to discredit McCarthy and his supporters than an accurate description of conditions in Wisconsin. McCarthy occasionally harassed anti-McCarthy newspapers, but this did not stop them from vigorously criticizing him. The Wisconsin legislature never enacted antisubversion measures urged by conservative groups after World War II. Nor did lawmakers conduct any major investigations or establish special procedures to test the loyalty of public servants. No state employees were fired, or at least no firings received publicity. No municipalities enacted loyalty measures such as those in Detroit and other cities. Milwaukee, Wisconsin's largest municipality, had a Socialist mayor from 1948 to 1960. Milwaukee socialism was a mild variety, but the mayor still identified himself as a Socialist at a time when anyone who walked downwind from a card-carrying Marxist was suspect. Yet no one supposed that Mayor Frank Zeidler was subversive. In 1952, during the height of McCarthyism, the soft-spoken, scholarly Zeidler won reelection by a larger majority than any previous candidate.[60]

Wisconsin endured strong attempts to curb basic freedoms, some ugly cases of terrorism, and some intimidation of opinion. The terrorism and intimidation were most prevalent from April to June 1954 and were confined mostly to the conservative Fox River valley.

On 4 July 1951, John Patrick Hunter, a young reporter for *The Capital Times*, asked 112 people at a Madison city park to sign a petition consisting exclusively of sections from the Declaration of Independence and the Bill of Rights. Despite the people's understandable reluctance to sign anything on the request of a stranger, and despite some evidence that Hunter discouraged people from signing to build dramatic impact for his story, the reaction to his project remains significant: only one person signed the petition. Twenty people asked Hunter if he were a Communist, and many others expressed fear of losing their job if they cooperated.[61]

In the Fox River valley, where pro-McCarthy sentiment dominated, fear was more extensive. George B. Green of Oshkosh turned down requests to organize a local chapter of Americans for Democratic Action in 1953 primarily because of the "local political temper."[62] A Neenah housewife, who campaigned against McCarthy in 1952, observed of those people associated with her tiny anti-McCarthy group:

> A few persons were even afraid to make anonymous contributions for fear they might be found out. Rumors spread of people being demoted or threatened with demotion because they opposed the senator. Business and professional men were afraid of losing customers and clients. Those who did take a public stand against him received phone calls accusing them of being Communist, telling them to "go back to Russia" and in at least one case intimating some sort of reprisal in the man's employment.[63]

Joe Must Go recall workers encountered some intense harassment in 1954. Some organizers were labeled Communists; others were threatened with loss of employment. Circulators in Milwaukee were spat on, called vile names, and threatened with physical violence. Hate mail and threatening phone calls deluged Leroy Gore.[64]

The treatment of Robert Houle by residents in his hometown of Green Bay was perhaps the worst example of this reaction. Houle, a tall, good-looking, thirty-four-year-old television announcer, accepted the leadership of the local recall drive on 6 May 1954, after four other nominees refused. The fact that Houle was a native of Green Bay, an Eisenhower Republican, a regular churchgoer, and the possessor of two Purple Hearts did not spare him abuse from aggressive McCarthyites. The local distributors for Houle's television sponsor received a torrent of protesting telephone calls warning them that they would never make another sale as long as Houle continued to broadcast. He resigned from the program after the Milwaukee offices of his sponsor received similar threats and demands. Residents labeled him a Communist and threatened him and his family. He finally left town for a while.

The terrorist campaign against Houle appalled a prominent bank president: "Doesn't it seem strange that a bigoted mob could be so riled by a demagogue as to apply Communistic tactics on a decent, innocent friend and neighbor?" Although the *Green Bay Press-Gazette* condemned the treatment of Houle—though questioning if it actually occurred—the dogged pro-McCarthy newspaper did little to alleviate the situation by speculating that anti-McCarthyites initiated the assault, "trying to arouse and anger their own followers."[65]

That McCarthy's opponents in Wisconsin emphatically proclaimed their anticommunism and broadcast their Americanism testified to the power of McCarthyism. Anti-McCarthy newspapers invariably prefaced virulent attacks on the senator by airing their equally strong opposition to communism and their determination to eradicate its influence in American life. McCarthy could not be dealt with on his demerits alone. When searching for sponsors for *The McCarthy Record* in 1952, promoters sought conservatives—preferably Catholics—whose anticommunism and integrity were beyond question. Authors of the anti-McCarthy booklet pointed out that they had quoted exclusively from official records and "from newspapers and magazines whose reputation for telling the truth or whose anti-Communist credentials are so impressive that informed Americans everywhere will accept their reporting in this field as unassailable."[66]

Organizers of the Joe Must Go movement in 1954 repeatedly reaffirmed their anticommunism and sought Republican and conservative leadership. They described State Sen. Harry Franke, a recall leader in Milwaukee, as a conservative Republican from Milwaukee's silk-stocking district. Harold Michael occasionally prefaced his attacks on McCarthy by assuring his correspondent that "there is nothing 'subversive' or 'pink' in my background," whereupon he described his service record and Republican party affiliation.[67]

Although McCarthy achieved most of his notoriety by attacking the Truman and Eisenhower administrations, he did not overlook what he termed "pro-Communist" sympathizers in Wisconsin. Most of his investigations and public assaults were designed to intimidate his critics, and he encouraged friends to investigate his Wisconsin enemies. Joseph Kriofske, a Milwaukee FBI agent and McCarthy's classmate in law school, and Otis Gomillion, McCarthy's bodyguard, apparently conducted secret investigations. So did Albert Shortridge, another bodyguard and a Milwaukee County sheriff's deputy. At McCarthy's urging, Shortridge investigated two politicians—one Democrat and one Republican—and two labor leaders, all of whom had publicly criticized McCarthy. McCarthy could not understand why the Republican had been "spouting off" about him, but he presumed that the attacks were Communist-inspired. Although Shortridge had no training for such work and the sheriff's department had not sanctioned his amateur sleuthing, he sought to get the lowdown on the critics by questioning neighbors and gas-station attendants and by surreptitiously listening to their conversations at bars. He reported to McCarthy that all four belonged to the Communist party.[68]

McCarthy continued to lash out at newspapers that criticized him. Because it still employed Cedric Parker, *The Capital Times* was called the "Madison *Daily Worker*."[69] After *The Sheboygan Press* criticized him, McCarthy told thirty Sheboygan schoolchildren that their local newspaper had pro-Communist sympathies. By the senator's estimate, the Communist *Daily Worker* and its "state editions" won the honor of having the largest newspaper circulation in the state. The *Milwaukee Journal* shared the same fate but with additional intimidation. After it published an article on McCarthy's failure to pay any tax on his 1949 income, he labeled the staid newspaper the "Milwaukee version of the *Washington Daily Worker*." Subsequently, he urged Milwaukee retail food dealers to withdraw advertising from the "Communist Sheet." "Keep in mind," he told them, "when you send your checks over to the *Journal* . . . you are contributing to bringing the Communist party line into the homes of Wisconsin." In April 1951, in an unusually peculiar accusation, he charged that the *Journal* had been dangerously influenced by a man named Louis Weiss, who before his death had been counsel for an alleged Communist newspaper. The Communist influence of the dead man over the *Journal* could be documented, McCarthy claimed, because Weiss had married the younger sister of the wife of one of the *Journal* executives. In another barrage, McCarthy accused two unnamed *Journal* editorial writers of contributing to the defense fund for Alger Hiss. The Milwaukee paper emphatically denied all the charges.[70]

The reasoning behind McCarthy's blasts at the *Journal* and other newspapers is perhaps revealed in a private interview Robert Fleming had with him in the summer of 1950. "I don't have any idea that I can break the *Journal*," McCarthy explained:

> Off the record, I don't know that I can cut its profits at all, let alone cut that million dollars down a hundred, so you don't have to worry about your stock. But if you can show a paper as unfriendly and having a reason for being antagonistic, you take the sting out of what it says about you. I think I can convince a lot of people that they can't believe what they read in the *Journal*.[71]

Although the *Journal* continued to serve as a breakwater against McCarthy's attacks and publicly refused to be intimidated, the assaults caused apprehension among its editors. Fleming observed in July 1950 that the *Journal* was a "very popular target." Crowd reaction to McCarthy's attack on the paper during one Milwaukee address amazed Fleming. He pointed out to *Journal* executives that McCarthy's raps at the *Journal* "drew greater audience response than anything else he said." Over a dozen people approached Fleming, holding McCarthy's handout, to say, "He's certainly shown *The Journal* up here." Some of the people knew Fleming, others were strangers, but "none seemed to doubt McCarthy's story." Publicly the *Journal* denied McCarthy's charge that two of their editorial writers had contributed to the defense fund for Alger Hiss. But, behind the scenes, *Journal* executives frantically sought information on people knowledgeable about the fund to determine whether any staff member appeared on the list.[72]

On the whole, however, despite the pressure, Wisconsin's institutions defeated action that threatened civil liberties. Like many states, Wisconsin had statutes to curb treason, rebellion, insurrection, and criminal anarchy. All of them had been enacted before 1921, and none had to be enforced during the McCarthy era. Between 1921 and 1961, legislators had made over fifty attempts to pass additional laws. The assembly approved fifteen and the senate sixteen. Only two measures became law—one to prevent sabotage and another to ban the Communist party from the Wisconsin ballot—and both were enacted in 1941. According to an authority on security legislation, the Wisconsin production of subversion laws was "limited . . . compared with the measures turned out by many state legislatures." The Wisconsin laws generally punished action but did not restrict opinion or association.[73]

The period from 1947 to 1949 was at least as threatening to traditional liberties in Wisconsin as the five years of McCarthy's prominence. In the 1947 session of the legislature, conservatives introduced three bills to curb Communists, including one that would have barred avowed Communists from becoming students or staff members at the University of Wisconsin. All were defeated. Four bills introduced but not passed in the 1949 session dealt with administering a non-Communist oath, prohibiting the use of public buildings by Communists and similar groups, registering Communists and "other revolutionaries," and establishing a legislative committee to investigate un-American activities.[74]

During the years that McCarthy rode the crest of his anti-Communist crusade, conservative (usually pro-McCarthy) organizations urged action against vaguely defined evils. In 1953 by a vote of fifty-six to thirty-one, the Wisconsin assembly approved a bill barring from public employment any person who claimed the protection of the Fifth Amendment and refused to testify before a government body investigating subversion. But the state senate did not concur, and the measure died.[75]

In 1955, Republican State Sen. Louis Prange, a farmer from Sheboygan Falls, introduced one of the most rigorous antisubversion bills in state history. It required loyalty oaths from all state employees as well as all candidates for public office. The bill made it a felony to belong to any subversive organization and barred from public office for life any person convicted of belonging to such an organization. It also prohibited individuals from refusing to testify on Fifth-Amendment grounds. The bill aroused a storm of editorial protest even from pro-McCarthy newspapers.

At a public hearing, twenty-five people showed up to oppose it; only Prange and a Madison woman appeared in support. The senate rejected the bill by voice vote.[76]

The only public case of apparent censorship by a library occurred in 1953 when a librarian in Madison refused to stock Jack Anderson and Ronald May's critical book, McCarthy: The Man, the Senator, the "Ism." The Capital Times howled its protest. The issue was the first to confront the new Madison chapter of the American Civil Liberties Union, but it handled the matter with relaxed confidence. The board of directors sent two board members—a state senator and a Catholic priest—to confer with the librarian and the library board. The incident proved less than controversial when the investigators discovered that the librarian's objection was practical not ideological: she had also refused to stock McCarthy's book on the theory that neither was worth purchasing.[77]

The undermining of Roman Reuter, the misguided Sauk City restaurant owner and the organizer of the Door for Gore activities in 1954–1955, illustrated how organized opinion put down serious encroachments on civil rights. Reuter became overconfident after his pressure apparently contributed to Leroy Gore's decision to sell his newspaper. Early in 1955, the Milwaukee Journal quoted Reuter as warning the new editors of The Sauk-Prairie Star, Elmer Anderson and his son Robert, to "stay neutral and don't take a stand in politics whatsoever." They would be all right, Reuter asserted, if they kept their noses clean and refrained from expressing political opinions. This time Reuter overextended himself. The Andersons rejected his intimidation. "We don't believe we would be doing our duty if we were to slink down the back alleys, afraid to . . . express our opinion on any subject that might be the least bit controversial." As a result of his arrogant warning to the Andersons, Reuter was castigated throughout the state by officers of the Wisconsin American Legion, the Wisconsin Civil Liberties Union, and by editors, clergymen, and public officials. Ten days after the interview, under a barrage of criticism, Reuter indignantly denied making the statements.[78]

Nowhere was concern for subversive thought and activity more steadily manifest than in education. Intense stress during the McCarthy era placed tremendous pressure on the academic community. Publicly supported schools were leading targets of state legislative investigations into un-American activities. Censorship of schoolbooks frequently occurred, but the primary concern focused on the political identification of teachers. The policy that Communists should not be allowed on faculties gained wide acceptance, not only from professional heresy hunters, but from the National Education Association and many educators. By 1951, over thirty states insisted on loyalty oaths for teachers.[79]

In late 1948 and early 1949, action at the University of Washington inspired attacks on academic freedom at the university level. The dean of the College of Arts and Sciences initiated complaints against six tenured members of the faculty because of past or present membership in the Communist party. Each faculty member had earlier been called to testify before the State of Washington's Legislative Committee on Un-American Activities, known as the Canwell committee. Raymond Allen, president of the university, subsequently sought their dismissal and the board of regents dismissed three of them.[80]

The Washington action, plus investigations by the California legislature, led to an explosive controversy at the University of California. Public opinion, newspapers, and regents demanded a loyalty oath. University administrators, primarily concerned with their relations with the public, did not deeply believe in freedom of speech. Pres. Robert Sproul had opposed the appearance of Harold Laski on campus in 1949 because his presence would "not be pleasing to the board of regents." A regent's oath was finally adopted. The controversy anticipated nearly all the issues that were to afflict other universities: oaths of loyalty and Communist disclaimers required of teachers on pain of dismissal; penalties levied on teachers for refusing to cooperate with legislative committees investigating subversion; and sanctions imposed by intramural bodies against colleagues for lack of candor when questioned about possible Communist ties. In addition, the controversy had implications for academic freedom and constitutional liberties because of rules disqualifying Communist and other alleged subversives from university employment.

Between 1949 and 1951, the University of California lost sixty-three faculty members who either refused to sign loyalty affidavits or signed and then resigned in protest. Rather than quieting public suspicion, the conflict amplified accusing whispers. The battle made adversaries of faculty and regents and also pitted faculty against faculty and regent against regent.[81]

Other states and universities took similar action. The Pennsylvania Board of Education fired twenty-six teachers on the technical grounds of incompetence after they had been questioned by the House Committee on Un-American Activities. In 1949, the New York legislature passed the Feinberg Bill, which sought to eliminate subversive individuals from the public-school system, and the board of regents drew up a list of five subversive organizations. Rutgers University dismissed some controversial professors because the administration feared public opinion and legislative action. Recent evidence suggests that even Harvard, which has long congratulated itself for stubbornly resisting McCarthy's onslaught, secretly pressured ex-Communist faculty members to inform on former party associates when asked to do so by the FBI or other government investigators. Moreover, Harvard's much-acclaimed defense of academic immunity did not extend to nontenured faculty, administrators, or graduate students.[82]

Some universities in states bordering Wisconsin shared the same fate. The presidents of three Big Ten universities—Minnesota, Northwestern, and Michigan State—sent letters to the Washington Board of Regents supporting their action against faculty. When three faculty members at the University of Michigan refused to testify before a state legislative committee in 1954, the president suspended all three, and an advisory committee recommended the dismissal of two. In 1947, the Illinois legislature created the Seditious Activities Investigation Commission, popularly known as the Broyles commission, which conducted secret investigations into subversive activities throughout the state. Major targets included the University of Chicago and Roosevelt College. In June 1949, the commission condemned conditions at both schools and recommended the withdrawal of tax exemptions from both. Robert M. Hutchins, president of the University of Chicago, eloquently criticized the commission. Although none of the commission bills became law, its investigation caused considerable disruption.[83]

In Wisconsin, despite heavy pressure on educational authorities, especially at the Madison campus, the university did not succumb to assaults on academic freedom. The state instituted no censorship. No legislative investigation harassed the University of Wisconsin. No professors were fired for political beliefs even though a few ex-Communists served on the faculty. In 1952, William Gorham Rice, a liberal Democrat and prominent member of the University of Wisconsin Law School, confidently speculated on what would happen if the regents imposed a loyalty oath on the faculty. "If a respected dean at the university who knows he can count on strong support from the teachers," Rice noted, "privately informs the right regent at the right time that he, the dean, will resign if the regents impose a loyalty oath on the faculty, the proposal will never see the light of day." No loyalty oath was imposed on teachers in Wisconsin.[84]

Response to McCarthy at state colleges, especially at the University of Wisconsin, was noticeably more critical than in the remainder of the state. The academic community had additional reasons to abhor him besides disgust with his personal ethics and methods and doubts about the validity of his anti-Communist campaign. McCarthy's widely publicized attacks on intellectuals and his proposals to investigate subversives on college campuses appeared to threaten academic freedom. President Truman was "merely the prisoner of a bunch of twisted intellectuals," McCarthy said. He urged the public to appoint themselves "to undo the damage which is being done by Communist infiltration of our schools and colleges through Communist-minded teachers and Communist textbooks."[85]

In a mock election held by students at thirteen state colleges (excluding the Madison campus of the University of Wisconsin) before the 1952 general election, Fairchild narrowly won with 50.5 percent of the vote to McCarthy's 49.5 percent. The same students preferred Eisenhower and Kohler by overwhelming majorities. Faculty and students at the University of Wisconsin in Madison vigorously attacked McCarthy. The same mock election on the Madison campus revealed that 58 percent of the students voted for Fairchild, while 42 percent preferred McCarthy. About twenty faculty members of the Law School and the College of Letters and Science publicly rebuked him. No professor publicly defended him. Campus chapters of Americans for Democratic Action, Young Democrats, and the student newspaper, *The Daily Cardinal*, actively labored to discredit and defeat him. Even Young Republicans were divided on his merits.[86]

On the other side were conservative organizations, some state legislators, and some regents who suspected Communist influence on the campuses and desired strong measures to root it out. In 1952, Wisconsin Young Republicans proposed to outlaw Communist and subversive groups from Wisconsin campuses and approved a platform that called for loyalty oaths for state teachers. The parent GOP organization urged an investigation of subversive teachers, textbooks, and "collateral reading material." The Wisconsin American Legion actively and persistently harassed the university. The university officially cooperated with all investigatory groups—the state legislature, the American Legion, the Federal Bureau of Investigation, and the House Committee on Un-American Activities—but apparently never endorsed or actively assisted their investigations.[87]

Edwin B. Fred, the president of the University of Wisconsin from 1945 to 1958, had to withstand the numerous assaults on academic freedom and freedom of speech. Earlier Fred had been professor of bacteriology and the dean of the Graduate School and the College of Agriculture. He had gained wide respect for his scholarly achievements and his calm, soft-spoken, dignified manner. As president, he cultivated excellent relations with the legislature, newspapers, students, faculty, and regents. He defended academic freedom with none of the passion and eloquence of Robert Hutchins but defended it nonetheless with consistency, subtlety, and effectiveness, changing rollers to ripples.

In 1952, the Wisconsin Union Forum Committee invited Prof. Owen Lattimore to speak on campus. Lattimore had been a major McCarthy target, and some Wisconsin McCarthyites protested his appearance. Fred did not admire Lattimore and probably wished that he had not accepted the invitation. Nevertheless, in a statement on 8 March 1952, Fred defended the university's "time-honored traditions" that provided a forum for the "free exchange of ideas." He reminded critics that the student group had invited other speakers, including prominent conservatives Gen. Douglas MacArthur, Sen. Robert Taft, and Col. Robert McCormick. Lattimore gave his speech.[88]

In the next two years, the Wisconsin American Legion strongly objected to scheduled appearances by Howard Mumford Jones, the distinguished Harvard English professor, and Joseph Starobin, editor of the Communist *Daily Worker*. The Legion even investigated the people responsible for the selection of Starobin. Both Jones and Starobin spoke at the university.[89]

The most serious incident that faced the university mushroomed out of the activities of the Labor Youth League, reputedly a Communist front organization, and its invitation to Abner Berry to speak on campus. Berry, the editor of the New York edition of the *Daily Worker*, was to appear on 14 January 1953. The day before his address, State Sen. Gordon Bubolz, Appleton Republican and chairman of the Wisconsin Legislative Council, strongly objected to permitting subversive groups on campus and promised to investigate the university. He threatened to hold up university funds if Berry appeared and hinted to university administrators that perhaps he would invite McCarthy to clean up the campus. On 14 January, President Fred promised to cooperate and supply information for any potential legislative investigation. He defended the university's role in combating communism and at the same time tried to uphold the principle of academic freedom. The university, he said,

> is dedicated to education and research. Each demands freedom of inquiry. This freedom of inquiry has produced a faculty and student body staunchly loyal to the state and nation. The contributions of the university to the strengthening of our nation have been of inestimable value. Freedom of inquiry at the University of Wisconsin has served to discredit communism, not to strengthen its insidious influence.

Fred did not believe that the university should censor ideas, but he personally would recommend the "termination of the services of any staff member whose activities are proved to be subversive of our government."[90]

The university allowed Berry to speak, whereupon conservative legislators pushed for an investigation of subversive activities on campus. The university had long feared such an investigation and had prepared for it. Fred and administrators Ira L. Baldwin, vice-president of academic affairs, and Leroy E. Luberg, assistant to the president, had carefully cultivated relations with government officials partly to forestall attacks on the university. A number of contacts who had graduated from the university and regarded it with affection served on Governor Kohler's staff. Twelve state senators and twenty-seven assemblymen were alumni. On the Democratic side, the university relied on Assemblyman Carl Thompson (Stoughton, U.W. Law School, 1939) and State Sen. Gaylord Nelson (Madison, U.W. Law School, 1942). State Sen. Warren Knowles (New Richmond, U.W. Law School, 1933) protected the university on the Republican side. Since Republicans controlled the legislature, Knowles's support was critical. Knowles had been the Republican floor leader since 1943 and would be elected lieutenant governor in 1954. In 1952, the Wisconsin Alumni Association selected him to lead its organization. Behind-the-scenes lobbying by university officials and alumni accounted for his selection, which was out of the order by which the association usually picked its president. They reasoned that Knowles would use his power and influence to protect the university's interests and philosophy; they were not disappointed.[91]

A resolution to investigate the university passed the legislature but only after an understanding between Knowles and university officials that Knowles would divert its focus toward an analysis of the university's overall needs. The legislature assigned the inquiry to the University of Wisconsin Policies Committee, a subcommittee of the Wisconsin Legislative Council. Knowles chaired the committee investigation. Friends of the university, including Nelson, dominated its membership. The committee's report ignored the problem of subversion but forcefully documented university needs in the areas of instruction, research, outreach, financing, and physical facilities.[92]

Conservative regents with close ties to McCarthy also pressured university officials. President Fred politely listened to their complaints but, with subtle firmness, defended academic freedom. Regent William J. Campbell, the founder of the RVC and a diligent fund raiser for McCarthy in 1952, worried about Communist infiltration of colleges. In 1949, he had urged that Wisconsin follow the example of the University of California and require loyalty oaths for teachers. University officials lobbied so effectively against his proposal that they not only defeated it but convinced the board to reaffirm its belief in the "intellectual right of students and teachers to explore and study critically our way of life and systems which challenge it." In 1952, Campbell became incensed after news accounts reported that history professor Fred H. Harrington had signed a petition protesting the trial of eleven American Communists. Fred pacified Campbell by patiently explaining that Harrington's protest had been misconstrued, that he had actually protested against the 1940 Smith Act. (Fred did not indicate what his action would have been if the news accounts had been accurate.)[93]

Some regents were irritated with university financing of the School for Workers, an extension division that trained trade-union members in running a union. Regents wanted the school to teach workers the virtues of free-enterprise capitalism. But university officials held their ground, informed the regents that the university also provided classes for management, and steadily increased the budget of the school.[94]

Of all the regents concerned with subversion, Fred occupied most of his time tactfully appeasing Frank J. Sensenbrenner. Sensenbrenner was a wealthy business executive and paper manufacturer from Neenah. He had risen from bookkeeper to become president, director, and then chairman of the board of the Kimberly-Clark Corporation, one of Wisconsin's largest corporations. For almost thirty years, he was also a director of the Wisconsin Manufacturers Association. First appointed to the board of regents in 1939, he served as president from 1945 until his death in 1952. Despite his advanced age—he was eighty-five years old in 1950—he was one of the most influential people in Wisconsin, a powerful member of the Republican party's finance committee, and a strong McCarthy partisan. He donated at least $500 to McCarthy's 1946 campaign, and, by McCarthy's estimate, as of July 1951, the senator owed Sensenbrenner $14,016.63 in personal loans.[95]

Sensenbrenner, like Campbell, suspected that universities tolerated subversive influences. He objected to what he thought were "pink" candidates being considered for membership on the board of the Wisconsin Alumni Association and worried that the School for Workers preached socialism and that professors in Illinois taught Keynesian economics. "The old slogan, academic freedom, is too frequently construed to give academic license to smart alecks," Sensenbrenner informed Fred in 1950. After this complaint, Fred sent Sensenbrenner information explaining the purpose of academic freedom. Sensenbrenner's preoccupation with subversion compelled Fred to put "communism" on the agenda of private meetings with him along with topics such as fund raising, outreach, and building-expansion projects.[96]

An example of Fred's superior gift for subtle persuasion and diversion occurred in 1951 when Sensenbrenner urged Fred's attention to a speech by Clarence Manion, the ultraconservative dean of the College of Law at the University of Notre Dame. Manion had cited the Declaration of Independence and other sources to warn of the dangers of "communism," "socialism," and "statism." "The wolves of despotism never advertise themselves as such. They hide in the sheep's clothing of 'democratic,' 'progressive,' 'liberal,' 'humanitarian,' or 'fraternal,' " Manion had argued. Sensenbrenner admired the address so much that he proposed to reprint three to four thousand copies, at his own expense, and distribute them to faculty and regents.[97]

Fred, responding with his usual cordiality, recommended a more tolerant authority on the subject of subversion and chided Manion for omitting "some phrases from his Declaration of Independence quotation." Fred eagerly agreed with the idea of reprinting important speeches but, rather than Manion's address, he suggested distributing pamphlets of the "best speeches given by some of our own staff members" for which funds were not currently available. Sensenbrenner dropped the subject.[98]

On some issues Wisconsin was in the forefront among universities in forcefully rejecting stringent loyalty measures. The U.S. Armed Forces Institute held contracts with many universities to provide correspondence courses for servicemen. During the height of the McCarthy fear, the institute added a clause to its contract stipulating that the "contractor shall not employ or retain . . . such persons as are disapproved by the government." Thirty-two universities agreed to the new provision in their 1954 contracts. Wisconsin was among fourteen dissidents that refused to sign.[99]

In 1954, the Defense Department required a loyalty oath for all entrants into the Reserve Officers Training Corps (ROTC). For land-grant colleges, student participation in ROTC was compulsory for two years. At Wisconsin, the army excluded a sophomore student, who was also a Sunday-school teacher, because he had admitted that he once knew a man who had been investigated by the FBI. Despite the state law requiring participation in the program, the army refused to issue the student a uniform and could only suggest that he take his training in civilian clothes. Liberal newspapers and the university protested the regulation. The head of the Wisconsin Civil Liberties Union complained that the oath was abhorrent, and even mis-named, because it tested "organizations joined, meetings attended, social functions participated in, and associations students have had." After weeks of controversy, an embarrassed army retreated and issued the student a uniform. The Wisconsin furor contributed to the army's decision to change its requirements so that ROTC trainees affirmed their support of the government and the constitution.*

Although some university officials continually expected McCarthy to attack the University of Wisconsin, he never did. Observers have pon-dered the reasons for his failure to attack the Madison campus as he did Harvard and other universities. As a Catholic and a graduate of Catholic Marquette University, McCarthy may not have wanted to arouse religious controversy in Wisconsin by assaulting the state's most prestigious public university. Mark Ingraham, dean of Letters and Science at the university during the McCarthy era, and other university spokesmen have specu-lated that, while McCarthy recognized the political value of attacking Harvard and "effete" Eastern schools, he was too politically astute to move against the University of Wisconsin and thereby alienate its loyal alum-ni.[101]

Perhaps McCarthy never considered investigating the university or felt any reason to do so. The laughter and pointed questions that so embar-rassed him during his address there in May 1951 may also have caused him to shy away from a second confrontation with the university.

Another consideration involved the problem of attacking a university whose board of regents was composed of prominent Wisconsin Republi-cans. Besides Campbell and Sensenbrenner, other important GOP officials who served as regents included Mrs. Melvin Laird, Sr., Wilbur Renk, Oscar Rennebohm, and Carl E. Steiger. Renk and Rennebohm were not McCarthy enthusiasts, but they were, nevertheless, leading figures in the Republican party. In retrospect, it is inconceivable that McCarthy would assault the university and thus embarrass and alienate GOP leaders and individuals who had significantly advanced his political career.

That Wisconsin avoided the serious encroachment on civil liberties that plagued other states was partly fortuitous. Geography and unique ethnic composition contributed to the hysteria in California when, during World War II, fear of Japanese along the coast and Japanese living within the state accentuated wartime nervousness. Nor did Wisconsin produce an influen-tial anti-Communist crusader—such as Jack Tenney in California or Albert Canwell in Washington—determined to root out subversives in the state. Nor did Wisconsin have major federal agencies within its borders, thus

---

*For some important evidence that the university was not a consistent defender of academic freedom, see the discussion in the notes to Chapter 10.[100]

avoiding Missouri's experience when the Red Scare was aggravated by the federal government's firing of about seventy-five people in a well-publicized housecleaning.[102]

The academic community in Wisconsin benefited from the fact that McCarthy's strong anti-intellectual sentiments were shared only to a limited degree by his followers in Wisconsin. This circumstance helped to restrain attacks on higher education. However, some attacks on intellectuals did take place. During the 1952 campaign, the McCarthy Club distributed an editorial by the *Vilas County News-Review* that lashed out at "pseudo intellectuals" who hid behind the "cloak" of liberalism but whose "twisted and distorted minds" wanted only "power." Only power would satisfy their "stinking little souls and assure them they are better than those they pretend to despise."[103] During the 1951 session of the state legislature, Democrat William Proxmire and Republican Arthur Peterson attempted to discredit McCarthy by introducing a bill to curb legislative immunity. Since both were studying for postgraduate degrees, they became targets for derision by some pro-McCarthy legislators. During debate on the measure, Assemblyman Elmer Genzmer, Republican from Mayville, referred to them disdainfully as "you college graduates and geniuses," and another legislator sarcastically called them "intellectual giants."[104] Such sentiments were the exception, however, and not the rule. McCarthy partisans showed, at most, moderate enthusiasm for his assault on Harvard's intellectuals. McCarthyites who commented on the controversy sided with former Lawrence College president, Nathan Pusey, after McCarthy denounced him.

Some McCarthy sympathizers even sought academic confirmation for their convictions. Wyngaard, for example, thought it significant that William McGovern, chairman of the Department of Political Science at Northwestern University, spoke and wrote on McCarthy's behalf. After McGovern's address at a McCarthy testimonial dinner, Wyngaard used his appearance to disprove the contention "some persons have that McCarthy's charges have been irresponsible." McGovern's introduction to McCarthy's book, *McCarthyism: The Fight for America,* Wyngaard thought, supplied a "highly responsible source" and should silence those who "spread the idea that responsible opinion is anti-McCarthy." The book itself, McCarthy's principal literary effort, had been "carefully prepared."[105]

Effective public relations helped the University of Wisconsin to maintain its principles. President Fred and his assistants were particularly adept at this. Deeply ingrained and proud traditions at the university probably served the same purpose. After some unhappy incidents in the early 1900s, Wisconsin had become a major bastion of academic freedom. The famed "Wisconsin Idea," first expanded during the presidency of Charles Van Hise (1903–1918), had provided two major contributions to higher education and to the residents of Wisconsin. First, Wisconsin had fostered the entry of the expert into government, both in technical and social planning. Second, the university had developed the extension movement, whereby university classes were held in every part of the state. These progressive measures may have created enough good will to sustain freedom of thought after World War II.[106]

Most important were the traditions, coordinated power, and constant vigilance of political forces in Wisconsin—ranging from Socialists to moderate Republicans. Between 1910 and 1960, Milwaukee had Socialist mayors for thirty-eighty years. Milwaukee Socialists had deemphasized philosophy to concentrate on the practical housekeeping problems of running a city. Although they socialized nothing in Milwaukee and experienced party decline by the end of World War II, their tradition of providing tolerant, honest, and efficient government moderated stereotypes of left-wing activity. In the 1930s, the La Follette Progressives had led the drive to oppose attacks on alleged subversives who held nonconformist opinions and were of a liberal mind.[107] After World War II, liberal Democrats and liberal groups allied with them—organized labor, some farm groups, anti-McCarthy newspapers—blamed every incident and every piece of legislation that threatened basic freedoms on reactionary Republicans or McCarthyism. Some moderate Republicans provided critical assistance as well. Governor Kohler showed no inclination to investigate subversion in the state, and Knowles provided timely aid to the University of Wisconsin.

Ironically, the state that provided the nation with a senator and an "ism" symbolizing serious infringement on basic freedoms preserved those freedoms better than other parts of the country. The tumultuous waves of civil-liberties violations that engulfed the country became breakers as they approached Wisconsin's political and educational shores.

# Chapter 11

# The Last Years: 1955–1957

Joe McCarthy never recovered from the disastrous political upheavals of 1954. Richard Rovere may have assumed correctly that in late 1954 or early 1955 McCarthy "suffered a kind of interior collapse."[1] His Senate colleagues ignored him and the measures he proposed, and he lost the power to panic that august body. He seldom spoke with much force, and, in any case, no one paid much attention. When he got the Senate floor, senators would drift from the chamber to the cloakroom or to other business. Reporters in Washington also ignored him, and his infrequent appearances in newspapers were on the back pages. A Gallup poll published in May 1955 disclosed that, if McCarthy ran on a third-party ticket for president in 1956, he would receive only 4 percent of the vote compared to 55 percent for Eisenhower and 37 percent for Stevenson. Gallup concluded that McCarthy had lost ground among the Republican rank and file.[2]

McCarthy's health seemed to decline along with his political power. He was sick much of the last years of his life and made frequent trips to the hospital. Back trouble, heart trouble, herniated-diaphragm trouble, alcohol trouble—all were mentioned, but none was confirmed. He was obviously sick. He would run alarmingly to fat and then grow gaunt. Wisconsin friends were shocked by his ghastly appearance. In Wisconsin tours, his legs seemed to bother him. He was unsteady on his feet. He leaned on the arm of his wife, and a bodyguard helped him up stairways. His catlike quickness, both in political sparring and in movement, seemed to have disappeared. He had a slow, ponderous manner, like a man carrying a heavy burden or suffering pain.[3]

In the company of old supporters and friends from Wisconsin, McCarthy tried to be jovial, but the old spark had gone. When Urban Van Susteren tried to prod him in to regaining his old momentum by attacking his censors, McCarthy rebuffed him. "No," he told Van Susteren, "What you want me to do is become a bitter old man." Not even his closest friends in Wisconsin knew what his problem was, but most assumed it had to do with alcohol. According to Van Susteren, by 1956 McCarthy consumed "at least a whole bottle a day—a fifth to a quart and maybe more." Wisconsin Republican leaders knew of his drinking problem and were greatly disturbed by it. During his infrequent state appearances, McCarthy sometimes cut his speeches short, and, although party officials sensed his predicament, most were reluctant to say anything. His drinking so embarrassed Leonard Hall, the Republican national chairman, that Hall pleaded with Claude Jasper to come to Washington and take McCarthy to an island to dry out. Jasper visited McCarthy in Washington but made only a feeble effort to talk about the problem because he sensed that McCarthy resented his intrusion. Rep. Alvin O'Konski frankly suggested that McCarthy control his drinking, but his suggestion met an even stronger rebuff.[4]

McCarthy had become so withdrawn and seemed so paranoid that party officials and some constituents found it difficult to communicate with him. One could never be certain that he would keep his appointments. In 1955, Lt. Gov. Warren Knowles and Henry Ringling went to Washington to talk with the Wisconsin congressional delegation about a possible judicial appointment for Knowles. They searched all over Washington for McCarthy and finally located him in the back of a bar, surrounded by his henchmen. His behavior was so bizarre that Knowles returned to Wisconsin convinced that McCarthy suffered from alcoholism and paranoia.[5]

In his last years, McCarthy became increasingly concerned with money and security. Earlier he had been quite astute at determining the underlying value of defaulted railroad companies. He now tried to regain his financial touch as he poured over the stock-market news. He began thinking in terms of a quiet, cozy old age. "Jean and I have enough money for a small cattle spread in Arizona," he said. Then disaster struck. He had trusted a friend with an investment in the Green Bay Uranium Company. In 1956 or early 1957, when the investors decided to liquidate, the friend absconded to South America with McCarthy's money, and he lost nearly everything. "He fell off the wagon in a heap," Rovere noted, "and never got on again."[6]

McCarthy's fall from grace in Wisconsin resembled the one he suffered after his Senate election in 1946, only this time his fall was much more precipitous. Wisconsinites were either apathetic, disenchanted, or harshly critical of him during his last two-and-a-half years in the Senate. Thousands of people in Wisconsin no doubt continued to regard McCarthy as a courageous fighter for right, but their voices were now silent. They no longer scribbled passionate letters to newspapers. The failure of the McCarthy Day celebration at Boscobel, Wisconsin, on 4 June 1955 illustrated the pervasive apathy. City fathers promoted the affair vigorously and predicted a turnout of fifty thousand people. When the event occurred, however, only five thousand people watched him pass in parade, and a mere fifteen hundred showed up for his speech. The curious but unenthusiastic crowd, which included band members and their admiring parents, dispersed immediately after the ceremonies. With the exception of *The Capital Times*, Wisconsin newspapers ignored the affair. Leroy Gore remarked sarcastically that "as a funeral director's son, I never saw so many pallbearers at one funeral in my life." Another critic called it an "Irish wake."[7]

Wisconsin interest groups and their publications either ignored McCarthy or criticized him. Although McCarthy now talked as a farmer's friend, he did not stick to it or capitalize on it politically. He had always had difficulty sticking with any issue except Communists in government, but in his declining years his power of concentration was more feeble than ever. Farm leaders and publications could find nothing to praise in his record. While Congress argued whether agricultural price supports should assure 85, 87.5, or 90 percent of parity, McCarthy continued to demand 100 or even 110 percent, leading the National Farmer's Union to caution Wisconsin farmers "not [to] be deceived by such demagoguery." *The Wisconsin Agriculturist and Farmer* heralded the decline of McCarthyism. State supporters of rural electric cooperatives condemned his attempt to eliminate the Rural Electrification Administration as a federal administrative agency. No farm leader, organization, or publication defended him.[8]

McCarthy's political appointments fared no better than his policy statements. In 1955, he recommended Thomas Miller as postmaster in Appleton. After learning that Miller was an ex-convict, convicted of bootlegging in 1931 and gambling in 1946 and 1950, Postmaster General Arthur Summerfield rejected him as unsuitable. State opinion castigated McCarthy for his dreadful choice. One Republican newspaper thought it instructive for the people of Wisconsin to discover "what kind of a man represents them in the U.S. Senate and what kind of people he thinks are qualified for public office."[9]

McCarthy's widely publicized friendship with Texas oil-and-gas magnates, and his votes in their interests, were another weak link in his political armor. On 11 February 1956, Howard B. Keck, president of the Superior Oil Company of Texas and California, was identified at a Senate inquiry as the source of a $2,500 campaign contribution to Sen. Francis Case, a Republican from South Dakota. Subsequent investigation disclosed that an "N. B. Keck" had donated $2,000 to McCarthy's campaign in 1952. Reporters tried to establish that the two Kecks were the same individual. When this proved fruitless, critics assumed that he was and that he had rewarded McCarthy for his faithful service to the oil-and-gas interests. Since 1950, McCarthy had voted for measures favored by the oil-and-gas industry, including tidelands-oil bills, a natural-gas bill, and a bill to continue the 27½-percent tax exemption for oil producers. In 1953 and 1954, McCarthy frequently took trips in planes owned by the Superior Oil Company. His critics pointed out that the Superior Oil Company had leases on submerged land in the Gulf of Mexico and in Galveston Bay and therefore benefited from the tidelands-oil legislation. The plane trips, campaign contributions, Texas vacations, and votes for oil-and-gas interests led to the charge that McCarthy was Wisconsin's "senator for Texas."[10]

McCarthy's relationship with prominent Republican leaders and newspapers, which had once supported him, deteriorated badly after 1954. Their main objection was his continuing criticism of Eisenhower. In May

1955, he attacked the president's advisers and sarcastically added: "If Eisenhower were alive. . . ." In the summer of 1955, McCarthy charged that Eisenhower had "betrayed his trust" and had advanced "the cause of tyranny" by offering friendship to Soviet leaders and by selling out Nationalist China. McCarthy's hometown newspaper, the *Appleton Post-Crescent*, objected to his careless propensity to level the charge of treason against people with whom he disagreed and disapproved of his "heavy-handed humor" and "lack of dignity." McCarthy's opposition to President Eisenhower and his Senate voting record so offended the *Wisconsin State Journal* that its editor, Roy Matson, was finally driven to say in February 1956 that "time and the public's good sense have taken care of McCarthy. He's a dead pigeon."[11]

The press angered McCarthy and probably intensified his paranoia by opposing his policies and by refusing to print his press releases. He sent reams of releases to Wisconsin newspapers, many of them attacking the Eisenhower administration, but most papers ignored them. The attitude of the *State Journal* bewildered McCarthy. He complained to Matson about the *Journal's* "sudden and apparent all-out opposition." "I cannot understand this for the reason that my politics and policies are exactly the same as when you were giving me all-out support." McCarthy's naive complaint failed to account for the political realities. The *State Journal* and other Republican newspapers had indeed supported him when he attacked the Democrat Truman but did not appreciate his pursuing exactly the same policies against the Republican Eisenhower.[12]

On 20 January 1956, McCarthy announced that he favored the bill to exempt natural-gas producers from federal regulation because such regulation was a step toward "socializing our economy." He conceded that his stance was "not the popular one in my state."[13] Indeed, his position met withering criticism in Wisconsin. His political stock dropped to a new low. The overwhelming preponderance of opinion in the state, both official and private, opposed the bill. Milwaukee and most of the state's larger cities used natural gas, and the bill McCarthy supported threatened to raise its price. Senator Wiley, Governor Kohler, Atty. Gen. Vernon Thomson, most other Republican leaders, and nearly all the mayors of Wisconsin supported the consumer in the natural-gas fight and argued that it was unfair and dangerous to decontrol the production of natural gas. Thomson, who on many past occasions had spoken on McCarthy's behalf, was "greatly disappointed" by his stand and added sharply that the "record is so replete with answers to these gas producers that it is difficult to see how anyone not beholden to these people for election can take a point of view contrary to the almost unanimous opinion of the officials of Wisconsin." A Republican and long-time friend of McCarthy, James Durfee, chairman of the Wisconsin Public Service Commission which fought the gas bill, was "much disappointed" by McCarthy's stand.[14]

At the state Republican convention in June 1955, McCarthy continued to arouse more support among convention delegates than President Eisenhower. Political necessity required that Republicans proclaim that they liked Ike, but a majority of the delegates showed, by endorsing the Bricker amendment and by opposing revision of the McCarran–Walter Immigration Act, that they did not like much of what Ike liked. The convention singled McCarthy out for personal praise and censured the U.S. Senate for censuring him. But the fanatical devotion to McCarthy had died. His appearance generated little enthusiasm and no standing ovation, and a substantial minority of delegates opposed the pro-McCarthy resolution.[15]

In general, McCarthy's backing within the Republican party and the state fell off to such an extent that John Wyngaard noted in March 1956 that McCarthy had the lowest popularity "since his election to the Senate an even decade ago." He had no relation whatever to current political management of his party, such as delegate selection to the national Republican convention in 1956.[16] The fact that he made few public appearances in the state and showed little concern for party problems also hurt him. In March 1956, Wayne Hood pointed out that McCarthy's deteriorating position was partly "due to the fact that [he has] not been back in the state frequently enough to keep the fences mended."[17]

At the 1956 Wisconsin Republican convention, delegates endorsed Rep. Glenn Davis over Senator Wiley for the U.S. Senate nomination. One scholar assumed that Republicans had struck at Wiley because "he had not voted against McCarthy's censure." Actually this was a minor factor. More often, Republicans expressed irritation with Wiley's pompous, arrogant personality and objected to his support of foreign aid and international cooperation and his opposition to the Bricker amendment. Wiley defeated Davis and won the general election.[18]

During the 1956 election campaign, state and national Republicans ignored McCarthy. He was not invited to the Republican convention in San Francisco and did not attend. Few if any missed him. When asked by a reporter if word had been received at the convention from McCarthy, a Wisconsin GOP official responded: "Not a word, not a word. Fact is, I haven't even heard his name mentioned."[19]

After the 11 September primary, McCarthy offered all GOP primary winners, including those for state legislative offices, campaign assistance "if you think I can be of any help." But his help, once valued so highly, was not sought after by Republican hopefuls in 1956. Only William Burke, running in the Fourth Congressional District, accepted the offer and invited McCarthy to appear at a West Allis dinner honoring Burke and Thomson, the Republican candidate for governor. But when Thomson learned that McCarthy had accepted Burke's invitation, he canceled his appearance at the gathering.[20]

Speculation about prospective candidates to run against McCarthy in 1958 started as early as 1956. The large number of potential candidates from both parties suggested that McCarthy would be ripe for defeat. Democratic hopefuls included James Doyle, Henry Reuss, Gaylord Nelson, William Proxmire, and Henry Maier. Among the Republicans, Knowles, Davis, and especially Kohler were likely prospects. Kohler had become more outspokenly critical of McCarthy and of the conservative wing of the party. "The real right wingers in Wisconsin think you have to be for McCarthy and against Eisenhower or you are not a Republican," he complained early in 1957. "Heaven forbid that I be included among that group." Kohler for Senator clubs sprang up around the state as early as December 1956. Some conservative Republicans believed that McCarthy could win reelection in 1958 if he could control his drinking, improve his health, and vigorously campaign.[21] But the speculation ended abruptly when, on 2 May 1957, Joe McCarthy died of acute hepatitis.

  *  *  *  *

During the five days following his death, McCarthy was once again the center of political attention in Wisconsin as observers sought to assess his controversial career. The years of bitterness and partisan wrangling resurfaced. Four Democratic legislators remained in their seats when the Wisconsin senate adopted a resolution paying tribute to McCarthy's life. Nelson left the chamber to avoid voting. Maier explained that the dissenters had objected to the language of the resolution, particularly to the part that said that "history will record [McCarthy] as one of the most aggressive and courageous fighters against communism." The Democrats' opposition was the "act of little men," reproached a Republican newspaper.[22]

In their eulogies, McCarthy's admirers concentrated on his intensely appealing image. Some noted the facts he had uncovered about communism. More often, his partisans commended his "burning patriotism" and his crusade for "Christian morality." "Everyone will concede his courage," one newspaper assumed. Most often, however, his saddened supporters dwelt on his rugged, fighting qualities. He was a "valiant," "saber-slashing warrior," the Milwaukee Sentinel stated, whose only motive had been to smash the Communist conspiracy. Others noted his rugged Marine Corps training and his motto that Communists could not be handled with kid gloves. To criticize McCarthy's tactics was "pretty much like criticizing the tactics of the United States Marine Corps."[23]

Despite the emotional reaction to McCarthy's death by his hardcore supporters, much of the response reflected the extent of his decline since 1952. At first, there had been adulation and anger. Recently, anger had turned to pity and the adulation to doubt. As expected, anti-McCarthyites dwelt on the evils of McCarthy and McCarthyism: fear, suspicion, ruined reputations, disruption of foreign policy, and unethical political tactics.[24] More significant was the attitude of many Republican newspapers that had seldom found fault with McCarthy in his heyday. Now many questioned his political morality and ethics. Some praised his crusade against the Democratic Truman administration, but, as one journal noted, long after the Eisenhower administration "began to get rid of the 'mess,' he was lashing out more and more recklessly." The same newspaper now maintained that he was "often unfair" and "frequently destructive." Another reflected that he "unnecessarily tore down reputations" and "overplayed his official position." The *Oshkosh Daily Northwestern*, which had never faulted him during his red-hunting days, suggested after his death that he might have gone beyond the duty and ethics of his position "for the sake oi personal advantage and prominence." The *Wisconsin State Journal* found that, while McCarthy made Americans dramatically conscious of Communists, he also made them aware of "conscience, the need for fair play, the basic Amiercan right to assumption of innocence until proved guilty."[25]

In death as well as in life, some Republican politicians found McCarthy's legacy politically sensitive. McCarthy's ghost remained, and politicians did not want to antagonize the virulent pro- and anti-McCarthy forces in the state. Kohler, who would subsequently try to capture McCarthy's vacated Senate seat, avoided comment on the senator's death altogether except to express his sympathy for McCarthy's family. Knowles, a rising political star in Wisconsin, contrived a carefully worded, fence-straddling comment that observed that Wisconsin citizens would have "mixed feelings" about McCarthy but that all could agree that he was "a colorful and controversial figure."[26]

After funeral services and elaborate official farewells in Washington, McCarthy's body was flown into Austin Straubel Airport in Green Bay on Monday, 6 May. Joined by a thirty-five-man Marine Corps honor guard, the cortege drove the twenty-eight miles to Appleton while thousands of onlookers watched at intersections along the route. That evening and the next morning, twenty-five thousand people filed through St. Mary's Catholic Church in Appleton to visit the bier. Twenty-one U.S. senators flew in for the funeral on 7 May. Over a thousand people packed the church for the requiem high mass, and another thousand stood outside. Rev. Adam Grill, McCarthy's long-time friend and former catechism instructor, delivered the funeral sermon. McCarthy was like a "man of old," Father Grill said, "who saw danger to his country and clothed in the shining armor of zeal and love and holding within his hands the sword of truth," marched "forward into battle with the cry on his lips, 'For God and for my Country.'"[27]

Peace, which Joe McCarthy had never sought and never stumbled on in his ten turbulent years in the Senate, finally enfolded him on 7 May as they buried him next to his mother and father. He was left in his grave on a grassy spruce-shaded bluff fifty feet above the Fox River in Appleton. "The only sound of strife came from the contending current and the shore and the only voices raised were those of the birds."[28]

*　　*　　*　　*

The McCarthy controversy had little direct effect on the 27 August 1957 special senatorial election, called to fill McCarthy's vacant seat. Kohler, the Republican hopeful, urged that McCarthy be allowed to "rest in peace." Philleo Nash, the Democratic state chairman, agreed and added that "when McCarthy died, the issue died with him." The legacy of McCarthy, though, indirectly contributed to William Proxmire's upset victory over Kohler. One of the four major reasons for Proxmire's triumph was dissension in GOP ranks, a situation that partly stemmed from the smoldering feud between conservative McCarthy Republicans and moderate Eisenhower supporters over the wisdom and expediency of McCarthy's attack on the Eisenhower administration.[29]

In addition, after McCarthy's death, the frustrating years of failure for Wisconsin Democrats came to an end as they experienced a period of unparalleled success. Besides Proxmire's victory (and subsequent reelections), Nelson defeated Wiley in 1962, and Democrats controlled the governorship from 1959 to 1965. After a Republican interlude, the Democrats assumed almost complete dominance of Wisconsin politics in the mid-1970s. Many factors accounted for the rise of the Wisconsin Democrats, but both Democratic and Republican leaders agree that McCarthy assisted this revitalization. In the early 1950s, Wisconsin Democrats had no dynamic leaders to rally around and had naturally been inclined to fight among themselves. McCarthy, however, threatened and angered Democrats by accusing them of being unpatriotic and un-American. Their contempt for him and for McCarthyism provided an issue that all Democrats could agree about. "Without Joe to zero in on," Patrick Lucey has observed, "we would never have pulled all our people together, and then keep [sic] them together through the middle 1950's while we were coming close to winning but not quite making it." Knowles and Claude Jasper, a state GOP chairman, agreed. Democrats "had never been able to get together on one issue," Jasper reflected, "and they got together on the issue of Joe McCarthy and it established the Democratic party of Wisconsin."[30] McCarthy also drove some young, idealistic, and hardworking people into the DOC because of their revulsion for him and their attraction to the character and integrity of Thomas Fairchild and Adlai Stevenson.[31]

Since McCarthy's death, historians and commentators have almost unanimously condemned his demagoguery and its damaging influence on the republic. Wisconsin Democrats have capitalized on history's judgment. When expedience dictated, they revived the specter of McCarthy to lash their Republican opponents. In 1961, Lucey excoriated the "Republican bosses" for calling up the "ghost of discredited McCarthyism." Democrats subsequently tagged the "McCarthyite" label on Republican congressmen Melvin Laird and Glenn Davis.[32]

The mute response of Wisconsin Republicans to McCarthy's life indicates their tacit acceptance of the verdict of history and their awareness of his divisive influence on their party. McCarthy's name is rarely mentioned at the state Republican party's annual conventions. Nor have Republicans done anything to officially memorialize him; they have raised no monuments to Joe McCarthy. In 1967, George Greeley, then the executive secretary of the party, explained that to memorialize McCarthy "might only serve to reopen old wounds. . . . We are a united party now; we want to stay that way."[33]

# Notes

## Notes to Chapter 1: Young Joe McCarthy

1. Richard Rovere, *Senator Joe McCarthy* (Cleveland and New York: The World Publishing Co., 1959), p. 78.

2. Weston A. Goodspeed, Melvin E. Bothwell, and Kenneth C. Goodspeed, *History of Outagamie County, Wisconsin* (Chicago: Goodspeed Historical Association, 1911), pp. 707–8, 1222–23. This source contains short biographies of two of Joseph McCarthy's uncles, William and Michael John McCarthy. I am indebted to James Heenan, Grand Chute, a neighbor of the McCarthys, for directing me to this source. Heenan has made a hobby of studying the McCarthy ancestry and has worked very closely with historian Thomas C. Reeves, who is writing a biography of Joe McCarthy.

3. Ibid.; Rovere, *Joe McCarthy*, p. 79; Interview, Stephen McCarthy, 3 March 1977.

4. Jack Anderson and Ronald May, *McCarthy: The Man, the Senator, the "Ism"* (Boston: The Beacon Press, 1952), p. 7; Saul Pett, ed., *The AP McCarthy Series* (New York: Associated Press, 1954), pp. 50–51; Interviews, James Heenan, 10 February 1977; Stephen McCarthy, 3 March 1977.

5. Anderson and May, *McCarthy*, pp. 7–8; Pett, *AP Series*, p. 52; Interviews, Stephen McCarthy, 3 March 1977; Mary (Hoolihan) Kools, 21 January 1977; and Mrs. Carl Radtke, 21 February 1977.

6. Interview, Stephen McCarthy, 3 March 1977.

7. Ibid.; Anderson and May, *McCarthy*, p. 8.

8. *Appleton Post-Crescent*, 1 May 1977; Interview, Stephen McCarthy, 3 March 1977.

9. Anderson and May, *McCarthy*, p. 8; Pett, *AP Series*, pp. 50–51; Interviews, Heenan, 10 February 1977; Stephen McCarthy, 3 March 1977.

10. Anderson and May, *McCarthy*, pp. 9, 11; Interviews, Heenan, 10 February 1977; Kools, 21 January 1977; and Stephen McCarthy, 3 March 1977. Heenan possesses McCarthy's grade-school records. He would not allow me to use them, but he has granted permission to Reeves. The reader should, therefore, consult Reeves's forthcoming biography.

11. Interviews, Radtke, 21 February 1977; Erwin Fickel, 21 February 1977; and Stephen McCarthy, 3 March 1977.

12. Anderson and May, *McCarthy*, pp. 11–12; Pett, *AP Series*, p. 52; *New York Post*, 5 September 1951; Interviews, Heenan, 10 February 1977; Stephen McCarthy, 3 March 1977.

13. Anderson and May, *McCarthy*, pp. 12–13; Pett, *AP Series*, p. 52; *New York Post*, 5 September 1951; Interview, Heenan, 10 February 1977.

14. Anderson and May, *McCarthy*, pp. 8–13; Eric Goldman, *The Crucial Decade: America, 1945–1955* (New York: Alfred A. Knopf, Inc., 1959), p. 137; Rovere, *Joe McCarthy*, p. 81.

15. Barron Beshoar to Robert Schwartz, 4 October 1951, Box 4, Robert Fleming Papers, State Historical Society of Wisconsin (S.H.S.W.); Interview, Stephen McCarthy, 3 March 1977.

16. *The Manawa Advocate*, 16 May 1929, 2 January 1930.

17. Anderson and May, *McCarthy*, pp. 14–17.

18. *Milwaukee Journal*, 16 March 1930; Interviews, Honor (Walch) Testin, 29 January 1977; Stephen McCarthy, 3 March 1977.

19. *Milwaukee Journal*, 16 March 1930; James Auer and Clark Kalvelage, "Joe McCarthy's School Days" (typescript, c. 1953), p. 2, in the Archives Division, S.H.S.W.; Interview, Leo Hershberger, 3 February 1977.

20. *The Manawa Advocate*, 12 September and 3, 10, and 31 October 1929; Anderson and May, *McCarthy*, p. 17; Interviews, Hershberger, 3 February 1977; Ione (Norton) Goetz, 18 April 1977; and Charles Middleton, 22 February 1977. The following summer, however, McCarthy secured a job at the Cash-Way in Shiocton.

21. Auer and Kalvelage, "McCarthy's School Days," pp. 3–4.

22. Ibid., pp. 4–5; Interviews, Hershberger, 3 February 1977; Goetz, 18 April 1977; Testin, 29 January 1977; George Kelley, 18 March 1977; Gordon Brown, 3 February 1977; Dorothy Henning, 4 February 1977; and Paul Sturm, 18 March 1977.

23. Auer and Kalvelage, "McCarthy's School Days," p. 5; Interviews, Hershberger, 3 February 1977; Kelley, 18 March 1977.

24. *The Manawa Advocate*, 21 November 1929, 13 February and 20 March 1930; Auer and Kalvelage, "McCarthy's School Days," p. 6; "McCarthy's Scholastic Records at Little Wolf High School, Manawa, Wisconsin," Archives Division, S.H.S.W.

25. Anderson and May, *McCarthy*, pp. 18–19; Interviews, Hershberger, 3 February 1977; Kelley, 18 March 1977; Goetz, 18 April 1977; Sturm, 18 March 1977; Testin, 29 January 1977; and Mary (McDermott) Stadler, 20 April 1977.

26. *Milwaukee Journal*, 16 March 1930; Anderson and May, *McCarthy*, p. 18; Interview, Hershberger, 3 February 1977.

27. *The Manawa Advocate*, 24 October 1929; Interviews, Testin, 29 January 1977; Harold Crane, 3 February 1977; and William Remmel, 3 February 1977.

28. *The Manawa Advocate*, 8 September 1929; Anderson and May, *McCarthy*, pp. 14–15, 19; Interviews, Kelley, 18 March 1977; Testin, 29 January 1977.

29. *The Manawa Advocate*, 1 August 1929, 13 March, 19 May, and 12 June 1930; Interviews, Middleton, 22 February 1977; Testin, 29 January 1977; Melda Mortenson, 10 April 1977; and Maurice Peterson, 9 February 1977.

30. Auer and Kalvelage, "McCarthy's School Days," p. 6; "McCarthy's Scholastic Records," Archives Division, S.H.S.W.; Interview, Hershberger, 3 February 1977.

31. *The Manawa Advocate*, 12 September and 10 October 1929; *Milwaukee Journal*, 16 March 1930.

32. Pett, *AP Series*, p. 53; "McCarthy's Scholastic Records," Archives Division, S.H.S.W.; Interviews, Robert Harland, 5 April 1977; Stephen McCarthy, 3 March 1977. McCarthy's grades in subsequent years are not known; probably they were average.

33. Anderson and May, *McCarthy*, p. 25.

34. Memorandum, "Information on Part-Time Employment," 9 July 1932, Box 21, Marquette University Papers, Marquette University Archives, Milwaukee, Wisconsin; *The Marquette Tribune*, 27 October 1932; Interviews, Middleton, 22 February 1977; Charles Curran, 13 April 1977; Hugh Gwin, 13 May 1977; Thomas Korb, 24 March 1977; Clifford Mullarky, 21 January 1977; Roman Papka, 25 April 1977; and Henry Schroeder, 25 May 1977.

35. Interviews, Mullarky, 21 January 1977; Joseph Kores, 12 May 1977; and William Schmit, 18 May 1977.

36. *The Marquette Tribune*, 19 February, 26 March, and 7 May 1931; Interviews, Kores, 12 May 1977; Schmit, 18 May 1977.

37. *The Marquette Tribune,* 17 and 24 March, 28 April, and 5 May 1932. Another report said that in the second fight Balcerzak knocked McCarthy down in the second round; *Milwaukee Sentinel,* 3 May 1932; Interview, Kores, 12 May 1977.

38. *The Marquette Tribune,* 13 and 20 October 1952; *The Hilltop* (yearbook), 1933, p. 191.

39. *The Marquette Tribune,* 13 October 1932, 25 May 1933; Interviews, Kores, 12 May 1977; Schmit, 18 May 1977; and Bernard O'Connor, 4 May 1977.

40. *The Hilltop* (yearbook), 1934, p. 195; Anderson and May, *McCarthy,* pp. 21–22; Interviews, Curran, 13 April 1977; Hershberger, 3 February 1977; and Kelley, 18 March 1977. McCarthy's subsequent rough-and-tumble technique may have been influenced by the Franklin Club's use of the Oregon style of debate, in which cross-examination separated the speech and the rebuttal, supposedly heightening the intensity of conflict between teams.

41. Anderson and May, *McCarthy,* pp. 22–23, 26–27; Interviews, Curran, 13 April 1977; Richard Drew, 19 May 1977; and Warren Kenney, 17 May 1977. Curran claimed that Anderson and May's account of the Franklin Club election was exaggerated.

42. *The Marquette Tribune,* 4 and 11 May 1933; Interview, Curran, 13 April 1977.

43. Interviews, Korb, 24 March 1977; Papka, 25 April 1977; Mrs. Bernadine Gomillion, 10 March 1977; Arlo McKinnon, 23 March 1977; and Joseph Kriofske, 23 March 1977.

44. *Shawano County Journal,* 7 May 1936; Interviews, Drew, 19 May 1977; Korb, 24 March 1977; Middleton, 22 February 1977; and Papka, 25 April 1977.

45. *The Hilltop* (yearbook), 1934, p. 245; 1935, p. 255; Pett, *AP Series,* p. 53; Interviews, Mullarky, 21 January 1977; Francis Reiske, 5 April 1977.

46. Anderson and May, *McCarthy,* p. 26; Interviews, Curran, 13 April 1977; Gwin, 13 May 1977; Harland, 5 April 1977; Korb, 24 March 1977; O'Connor, 4 May 1977; Papka, 25 April 1977; Schroeder, 25 May 1977; Gerrit Foster, 5 April 1977; Irene Gyzinski, 23 March 1977; and Rosalie (Stein) Horwitz, 4 April 1977.

47. Interviews, Curran, 13 April 1977; Gwin, 13 May 1977; Foster, 5 April 1977; Korb, 24 March 1977; Mullarky, 21 January 1977; Papka, 25 April 1977; and Schroeder, 25 May 1977.

48. Interviews, Harland, 5 April 1977; Mullarky, 21 January 1977; and Schroeder, 25 May 1977.

49. Van Susteren quoted in *Appleton Post-Crescent,* 1 May 1977.

Notes to Chapter 2: First Steps and Missteps in Public Life

1. Jack Anderson and Ronald May, *McCarthy: The Man, the Senator, the "Ism"* (Boston: The Beacon Press, 1952), p. 29; Interviews, Edward Hart, 3 February 1977; Helen Hobart, 27 April 1977; and William Remmel, 3 February 1977.

2. Barron Beshoar to Robert Schwartz, 4 October 1951, Box 4, Robert Fleming Papers, State Historical Society of Wisconsin (S.H.S.W.); *Waupaca County Post,* 15 August 1935; Anderson and May, *McCarthy,* pp. 30–31; Interviews, Remmel, 3 February 1977; Irving Hansen, 10 February 1977; and Andrew Parnell, 21 January 1977.

3. Interview, Remmel, 3 February 1977.

4. Beshoar to Schwartz, 4 October 1951, Box 4, Fleming Papers; Anderson and May, *McCarthy,* p. 30; Interviews, Louis Cattau, 1 March 1977; Hugh Gwin, 13 May 1977; Clifford Mullarky, 21 January 1977; and Remmel, 3 February 1977.

5. Interview, Henry Van Straten, 7 February 1977.

6. *Waupaca County Post,* 26 September and 26 December 1935, 16 January 1936.

7. Anderson and May, *McCarthy*, pp. 31–32; Interview, Hansen, 10 February 1977.

8. *Shawano County Journal*, 13 January 1938; *Waupaca County Post*, 5 March 1936; Anderson and May, *McCarthy*, p. 32; Interviews, Parnell, 21 January 1977; Mae (Beyer) Voy, 18 March 1977; and Francis Werner, 26 January 1977. McCarthy kept his Waupaca office open for another two months after moving to Shawano.

9. *New York Post*, 5 September 1951; Interviews, Mullarky, 21 January 1977; Parnell, 21 January 1977; and Werner, 26 January 1977.

10. *Shawano County Journal*, 26 May 1938; *Milwaukee Journal*, 10 November 1946. Almost everyone I interviewed who knew Eberlein considered him arrogant and overbearing.

11. *Waupaca County Post*, 20 February 1936; Weston A. Goodspeed, Melvin E. Bothwell, and Kenneth C. Goodspeed, *History of Outagamie County, Wisconsin* (Chicago: Goodspeed Historical Association, 1911), pp. 708, 1223; Interviews, Roman Papka, 25 April 1977; Remmel, 3 February 1977; and Stephen McCarthy, 3 March 1977.

12. Robert C. Nesbit, *Wisconsin: A History* (Madison: The University of Wisconsin Press, 1973), pp. 489, 526.

13. Interview, Charles Curran, 13 April 1977.

14. *Shawano County Journal*, 6, 8, and 12 August 1936; *The Shawano Evening Leader*, 3 August 1936.

15. *The Shawano Evening Leader*, 24 October 1936; *The Bonduel Times*, 8 October 1936; William Flarity, "Recollections of Joe McCarthy" (typescript, 1966), a copy of which was given to me by historian Robert Griffith; Interviews, Voy, 18 March 1977; Clarence Graves, 2 March 1977; and Grover Meisner, 1 March 1977.

16. *The Shawano Evening Leader*, 9 October 1936.

17. Ibid.; Interview, Voy, 18 March 1977.

18. *The Shawano Evening Leader*, 31 October 1936; *Shawano County Journal*, 22 October 1936.

19. *The Shawano Evening Leader*, 14 and 23 October 1936; *The Shawano County Journal*, 6 and 20 August 1936; *The Bonduel Times*, 5 August 1936.

20. *The Shawano Evening Leader*, 2 November 1936.

21. *Shawano County Journal*, 15 October 1936; Anderson and May, *McCarthy*, p. 36.

22. *Shawano County Journal*, 13 February 1936; *The Shawano Evening Leader*, 13 April 1939.

23. Interviews, Graves, 2 March 1977; Meisner, 1 March 1977.

24. *Shawano County Journal*, 10 February 1938.

25. Interviews, Cattau, 1 March 1977; Werner, 26 January 1977; Herman Koehler, 18 March 1977; and Helen (Ludolph) Wagner, 21 April 1977.

26. *Shawano County Journal*, 8 April 1937; Interviews, Cattau, 1 March 1977; Koehler, 18 March 1977.

27. *Shawano County Journal*, 10 February 1938.

28. Interviews, Cattau, 1 March 1977; Hart, 3 February 1977; Remmel, 3 February 1977; and Werner, 26 January 1977.

29. Interviews, Voy, 18 March 1977; Wagner, 21 April 1977; Dottie (Druckery) Anderson, 1 March 1977; Peter Frei and Lorraine Frei, 1 March 1977; and John Reed, 12 April 1977.

30. Interviews, P. Frei and L. Frei, 1 March 1977.

31. Interviews, Koehler, 18 March 1977; Meisner, 1 March 1977; Wagner, 21 April 1977; and P. Frei and L. Frei, 1 March 1977.

32. *Shawano County Journal*, 14 April 1938.

33. *Shawano County Journal*, 14 January 23 and 30 September 1937, and 13 January 1938; *The Shawano Evening Leader*, 22 October 1936.

34. *Shawano County Journal,* 10 November 1938.

35. Flarity, "Recollections of Joe McCarthy."

36. See, for example, Anderson and May, *McCarthy,* pp. 37–38.

37. Robert Fleming memorandum, "McCarthy's Early Background," Box 3, Fleming Papers; Interviews, Koehler, 18 March 1977; Parnell, 21 January 1977; Voy, 18 March 1977; and Dottie Anderson, 1 March 1977.

38. *Appleton Post-Crescent,* 20, 23, and 31 March and 1 April 1939; *The Antigo Daily Journal,* 28 March 1939.

39. Interviews, Cattau, 1 March 1977; Koehler, 18 March 1977; Mullarky, 21 January 1977; Werner, 26 January 1977; Mark Catlin, Jr., 24 February 1977; Patrick Howlett, 7 January 1977; and Gerard Van Hoof, 24 January 1977.

40. *Shawano County Journal,* 10 March 1938.

41. Interview, Voy, 18 March 1977.

42. Interview, Dottie Anderson, 1 March 1977.

43. Interviews, Koehler, 18 March 1977; Reed, 12 April 1977; Voy, 18 March 1977; Dottie Anderson, 1 March 1977; and Urban Van Susteren, 4 September 1969, 22 March 1977.

44. "Election Financial Statements," Series 209, Box 19, Papers of the Secretary of State, Wisconsin State Archives, S.H.S.W.; memorandum, "McCarthy's Early Tax Returns," Box 3, Fleming Papers; Flarity, "Recollections of Joe McCarthy." In his recollections, Flarity, a lawyer and an acquaintance of McCarthy in Shawano, stated that McCarthy borrowed $7,000 from the First National Bank of Tigerton in 1939–1940. To pay off the loan, according to Flarity, McCarthy's monthly checks as judge were assigned to the bank, which had the power of attorney to cash them. The bank took out its interest and some of the principal and gave Joe enough to live on. Flarity's recollections of the loan seem unreliable, however, because his knowledge is secondhand and because McCarthy's tax returns during these years do not indicate large interest payments to the Tigerton bank.

45. Interviews, Reed, 12 April 1977, Van Hoof, 24 January 1977; Van Straten, 7 February 1977; Van Susteren, 4 September 1969, 22 March 1977; Voy, 18 March 1977; Werner, 26 January 1977; and Dottie Anderson, 1 March 1977.

46. Anderson and May, *McCarthy,* pp. 38–39; Interview, Reed, 12 April 1977.

47. Interviews, Reed, 12 April 1977; Dottie Anderson, 1 March 1977.

48. *Appleton Post-Crescent,* 1 May 1977.

49. Interviews, Mullarky, 21 January 1977; Reed, 12 April 1977; Van Hoof, 24 January 1977; Dottie Anderson, 1 March 1977; and Stephen McCarthy, 3 March 1977.

50. *Appleton Post-Crescent,* 22 February 1939.

51. *Appleton Post-Crescent,* 1 April 1939.

52. *Appleton Post-Crescent,* 18 April 1939.

53. Richard Rovere, *Senator Joe McCarthy* (Cleveland and New York: The World Publishing Co., 1959), p. 88; Sharon Coady, "The Wisconsin Press and Joseph McCarthy: A Case Study" (Master's thesis, University of Wisconsin, 1965), p. 78. After McCarthy began to insinuate that Werner had lied about his age, Werner produced a birth certificate showing that he had been born on 24 July 1872 in Black River Falls, Wisconsin. That would make him, as he claimed, sixty-six years old in 1939. Werner's birth certificate was certified on 6 February 1939. I obtained a copy of the certificate from the Wisconsin Department of Health and Social Services, Division of Health, Madison, Wisconsin.

54. Coady, "Wisconsin Press," pp. 30–32.

55. *The Shawano Evening Leader,* 4 January 1940; Anderson and May, *McCarthy,* p. 43.

56. *The Shawano Evening Leader,* 6 January 1940; Interview, Howlett, 7 January 1977.

57. *The Shawano Evening Leader,* 6 January 1940; Joseph McCarthy to Dottie Druckery, 6 August 1942 (unprocessed), Dottie (Druckery) Anderson Papers, Dottie Anderson's home, Shawano, Wisconsin; Interview, Parnell, 21 January 1977.

58. Saul Pett, ed., *The AP McCarthy Series* (New York: Associated Press, 1954), p. 55; Anderson and May, *McCarthy,* p. 44; *Appleton Post-Crescent,* 1 May 1977; Interviews, Howlett, 7 January 1977; Parnell, 21 January 1977; and Van Hoof, 24 January 1977.

59. Pett, *AP Series,* pp. 54–55; Interviews, Howlett, 7 January 1977; Parnell, 21 January 1977; Van Hoof, 24 January 1977; Werner, 26 January 1977; and Elmer Honkamp, 10 February 1977.

60. Interviews, Howlett, 7 January 1977; Koehler, 18 March 1977; and Parnell, 21 January 1977.

61. Lately Thomas, *When Even Angels Wept: The Senator Joseph McCarthy Affair—A Story without a Hero* (New York: William Morrow & Co., 1973), p. 19; Interview, Parnell, 21 January 1977.

62. Anderson and May, *McCarthy,* p. 76; Interviews, Cattau, 1 March 1977; Koehler, 18 March 1977; Mullarky, 21 January 1977; Parnell, 21 January 1977; and Wagner, 21 April 1977.

63. Interviews, Harland, 5 April 1977; Howlett, 7 January 1977; Mullarky, 21 January 1977; Van Susteren, 4 September 1969, 22 March 1977; Werner, 26 January 1977; and Mary Ellen Ducklow, 20 January 1977.

64. Anderson and May, *McCarthy,* pp. 44–45; *Appleton Post-Crescent,* 1 May 1977; Interviews, Howlett, 7 January 1977; Arlo McKinnon, 23 March 1977; Parnell, 21 January 1977; Van Susteren, 4 September 1969, 22 March 1977; and John Wyngaard, 30 December 1969.

65. *Appleton Post-Crescent,* 12 April 1940, 14 July 1941; "Amended Complaint," 3 December 1940, State of Wisconsin, *Department of Agriculture* v. *Quaker Dairy Company,* Series 733, Box 5, General Legal Files, Papers of the Wisconsin Department of Agriculture, Archives, S.H.S.W. (hereafter cited as Quaker Dairy Case, Department of Agriculture Papers). The original complaint was filed on 4 November 1940.

66. Joseph McCarthy to Gilbert Lappley, 9 April 1941; Mark Catlin to Ralph Ammon, "Notice of Appearance," 9 April 1941; Isadore Alk to Joseph McCarthy, 10 April 1941; Mark Catlin, "Notice of Motion," 16 April 1941, all in Quaker Dairy Case, Department of Agriculture Papers.

67. Joseph McCarthy to Gilbert Lappley and Mark Catlin, 13 May 1941; Edgar Zobel to Verlyn Sears, 20 May 1941; Joseph McCarthy, "Temporary Injunction and Restraining Order," [20] May 1941; Ben Cherkasky, "Affidavit," 3 June 1941; Joseph McCarthy, "Order to Show Cause," 4 June 1941; all in Quaker Dairy Case, Department of Agriculture Papers; Interview, Howlett, 7 January 1977.

68. Gilbert Lappley, "Petition for Writ of Mandamus," 10 June 1941, *State of Wisconsin* ex rel. *Department of Agriculture, Petitioner* v. *Joseph McCarthy, Respondent,* Series 733, Box 5, General Legal Files, Papers of the Wisconsin Department of Agriculture, Archives, S.H.S.W.; Gilbert Lappley, "Brief," n.d., *Department of Agriculture* v. *McCarthy,* Department of Agriculture Papers; Oliver Pilat and William Shannon, *New York Post,* 6 September 1951; Interview, Howlett, 7 January 1977.

69. Gilbert Lappley, "Petition for Writ of Mandamus," 10 June 1941, *Department of Agriculture* v. *McCarthy,* Department of Agriculture Papers; Gilbert Lappley, "Brief," n.d., *Department of Agriculture* v. *McCarthy,* Department of Agriculture Papers.

70. Ibid.; "Writ of Certiorari," n.d., *State of Wisconsin* ex rel. *Department of Agriculture* v. *Quaker Dairy Company* and *State of Wisconsin* ex rel. *Department of Agriculture*

v. *John Richter and Mrs. John Richter*, Department of Agriculture Papers. (The Richters were involved in a related case that had no bearing on the main Quaker Dairy case or the entire controversy.) Joseph McCarthy, "Sworn Affidavit," 13 June 1941, *Department of Agriculture* v. *McCarthy*; Joseph McCarthy's counsel, "Brief" [14 June 1941], *Department of Agriculture* v. *McCarthy*, Department of Agriculture Papers.

71. Judge Marvin Rosenberry's opinion (18 January 1941), *Department of Agriculture* v. *McCarthy*, Department of Agriculture Papers.

72. Joseph McCarthy, "Order," 18 June 1941, *State of Wisconsin* ex rel. *Department of Agriculture and Markets, Plaintiff* v. *Ben Cherkasky and the Quaker Dairy Company, Defendants*, Quaker Dairy Case, Department of Agriculture Papers.

73. Gilbert Lappley to William Kirsch, 15 October 1941, Quaker Dairy Case, Department of Agriculture Papers; *The Capital Times*, 20 June 1941; *Milwaukee Sentinel*, 19 June 1941; *Wisconsin State Journal*, 19 June 1941; *Appleton Post-Crescent*, 19 June 1941; *Kenosha News*, 19 June 1941.

74. Gilbert Lappley to William Kirsch, 15 October 1941, Quaker Dairy Case, Department of Agriculture Papers. This yes-or-no technique was used to great effect by McCarthy as chairman of the U.S. Senate Permanent Subcommittee on Investigations.

75. Andrew Parnell to Department of Agriculture, 7 July 1941; Andrew Parnell, "Brief of Defendant," n.d.; Gilbert Lappley, "Department's Brief" [3 July 1941]; and Gilbert Lappley and R. M. Orchard, "Reply Brief," n.d., all Quaker Dairy Case, Department of Agriculture Papers.

76. Joseph McCarthy, "Decision," 8 July 1941, Quaker Dairy Case, Department of Agriculture Papers.

77. Gilbert Lappley to William Kirsch, 15 October 1941, Quaker Dairy Case, Department of Agriculture Papers. On 2 July 1941, the Wisconsin Department of Agriculture held a hearing in the Appleton courthouse at which testimony was given against continuation of state control of milk prices. The hearing had no direct connection with the Quaker Dairy case. Nevertheless, McCarthy may have attended that hearing and used some of the testimony in his decision on 8 July 1941. *Kaukauna Times*, 16 July 1941; *Appleton Post-Crescent*, 12 July 1941.

78. *Appleton Post-Crescent*, 9, 10, and 14 July 1941; *Eau Claire Leader*, 20 July 1941.

79. Gilbert Lappley to William Kirsch, 15 October 1941, Quaker Dairy Case, Department of Agriculture Papers; *Appleton Post-Crescent*, 12 July 1941.

80. Gilbert Lappley to William Kirsch, 15 October 1941, Quaker Dairy Case, Department of Agriculture Papers.

81. Interview, Catlin, 24 February 1977.

82. Anderson and May, *McCarthy*, p. 50; Gilbert Lappley to William Kirsch, 15 October 1941, Quaker Dairy Case, Department of Agriculture Papers.

## Notes to Chapter 3: The Birth of "Tail-Gunner Joe"

1. Interview, John Wyngaard, 30 December 1969.

2. *Appleton Post-Crescent*, 5 November 1938, 30 March 1939; Interview, Lillian Mackesy, 29 March 1977.

3. Saul Pett, ed., *The AP McCarthy Series* (New York: Associated Press, 1954), p. 55; Lately Thomas, *When Even Angels Wept: The Senator Joseph McCarthy Affair—A Story without a Hero* (New York: William Morrow & Co., 1973), p. 20; Interview, Urban Van Susteren, 4 September 1969, 22 March 1977.

4. *Milwaukee Journal*, 4 June 1942. Most accounts have said that McCarthy went to Milwaukee on 4 June, but the *Journal* reported his visit there on 3 and 4 June.

5. *Appleton Post-Crescent*, 4 and 6 June 1942; Jack Anderson and Ronald May, *McCarthy: The Man, the Senator, the "Ism"* (Boston: The Beacon Press, 1952), p. 56; Interviews, Margaret Hagene, 1 June 1977; Andrew Parnell, 21 January 1977. Judge Murphy was probably not too angry at McCarthy; in 1944 he acted as a major adviser in McCarthy's campaign.

6. Joseph McCarthy to Dottie Druckery, 16 September 1942, Dottie (Druckery) Anderson Papers, Dottie Anderson's home, Shawano, Wisconsin. Joseph McCarthy to Albert O'Melia, 21 May 1943, Box 1, Albert O'Melia Papers, State Historical Society of Wisconsin (S.H.S.W.); Anderson and May, *McCarthy*, p. 58.

7. Anderson and May, *McCarthy*, pp. 59, 63; Thomas, *When Even Angels Wept*, p. 25; *Milwaukee Journal*, 8 June 1952; Adm. Chester Nimitz, "Citation for Capt. McCarthy," 1 September 1944, Box 4, Robert Fleming Papers, S.H.S.W.; Thomas C. Reeves, "Tail Gunner Joe: Joseph R. McCarthy and the Marine Corps," *Wisconsin Magazine of History* 62 (Summer 1979): 303, 306.

8. E. E. Munn to the Commandant, U.S. Marine Corps, 11 February 1944, Box 4, Fleming Papers; Anderson and May, *McCarthy*, pp. 63–64; Reeves, "Tail Gunner Joe," pp. 304–5.

9. U.P. dispatch, 25 July (probably 1952), reported the recollection of Capt. Glenn Cooper, Box 4, Fleming Papers; Anderson and May, *McCarthy*, pp. 59–60; Thomas, *When Even Angels Wept*, p. 24; Reeves, "Tail Gunner Joe," pp. 307–9.

10. *Milwaukee Journal*, 8 June 1952; Reeves, "Tail Gunner Joe," p. 304.

11. Ibid.; Pett, *AP Series*, pp. 56–57; Michael O'Brien, "Robert Fleming, Senator McCarthy and the Myth of the Marine Hero," *Journalism Quarterly* 50:1 (Spring 1973): 48–53; Reeves, "Tail Gunner Joe," pp. 305–6.

12. *New York Post*, 5 September 1951; Anderson and May, *McCarthy*, pp. 65–66; Interview, Louis Cattau, 1 March 1977.

13. *Appleton Post-Crescent*, 9 July 1943; clipping, probably the *Milwaukee Sentinel* (Autumn 1943), in the Stephen McCarthy scrapbook (unprocessed), Stephen McCarthy Papers, Stephen McCarthy's home, Appleton, Wisconsin.

14. *Appleton Post-Crescent*, 15 November 1943.

15. *Appleton Post-Crescent*, 20 January 1944; *Milwaukee Journal*, 8 June 1952; Thomas, *When Even Angels Wept*, p. 25.

16. *Wisconsin State Journal*, 10 April 1944; Anderson and May, *McCarthy*, p. 61.

17. Interviews, Hagene, 1 June 1977; Arlo McKinnon, 23 March 1977; and Henry Van Straten, 7 February 1977.

18. *New York Post*, 5 September 1951; Anderson and May, *McCarthy*, pp. 251–52; Interviews, Hagene, 1 June 1977; Van Susteren, 4 September 1969, 22 March 1977.

19. *The Capital Times*, 21 and 25 April 1944; *Appleton Post-Crescent*, 21 March and 28 April 1944; *Milwaukee Journal*, 25 April 1944.

20. *Appleton Post-Crescent*, 8 June 1944.

21. *Appleton Post-Crescent*, 3 and 4 May 1944; *Milwaukee Journal*, 4 May 1944.

22. *Milwaukee Journal*, 4 August 1944; *Wisconsin State Journal*, 21 July 1944.

23. *Milwaukee Journal*, 14 August 1944; *Wisconsin State Journal*, 3 and 13 August 1944; Sharon Coady, "The Wisconsin Press and Joseph McCarthy: A Case Study" (Master's thesis, University of Wisconsin, 1965), p. 44.

24. *The Shawano Evening Leader*, 26 July 1944; *Wisconsin State Journal*, 3 August 1944.

25. Coady, "Wisconsin Press," pp. 39–42; *The Capital Times*, 13 August 1944.

26. *Appleton Post-Crescent*, 2 May and 27 July 1944; among the newspapers that endorsed McCarthy were the *Appleton Post-Crescent*, *Green Bay Press-Gazette*, *Shawano Evening Leader*, and, implicitly, the *Wisconsin State Journal*.

27. Coady, "Wisconsin Press," pp. 32–45.

28. *Appleton Post-Crescent*, 11 August 1944; *Wisconsin State Journal*, 11 August 1944; *Milwaukee Journal*, 13 August 1944.

29. *Appleton Post-Crescent,* 18 August 1944; Harold Meyer to Alexander Wiley, 27 August 1944, Box 17 (not completely processed), Alexander Wiley Papers, S.H.S.W.

30. Arthur Tiller to Alexander Wiley, 6 September 1944, Box 17, Wiley Papers; Elmer Honkamp to Alexander Wiley, 15 September 1944, Box 17, Wiley Papers; Interview, Mark Catlin, Jr., 24 February 1977.

## Notes to Chapter 4: The 1946 Election

1. Charles Backstrom, "The Progressive Party of Wisconsin, 1934–1946" (Ph.D. diss., University of Wisconsin, 1956), pp. 462, 529; Richard Rovere, *Senator Joe McCarthy* (Cleveland and New York: The World Publishing Co., 1959), p. 99; John Miller, "Governor Philip F. La Follette, the Wisconsin Progressives, and the New Deal, 1930–1939" (Ph.D. diss., University of Wisconsin, 1973), pp. 10–11; Isabel La Follette to Morris Rubin, 12 October 1945, Series 3, Box 161, Philip La Follette Papers, State Historical Society of Wisconsin (S.H.S.W.); Interview, Gordon Sinykin, 11 November 1970.

2. Patrick J. Maney, " 'Young Bob' La Follette: A Biography of Robert M. La Follette, Jr. (1895–1953)" (Ph.D. diss., University of Maryland, 1976), pp. 342–43. Maney did not discuss La Follette's alleged drinking problem. For more on this, consult Box 69, William T. Evjue Papers, S.H.S.W.; Interview; Donald Anderson, 15 February 1977.

3. Maney, "Robert M. La Follette, Jr.," pp. 350–51; Glenn Roberts to Robert La Follette, 12 May 1945, Series A, Box 49, The La Follette Family Collection (L.F.C.), Library of Congress.

4. Robert Nesbit, *Wisconsin: A History* (Madison: The University of Wisconsin Press, 1973), pp. 489–90.

5. Miller, "Governor Philip F. La Follette," pp. 4–5, 223, 377.

6. Ibid., pp. 347, 349; Nesbit, *Wisconsin,* pp. 493, 526–27; Carolyn Mattern, "The Man on the Dark Horse: The Presidential Campaigns for General Douglas MacArthur: 1944 and 1948" (Ph.D. diss., University of Wisconsin, 1976), p. 89.

7. Miller, "Governor Philip F. La Follette," pp. 367, 377-78, 383.

8. Ibid., p. 411; Backstrom, "Progressive Party," p. 466.

9. Miller, "Governor Philip F. La Follette," p. 411; David Oshinsky, *Senator Joseph McCarthy and the American Labor Movement* (Columbia: University of Missouri Press, 1976), p. 11; Backstrom, "Progressive Party," pp. 504–23, 530; *Green Bay Press-Gazette,* 18 January 1946.

10. Francis Sorauf, "The Voluntary Committee System in Wisconsin: An Effort to Achieve Party Responsibility" (Ph.D. diss., University of Wisconsin, 1953), pp. 136–37; Alfred Bowman (pseudonym), "The Man behind McCarthy," *The Nation* (20 March 1954): 230–37; this description of Coleman is also based on about fifteen personal interviews with people who knew him.

11. Backstrom, "Progressive Party," pp. 201–2.

12. Glenn Roberts to Robert La Follette, 24 May 1945, Series A, Box 49, L.F.C.; *Milwaukee Journal,* 17 March 1946; *Wisconsin State Journal,* 30 January 1946.

13. Roger Johnson, *Robert M. La Follette, Jr. and the Decline of the Progressive Party in Wisconsin* (Madison: The State Historical Society of Wisconsin, 1964), p. 119.

14. Isabel La Follette's Political Diary, 16 March 1952, Series 3, Box 161, Philip La Follette Papers; Interview, Sinykin, 11 November 1970.

15. Johnson, *La Follette, Jr.,* p. 112; *Green Bay Press-Gazette,* 12 and 18 March 1946.

16. *Milwaukee Journal,* 24 March 1946.

17. Thomas Amlie to Howard McMurray, 10 October 1947, Box 51, Thomas R.

Amlie Papers, S.H.S.W.; Daniel Hoan to Thomas Stodola, 23 January 1946, Box 4, File 15, Daniel Hoan Papers, Milwaukee County Historical Society; *Racine Labor*, 29 March 1946.

18. *Kenosha Labor*, 14 March 1946; *Union Labor News* (Madison), April 1946; Gerald Flynn to Daniel Hoan, 6 March 1946, Box 4, File 15, Hoan Papers.

19. *Milwaukee Journal*, 27 April 1946.

20. Johnson, *La Follette, Jr.*, pp. 125–26; *The Capital Times*, 4 April 1946; Interview, Urban Van Susteren, 4 September 1969, 22 March 1977.

21. Interview, Alvin O'Konski, 4 March 1977.

22. Sorauf, "Voluntary Committee System," p. 143; *Milwaukee Journal*, 27 April 1946; Interviews, Loyal Eddy, 11 March 1977; Lloyd Tegge, 24 March 1977.

23. *Milwaukee Journal*, 29 April 1946; Interview, Van Susteren, 4 September 1969, 22 March 1977.

24. Thomas Coleman memorandum, "Conference with Governor Goodland," 19 April 1946, Box 4, Thomas Coleman Papers, S.H.S.W.; Interviews, Eddy, 11 March 1977; John Wyngaard, 30 December 1969.

25. A. J. Fiore to Alexander Wiley, 7 May 1946, Box 22 (not completely processed), Alexander Wiley Papers, S.H.S.W.

26. Interviews, Eddy, 11 March 1977; Walter Kohler, Jr., 5 September 1969. Six years later, Governor Kohler again considered running against McCarthy. At that time, a story circulated that Kohler disliked McCarthy because of an unpleasant encounter they had had before the 1946 RVC convention. In order to discourage Kohler from challenging him for the endorsement, McCarthy had allegedly threatened to publicize Kohler's divorce, which would ruin his budding political career by alienating Catholic voters. Because of this affront, so the story went, Kohler's bitterness intensified, almost leading him to challenge McCarthy's renomination in 1952.

Actually, when Kohler and McCarthy met, Kohler revealed nothing about his plans, but McCarthy left the meeting confident that he would not enter the race. They did discuss the divorce issue, but McCarthy made no threat of any kind and Kohler held no resentment; Interviews, Kohler, 5 September 1969; Van Susteren, 4 September 1969, 22 March 1977.

The story originated with reporter Miles McMillin, *The Capital Times*, 25 September 1951. In an interview, McMillin told me that McCarthy himself told him at the 1946 RVC convention that Kohler would not become a candidate because he had threatened to smear him on the divorce issue. McMillin admitted, however, that McCarthy could have made up the story; Interview, Miles McMillin, 2 September 1969.

27. Interviews, Eddy, 11 March 1977; Tegge, 24 March 1977; and Van Susteren, 4 September 1969, 22 March 1977.

28. Johnson, *La Follette, Jr.*, p. 127; Coleman memorandum, "Conference with Governor Goodland," 19 April 1946, Box 4, Coleman Papers. On Goodland's senility I relied also on interviews with Mark Catlin, Jr. (24 February 1977) and Donald Anderson (15 February 1977).

29. *Green Bay Press-Gazette*, 6 and 7 May 1946; *The Capital Times*, 6, 7, and 16 May 1946.

30. *The Capital Times*, 20 June 1946; see also John Steinke, "The Rise of McCarthyism" (Master's thesis, University of Wisconsin, 1960), p. 77. For examples of the optimism pervading the La Follette campaign, see Herbert Mount to Herman Ekern, 26 July 1946, Box 77, Herman Ekern Papers, S.H.S.W.; Morris Rubin to Robert La Follette, 26 May 1945, Series C, Box 23, L.F.C.; Robert La Follette to Thurman Arnold, 19 July 1946, Series C, Box 533, L.F.C.

31. *Green Bay Press-Gazette*, 29 May 1946; *Wisconsin State Journal*, 23 June 1946; "Special La Follette Edition," *Labor*, 27 July 1946; Sharon Coady, "The Wisconsin

Press and Joseph McCarthy: A Case Study" (Master's thesis, University of Wisconsin, 1965), pp. 50–51.

32. "Special La Follette Edition," *Labor*, 27 July 1946.

33. *Wisconsin State Journal*, 20 and 28 July and 1 August 1946; *Green Bay Press-Gazette*, 7 August 1946; Coady, "Wisconsin Press," pp. 46–47.

34. Coady, "Wisconsin Press," pp. 47–48; *Wisconsin State Journal*, 19 July 1946; *Milwaukee Journal*, 26 July and 12 August 1946.

35. *The Capital Times*, 23 December 1945, 6 May and 6 August 1946; *Milwaukee Journal*, 9 May 1946; *Green Bay Press-Gazette*, 22 July 1946.

36. *The Beloit Daily News*, 26 July 1946; *The Capital Times*, 30 June 1946; Johnson, *La Follette, Jr.*, p. 132; *Milwaukee Journal*, 13 June 1946; Coady, "Wisconsin Press," p. 49.

37. Maney, "Robert M. La Follette, Jr.," pp. 377–78.

38. *Wisconsin State Journal*, 2 June and 23 and 28 July 1946; Jack Anderson and Ronald May, *McCarthy: The Man, the Senator, the "Ism"* (Boston: The Beacon Press, 1952), pp. 98–99.

39. Anderson and May, *McCarthy*, pp. 98–99; Coady, "Wisconsin Press," p. 49; Maney, "Robert M. La Follette, Jr.," p. 378.

40. Alexander Wiley to Harold Wilde, 25 February 1946, Personal Correspondence with Harold Wilde, Wiley Papers.

41. Thomas Amlie to Howard McMurray, 10 October 1947, Box 51, Amlie Papers.

42. *Milwaukee Journal*, 7 July 1946; Thomas Coleman memorandum, "Report to the Finance Committee," 23 July 1946, Box 9, Coleman Papers.

43. *Green Bay Press-Gazette*, 9 August 1946; *Milwaukee Sentinel*, 26 July 1946; *Milwaukee Journal*, 26 July and 9 August 1946; *Racine Labor*, 29 March 1946; *Appleton Post-Crescent*, 5 August 1946; *The Capital Times*, 15 April 1946; Johnson, *La Follette, Jr.*, p. 135.

44. *Green Bay Press-Gazette*, 15 April 1946.

45. Oshinsky, *McCarthy and Labor*, pp. 1–2; Gerald Flynn to Daniel Hoan, 6 March 1946, Box 4, File 15, Hoan Papers; *Racine Labor*, 26 April 1946; *Kenosha Labor*, 14 March 1946.

46. Oshinsky, *McCarthy and Labor*, pp. 16, 33.

47. Ibid., p. 42; *Racine Labor*, 7 June 1946. For details on Taft's endorsement of La Follette, consult Lester Bradshaw to Robert Taft, 6 April 1946; Robert Taft to Lester Bradshaw, 11 April 1946; and Robert Taft to Robert La Follette, 29 June 1946, all Series C, Box 533, L.F.C.

48. For a fascinating view of Schoeman's position and, in general, of labor's relations with La Follette, consult the memorandum entitled "Senator Robert M. La Follette's Political Situation in Wisconsin," Joe Ozanic to William Green, 25 May 1946, Series C, Box 432, L.F.C. See also the *Milwaukee Journal*, 5 June and 15 August 1946; Johnson, *La Follette, Jr.*, p. 143.

49. Oshinsky, *McCarthy and Labor*, pp. 18–19; *Racine Labor*, 2 and 9 August 1946; *Kenosha Labor*, 8 August 1946.

50. *The Wisconsin CIO News*, 13 May 1944, 11 and 18 June 1945, and 6 April, 14 June, and 19 July 1946; *Milwaukee Journal*, 10 April 1946.

51. Johnson, *La Follette, Jr.*, p. 145.

52. Maney, "Robert M. La Follette, Jr.," pp. 382–84.

53. Johnson, *La Follette, Jr.*, p. 155; Coleman memorandum, "Conference with Governor Goodland," 19 April 1946, Box 4, Coleman Papers.

54. See the (unprocessed) John (Jack) Kyle Papers, S.H.S.W. Kyle was chairman of the Progressive Republican Association headquartered in Madison; *Milwaukee Journal*, 16 June and 9 August 1946; Johnson, *La Follette, Jr.*, pp. 155–56; Interview, Tegge, 24 March 1977.

55. Interviews, Patrick Howlett, 7 January 1977; Ray Kiermas, 7 April 1977.

56. Interviews, Llewellyn Morack, 11 March 1977; Harold Townsend, 10 March 1977.

57. "The Newspapers Say," Library Collection, S.H.S.W.; Interview, Van Susteren, 4 September 1969, 22 March 1977.

58. Interviews, Kiermas, 7 April 1977; Van Susteren, 4 September 1969, 22 March 1977.

59. *Green Bay Press-Gazette*, 6 September 1946.

60. *Milwaukee Journal*, 26 July 1946; Saul Pett, ed., *The AP McCarthy Series* (New York: Associated Press, 1954), p. 58.

61. This information came from interviews with about ten people who knew McCarthy.

62. Jack Alexander, "The Senate's Remarkable Upstart," *The Saturday Evening Post* (9 August 1947): 57.

63. *The Capital Times*, 24 August 1946; Steinke, "Rise of McCarthyism," p. 89; Interview, Eddy, 11 March 1977.

64. *The Capital Times*, 11 April 1946; *Appleton Post-Crescent*, 9 August 1946; *Green Bay Press-Gazette*, 8 August 1946.

65. *Wisconsin State Journal*, 6 May 1946; *Waukesha Daily Freeman*, 10 August 1946; *The LaCrosse Tribune*, 9 August 1946; *The Beloit Daily News*, 10 August 1946; *The Janesville Gazette*, 10 August 1946; *Marinette Eagle-Star*, 10 August 1946.

66. Newspapers that were neutral in the Republican senatorial primary included *Milwaukee Sentinel, Milwaukee Journal, The Eau Claire Leader, Fond du Lac Commonwealth Reporter, Wausau Daily Record-Herald, The Sheboygan Press, The Evening Telegram* (Superior), *Racine Journal-Times*, and the *Oshkosh Daily Northwestern*.

67. Coady, "Wisconsin Press," pp. 45, 61.

68. Johnson, *La Follette, Jr.*, p. 136; Maney, "Robert M. La Follette, Jr.," pp. 387–88.

69. Karl Ernest Meyer, "The Politics of Loyalty from La Follette to McCarthy in Wisconsin, 1918–1952" (Ph.D. diss., Princeton University, 1956), p. 137; Oshinsky, *McCarthy and Labor*, pp. 43, 44, and 47.

70. Anderson and May, *McCarthy*, p. 104; William T. Evjue book review in the *Saturday Review* (25 October 1952): 17; *The Wisconsin CIO News*, 26 November 1954; typescript of a tape-recorded interview of Miles McMillin by Robert Griffith on 25 July and 1 August 1967, for the Cornell University Oral History Program, pp. 15–16; "McCarthy: A Documented Record," special edition of *The Progressive* (April 1954): 64, 75; *A.F. of L. Milwaukee Labor Press*, 24 June 1954.

71. *Milwaukee Journal*, 13 September 1946.

72. At least two McCarthy critics finally realized that no such statement could be documented; Robert Fleming to Susanna Davis, 7 December 1953, Series 7, Box 81, Folder 3, ADA Papers, S.H.S.W.; Miles McMillin to Susanna Davis (approximately December 1953), Series 7, Box 81, Folder 3, ADA Papers.

73. Roy Reuther to Lucille Lang, 24 July 1953, File 4, Drawer 1 (unprocessed), National Committee for an Effective Congress Papers, Maurice Rosenblatt's home, Washington, D.C. Reuther was the political action coordinator of the UAW–CIO; *Green Bay Press-Gazette*, 23 March 1954.

74. Interview, Van Susteren, 4 September 1969, 22 March 1977.

75. Gerald Clifford to Daniel Hoan, 7 November 1946, Box 4, File 15, Hoan Papers; Sorauf, "Voluntary Committee System," p. 39; also consult Richard Haney, "A History of the Democratic Party of Wisconsin since World War Two" (Ph.D. diss., University of Wisconsin, 1970).

76. The description of McMurray was based on comments made to me in interviews with people who knew him.

77. *Kenosha Labor*, 20 September 1946; *Milwaukee Journal*, 10 October 1946; *The Capital Times*, 4 and 29 September 1946.

78. *The Capital Times*, 29 October and 3 November 1946.

79. *The Capital Times*, 16 September 1946; *Green Bay Press-Gazette*, 17 September 1946; *The LaCrosse Tribune*, 3 November 1946. In McCarthy's defense, there apparently was no basis to McMurray's allegations during the campaign that McCarthy drew his judicial salary without returning services. In 1948–1949, the Wisconsin Board of Bar Commissioners investigated whether McCarthy should be disbarred for running for political office while a judge. Harlan Rodgers, counsel for the bar commissioners, checked the minute book of the clerk of the court of Outagamie County and found that McCarthy had consistently made appearances in court from June through November 1946; Harlan Rodgers to Members of the Wisconsin Board of Bar Commissioners, 11 November 1948, Microfilm Reel 11, Edward Dempsey Papers, S.H.S.W.

80. *The Capital Times*, 26 September 1946; Interview, McMillin, 2 September 1969.

81. *The Capital Times*, 26 September and 11 October 1946; memorandum by Robert Fleming, "McCarthy as a Judge," 17 September 1951, Box 3, Fleming Papers; Interview, Arlo McKinnon, 23 March 1977.

82. *The Capital Times*, 11 October 1946; *Milwaukee Journal*, 28 September 1946.

83. *Green Bay Press-Gazette*, 7 and 17 October 1946; *Waukesha Daily Freeman*, 6 November 1946.

84. *The Capital Times*, 24 October 1946.

85. *Green Bay Press-Gazette*, 7 November 1946.

86. Conservative newspapers assisted McCarthy's candidacy with their biased and inadequate handling of campaign news. While much information was printed on McCarthy's views and background, readers were not given sufficient information on McMurray to judge him. In the *Wisconsin State Journal*, for example, only two stories on McMurray were longer than five inches, while several stories on McCarthy reached forty inches. When McMurray was accused of pro-Communist sympathies, many newspapers printed the charges against him but ignored his rebuttals. Most voters could not comprehend McMurray's references to "quick divorces" because the issue had been discussed in only four newspapers. Only *The Capital Times* published the significant account of McCarthy's censure by the state supreme court in 1941. Few publications reported the other disclosures by the liberal Madison daily. As in the primary, no newspaper sought to investigate the exaggerated stories of McCarthy's war record.

87. *Wisconsin State Journal*, 27 October 1946; see also Steinke, "Rise of McCarthyism," pp. 82–84; Coady, "Wisconsin Press," p. 66. For McMurray's appeal to former Progressives, see the advertisement in the *Appleton Post-Crescent*, 25 October 1946.

88. *Milwaukee Journal*, 13 September and 5 October 1946; Gerald Clifford to Daniel Hoan, 7 November 1946, Box 4, File 15, Hoan Papers.

89. As examples, see *Green Bay Press-Gazette*, 6 September and 9, 22, and 24 October 1946; *Milwaukee Sentinel*, 2 November 1946. For McMurray's repudiation of communism, see *Milwaukee Journal*, 5 October 1946.

90. *Appleton Post-Crescent*, 31 October 1946; *Milwaukee Journal*, 24 October 1946; *The Evening Telegram* (Superior), 4 November 1946.

91. *Milwaukee Journal*, 17 October 1946; *The Capital Times*, 25 October 1946; *The Beloit Daily News*, 30 October 1946; Anderson and May, *McCarthy*, pp. 106–10; Steinke, "The Rise of McCarthyism," p. 214. To prove his preoccupation with and emphasis on the Communist issue in the 1946 election, one secondary account cited the campaign advertisement "Joe placed" in the *Wausau Daily Record-Herald*. The ad charged that, while many Democratic candidates were suspected of Communist sympathies, McCarthy was a "100 percent American in thought and deed." Actually, the advertisement had not been inserted by McCarthy himself, but by the

Marshfield McCarthy Club and was the only such ad to appear in a state newspaper. Moreover, the five previous ads placed in the same newspaper by the same organization discussed McCarthy's background, the danger of bureaucracy (twice), OPA, and foreign policy; Anderson and May, *McCarthy*, p. 110; *Wausau Daily Record-Herald*, 25, 26, 29, 30, and 31 October and 1 November 1946.

92. Interview, Van Susteren, 4 September 1969, 22 March 1977.

93. *Wisconsin State Journal*, 18 July and 26 October, 1946; *Milwaukee Journal*, 8 August 1946; *Appleton Post-Crescent*, 17 October 1946; *Green Bay Press-Gazette*, 17 October 1946.

94. *Wisconsin State Journal*, 18 July 1946.

95. *Milwaukee Journal*, 7 July 1946; *Green Bay Press-Gazette*, 17 October 1946.

96. Coady, "Wisconsin Press," p. 66; *Green Bay Press-Gazette*, 31 October 1946.

97. See, for example, *Wisconsin State Journal*, 16 and 17 July 1946; *Green Bay Press-Gazette*, 22 August 1946; *Appleton Post-Crescent*, 16 August 1946; *New York Times*, 15 August 1946.

98. *Appleton Post-Crescent*, 16 August 1946.

99. "The Newspapers Say," Library Collection, S.H.S.W.; *Milwaukee Journal*, 6 November 1946.

100. *The Capital Times*, 29 September 1946.

101. *Wisconsin State Journal*, 6 May 1946; *Green Bay Press-Gazette*, 15 August 1946.

102. *Janesville Gazette*, 30 October 1946; *The Rhinelander News* quoted in "The Newspapers Say," Library Collection, S.H.S.W.; *The Shawano Evening Leader* quoted in "The Newspapers Say"; *Green Bay Press-Gazette*, 16 October 1946; *Wisconsin State Journal*, 23 October 1946; *Appleton Post-Crescent*, 1 November 1946.

103. *Milwaukee Sentinel* quoted in "The Newspapers Say," Library Collection, S.H.S.W.; *Wisconsin State Journal*, 23 July and 3 October 1946.

104. *Milwaukee Journal*, 10 November 1946.

105. Robert Griffith, *The Politics of Fear: Joseph R. McCarthy and the Senate* (Lexington: The University Press of Kentucky, 1970), p. 12; Louis H. Bean, *Influences in the 1954 Mid-Term Elections* (Washington, D.C.: Public Affairs Institute, 1954), pp. 10–13.

## Notes to Chapter 5: Decline and Comeback: 1947–1949

1. *Wisconsin State Journal*, 5 January 1947.

2. Richard Rovere, *Senator Joe McCarthy* (Cleveland and New York: The World Publishing Co., 1959), pp. 108–9; *Milwaukee Journal*, 10 November 1946; Robert Griffith, *The Politics of Fear* (Lexington: The University Press of Kentucky, 1970), pp. 12–13; David Oshinsky, *Senator Joseph McCarthy and the American Labor Movement* (Columbia: University of Missouri Press, 1976), p. 82.

3. Griffith, *Politics of Fear*, pp. 13, 17.

4. *Wisconsin State Journal*, 28 January, 22 March, and 7 November 1947; *Milwaukee Journal*, 13 September 1947.

5. *Green Bay Press-Gazette*, 7 August 1947.

6. *Milwaukee Journal*, 7 September 1947; *The Capital Times*, 25 May 1947.

7. Carolyn Mattern, "The Man on the Dark Horse: The Presidential Campaigns for General Douglas MacArthur: 1944 and 1948" (Ph.D. diss., University of Wisconsin, 1976), p. 192.

8. Ibid., p. 219.

9. Joseph McCarthy to (his constituents), 31 March 1948, File 4, Drawer 2 (unprocessed), National Committee for an Effective Congress Papers, Maurice Rosenblatt's home, Washington, D.C.; *Milwaukee Journal*, 1 April 1948.

10. William J. Campbell to Henry Ringling, 15 April 1948, Box 1, William J. Campbell Papers, State Historical Society of Wisconsin (S.H.S.W.); George Gilkey to Joseph McCarthy, 3 April 1948, Box 1, Campbell Papers; Interview, Loyal Eddy, 11 March 1977.

11. *The Capital Times*, 9 May 1948; Interviews, Eddy, 11 March 1977; Wilbur Renk, 3 September 1969, 24 May 1977.

12. William J. Campbell to Courtney Whitney, 29 June 1948, Box 1, Campbell Papers; Campbell to Thomas Dewey, 22 July 1948, Box 1, Campbell Papers.

13. *Wisconsin Farmers Union News*, 12 December 1949.

14. Milton Campbell to Walter Rose, 16 April 1946, Box 46, American Legion Papers, Department of Wisconsin, S.H.S.W.; Rose to Campbell, 21 April 1947, Box 46, Legion Papers. Campbell was the director of the Division of National Defense of the American Legion; Walter Rose to Milton Campbell, 28 April 1947, Box 46, Legion Papers; *The Badger Legionnaire*, May 1947.

15. Bradley Taylor to William Sayer, 1 February 1950, Box 4, Bradley Taylor Papers, S.H.S.W. Taylor was an influential leader in the Wisconsin American Legion.

16. *Milwaukee Journal*, 12 February and 8 August 1948.

17. *Milwaukee Journal*, 3 September 1947, 12 June 1948; *Wisconsin State Journal*, 27 August 1947; *The Capital Times*, 15 September 1947, 13 February 1948.

18. *The Capital Times*, 20 April and 20 July 1947; Rovere, *Joe McCarthy*, pp. 106–7.

19. *Milwaukee Journal*, 13 February 1947; *The Capital Times*, 13 February 1947. Initial news stories reported McCarthy's profits as $30,000.

20. *The Capital Times*, 14 February and 31 July 1947.

21. *Wisconsin State Journal*, 14 February 1947.

22. *Waukesha Daily Freeman*, 21 February 1947.

23. *Milwaukee Journal*, 25 May 1947.

24. Ibid.

25. *The Capital Times*, 2 June 1947, 17 September 1949.

26. Typescript of a tape-recorded interview of Miles McMillin by Robert Griffith on 25 July and 1 August 1967 for the Cornell University Oral History Program, pp. 20–21. McMillin lent me a copy of the typescript.

27. Miles McMillin to Arthur McLeod, 7 July 1948, Microfilm Reel 11, Dempsey Papers, S.H.S.W. McLeod was secretary and Dempsey was president of the Wisconsin Board of Bar Commissioners.

28. McMillin interview by Griffith, 25 July and 1 August 1967, p. 24.

29. Joseph McCarthy to Arthur McLeod, 27 July 1948, Microfilm Reel 11, Dempsey Papers; Richard Reinholdt to Edward Dempsey, 2 August 1948, Microfilm Reel 11, Dempsey Papers.

30. Richard Reinholdt to Harlan Rodgers, 23 August 1948, Microfilm Reel 11, Dempsey Papers. Rodgers was the legal counsel for the Wisconsin Board of Bar Commissioners.

31. Ibid.; W. T. Doar, Sr., to members of the Wisconsin Board of Bar Commissioners, 10 January 1949, Microfilm Reel 11, Dempsey Papers.

32. *State of Wisconsin* v. *Joseph R. McCarthy*, 255, Wis. 234, 12 July 1949. A copy of the case is in Microfilm Reel 11, Dempsey Papers.

33. Robert Schwartz to Barron Beshoar, 4 October 1951, Box 4, Robert Fleming Papers, S.H.S.W. Schwartz was a *Time* magazine reporter who interviewed Rosenberry in 1951.

34. *Wisconsin State Journal*, 13 July 1949.

35. *Green Bay Press-Gazette*, 18 July 1949.

36. *Milwaukee Journal*, 15 July 1949.

37. Reprint of a *Rhinelander News* editorial in *The Capital Times*, 20 July 1949; *Marshfield News-Herald*, 14 July 1949; *Wisconsin State Journal*, 13 July 1949. The

*Journal* also defended McCarthy by charging that the case was inspired by McCarthy's political opponents. In addition, another conservative newspaper criticized his "irrational" and "unwarranted" statement on the integrity of the bar commissioners; *Waukesha Daily Freeman,* 13 July 1949.

38. *Green Bay Press-Gazette,* 14 July 1949. Most state newspapers that syndicated John Wyngaard's column printed his entire article and captioned it (as *The LaCrosse Tribune* did) "Supreme Court Censure Likely to Plague McCarthy." But the ultraconservative *Appleton Post-Crescent,* whose managing editor John Reidl was a fervent McCarthy supporter and friend of the McCarthy family, did not want its subscribers to read about that unpleasant development. Consequently, Reidl deleted the four pertinent paragraphs of Wyngaard's column, leaving only his account of the partisan origins of the case and the court's decision not to disbar the senator. With the article straightened out, Reidl captioned it "McCarthy Wins Another Round"; *Appleton Post-Crescent,* 14 July 1949; *The LaCrosse Tribune,* 14 July 1949.

39. *The Capital Times, Wisconsin State Journal, Milwaukee Journal, Marshfield News-Herald, The Rhinelander News, Green Bay Press-Gazette, Appleton Post-Crescent, Waukesha Daily Freeman, Oshkosh Northwestern, The Sheboygan Press.*

40. *Green Bay Press-Gazette,* 18 July 1949; *Appleton Post-Crescent,* 18 July 1949; *Oshkosh Northwestern,* 20 July 1949.

41. *Milwaukee Journal,* 7 and 9 May 1948; Francis Sorauf, "The Voluntary Committee System in Wisconsin: An Effort to Achieve Party Responsibility" (Ph.D. diss., University of Wisconsin, 1953), pp. 46–47.

42. Robert Tehan and Julia Boegholt to Harry S. Truman, 15 November 1948, Official File 300, Harry S. Truman Papers, Harry S. Truman Library, Independence, Mo.

43. Sorauf, "The Voluntary Committee System," pp. 47–48.

44. Ibid., pp. 48–49; John Fenton, *Midwest Politics* (New York: Holt, Rinehart and Winston, 1966), p. 55.

45. Alexander Wiley to Harold R. Wilde, 15 June 1949 (not completely processed), Personal Correspondence with Harold Wilde, Alexander Wiley Papers, S.H.S.W.

46. *Green Bay Press-Gazette,* 7 August 1947.

47. John Addison Ricks III, "Mr. Integrity and McCarthyism: Senator Robert A. Taft and Senator Joseph R. McCarthy" (Ph.D. diss., The University of North Carolina at Chapel Hill, 1974), p. 81; Interviews, Renk, 3 September 1969, 24 May 1977; Wayne Hood, 10 September 1969; and Ray Kiermas, 7 April 1977.

48. *The Capital Times,* 14 June 1949.

49. William T. Evjue, "Joe McCarthy in Wisconsin," *The Nation* (5 April 1952):315.

50. *The Capital Times,* 1 October 1949. When asked specifically which Republican leaders in 1949 disliked McCarthy's activities, McMillin named Claude Jasper and Warren Knowles, both of whom were influential state Republicans; Interview, Miles McMillin, 2 September 1969.

51. *Green Bay Press-Gazette,* 26 April 1950; Wyngaard's sentiments were echoed by pro-McCarthy columnist Sanford Goltz; *Wisconsin State Journal,* 11 June 1950.

52. Jack Anderson and Ronald May, *McCarthy: The Man, the Senator, the "Ism"* (Boston: The Beacon Press, 1952), pp. 108, 110; *The Capital Times,* 17 and 25 October 1946; Les Adler, "McCarthyism: The Advent and the Decline, Part I," *Continuum* (Autumn 1968):404–10.

53. Roy Cohn, *McCarthy* (New York: New American Library, 1968). I have written two letters to Cohn, asking him to substantiate his vague claims, but I have received no response.

54. Ibid., pp. 8–11.

55. Promoters of the Washington dinner interpretation have exaggerated its significance. They mistakenly assumed that McCarthy first thought of exploiting the issue at the suggestion of Father Walsh, and that he never seriously used or considered it before 7 January 1950. Drew Pearson insisted that Father Walsh, "first planted the idea in Joe's mind"; *The Capital Times*, 6 May 1957. A McCarthy scholar has recently maintained that McCarthy "pounced upon the suggestion"; Griffith, *Politics of Fear*, p. 29. Newspaper editor William T. Evjue assumed that Father Walsh's remark "was the inspiration for the launching of the McCarthy campaign against communism"; *The Capital Times*, 19 August 1954. "The suggestion struck a responsive chord in McCarthy," Fred Cook declared. McCarthy's three friends "had no idea at the time of what they had started"; Fred Cook, *The Nightmare Decade* (New York: Random House, 1971), p. 141. Richard Rovere also wrote that McCarthy "seized upon the idea" and that it led him to start his national crusade. He did so with the "simple hope that it would help him hold his job in 1952"; Rovere, *Joe McCarthy*, pp. 120, 123.

56. Typed copy of memorandum, Joseph McCarthy to School Clerks of Dane County, 10 November 1949, File 4, Drawer 3, National Committee for an Effective Congress Papers.

57. Type copy of Joseph McCarthy, "Important Questions for the People of Dane County," n.d., File 4, Drawer 3, National Committee for an Effective Congress Papers.

58. Ibid.

59. *The Capital Times*, 11 November 1949; *Wisconsin State Journal*, 12 November 1949; *Milwaukee Journal*, 12 November 1949; *Green Bay Press-Gazette*, 12 November 1949.

60. *Wisconsin State Journal*, 10 November 1949; *The Capital Times*, 9 November 1949.

61. *Wisconsin State Journal*, 19 November 1949; *The Capital Times*, 9 November 1949; *Milwaukee Journal*, 12 November 1949; Claude B. Calkin to Joseph McCarthy, 10 November 1949, President's File 200, Truman Papers. A copy of the letter was enclosed with Joseph McCarthy to Harry S. Truman, 3 August 1951, President's File 200, Truman Papers. Evjue later explained or rationalized this embarrassing discrepancy: Parker became ineligible for membership in the Newspaper Guild when he became city editor of *The Capital Times*; therefore, although he signed the affidavit he did not file it with the National Labor Relations Board; *The Capital Times*, 6 August 1951. The Madison newspaper had given much publicity to Parker's signing of the affidavit. After he signed it, Parker proclaimed: "This is my answer to the old 'Red' charge"; *The Capital Times*, 31 January 1948.

62. *The Capital Times*, 15 November 1949.

63. *Milwaukee Journal*, 11 November 1949.

64. *The Capital Times*, 14 March 1941. The relations between Parker and Evjue improved thereafter. In a friendly letter written while in naval training in 1943, Parker told Evjue that despite "our little clashes and misunderstandings," they both shared antifascist sentiments; Cedric Parker to William T. Evjue, 9 January 1943, Box 106, William T. Evjue Papers, S.H.S.W.

65. Later Evjue rationalized that when he wrote the editorial "the word Communist had different connotations than it has today. Today a man can be sued for libel for calling a person a Communist. Ten years ago that label Communist was used broadly in the same sense that the words reactionary, Tory, radical, or Red were used, and the average citizen dismissed these charges as politics"; *The Capital Times*, 6 August 1951.

66. Evjue memorandum, 9 November 1949, Box 106, Evjue Papers; typescript of a tape-recorded interview of Miles McMillin by Robert Griffith, 25 July and 1 August 1967, p. 74.

67. Because McCarthy did not document his "document" on Parker, I had difficulty tracing his allegations. In the order of McCarthy's listing, here are his probable sources. Evjue's charge: *The Capital Times*, 14 March 1941; Farrell Schnering: *Record of the Proceedings of the Wisconsin State Assembly*, 22 June 1939; Kenneth Goff: *The Capital Times*, 10 April 1947, and the *Wisconsin State Journal*, 11 April 1947; American League for Peace and Democracy: *Milwaukee News*, 4 June 1938; Eugene Dennis: *Committee on Un-American Activities, House of Representatives, Hearings*, 76th Cong., 1st sess., vol. 9, 1939, pp. 5670–72; Wisconsin Conference on Social Legislation: ibid., 77th Cong., app. IX, vol. 54-1, 1944, pp. 1746–48; Earl Browder: ibid., p. 625. Using the Wisconsin State Conference on Social Legislation as an example, it can be seen that McCarthy exaggerated and distorted his evidence. Many outstanding citizens as well as many people later reputed to be Communists participated in the conference. Among them were Thomas Fairchild, the Democratic candidate against McCarthy in 1952, whose integrity was beyond question, and Perry Hill, who in 1949 was chief of the Madison bureau of the ultraconservative *Milwaukee Sentinel*. Similarly, McCarthy stated that Eugene Dennis and Parker organized and sponsored the statewide conference on farm and labor legislation. Actually, the conference had many sponsors, and there is no evidence that Parker and Dennis organized it. The conference was chaired by Paul Alfonsi who later became a conservative Republican state legislator. Rep. Alvin O'Konski, who also had bitter clashes with Evjue, provided McCarthy with some of the material on Parker. Interview, Alvin O'Konski, 4 March 1977.

68. Memorandum, Aldric Revell to William T. Evjue, n.d., Box 82, Evjue Papers.

69. *Wisconsin State Journal*, 10 and 12 November 1949; *The Capital Times*, 9, 11, 14, 15, and 23 November 1949; *Milwaukee Journal*, 9, 10, 11, and 12 November and 5 December 1949; *Green Bay Press-Gazette*, 10, 12, and 14 November 1949; *Appleton Post-Crescent*, 10 and 15 November 1949. As examples, see the *Waukesha Daily Freeman*, 10 and 12 November 1949; *Oshkosh Daily Northwestern*, 10, 11, and 12 November 1949. "Mud for Muckrakers," *Time* (28 November 1949):34–38.

70. *Appleton Post-Crescent*, 15 November 1949; *Milwaukee Sentinel*, 11 and 12 November 1949; *The LaCrosse Tribune*, 10 November 1949; *Milwaukee Journal*, 11 November 1949.

71. *Milwaukee Journal*, 11 and 12 November 1949.

72. "Mud for Muckrakers," *Time* (28 November 1949): 34–38.

73. *Racine Labor*, 25 November 1949; *Milwaukee Sentinel*, 10 November 1949; *The Capital Times*, 14 November 1949; reprint of a *Medford-Star News* editorial in *The Capital Times*, 23 November 1949.

74. *Milwaukee Sentinel*, 11 November 1949; *Green Bay Press-Gazette*, 12 November 1949.

75. During the next five years, McCarthy repeated his allegations against Parker and Evjue at least fifteen times. Evjue dolefully observed on one occasion that, everytime McCarthy rehashed his "old charges about Parker, the Associated Press and the United Press dutifully send it out over the country as news"; *The Capital Times*, 6 August 1951. McCarthy's language became more extreme after 1949 as he accused Evjue of running a "disguised poisoned waterhole of dangerous Communist propaganda"; *The Capital Times*, 28 April 1950.

76. *Kenosha Evening News*, 16 November 1949.

77. *The Evening Bulletin* (Philadelphia), 4 December 1949.

78. *The Eau Claire Leader*, 8 December 1949; *Milwaukee Journal*, 7 December 1949.

79. *Congressional Record*, vol. 96, part 1, 5 January 1950, p. 86.

80. *Milwaukee Sentinel*, 22 January 1950.

81. *Congressional Record*, vol. 96, part 1, 25 January 1950, p. 895.

82. Only three commentators have discussed the Parker controversy. Whether intentionally or not, the entire story and its full implications were not brought out.

Jack Anderson and Ronald May (who had formerly worked for *The Capital Times*) severely distorted the affair in their book. First, they neglected to give the date of the incident, thus leading the reader to believe it occurred sometime after 1949. Second, they discussed it only as an example of McCarthy's reckless attacks on newspapers that opposed him. Third, they mistakenly assumed that Parker and Evjue effectively rebutted McCarthy's accusations and that his offensive was a failure; Anderson and May, *McCarthy*, pp. 272–73. In 1954, Miles McMillin associated McCarthy's barrage with his later crusade on Communists in government. Although McMillin's account displayed some insight, it was superficial and failed to grasp the full implications of the incident; *The Capital Times*, 13 December 1954. The controversy was again reviewed by Morris Rubin in 1967 for the fiftieth-anniversary edition of *The Capital Times*, but he merely repeated McMillin's earlier account; Morris Rubin, "The Fight against McCarthy: Finest Hour of *The Capital Times*," *The Capital Times: Fiftieth Anniversary Edition*, 13 December 1967.

## Notes to Chapter 6: The Issue, Politics, and Debate: 1950–1952

1. Interview, Urban Van Susteren, 4 September 1969, 22 March 1977.

2. Robert Griffith, *Politics of Fear: Joseph R. McCarthy and the Senate* (Lexington: The University Press of Kentucky, 1970), p. 58; Alan Harper, *The Politics of Loyalty: The White House and the Communist Issue, 1946–1952* (Westport, Conn.: Greenwood Publishing Corp., 1969), p. 134; Richard Fried, *Men against McCarthy* (New York: Columbia University Press, 1976), pp. 71–72, 89.

3. Griffith, *Politics of Fear*, p. 58; Fried, *Men against McCarthy*, pp. ix-x; Richard Fried, "Democrats against McCarthy," *Continuum* 6 (Autumn 1968): 347.

4. Fried, *Men against McCarthy*, pp. 14, 21, 30, 154, 182–83, and 196.

5. Ibid., pp. 102–3.

6. Ibid., pp. 166–67, 170–71.

7. *Green Bay Press-Gazette*, 26 April 1950; *Congressional Record*, vol. 96, part 3, 28 March 1950, p. 4233; *Congressional Record*, vol. 96, part 4, 29 March 1950, p. 4311; Interview, Wayne Hood, 10 September 1969.

8. One columnist reported that rural politicians felt that rank-and-file Republicans thought the same way; *Green Bay Press-Gazette*, 26 April 1950; Interview, Hood, 10 September 1969.

9. *The Capital Times*, 12 April 1950.

10. Wayne Hood to Joseph McCarthy, 13 April 1950, Box 6 (unprocessed), Wayne Hood Papers, State Historical Society of Wisconsin (S.H.S.W.).

11. *New York Times*, 19 May 1950.

12. See the series of correspondence in 1950 in Box 13, Thomas Coleman Papers, S.H.S.W.

13. Thomas Coleman, "Report to the National Republican Strategy Committee," 20 April 1950, Box 5, Coleman Papers.

14. Thomas Coleman, "Memorandum to the Wisconsin Republican Party Finance Committee," 6 May 1950, Box 4, Hood Papers.

15. Wayne Hood to Joseph McCarthy, 13 April 1950, Box 6, Hood Papers.

16. *Proceedings of the 1950 Republican State Convention* (Republican Party of Wisconsin, Madison, Wisconsin), p. 40; *Milwaukee Journal*, 9 and 10 June 1950; *The LaCrosse Tribune*, 9 and 15 June 1950; *Wisconsin State Journal*, 11 June 1950; *Green Bay Press-Gazette*, 13 June 1950.

17. Thomas Coleman to Joseph McCarthy, 7 July 1950; McCarthy to Coleman, 15 July 1950; and Coleman to McCarthy, 17 July 1950, all Box 13, Coleman Papers.

18. Fried, *Men against McCarthy*, p. 119; John Addison Ricks III, "Mr. Integrity

and McCarthyism: Senator Robert A. Taft and Senator Joseph R. McCarthy" (Ph.D. diss., University of North Carolina at Chapel Hill, 1974), p. 111.

19. *Milwaukee Journal*, 1 and 15 October 1950; *Green Bay Press-Gazette*, 28 October 1950.

20. Joseph McCarthy to Wayne Hood, 27 July 1950, Box 2, Hood Papers; *Green Bay Press-Gazette*, 2 September and 15 November 1950.

21. *Milwaukee Journal*, 17 and 22 October 1950; *Green Bay Press-Gazette*, 15 November 1950.

22. *Milwaukee Journal*, 9 October 1950; Interview, James Doyle, 3 September 1969.

23. Wayne Hood to Joseph McCarthy, 16 November 1950, Box 2, Hood Papers; *Green Bay Press-Gazette*, 24 July 1951.

24. *The Capital Times*, 11 November 1950; *The Wisconsin Democrat*, November 1950; *The Progressive* (December 1950): 4; Fried, *Men against McCarthy*, pp. 115–16.

25. Interviews, Patrick Lucey, 28 August 1969; Carl Thompson, 10 April 1969.

26. Fried, *Men against McCarthy*, pp. 119, 139.

27. *Green Bay Press-Gazette*, 9 July 1951, 6 January 1952; *Milwaukee Journal*, 20 February 1952.

28. James T. Patterson, *Mr. Republican: A Biography of Robert A. Taft* (Boston: Houghton Mifflin Co., 1972), pp. 445–49.

29. Ibid., p. 527; Leo Katcher, *Earl Warren: A Political Biography* (New York: McGraw-Hill Book Co., 1967), p. 282.

30. Patterson, *Robert A. Taft*, pp. 511–12; Ricks, "Taft and McCarthy," pp. 185–87.

31. Ricks, "Taft and McCarthy," pp. 118–19.

32. Ibid., pp. 123–24; *Green Bay Press-Gazette*, 23 October 1951; *Milwaukee Journal*, 6 November 1951.

33. *Milwaukee Journal*, 16 December 1951; *Green Bay Press-Gazette*, 27 December 1951.

34. Ricks, "Taft and McCarthy," p. 127.

35. Ibid., pp. 127–28; memorandum, John Hamilton to Robert Taft, 19 December 1951, Box 14, Coleman Papers.

36. Ricks, "Taft and McCarthy," pp. 122, 129; Patterson, *Robert A. Taft*, p. 530.

37. *Green Bay Press-Gazette*, 9 and 24 July and 27 December 1951.

38. *Milwaukee Journal*, 17 May 1950, 23 August 1951; *The Capital Times*, 11 December 1951; see also Fred Zimmerman, "Why McCarthy Should Be Repudiated," *The Nation* (20 August 1952): 168–69.

39. Interviews, Walter Kohler, Jr., 5 September 1949; John Wyngaard, 30 December 1969.

40. Interview, Kohler, 5 September 1969.

41. *Green Bay Press-Gazette*, 20 June 1950; memorandum, John Hunter to William T. Evjue, 3 April 1951, Box 24, William T. Evjue Papers, S.H.S.W.

42. *Milwaukee Journal*, 1 April 1950.

43. *Milwaukee Journal*, 24 September and 5 October 1950; *Wisconsin State Journal*, 9 November 1950.

44. Interview, Wyngaard, 30 September 1969.

45. *Green Bay Press-Gazette*, 20 June 1950.

46. Alexander Wiley to Marshall A. Wiley, 6 April 1950, Personal Correspondence with Marshall Wiley (not completely processed), Alexander Wiley Papers, S.H.S.W.

47. *Milwaukee Journal*, 24 September 1950; *The Sheboygan Press*, 17 January 1951.

48. *Milwaukee Journal*, 20 April 1952; Claude Jasper to Alexander Wiley, 5 May 1952, Box 2, Hood Papers; Wayne Hood to Claude Jasper, 6 May 1952, Box 2, Hood Papers; *Green Bay Press-Gazette*, 13 May and 4 August 1952.

49. Interview, Van Susteren, 4 September 1969, 22 March 1977.

50. *Ashland Daily Press*, 25 February 1950, 31 January 1952; *Vilas County News-Review*, 21 February 1952; *Green Bay Press-Gazette*, 31 July 1950.

51. As an example, see the *Wisconsin State Journal*, 28 April 1950.

52. *Wisconsin State Journal*, 15 March and 29 April 1950; *Monroe Times*, 21 July 1950.

53. *Green Bay Press-Gazette*, 8 June 1950; *Wisconsin State Journal*, 29 April 1950, 4 September 1951.

54. *Green Bay Press-Gazette*, 19 July 1950; *Wisconsin State Journal*, 9 February, 16 April, 4 September, and 17 December 1951.

55. *Major Speeches and Debates of Senator Joe McCarthy Delivered in the United States Senate, 1950–1951*, reprinted from the *Congressional Record* (Washington, D.C.: United States Government Printing Office, n.d.), p. 215.

56. Richard Rovere, *Senator Joe McCarthy* (Cleveland and New York: The World Publishing Co., 1959), p. 171; *Green Bay Press-Gazette*, 3 September 1952; *Wausau Record-Herald*, 17 October 1952.

57. Letter to the editor by William J. Campbell, *Oshkosh Daily Northwestern*, 6 September 1952.

58. Robert Schwartz to Barron Beshoar, 4 October 1951, Box 4, Robert Fleming Papers, S.H.S.W. Schwartz, the *Time* magazine reporter, interviewed Coleman.

59. Bradley Taylor to John [?], 15 September 1952, Box 5, Bradley Taylor Papers, S.H.S.W.

60. *The Wisconsin Democrat*, November 1951.

61. *The Wisconsin Democrat*, May and June 1951; *The Capital Times*, 25 May 1950.

62. *The Wisconsin Democrat*, May and June 1951; *Racine Labor*, 28 July 1950; *The Capital Times*, 18 July 1950; *Milwaukee Journal*, 18 July 1950; *Wisconsin CIO News*, 28 July 1950; *Kenosha Labor*, 16 March 1950, 16 August 1951.

63. *Milwaukee Journal*, 10 June 1950; *Manitowoc Herald-Times*, 16 March 1950; *The Capital Times*, 16 December 1950; for an example of Evjue's anger at McCarthy's use of congressional immunity, see William T. Evjue to Alexander Wiley, 31 July 1951, Box A, Wiley Papers.

64. *The Wisconsin Democrat*, May and June 1951; *Union Labor News*, April 1950; *The Capital Times*, 14 December 1951.

65. *Racine Labor*, 31 March 1950; *Milwaukee Journal*, 15 June 1951; Lindsay Hoben, "An Independent Editorial Page: The Milwaukee Journal," *Nieman Reports* (January 1953): 29; Karl Meyer, "Students Speak Up on McCarthyism," *The Progressive* (October 1950): 28–29.

66. *The Daily Cardinal* (University of Wisconsin–Madison), 28 March 1950; *The Capital Times*, 26 April 1950, 20 August 1951; *The Sheboygan Press*, 31 July 1950.

67. Rovere, *Joe McCarthy*, p. 38; *Investigations of Senators Joseph R. McCarthy and William Benton*, Report of the Subcommittee on Privileges and Elections to the Committee on Rules and Administration (Washington, D.C., 1952), pp. 15–19; *Milwaukee Journal*, 23 April 1950; *The Sheboygan Press*, 20 June 1950; *The Capital Times*, 25 April 1950.

68. *Milwaukee Journal*, 10 January, 2 March, and 3 August 1951; *The Capital Times*, 27 December 1950.

69. Morris Rubin to Clough Gates, 14 February 1951; Rubin to John Hoving, 20 June 1951; Rubin to Clarence H. Low, 27 March 1952, all (unprocessed), *The Progressive* Magazine Papers, S.H.S.W.; Morris Rubin, ed., *The McCarthy Record* (Madison: The Wisconsin Citizens' Committee on McCarthy's Record, 1952).

70. John Hoving, "My Friend McCarthy," *The Reporter* (25 April 1950): 30.

71. Memorandum, Robert Fleming to Harvey and Wally [?], Fall 1950, Box 3, Fleming Papers.

72. Robert Fleming memorandum on McCarthy's taxes, 17 September 1951, Box 3, Fleming Papers.

73. Robert Fleming to [?] Gonzales, 19 July 1950, Box 1, Fleming Papers.

74. Robert Fleming memorandum on cooperative effort against McCarthy (probably May–June 1951), Box 3, Fleming Papers.

75. Ibid.

76. Memorandum, Robert Fleming to Harvey and Wally [?], Fall 1950, Box 3, Fleming Papers.

77. Robert Fleming to Murrey Marder, 6 July 1950, Box 1, Fleming Papers.

78. Memorandum, Robert Sherrod to [?] Berger, 15 October 1951, Box 4, Fleming Papers.

79. Ibid.

80. Jean Franklin Deaver, "A Study of Senator Joseph R. McCarthy and 'McCarthyism' as Influences upon the News Media and the Evolution of Reportorial Method" (Ph.D. diss., University of Texas at Austin, 1969), p. 162. Deaver interviewed Fleming for her study. For information on assistance given Fleming by national Democratic leaders and the Truman administration, see Kenneth Heckler to David Lloyd, 27 May 1952, David Lloyd Files, "Senator Joseph McCarthy" Folder, Harry S. Truman Library, Independence, Mo.

81. Deaver, "McCarthy and News Media," p. 162.

82. *Milwaukee Journal*, 8 June 1952.

83. Deaver, "McCarthy and News Media," p. 162.

84. Robert Fleming to Maxwell P. Aley, 18 September 1951, Box 3, Fleming Papers.

85. Patrick Lucey to Robert Fleming, 13 June 1952, Box 4, Fleming Papers.

86. William Benton to Robert Fleming, 26 November 1952, Box 3, Fleming Papers. Fleming's earlier letter to Benton is not available. I have quoted from Benton's letter in which he in turn quoted from an earlier letter from Fleming.

87. Assorted memoranda probably compiled in 1951 by Ronald May who in conjunction with Jack Anderson wrote *McCarthy: The Man, the Senator, the "Ism"* (Boston: The Beacon Press, 1952). This material is found in File 4, Drawers 1, 2, and 3 (unprocessed), National Committee for an Effective Congress Papers, Maurice Rosenblatt's home, Washington, D.C. Among the leading opponents of McCarthy who investigated the McCarthy–Capone case were James Doyle and William T. Evjue.

88. *The Capital Times*, 18 December 1950; *Milwaukee Journal*, 27 April 1950; *The Sheboygan Press*, 17 January 1951; *Union Labor News*, January 1951.

89. *Union Labor News*, June 1950.

90. *Union Labor News*, September 1951.

91. The state union was the Wisconsin Council of the International Association of Machinists; their proposal was contained in Henry J. Winkel (Secretary) to President Harry Truman, 27 May 1950, Official File 3371, Harry S. Truman Papers, Truman Library.

92. *The Capital Times*, 19 August 1952.

93. Typed copy of a letter from David Rabinowitz to Joseph McCarthy, 6 June 1950, File 4, Drawer 3, National Committee for an Effective Congress Papers. *Wisconsin Jewish Chronicle*, 6 April 1951; *The Capital Times*, 8 February 1951.

94. *The Capital Times*, 8 February 1951.

95. See, for example, Rubin, *The McCarthy Record*; and Morris Rubin, ed., "McCarthy: A Documented Record," special edition of *The Progressive* (April 1954).

96. Immanuel Wallerstein, "McCarthyism and the Conservative" (Master's thesis, Columbia University, 1954), p. 56; Interview, Harold Townsend, 10 March 1977.

97. *The Daily Cardinal* (University of Wisconsin–Madison), 15 May 1951; *The Capital Times*, 14 May 1951; tape-recorded interview with Carlisle Runge by Edward Coffman, 22 March 1963, deposited in S.H.S.W.

## Notes to Chapter 7: The 1952 Election

1. Richard Fried, *Men against McCarthy* (New York: Columbia University Press, 1976), p. 220.

2. *Minneapolis Tribune*, 30 April 1967; typescript of a tape-recorded interview of Miles McMillin by Robert Griffith, 25 July and 1 August 1967; Interviews, James Doyle, 3 September 1969; Claude Jasper, 22 June 1977; Patrick Lucey, 28 August 1969; and Carl Thompson, 10 April 1969.

3. *The Capital Times*, 18 June, 24 August, and 12 December 1951.

4. William T. Evjue to Joseph Short, 7 August 1951, President's Personal File 200, Harry S. Truman Papers, Harry S. Truman Library, Independence, Mo. Short was secretary to President Truman; Evjue to Short, 11 September 1951, Official File 300, Truman Papers.

5. *Milwaukee Journal*, 7 November 1951.

6. Interview, Lucey, 28 August 1969.

7. *The Wisconsin Democrat*, May 1951; *Union Labor News*, October 1951.

8. Morris Rubin, ed., *The McCarthy Record* (Madison: The Wisconsin Citizens' Committee on McCarthy's Record, 1952); *Milwaukee Journal*, 3 June 1951; *The Capital Times*, 28 June 1951; Interview, Doyle, 3 September 1969.

9. *A.F. of L. Milwaukee Labor Press*, 24 July 1952; *Racine Labor*, 5 September 1952; *Union Labor News*, October 1951.

10. James Doyle to William Benton, 17 June 1952, Box 4, William Benton Papers, State Historical Society of Wisconsin (S.H.S.W.).

11. *The Capital Times*, 23 August 1951.

12. Daniel Hoan to Gerald Clifford and Jerome Fox, 13 June 1951, Box 14, File 51, Daniel Hoan Papers, Milwaukee County Historical Society, Milwaukee, Wisconsin.

13. Frank Henson and Henry Reuss to Daniel Hoan, 18 April 1951, Box 14, File 51, Hoan Papers; Daniel Hoan to Gerald Clifford and Jerome Fox, 13 June 1951, Box 14, File 51, Hoan Papers.

14. Francis Henson to Daniel Hoan, 2 July 1951; James Doyle to Francis Henson, 23 June 1951; and Daniel Hoan to Francis Henson, 6 July 1951, all Box 14, File 51, Hoan Papers.

15. Interview, Doyle, 3 September 1969.

16. *Congressional Report*, 15 July 1952. This was a biweekly bulletin published by the National Committee for an Effective Congress, Washington, D.C.; *Milwaukee Journal*, 12 November 1951; Francis Sorauf, "The Voluntary Committee System in Wisconsin: An Effort to Achieve Party Responsibility" (Ph.D. diss., University of Wisconsin, 1953), pp. 195–96.

17. *Wisconsin State Journal*, 28 January 1952; *Milwaukee Journal*, 10 February 1952.

18. *The Capital Times*, 10 November 1952; *The Daily Cardinal* (University of Wisconsin–Madison), 23 January 1952; Interview, Miles McMillin, 2 September 1969.

19. Miles McMillin to Thomas N. Duncan, 10 April 1952, Series 1, File A, Box 8, Correspondence of the Committee on Political Education, American Federation of Labor Papers, S.H.S.W.

20. David Oshinsky, "Wisconsin Labor and the Campaign of 1952," *Wisconsin Magazine of History* (Winter 1972–1973):110.

21. *Wisconsin State Journal*, 8 July 1951; *Milwaukee Sentinel*, 7 July 1951; *The Capital Times*, 13 July 1951.

22. *Milwaukee Journal*, 12 July 1951.

23. Wayne Hood to Walter Kohler, Jr., 18 July 1951, Box 2 (unprocessed), Wayne Hood Papers, S.H.S.W. For an example of Republican anger at Kohler, see George Larkin to Wayne Hood, July 1951, Box 2, Hood Papers.

24. *The Capital Times*, 19 July 1951; for Republican efforts to get Kohler to change his mind, see Box 11 (unprocessed), Warren Knowles Papers, S.H.S.W.

25. *Wisconsin State Journal*, 25 July 1951.

26. Interview, Walter Kohler, Jr., 5 September 1969.

27. Robert Schwartz to Barron Beshoar, 4 October 1951, Box 4, Robert Fleming Papers, S.H.S.W.

28. Interview, Kohler, 5 September 1969.

29. *The Capital Times*, 15 September 1951; *Wisconsin State Journal*, 26 September 1951.

30. Graham Hovey, "McCarthy Faces the Voters," *New Republic* (3 December 1951):16; *The Wisconsin Democrat*, October 1951.

31. *The Capital Times*, 3 November 1951; Hovey, "McCarthy Faces the Voters," p. 15.

32. Hovey, "McCarthy Faces the Voters," p. 15.

33. Quoted in Alfred Steinberg, "Is This the Man to Beat McCarthy?" *Collier's* (24 November 1951): 26.

34. Hovey, "McCarthy Faces the Voters," p. 15; reprint of an editorial in the *Glenwood City Tribune* by *The Capital Times*, 16 November 1951; reprint of an editorial in the *Whitewater Register* by the *Milwaukee Journal*, 12 October 1951; *Wisconsin State Journal*, 30 October 1951; *New York Times*, 25 October 1951; *Wisconsin Agriculturist and Farmer* (Racine), 6 October 1951; *The Daily Cardinal* (University of Wisconsin–Madison), 13 and 14 November 1951.

35. Robert Fleming to Sen. Estes Kefauver, 26 November 1951, Box 3, Fleming Papers.

36. George Haberman to Thomas Duncan, 25 October 1951, Series 1, File A, Box 8, C.O.P.E. Correspondence, American Federation of Labor Papers; Interview, Kohler, 5 September 1969.

37. *Green Bay Press-Gazette*, 11 October 1951.

38. William James to Walter Kohler, 9 January 1952, Box 41, Walter Kohler, Jr., Papers, S.H.S.W.; Charles Peterson to Walter Kohler, 10 January 1952, Box 41, Kohler Papers; Wayne Hood to Jean Kerr, 16 November 1951, Box 2, Hood Papers. Jean Kerr was McCarthy's secretary and later became his wife. Interviews, Kohler, 5 September 1969; Wayne Hood, 10 September 1969.

39. Memorandum, Walter Kohler to Sherman Adams, 27 April 1959. Kohler gave me a copy of the memorandum.

40. Ibid.; *The Capital Times*, 13 and 19 July 1951; *Milwaukee Sentinel*, 13 July 1951; *Wisconsin State Journal*, 8 July 1952; Interview, Kohler, 5 September 1969.

41. Richard Haney, "A History of the Democratic Party of Wisconsin since World War Two" (Ph.D. diss., University of Wisconsin, 1970), p. 164; *Wisconsin State Journal*, 3 August 1952.

42. Memorandum, William Benton to John Howe, 11 July 1952, Box 5, William Benton Papers, S.H.S.W.; Howe to Benton, 8 July 1952, Box 5, Benton Papers.

43. Interviews, McMillin, 2 September 1969; Leonard Schmitt, 5 September 1969.

44. *The Capital Times*, 7 August 1952.

45. *The Capital Times*, 6 September 1952; James Doyle to Thomas Duncan, 29 July 1952, Series 1, File A, Box 8, C.O.P.E. Correspondence, American Federation of Labor Papers.

46. *The Capital Times*, 7 and 13 August 1952.

47. *Milwaukee Journal*, 31 August 1952; Interview, Schmitt, 5 September 1969.

48. *The Eau Claire Leader*, 3 September 1952; for examples of labor apathy toward Schmitt and support of Democrats, see the *Union Labor News*, May–September 1952, and the *Kenosha Labor*, August–September 1952.

49. As an example, see the *Wisconsin State Journal*, 14 August 1952.

50. Additional confirmation of Cohen's visit comes from Luke P. Carroll, assistant to the editor of the *New York Herald-Tribune*. On 3 July 1952, Cohen appeared in Carroll's office looking for some help, meaning either publicity, money, or both. Cohen argued that Schmitt had a real chance to knock McCarthy off in the primary. Cohen said that the vote for Robert Taft in the Wisconsin presidential primary in 1952 was smaller than the anti-Taft vote and that this was the maximum McCarthy vote. Cohen believed that the votes for Harold Stassen and Earl Warren in the Republican presidential primary, plus 100,000 Democratic presidential primary votes would cross over and vote against McCarthy and give Schmitt the victory; Luke Carroll to Robert Fleming, 3 July 1952, Box 1, Fleming Papers; Interview, Schmitt, 5 September 1969.

51. Interviews, Ray Kiermas, 7 April 1977; Lloyd Tegge, 24 March 1977.

52. Interview, Harold Townsend, 10 March 1977.

53. Wayne Hood to Anne Hale Wilson, 1 November 1951, Box 2, Hood Papers.

54. Harold Hornburg to Wayne Hood, 29 February 1952, Box 2, Hood Papers.

55. Warren Knowles to Bill Drotning, 2 September 1952, Box 7, Knowles Papers; Robert Schwartz to Barron Beshoar, 4 October 1951, Box 4, Fleming Papers.

56. "Election News," September 1952, p. 7, contained in Box 13, Richard Rovere Papers, S.H.S.W.; *Milwaukee Journal*, 23 August 1952.

57. *Wisconsin State Journal*, 12 August 1952; "Election News," September 1952, p. 1, Box 13, Rovere Papers.

58. "Election News," September 1952, pp. 5, 7, Box 13, Rovere Papers; "The Truth about Senator Joe McCarthy," McCarthy Club campaign brochure found in Box 12, Rovere Papers.

59. *Appleton Post-Crescent*, 8 September 1952.

60. *Green Bay Press-Gazette*, 10 July 1952.

61. See, for example, the form letter written by William J. Campbell to Republicans, 21 August 1952 (unprocessed), Leonard Schmitt Papers.

62. Steve Miller to fellow Republican, 15 August 1952 (unprocessed), Harold Townsend Papers.

63. *Milwaukee Journal*, 4 September 1952; *The Capital Times*, 2 September 1952.

64. Robert Griffith, *The Politics of Fear* (Lexington: The University Press of Kentucky, 1970), pp. 176–77.

65. Quoted in Graham Hovey, "How McCarthy Sold Wisconsin," *New Republic* (22 September 1952): 10.

66. *Milwaukee Sentinel*, 11 September 1952.

67. Karl Meyer, "The Politics of Loyalty from La Follette to McCarthy in Wisconsin 1918–1952" (Ph.D. diss., Princeton University, 1956), pp. 191–92.

68. *Green Bay Press-Gazette*, 3 October 1952.

69. Quoted in the *Union Labor News*, November 1952.

70. *Waukesha Daily Freeman*, 3 November 1952.

71. *The Beloit Daily News*, 1 November 1952; "To Those Who Say: We Never Had It So Good," campaign brochure for William K. Van Pelt, Republican candidate for Congress, Box 12, Rovere Papers.

72. Fried, *Men against McCarthy*, p. 324; *Milwaukee Sentinel*, 29 and 30 October 1952; *Ashland Daily Press*, 28 October 1952.

73. Sherman Adams, *Firsthand Report: The Story of the Eisenhower Administration* (New York: Harper and Brothers, 1961), p. 137.

74. Robert Griffith, "The General and the Senator: Republican Politics and the 1952 Campaign in Wisconsin," *Wisconsin Magazine of History* 24 (Autumn 1970):24.

75. Copy of the text of Eisenhower's press conference at Denver, Colorado, 22 August 1952, Box 36, Sherman Adams Papers, Dwight D. Eisenhower Library, Abilene, Kans.; *New York Times*, 24 August 1952.

76. Bradley Taylor to Devin Garrity, 12 September 1952, Box 5, Bradley Taylor Papers, S.H.S.W.; see also *Waukesha Daily Freeman*, 10 September 1952; *Oshkosh Daily Northwestern*, 25 August 1952; *Wisconsin State Journal*, 3 October 1952.

77. Interview, Hood, 10 September 1969.

78. The sixth draft of Eisenhower's proposed speech in Milwaukee, October 1952, in Official File 101-GG, Dwight Eisenhower Papers, Eisenhower Library; Griffith, "The General and the Senator," p. 25.

79. Griffith, "The General and the Senator," p. 25.

80. Memorandum, Kohler to Adams, 27 April 1959.

81. Adams, *Firsthand Report*, pp. 30–31.

82. *Milwaukee Journal*, 3 October 1952; memorandum, Kohler to Adams, 27 April 1959; Griffith, "The General and the Senator," p. 26.

83. Memorandum, Kohler to Adams, 27 April 1959.

84. Adams, *Firsthand Report*, pp. 31–32; memorandum, Kohler to Adams, 27 April 1959.

85. Griffith, "The General and the Senator," p. 29.

86. *The Capital Times*, 15 September 1952.

87. Memorandum, Democratic Organizing Committee of Wisconsin, "The 1952 Wisconsin Primary with Special Emphasis on the 5th District," September 1952, Series 1, File A, Box 8, C.O.P.E. Correspondence, American Federation of Labor Papers; *Green Bay Press-Gazette*, 16 September 1952.

88. Morris Rubin to Marquis Childs, 16 September 1952, Box 10, Marquis Childs Papers, S.H.S.W.

89. Memorandum by the D.O.C., "The 1952 Wisconsin Primary"; memorandum, Finance Committee of the Democratic Organizing Committee of Wisconsin, 15 October 1952, Series 5, Box 39, Americans for Democratic Action Papers, S.H.S.W.; memorandum, Democratic Organizing Committee of Wisconsin, 5 September 1952, Series 1, File A, Box 8, C.O.P.E. Correspondence, American Federation of Labor Papers.

90. Interview, Lucey, 28 August 1969.

91. Memorandum, Democratic Organizing Committee of Wisconsin, 4 September 1952, Series 1, File A, Box 8, C.O.P.E. Correspondence, American Federation of Labor Papers.

92. Haney, "Democratic Party of Wisconsin since World War Two," p. 178.

93. Meyer, "The Politics of Loyalty," p. 195.

94. Interviews, Doyle, 3 September 1969; Lucey, 28 August 1969.

95. *Appleton Post-Crescent*, 22 October 1952; *The Capital Times*, 24 October 1952.

96. *The Beloit Daily News*, 1 November 1952.

97. *The Capital Times*, 21 and 29 September and 21 and 24 October 1952; *The Evening Telegram* (Superior), 10 October 1952; *The La Crossee Tribune*, 3 November 1952; *The Beloit Daily News*, 1 November 1952; *Wisconsin State Journal*, 16 October 1952.

98. *Milwaukee Journal*, 3 and 4 November 1952; Robert Fleming to Stephen J. Spingarn, 15 November 1952, Internal Security File, Box 37, Stephen Spingarn Papers, Truman Papers, Truman Library; Morris Rubin to Edward P. Morgan, 6 November 1952, Political Campaign Material, Box 61, Spingarn Papers; Interview, Lucey, 28 August 1969.

99. This observation was based on copies of a large number of thank-you letters

to contributors to the Fairchild campaign found in the papers of the National Committee for an Effective Congress.

100. Oshinsky, "Wisconsin Labor and Campaign of 1952," p. 117.

101. See the series of memos and financial statements in Box 9, Thomas Coleman Papers, S.H.S.W.; Interviews, Townsend, 10 March 1977; Claude Jasper, 22 June 1977; and Llewellyn Morack, 11 March 1977.

102. Leroy Ferguson and Ralph Smuckler, *Politics in the Press: An Analysis of Press Content in 1952 Senatorial Campaigns* (East Lansing, Mich.: The Government Research Bureau, 1954), pp. 60–67.

103. Nelson Polsby, "Towards an Explanation of McCarthyism," *Political Studies* 8 (1960): 263.

104. Meyer, "Politics of Loyalty," p. 205.

105. Michael Rogin, *The Intellectuals and McCarthy: The Radical Specter* (Cambridge, Mass.: The M.I.T. Press, 1967), p. 96.

106. Ibid., pp. 94, 97.

107. Ibid., pp. 91, 94.

108. Ibid., pp. 93–94.

109. David Oshinsky, *Senator Joseph McCarthy and the American Labor Movement* (Columbia: University of Missouri Press, 1976), pp. 147–50.

110. Martin Trow, "Right-Wing Radicalism and Political Intolerance: A Study of Support for McCarthy in a New England Town" (Ph.D. diss., Columbia University, 1957); Oshinsky, *McCarthy and Labor*, pp. 154–55.

111. *The Capital Times*, 5 November 1952.

112. Ibid.

## Notes to Chapter 8: Doubt and Criticism: 1953

1. Richard Rovere, *Senator Joe McCarthy* (Cleveland and New York: The World Publishing Co., 1959), pp. 186–87.

2. *Green Bay Press-Gazette*, 11 November 1952; *Wisconsin State Journal*, 13 November 1952; *Waukesha Daily Freeman*, 5 November 1952.

3. *Waukesha Daily Freeman*, 5 November 1952.

4. *Green Bay Press-Gazette*, 11 November 1952.

5. *The Capital Times*, 8 November 1952.

6. Rovere, *Joe McCarthy*, p. 187.

7. Ibid., pp. 187–89.

8. *Milwaukee Journal*, 11 December 1952.

9. *Investigations of Senators Joseph R. McCarthy and William Benton*, Report of the Subcommittee on Privileges and Elections to the Committee on Rules and Administration (Washington, D.C., 1952); Richard Fried, *Men against McCarthy* (New York: Columbia University Press, 1976), pp. 213–14.

10. *Racine Journal-Times*, 5 January 1953.

11. *Wausau Daily Record-Herald*, 7 January 1953.

12. *The Capital Times*, 1 July 1953.

13. Ibid.; *Appleton Post-Crescent*, 1 July 1953; Charles Murphy, "McCarthy and the Businessman," *Fortune* (April 1954): 156; Charles Seaborn to Joseph McCarthy, 25 July 1953, Box 62, William T. Evjue Papers, State Historical Society of Wisconsin (S.H.S.W.).

14. *Marinette Eagle-Star*, 3 July 1953; *Racine Journal-Times*, 3 July 1953; *Stevens Point Journal*, 2 July 1953.

15. *Appleton Post-Crescent*, 6 July 1953.

16. *Green Bay Press-Gazette,* 30 March 1953; *Oshkosh Daily Northwestern,* 15 April 1953.

17. *Wisconsin State Journal,* 27 March 1953.

18. *Waukesha Daily Freeman,* 23 March 1953; other Republican newspapers that criticized the senator were the *Fond du Lac Commonwealth Reporter,* 28 March 1953; the *Marinette Eagle-Star,* 25 March 1953; and *The Beloit Daily News,* 27 March 1953.

19. Rovere, *Joe McCarthy,* pp. 33–34.

20. *Green Bay Press-Gazette,* 1 April 1953.

21. *Wisconsin State Journal,* 23 April 1953.

22. *The Beloit Daily News,* 11 July 1953; *Waukesha Daily Freeman,* 14 July 1953.

23. Thomas Coleman to Leonard Hall, 15 June 1953, Box 2 (unprocessed), Wayne Hood Papers, S.H.S.W.

24. Interview, Walter Kohler, Jr., 5 September 1969.

25. *Milwaukee Journal,* 14 June 1953.

26. Wayne Hood to Alexander Wiley, 4 June 1953, Box 2, Hood Papers; see also Hood to Wiley, 22 May 1953, Box 2, Hood Papers.

27. Thomas Coleman to Leonard Hall, 15 June 1953, Box 2, Hood Papers.

28. Bradley Taylor to Richard O'Melia, 15 June 1953, Box 5, Bradley Taylor Papers, S.H.S.W.

29. *Proceedings of the Republican State Convention: 1953* (Republican Party of Wisconsin, Madison, Wisconsin); *Green Bay Press-Gazette,* 15 June 1953; Edwin Bayley, "Wisconsin: The War against Eisenhower," *New Republic* (6 July 1953): 16.

30. Miles McMillin, "Revolt against Ike," *The Nation* (4 July 1953):12.

31. Ibid.; Bayley, "The War against Eisenhower," p. 15; *Proceedings: 1953.*

32. Alexander Wiley to Harold Wilde, 24 April 1953, Series 1, Box 35, Personal Correspondence (not completely processed), Alexander Wiley Papers, S.H.S.W.

33. Quoted in Richard J. Steffens to Alexander Wiley, 6 July 1953, Series 1, Box 36, Personal Correspondence, Wiley Papers.

34. Alexander Wiley to Herbert Brownell, 6 July 1953, General File 109-A-2, Dwight Eisenhower Papers, Dwight Eisenhower Library, Abilene, Kans.

35. Fried, *Men against McCarthy,* p. 273; *Milwaukee Journal,* 25 November 1953.

36. Robert Branyan, "McCarthy and Eisenhower," *Continuum* 6 (Autumn 1968): 355–56.

37. *The Beloit Daily News,* 25 November and 8 December 1953.

38. *Racine Journal-Times,* 3 December 1953.

39. *Oshkosh Daily Northwestern,* 2 December 1953.

40. Fried, *Men against McCarthy,* pp. 255–56.

41. *Waukesha Daily Freeman,* 10 December 1953.

42. Interview, Talbot Peterson, 22 February 1977.

43. Ellis Dana to Sherman Adams, 29 November 1953, General File 171, 1953–1954 C, Eisenhower Papers.

44. James H. LaChance to Alexander Wiley, 10 December 1953, Series 2, Box 15, General Correspondence, Wiley Papers.

45. Interviews, Wayne Hood, 10 September 1969; Alvin O'Konski, 4 March 1977.

46. Richard Haney, "A History of the Democratic Party of Wisconsin since World War Two" (Ph.D. diss., University of Wisconsin, 1970), p. 210.

47. Ibid., pp. 216–18.

48. Thomas Coleman to A.L. Shultz, 19 October 1953, Box 5, Thomas Coleman Papers, S.H.S.W.; Coleman memorandum to five Wisconsin Republicans, 23 October 1953, Box 5, Coleman Papers.

49. *The Capital Times,* 22 December 1953.

50. *Green Bay Press-Gazette,* 22 December 1953.

51. Fried, *Men against McCarthy,* pp. 272–73.

Notes to Chapter 9: The Senator Becomes a Liability: 1954

1. Robert Griffith, *The Politics of Fear* (Lexington: The University Press of Kentucky, 1970), p. 248.
2. Richard Rovere, *Senator Joe McCarthy* (Cleveland and New York: The World Publishing Co., 1959), p. 30.
3. *Milwaukee Journal,* 12 March 1954.
4. Memorandum, Charles F. Willis to Sherman Adams, 4 March 1954, General File 171, Dwight Eisenhower Papers, Dwight Eisenhower Library, Abilene, Kans. The memo discussed the action of Jasper and other Wisconsin Republicans. Adams responded, "Good."
5. Richard Fried, *Men against McCarthy* (New York: Columbia University Press, 1976), p. 283; *Milwaukee Journal,* 12 March 1954.
6. *Milwaukee Journal,* 6 March 1954.
7. *The Sheboygan Press,* 20 March 1954; *The Capital Times,* 1 March 1954; *Milwaukee Journal,* 23 February and 10 March 1954.
8. *Waukesha Daily Freeman,* 25 February 1954; *The LaCrosse Tribune,* 28 February 1954; *The Beloit Daily News,* 26 February 1954. An editorial satirizing McCarthy for his criticism of Zwicker appeared in the *Wausau Record-Herald,* 6 March 1954.
9. *The Beloit Daily News,* 15 March 1954.
10. Rovere, *Joe McCarthy,* p. 239; Griffith, *Politics of Fear,* p. 254.
11. Griffith, *Politics of Fear,* pp. 254–58.
12. *Racine Journal-Times,* 11 June 1954; *Janesville Gazette,* 11 June 1954.
13. *Wisconsin State Journal,* 11 June 1954.
14. David P. Thelen and Esther S. Thelen, "Joe Must Go: The Movement to Recall Senator Joseph R. McCarthy," *Wisconsin Magazine of History* (Spring 1966): 186–87; *The Sauk-Prairie Star,* 7 January and 11 February 1954.
15. Thelen and Thelen, "Joe Must Go," pp. 189, 191; *The Capital Times,* 29 March 1954.
16. Leroy Gore, *Joe Must Go* (New York: Julian Messner, Inc., 1954), p. 50.
17. Thelen and Thelen, "Joe Must Go," p. 189.
18. Ivan Nestingen to Mr. Edwards, 21 June 1954, Series 1, File B, Box 1, C.O.P.E. Correspondence, A.F.L.–C.I.O. Papers, State Historical Society of Wisconsin (S.H.S.W.).
19. Ted Cloak and Jane Cloak, " 'Joe Must Go': The Story of Dane County in the 1954 Recall against McCarthy" (typescript, 1954, written for a University of Wisconsin sociology course), Manuscript Library, S.H.S.W., pp. 43–44.
20. *Wisconsin State Journal,* 31 March 1954.
21. Thelen and Thelen, "Joe Must Go," pp. 193, 198; Ivan Nestingen, "The McCarthy Recall Effort," *The Intercollegian* (October 1954); Ivan Nestingen, memorandum, 21 April 1954, Box 3, Ivan Nestingen Papers, S.H.S.W.; Ivan Nestingen to The Anti-Defamation League of B'nai B'rith, 21 April 1954, Box 3, Nestingen Papers.
22. Ivan Nestingen to Mr. Edwards, 21 June 1954, Series 1, File B, Box 1, C.O.P.E. Correspondence, A.F.L.–C.I.O. Papers; Ivan Nestingen to George Agree, 18 May 1954, Box 3, Nestingen Papers.
23. Thelen and Thelen, "Joe Must Go," p. 200.
24. Irving T. Cherdron, memorandum, 5 June 1954, Box 3, Nestingen Papers; Ivan Nestingen to Morris Novik and Harry Bovshow, 2 October 1954, Box 3, Nestingen Papers.
25. *The Sauk-Prairie Star,* 20 May 1954.
26. *The Capital Times,* 22 March 1954.
27. Memorandum, John Howe to William Benton, 1 August 1954, Box 4, William Benton Papers, S.H.S.W.; Thelen and Thelen, "Joe Must Go," p. 202.

28. *The LaCrosse Tribune*, 12 April 1954.

29. Thelen and Thelen, "Joe Must Go," p. 202.

30. Ibid., p. 203; *Milwaukee Journal*, 24 May 1954; Minutes of the Joe Must Go Steering Committee, 17 April 1954, Box 3, Nestingen Papers.

31. Thelen and Thelen, "Joe Must Go," p. 204.

32. Ibid., p. 205.

33. Ibid.

34. Minutes of Steering Committee, 29 June 1954, Box 3, Nestingen Papers; Leroy Gore to Morris Novik, 15 October 1954, Box 3, Nestingen Papers; Ivan Nestingen to Morris Novik, 19 October 1954, Box 3, Nestingen Papers.

35. Thelen and Thelen, "Joe Must Go," p. 209.

36. Ibid.

37. Karl Butler to Victor Emanuel, 27 December 1954, Box 5, John W. Hill Papers, S.H.S.W.

38. Thelen and Thelen, "Joe Must Go," p. 186.

39. Letter to the *Wisconsin Agriculturist and Farmer*, 6 March 1954.

40. Miles McMillin, "Calling the Roll on McCarthy," *The Progressive*, (May 1954): 13–14; *The Capital Times*, 5 April 1954.

41. Jerome Blaska, letter to *The Capital Times*, 22 February 1954; Thelen and Thelen, "Joe Must Go," p. 194.

42. *Wisconsin State Journal*, 9 May 1954. McCarthy had made a similar proposal on 12 January 1954, but it had not received publicity.

43. *Proceedings of the Republican State Convention: 1954* (Republican Party of Wisconsin, Madison, Wisconsin).

44. Thelen and Thelen, "Joe Must Go," p. 195.

45. Reprint of an editorial from *The Farmer's Friend* in *The Capital Times*, 12 May 1954; *Wisconsin Agriculturist and Farmer*, 5 June 1954; *Wisconsin Farmer's Union News*, 25 October 1954.

46. James Green to Karl Butler, [December 1954], Box 5, Hill Papers.

47. *Wisconsin Agriculturist and Farmer*, 17 July 1954.

48. Gore, *Joe Must Go*, p. 67.

49. Thelen and Thelen, "Joe Must Go," p. 195.

50. *The Capital Times*, 8 February 1954; *Wisconsin State Journal*, 8 February 1954.

51. *Green Bay Press-Gazette*, 14 June 1954; *Wisconsin State Journal*, 13 June 1954; *The Capital Times*, 12 June 1954.

52. *The Capital Times*, 21 June 1954; Thomas Coleman to Arthur Summerfield, 27 January 1954, Box 5, Thomas Coleman Papers, S.H.S.W.

53. Wilbur Renk to Sherman Adams, 18 June 1954, General File 109-A-2, Eisenhower Papers.

54. *Wisconsin State Journal*, 3 December 1954; *Green Bay Press-Gazette*, 15 March 1954; Miles McMillin, "Wisconsin Double-Take," *The Nation* (22 May 1954): 440.

55. Interviews, Mark Catlin, Jr., 24 February 1977; Claude Jasper, 22 June 1977.

56. Godfrey Sperling, Jr., "Wisconsin Rumblings," *The Christian Science Monitor*, 24 March 1954.

57. Wayne Hood to Carl E. Steiger, 30 March 1954, Box 2, Wayne Hood Papers, S.H.S.W.; Thomas Coleman to William Lloyd, 12 April 1954, Box 2, Hood Papers.

58. *Green Bay Press-Gazette*, 18 March 1954.

59. *Green Bay Press-Gazette*, 21 May 1954.

60. *Green Bay Press-Gazette*, 18 May 1954; Bernard Shanley to Sherman Adams, 23 June 1954, General File 109-A-2, Eisenhower Papers.

61. *Green Bay Press-Gazette*, 18 March 1954; *Wisconsin State Journal*, 27 April and 6 May 1954.

62. Thelen and Thelen, "Joe Must Go," pp. 205–6; Harry Franke to Dwight

Eisenhower, 26 April 1954, General File 171, Eisenhower Papers; Irving Cherdron memorandum, 5 June 1954, Box 3, Nestingen Papers.

63. *Milwaukee Journal*, 12 and 13 June 1954.

64. *Milwaukee Journal*, 27 June 1954.

65. Congressman John W. Byrnes to Dwight Eisenhower, 6 July 1954, General File 109-A-2, Eisenhower Papers; Congressman Glenn Davis to Sherman Adams, 3 July 1954, General File 109-A-2, Eisenhower Papers.

66. *Milwaukee Journal*, 30 June 1954; Congressman Melvin Laird to Sherman Adams, 1 July 1954, General File 109-A-2, Eisenhower Papers.

67. James Doyle, "McCarthyism," in Quincy Howe and Arthur M. Schlesinger, Jr., eds., *Guide to Politics 1954* (New York: The Dial Press, 1954), pp. 25–29; *The Capital Times*, 3 August 1954.

68. *Milwaukee Journal*, 6 August 1954; memorandum, John Howe to William Benton, 1 August 1954, Box 4, Benton Papers, S.H.S.W.

69. *The Christian Science Monitor*, 18 September 1954.

70. *Green Bay Press-Gazette*, 27 September 1954.

71. *Milwaukee Journal*, 1 and 19 October 1954.

72. Griffith, *The Politics of Fear*, p. 297.

73. Alexander Wiley to H. E. Ihlenfeld, 2 December 1954, McCarthy Subject File (not completely processed), Alexander Wiley Papers, S.H.S.W.; form letter by Wiley to his constituents, November 1954, Wiley Papers.

74. For examples, see *The LaCrosse Tribune*, 2 December 1954; *Milwaukee Sentinel*, 3 November 1954; *Appleton Post-Crescent*, 3 December 1954.

75. *Wisconsin State Journal*, 3 December 1954.

76. *The Beloit Daily News*, 3 December 1954; *Racine Journal-Times*, 4 December 1954; *Marshfield News-Herald*, 3 December 1954; *The Capital Times*, 3 December 1954.

77. *Wisconsin State Journal*, 8 December 1954; Griffith, *The Politics of Fear*, p. 316.

78. *Oshkosh Daily Northwestern*, 9 December 1954.

79. *Wausau Record-Herald*, 8 December 1954; *Marinette Eagle-Star*, 22 December 1954; *Fond du Lac Commonwealth Reporter*, 15 December 1954.

80. *The Capital Times*, 11 December 1954.

81. *Wisconsin State Journal*, 9 and 25 December 1954; *Milwaukee Journal*, 12 December 1954; *The Capital Times*, 8 December 1954; *Green Bay Press-Gazette*, 20 December 1954.

Notes to Chapter 10: Profiles: Catholics, Charisma, and "McCarthyism"

1. Donald Crosby, S.J., "The Angry Catholics: American Catholics and Senator Joseph R. McCarthy, 1950–1957" (Ph.D. diss., Brandeis University, 1973), p. 124; Robert Schwartz to Barron Beshoar, 4 October 1951, Box 4, Robert Fleming Papers, State Historical Society of Wisconsin (S.H.S.W.); W. Henry Johnston to Alexander Wiley, 18 April 1947, Box 24 (not completely processed), Alexander Wiley Papers, S.H.S.W.; *Wisconsin State Journal*, 30 January 1946; *The Capital Times*, 23 October 1946; *Appleton Post-Crescent*, 2 November 1946.

2. Crosby, "Angry Catholics," pp. x, 275.

3. Vincent P. De Santis, "American Catholics and McCarthyism," *The Catholic Historical Review*, 7 (April 1965):24.

4. Ibid., pp. 10–11; Crosby, "Angry Catholics," p. 108.

5. De Santis, "American Catholics," pp. 4–5; Crosby, "Angry Catholics," p. 49; Erma Melawn to Sen. Ralph Flanders, 2 June 1954, Box 6, Ralph Flanders Papers, S.H.S.W.

6. Crosby, "Angry Catholics," pp. 98–99, 157; *The Catholic Herald Citizen* (Madison), 18 March 1950.

7. *The Catholic Herald Citizen* (Madison), 13 May and 3 June 1950.

8. Wisconsin Civic Leaders, "Why McCarthy Should Be Repudiated," *The Nation* (30 August 1952): 170; *The Capital Times*, 15 March 1954; Ted Cloak and Jane Cloak, " 'Joe Must Go': The Story of Dane County in the 1954 Recall against McCarthy" (typescript, 1954, written for a University of Wisconsin sociology course), Manuscript Library, S.H.S.W., pp. 54–55.

9. *The Capital Times*, 28 November 1950, 28 October 1952, and 13 January 1954.

10. "Statements on McCarthyism by Religious Leaders," in Cloak and Cloak, " 'Joe Must Go,' " app. II; Morris Rubin, ed., *McCarthy: A Documented Record*, special edition of *The Progressive* (April 1954): 31; Morris Rubin to Michel Gordey, 24 December 1953 (unprocessed), *The Progressive* Magazine Papers, S.H.S.W.; *The Capital Times*, 17 May 1950, 19 and 23 April 1954.

11. *The Progressive* (May 1954): 10–12.

12. De Santis, "American Catholics," p. 10.

13. *Green Bay Press-Gazette*, 17 May 1954.

14. *The Capital Times*, 13 April 1954.

15. *Green Bay Press-Gazette*, 15 June 1953.

16. Typescript of a tape-recorded interview with Morris Rubin by Robert Griffith, 23 June 1967. A copy of the typescript was loaned to me by Rubin.

17. Karl Meyer, "The Politics of Loyalty from La Follette to McCarthy in Wisconsin 1918–1952" (Ph.D. diss., Princeton University, 1956), pp. 184–85.

18. *Wisconsin State Journal*, 10 July 1952; *The LaCrosse Tribune*, 9 June 1950; *Green Bay Press-Gazette*, 2 September 1950, 27 February 1951.

19. *Ashland Daily Press*, 28 October 1952; *Green Bay Press-Gazette*, 1 November 1952; *Milwaukee Sentinel*, 29 and 30 October 1952.

20. These terms were used often in letters to Wisconsin newspapers; *Milwaukee Sentinel*, 28 November 1953.

21. *Ashland Daily Press*, 23 March 1954.

22. *Milwaukee Journal*, 9 May 1952; *Wisconsin Agriculturist and Farmer*, 6 September 1952.

23. *The Shawano Evening Leader*, 3 December 1951.

24. *Milwaukee Journal*, 31 August 1950.

25. *Milwaukee Journal*, 8 July 1951.

26. Memorandum, excerpts from a number of letters received by Sen. Alexander Wiley on the McCarthy censure issue, McCarthy Subject File, Wiley Papers.

27. Francis Johnson to Dwight Eisenhower, 23 April 1954, GF 171, Dwight Eisenhower Papers, Dwight Eisenhower Library, Abilene, Kans. The quotation, which was enclosed in Johnson's letter, came from a resolution passed unanimously at a meeting of the Vilas County Republican party.

28. *The Beloit Daily News*, 12 November 1954.

29. *Appleton Post-Crescent*, 8 September 1952; *Wisconsin State Journal*, 2 May 1950; *Waukesha Daily Freeman*, 10 September 1952; *The Beloit Daily News*, 4 September 1952.

30. *Green Bay Press-Gazette*, 17 October 1950.

31. David Goodman to Leonard Schmitt, 10 September 1952 (unprocessed), Leonard Schmitt Papers, Leonard Schmitt's office, Merrill, Wisconsin.

32. *Green Bay Press-Gazette*, 9 July 1951.

33. *Green Bay Press-Gazette*, 14 June 1954.

34. *Congressional Record*, 83d Cong., 2d sess. (19 May 1954), vol. 100, p. 6819.

35. *Green Bay Press-Gazette*, 8 June 1950, 14 June 1954; letter to *The Progressive* (January 1953).

36. *Milwaukee Journal,* 14 November 1954.

37. *The Wisconsin Democrat,* June 1951.

38. Richard Rovere, *Senator Joe McCarthy* (Cleveland and New York: The World Publishing Co., 1959), p. 51.

39. *Milwaukee Journal,* 25 June 1954.

40. *Major Speeches and Debates of Senator Joe McCarthy: Delivered in the United States Senate 1950–1951* (Washington, D.C.: United States Government Printing Office), p. 161.

41. *Milwaukee Journal,* 10 May 1950.

42. *The Badger Legionnaire,* October 1952; *Green Bay Press-Gazette,* 22 August 1952; *Wisconsin State Journal,* 18 August 1952.

43. For examples of this terminology, see *Green Bay Press-Gazette,* 9 June 1950; survey report in the *Wisconsin Agriculturist and Farmer,* 3 June 1950; *Milwaukee Sentinel,* 4 February 1952; *Wisconsin State Journal,* 23 June 1954.

44. Leroy Gore, *Joe Must Go* (New York: Julian Messner, Inc., 1954), p. 130.

45. *Kenosha Labor,* 28 June 1951; *Racine Labor,* 12 September 1952; *Wisconsin State Journal,* 18 July 1952; *The Capital Times,* 7 August 1952.

46. *New York Times,* 2 November 1952.

47. *Proceedings of the Wisconsin State Republican Convention: 1950* (Republican Party of Wisconsin, Madison, Wisconsin), p. 39.

48. *Milwaukee Sentinel,* 10 July 1952.

49. *Chicago Daily News,* 11 September 1952.

50. Bradley Taylor to William C. Brooker, 19 April 1954, Box 5, Bradley Taylor Papers, S.H.S.W.

51. *Vilas County News-Review,* 28 February 1952.

52. *Milwaukee Journal,* 12 December 1951.

53. Ibid.; *The Capital Times,* 12 December 1951.

54. Alan D. Harper, *The Politics of Loyalty: The White House and the Communist Issue, 1946–1952* (Westport, Conn.: Greenwood Publishing Corp., 1969), pp. 48–49; Harold M. Hyman, *To Try Men's Souls: Loyalty Tests in American History* (Berkeley and Los Angeles: University of California Press, 1959), pp. 335–36; Ralph Brown, Jr., *Loyalty and Security: Employment Tests in the United States* (New Haven: Yale University Press, 1958), pp. 487–88.

55. Mary S. McAuliffe, "Liberals and the Communist Control Act of 1954," *The Journal of American History* 63:2 (September 1976): 351–67.

56. Hyman, *To Try Men's Souls,* pp. 338, 340; Walter Gellhorn, ed., *The States and Subversion* (Ithaca, N.Y.: Cornell University Press, 1952), pp. 382–83, 391.

57. Gellhorn, *States and Subversion,* pp. 363–64.

58. Ibid., pp. 203–16.

59. Gore, *Joe Must Go,* p. 130; *Wisconsin State Journal,* 12 July 1954; *Milwaukee Journal,* 2 May 1954.

60. Robert W. Wells, *This Is Milwaukee* (Garden City, N.Y.: Doubleday & Co., 1970), pp. 244–46.

61. *The Capital Times,* 5 July 1951; *Wisconsin State Journal,* 1 August 1951.

62. Violet Gunther to James Doyle, 3 February 1953, Series 5, Box 39, Americans for Democratic Action Papers, S.H.S.W.

63. Mary Jane Dunwiddie to Sherman Adams, 17 January 1953, GF 171, 1953–1954 C, Eisenhower Papers.

. 64. For examples, see Gore, *Joe Must Go; The Capital Times,* 11 May 1954; *The Sauk-Prairie Star,* 1 April 1954.

65. J. M. Rose to Dwight Eisenhower, 12 May 1954, GF 171, Eisenhower Papers; *Green Bay Press-Gazette,* 7 and 29 May 1954; *The Capital Times,* 25 May 1954.

66. Morris Rubin, ed., *The McCarthy Record* (Madison: The Wisconsin Citizens' Committee on McCarthy's Record, 1952), pp. 4–7; Interviews, Miles McMillin, 2

September 1969; Morris Rubin, 14 April 1969; and Griffith interview with Rubin, 23 July 1967.

67. Gore, *Joe Must Go*, pp. 18, 50; Harold Michael to Edward R. Murrow, 1 April 1954 (microfilmed), Harold Michael Papers, S.H.S.W.

68. Interviews, Joseph Kriofske, 23 March 1977; Albert Shortridge, 5 April 1977.

69. Jack Anderson and Ronald May, *McCarthy: The Man, the Senator, the "Ism"* (Boston: The Beacon Press, 1952), p. 285.

70. Ibid., p. 274; *Milwaukee Journal*, 3 July 1950, 8 April 1951.

71. Robert Fleming, memorandum, 6 August 1950, Box 3, Fleming Papers.

72. Robert Fleming to Tottie and Louie [?], 1 July 1950, Box 1, Fleming Papers; Fleming memorandum on McCarthy's speech of 27 January 1951, n.d., Box 3, Fleming Papers; Richard H. Field to Robert Fleming, 20 April 1951, Box 3, Fleming Papers; Fleming memorandum on McCarthy and Louis Weiss, n.d., Box 3, Fleming Papers; Fleming memorandum on the Hiss List, n.d., Box 3, Fleming Papers.

73. Gellhorn, *States and Subversion*, p. 439; *Digest of the Public Record of Communism in the United States* (New York: The Fund for the Republic, Inc., 1955), pp. 249, 256, 265, 295, 314, 341, 382; James F. Scotton, "Loyalty and the Wisconsin Legislature" (M.A. thesis, University of Wisconsin, 1966), pp. 73, 184–95.

74. Scotton, "Loyalty and the Wisconsin Legislature," pp. 118–19; *The Capital Times*, 23 February 1947, 26 May 1949; Walter Kohler, Jr., to H. Harris Nukes, 3 April 1951, Box 40, Walter Kohler, Jr., Papers, S.H.S.W.

75. Scotton, "Loyalty and the Wisconsin Legislature," pp. 74, 194.

76. Ibid., pp. 119–20.

77. Morris Rubin to Jeffrey Fuller, 15 April 1953, *The Progressive* Magazine Papers.

78. *The Progressive* (April 1955): 5–6; William E. Bohn, " 'Joe Must Go' and Leroy Gore," *The New Leader* (5 September 1955):7.

79. Gellhorn, *States and Subversion*, pp. 375, 377; Peter C. Schaehrer, "McCarthyism and Academic Freedom—Three Case Studies" (Ph.D. diss., Columbia University, 1974), pp. 243, 281.

80. David P. Gardner, *The California Oath Controversy* (Berkeley: University of California Press, 1967), p. 12.

81. Ibid., pp. vii, 245–47; Verne A. Stadtman, *The University of California: 1868–1968* (New York: McGraw-Hill Book Co., 1970), pp. 324, 327, 338; Scotton, "Loyalty and the Wisconsin Legislature," p. 28.

82. Scotton, "Loyalty and the Wisconsin Legislature," p. 28; Schaehrer, "McCarthyism and Academic Freedom," pp. 25–27, 240–41; Sigmund Diamond, "Veritas at Harvard," *The New York Review of Books*, 28 April 1977, pp. 13–17; "Incomplete Candor," *Newsweek* (25 July 1977): 77.

83. Gellhorn, *States and Subversion*, pp. 55, 138–39; Schaehrer, "McCarthyism and Academic Freedom," pp. 27–30, 107, 144–45.

84. William G. Rice, "The Meaning of McCarthyism," *The Nation* (30 August 1952): 166.

85. *Major Speeches and Debates of Senator Joe McCarthy: Delivered in the United States Senate: 1950–1951* (Washington, D.C.: United States Government Printing Office), p. 17; Joseph McCarthy, *McCarthyism: The Fight for America* (New York: Devin-Adair Co., 1952), p. 101.

86. *The Daily Cardinal* (University of Wisconsin–Madison), 30 October 1952; *Wisconsin State Journal*, 1 November 1952.

87. *Wisconsin State Journal*, 5 May 1952; Edwin Bayley, "Wisconsin: The War against Eisenhower," *New Republic* (6 July 1953): 16; *The Capital Times*, 27 July 1954. In April 1952, the six-man board of the Madison Vocational and Adult School voted unanimously to deny use of school facilities to any group labeled subversive, "either directly or by association"; *Wisconsin State Journal*, 29 April 1952.

88. Edwin B. Fred to R. M. Schlabach, 7 April 1952, Box 169, E. B. Fred, Presidential Papers, University of Wisconsin Archives, University of Wisconsin Library, Madison, Wisconsin; E. B. Fred statement, 8 March 1952, Box 169, Fred Papers.

89. *The Badger Legionnaire,* April 1954; Robert G. Wilke to Hans Kruger, 13 October 1954; Robert Wilke to E. B. Fred, 12 February 1954; and Robert Wilke to Lee Pennington, 12 February 1954, all Box 50, American Legion Papers, Department of Wisconsin, S.H.S.W.

90. "A Statement by University of Wisconsin President Edwin B. Fred," 14 January 1953, Box A-19, Fred Papers; *The Capital Times,* 13 January 1953; Interview, Leroy Luberg, 3 April 1969, 15 February 1977.

91. Interviews, Luberg, 3 April 1969, 15 February 1977; Donald Anderson, 15 February 1977; Mark Catlin, Jr., 24 February 1977; Mark Ingraham, 1 April 1969; and Warren Knowles, 10 March 1977.

92. "University of Wisconsin Policies," *Wisconsin Legislative Council 1955 Report,* vol. I; *Wisconsin State Journal,* 13 March 1953; Interviews, Ingraham, 24 February 1977; Luberg, 3 April 1969, 15 February 1977; and Knowles, 10 March 1977. For more on the University of Wisconsin's public-relations efforts with the legislature, see the Leroy Luberg File, Box 214, Fred Papers.

93. Frank J. Sensenbrenner to E. B. Fred, 13 March 1950, Box 135, Fred Papers; E. B. Fred statement of 8 March 1952, Box 169, Fred Papers; William J. Campbell to Fred, 15 July 1952, Box 163, Fred Papers; Fred to Campbell, 22 July 1952, Box 163, Fred Papers; William J. Campbell to Edgar Robinson, 4 December 1953, Box 1, William J. Campbell Papers, S.H.S.W.

94. F. J. Sensenbrenner to E. B. Fred, 8 June 1950, Box 135, Fred Papers; John D. Jones to F. J. Sensenbrenner, 30 March 1950, Box 135, Fred Papers; Interview, Robert Ozanne, 15 July 1977.

95. Copy of Election Financial Statement of the McCarthy for Senator Club, File 4, Drawer 1 (unprocessed), National Committee for an Effective Congress Papers, Maurice Rosenblatt's home, Washington, D.C.; Joseph McCarthy to Matt Schuh, 11 October 1951, File 4, Drawer 1 (unprocessed), National Committee for an Effective Congress Papers; "Frank J. Sensenbrenner," *Dictionary of Wisconsin Biography* (Madison: The State Historical Society of Wisconsin, 1960), p. 324.

96. F. J. Sensenbrenner to E. B. Fred, 8 June 1950; Sensenbrenner to Fred, 3 July 1950; Fred to Sensenbrenner, 10 July 1950; Fred memorandum, "Items to Discuss with F. J. Sensenbrenner" [probably June 1950], all Box 135, Fred Papers; Sensenbrenner to John Berge, 20 June 1951, Box 11 (unprocessed), Warren Knowles Papers, S.H.S.W.

97. F. J. Sensenbrenner to E. B. Fred, 27 July 1951, Box 156, Fred Papers.

98. E. B. Fred to F. J. Sensenbrenner, 10 August 1951, Box 156, Fred Papers.

99. Brown, *Loyalty and Security,* p. 134.

100. Ibid., pp. 89–90; Morris Rubin to A. Matt Werner, 22 March 1955, *The Progressive* Magazine Papers; E. B. Fred to Morris Rubin, 22 October 1954, *Progressive* Papers; Scotton, "Loyalty and the Wisconsin Legislature," p. 122; *The Capital Times,* 29 September 1954.

There is some evidence that the University of Wisconsin may not have been a consistently courageous defender of academic freedom. Wilbur Renk, a regent from 1951 to 1960, has recalled an informal policy adopted by unspecified university administrators to deal with students and faculty suspected of having been Communists. According to Renk, the university quietly dismissed alleged Communist professors, claiming that their work was unsatisfactory. The university also flunked students suspected of having Communist beliefs and affiliations. "Hell, we flunked A students," Renk recalled. (Interview, Wilbur Renk, 3 September 1969.)

If Renk's recollection is correct, it raises important questions about the extent of academic freedom at the university. Were the students and faculty who were dismissed actually Communists? What individuals, committees, or procedures determined this? Were political and ideological views sufficient bases for the drastic action taken against them? And, finally, was the university actually a courageous defender of academic freedom?

To date, there is no additional evidence to corroborate Renk's remarkable account. The voluminous Edwin B. Fred Papers (University of Wisconsin Archives, Madison) contain nothing on the subject. When I confronted prominent university administrators with Renk's charges, they responded with what appeared to be sincere incredulity. They could recall no such policy, claimed they would have opposed it had it been implemented, and doubted that such a policy could have been implemented secretly. (Interviews, Mark Ingraham, 27 July 1970; Leroy Luberg, 15 February 1977; and Robert Ozanne, 15 July 1977.) In a follow-up interview, Renk insisted that university officials had told him that an informal policy existed, that they "fired . . . people who were professing communism," but did not want to make a "big [public] stink" about it as McCarthy had done. (Interview, Wilbur Renk, 24 May 1977.)

Until more sources become available, I must conclude that Renk was misinformed. Some administrators may have told him that there was such a policy, but none in fact existed.

101. Interviews, Ingraham, 24 February 1977; Luberg, 3 April 1969, 15 February 1977; Rubin, 14 April 1969; and David Fellman, 3 April 1969.

102. See Schaehrer, "McCarthyism and Academic Freedom"; Ronald W. Johnson, "The Communist Issue in Missouri: 1946–1956" (Ph.D. diss., University of Missouri, 1973); Ingrid W. Scobie, "Jack Tenney: Molder of Anti-Communist Legislation in California: 1940–1949" (Ph.D. diss., University of Wisconsin, 1970).

103. *Vilas County News-Review,* 21 February 1952, see also 28 February 1952; *Green Bay Press-Gazette,* 1 August 1951.

104. *Milwaukee Journal,* 7 March 1951.

105. *Green Bay Press-Gazette,* 14 December 1951, 12 August 1952.

106. Laurence R. Veysey, *The Emergence of the American University* (Chicago and London: The University of Chicago Press, 1965), pp. 108–9; Merle Curti and Vernon Carstensen, *The University of Wisconsin: 1848–1925,* vol. II, pp. 53–57, 69–71, 285, 288–89.

107. Scotton, "Loyalty and the Wisconsin Legislature," p. 118; Wells, *This Is Milwaukee,* pp. 169–79; Thomas W. Gavett, *Development of the Labor Movement in Milwaukee* (Madison and Milwaukee: The University of Wisconsin Press, 1965), pp. 205–6.

## Notes to Chapter 11: The Last Years: 1955–1957

1. Richard Rovere, *Senator Joe McCarthy* (Cleveland and New York: The World Publishing Co., 1959), p. 239.

2. Ibid.; *The Capital Times,* 9 May 1955.

3. Rovere, *Joe McCarthy,* p. 244; *Milwaukee Journal,* 3 May 1957. Many people that I interviewed noted his ghastly appearance.

4. Interviews, Karl Baldwin, 3 March 1977; Wayne Hood, 10 September 1969; Claude Jasper, 22 June 1977; Alvin O'Konski, 4 March 1977; Urban Van Susteren, 4 September 1969, 22 March 1977; and John Wyngaard, 30 December 1969.

5. Interview, Warren Knowles, 10 March 1977.

6. Rovere, *Joe McCarthy,* pp. 245–46; Interview, Llewellyn Morack, 11 March 1977.

7. *The Capital Times*, 6 June 1955.

8. Reprint of a broadcast by the National Farmer's Union entitled "Farmer's Union on the Air," in *The Capital Times*, 3 November 1955; *Wisconsin Agriculturist and Farmer*, 18 June 1955; *The Capital Times*, 5 December 1956, 13 February 1957; Rovere, *Joe McCarthy*, p. 242.

9. *Racine Journal-Times*, 29 November 1955.

10. *New York Times*, 19 February 1956; *Milwaukee Journal*, 25 January and 12 and 19 February 1956; *The Capital Times*, 23 January and 14 February 1956.

11. Matson's statement appeared in *The Capital Times*, 1 March 1956; *Wisconsin State Journal*, 2 and 3 August 1955; *Milwaukee Journal*, 3 May 1957; *Appleton Post-Crescent*, 1 April 1955, 20 October 1956.

12. Joseph McCarthy to Roy Matson, 9 January 1957 (unprocessed), *Wisconsin State Journal* Papers, State Historical Society of Wisconsin (S.H.S.W.); Roy Matson to Joseph McCarthy, 18 January 1957, *Journal* Papers; Interview, Ray Kiermas, 7 April 1977. In his letter to Matson, McCarthy assumed that Matson's criticism stemmed from the fact that McCarthy had objected to a television license that Matson and others had applied for. McCarthy explained that he objected because William T. Evjue had joined Matson's group in applying for the license and because Cedric Parker was Evjue's assistant. Matson replied that this was not the reason for the *State Journal's* criticism of McCarthy.

13. *Milwaukee Journal*, 21 January 1956.

14. *New York Times*, 19 February 1956.

15. *Milwaukee Journal*, 26 and 29 June 1955; *The Capital Times*, 25 June 1955.

16. *Green Bay Press-Gazette*, 23 March 1956.

17. Wayne Hood to Mrs. Joseph McCarthy, 30 March 1956, Box 2 (unprocessed), Wayne Hood Papers, S.H.S.W.

18. Michael Rogin, *The Intellectuals and McCarthy: The Radical Specter* (Cambridge, Mass.: The M.I.T. Press, 1967), p. 251; see the series of memos probably written by Thomas Coleman, November–December 1955, Box 8, Thomas Coleman Papers, S.H.S.W.; *Wisconsin State Journal*, 6 and 29 May and 9 September 1956; *The Capital Times*, 28 May 1956.

19. *Milwaukee Journal*, 22 August 1956.

20. *Milwaukee Journal*, 28 September 1956, 3 May 1957.

21. *Green Bay Press-Gazette*, 23 March 1956; *The Christian Science Monitor*, 16 March 1957; Taylor Benson to James Hagerty, 7 December 1956, General File 109–A–2, Dwight Eisenhower Papers, Dwight Eisenhower Library, Abilene, Kans.; Walter Kohler to Edwin Bayley, 21 January 1957 (unprocessed), Edwin Bayley Papers, S.H.S.W.

23. *Fond du Lac Commonwealth Reporter*, 4 May 1957; *The Janesville Gazette*, 4 May 1957; *Green Bay Press-Gazette*, 4 May 1957; *Milwaukee Sentinel*, 3 May 1957.

24. *The Progressive* (June 1957); *The Capital Times*, 3 May 1957; *Milwaukee Journal*, 3 May 1957.

25. *The Janesville Gazette*, 4 May 1957; *Waukesha Daily Freeman*, 3 May 1957; *Oshkosh Daily Northwestern*, 3 May 1957; *Wisconsin State Journal*, 3 May 1957.

26. *Wisconsin State Journal*, 3 May 1957; *Green Bay Press-Gazette*, 1 May 1967.

27. *Milwaukee Journal*, 7 May 1957; *Appleton Post-Crescent*, 7 May 1957.

28. *Milwaukee Journal*, 7 May 1957.

29. *Report on Special Senatorial Election in Wisconsin, August 27, 1957* (New York: Public Opinion Polls, Inc., 1957), introduction and pp. 23 and 32. I used a copy located in the Dwight Eisenhower Library. Other reasons for Proxmire's victory were the cumulative effects of Proxmire's ceaseless campaigning, the swing of the farm vote to Proxmire in small towns and rural areas, and the massive drive by organized labor in urban areas. See also *The Progressive* (October 1957); Richard

Haney, "A History of the Democratic Party of Wisconsin since World War Two" (Ph.D. diss., University of Wisconsin, 1970), p. 286.

30. *Minneapolis Tribune,* 30 April 1967; Interviews, Jasper, 22 June 1977; Knowles, 10 March 1977. Other Democratic leaders who agreed with this view were John Reynolds and Elliot Walstead; *The New Wisconsin Democrat,* 20 April 1960; Interview, Elliot Walstead, 4 April 1977.

31. Haney, "Democratic Party of Wisconsin since World War Two," pp. 145–47; Interviews, James Doyle, 3 September 1969; Patrick Lucey, 28 August 1969; and Carl Thompson, 10 April 1969. In Marathon County, the DOC found that antipathy to McCarthy, combined with the appeal of Adlai Stevenson, attracted many people to the party. Leaders reported that in 1953 over half their members had not been previously active in Democratic politics; Howard R. Klueter and James J. Lorence, *Woodlot and Ballot Box: Marathon County in the Twentieth Century* (Stevens Point: Worzalla Publishing Co., 1977), p. 372.

32. Haney, "Democratic Party of Wisconsin since World War Two," pp. 147–48.

33. *Minneapolis Tribune,* 30 April 1967. Major Republicans who agreed on McCarthy's divisive influence included Donald Anderson, Claude Jasper, Warren Knowles, and Talbot Peterson; Interviews, Donald Anderson, 15 February 1977; Jasper, 22 June 1977; Knowles, 10 March 1977; and T. Peterson, 22 February 1977.

# Essay on Sources

This essay does not include all the sources used for this study. Readers should consult footnote citations for specific sources.

## Manuscripts

Some scholars may profit from a brief account of my experiences in attempting to secure access to the Joseph McCarthy Papers as well as my observations on the quality and availability of that much sought-after collection. Like other researchers, I did not receive permission to use the manuscripts that are committed to and partially possessed by Milwaukee's Marquette University, McCarthy's alma mater. McCarthy's widow, Mrs. Jean Minetti, who died in 1980, restricted access to the collection.

Father Raphael N. Hamilton, Marquette archivist and historian, told me in 1969 that the papers held by the university were "very good," but his description of them was less impressive: newspaper clippings, tape-recorded speeches, and mimeographed material. What Father Hamilton described as memos appeared to be the only valuable part of the collection.

The card catalogue at the Marquette University Archives indicates that (as of March 1977) the processed McCarthy Collection includes:

Series 1—Bills Introduced and Voting Record
Series 2—Biographical Manuscripts
Series 3—Correspondence Out
Series 4—Correspondence In
Series 5—Invitations to Speak
Series 6—Speeches Made by McCarthy
Series 7—Tapes and Phonograph Records
Series 8—Miscellaneous (Awards and Pictures)
Series 9—Newspaper Clippings
Series 10—Personal Library Related to McCarthy's Public Life
Series 11—McCarthy's Publications
Series 12—Additions to the Collection from Persons Other Than the Heirs of the Senator, and Publications about McCarthy and Those Associated with Him

Mrs. Minetti possessed the personal correspondence, and, based on a telephone conversation with her (12 March 1969), I suspect that her efforts to prepare the private papers may appreciably lessen their value for future historians. In 1966 or 1967, Mrs. Minetti commissioned right-wing author and one-time McCarthy assistant, J. B. Matthews, to write a biography of the senator using all the McCarthy Papers. Understandably, the senator's widow expected a sympathetic account. The project collapsed, however, when Matthews died unexpectedly before he had barely begun his research.

The length of time before all or part of the collection is opened is subject to speculation. In conversation with me, Father Hamilton placed the figure as long as "twenty-five to fifty years." He told *Newsweek* (5 May 1969) that the wait would be a "rather long one." Mrs. Minetti was indefinite. She told me that the entire collection would be opened when the preparation of the personal papers in her possession was ready. She explained to *Newsweek* that the private papers had not been "wholly put together" and that it would be useless for researchers to see "only part of the picture."

More recently, historian Thomas C. Reeves has encountered similar difficulties and frustrations. Mrs. Minetti told him in 1975 that the papers would be closed during her own and her daughter's lifetimes. He learned that the papers at Marquette are materials exclusively from the 1950s and contain no diaries or personal memorabilia and he judged that their contents are "qualitatively unimpressive." (Thomas C. Reeves, "The Search for Joe McCarthy," *Wisconsin Magazine of History* 60 [Spring 1977]: 185–96.)

In view of the fact that the Joseph McCarthy Papers are unavailable—and probably will remain so for many years—and that their quality is unknown, other collections dealing with the senator's career assume more importance. My foremost research aim was to consult all such collections. While, admittedly, these were not always as helpful as I desired, they nevertheless threw much light on an otherwise obscure historical subject. Most of the manuscript collections I consulted illuminated all aspects of McCarthy's career as well as my specific concern, Wisconsin's response to McCarthy.

For important insights into the relationship between McCarthy and Wisconsin Republicans, see the Thomas Coleman Papers (State Historical Society of Wisconsin, Madison, Wisconsin); Wayne Hood Papers (unprocessed, S.H.S.W.); and the voluminous Alexander Wiley Papers (S.H.S.W.). The William J. Campbell Papers (S.H.S.W.) are few in number but high in quality. Also useful for the same subject are the Sherman Adams Papers (Dwight Eisenhower Library, Abilene, Kansas); Dwight Eisenhower Papers (Eisenhower Library); Warren Knowles Papers (unprocessed, S.H.S.W.); and the Bradley Taylor Papers (S.H.S.W.). With the exception of material on his near decision to challenge McCarthy in the 1952 Republican primary, the Walter Kohler, Jr., Papers (S.H.S.W.) are disappointing. However, a six-page memorandum from Kohler to Adams, 27 April 1959, discloses Kohler's views on state GOP politics from 1950 to 1952. Kohler gave me a copy of the memorandum.

For important material on Robert M. La Follette, Jr., the Wisconsin Progressives, and the 1946 election, consult the La Follette Family Collection (Library of Congress, Washington, D.C.). Less useful for the same subjects are the Philip La Follette Papers (S.H.S.W.).

Papers dealing with anti-McCarthy forces in Wisconsin provide insights into state Democrats, journalists, labor unions, and political independents. Collections that shed light on one or more of these groups are the A.F.L.–C.I.O. Committee on Political Education Papers (S.H.S.W.); William Benton Papers (S.H.S.W.); National Committee for an Effective Congress Papers (Maurice Rosenblatt's home, Washington, D.C.); Stephen Spingarn Papers (Harry S. Truman Library, Independence, Missouri); and the Harry S. Truman Papers (Truman Library). The Ivan Nestingen Papers (S.H.S.W.) are revealing on the Joe Must Go recall movement. *The Progressive* Magazine Papers (not completely processed, S.H.S.W.) provide useful insight into anti-McCarthy groups and strategy. The Daniel Hoan Papers (Milwaukee County Historical Society, Milwaukee, Wisconsin) have important material on Wisconsin Democrats from 1946 to 1952. Less rewarding are Americans for Democratic Action Papers (S.H.S.W.), and the Richard Rovere Papers (S.H.S.W.).

A fascinating and important record of the efforts of a prominent anti-McCarthy journalist in Wisconsin, as well as significant materials on national and state opponents of McCarthy, can be found in the Robert Fleming Papers (S.H.S.W.).

The large collection of the William T. Evjue Papers (S.H.S.W.) are moderately helpful, but, considering the prominent role Evjue played in the anti-McCarthy movement, ultimately disappointing.

The Wisconsin Department of Agriculture Papers (S.H.S.W.) contain critically important records of the Quaker Dairy case of 1941. It has long been thought that these records were lost or stolen. Material on the state supreme court's censure of McCarthy in 1949 appears in the Edward Dempsey Papers (microfilm, S.H.S.W.). The John W. Hill Papers (S.H.S.W.) contain a few valuable letters discussing McCarthy's relationship with state farm leaders. The American Legion Papers, Department of Wisconsin (S.H.S.W.), detail the attitude toward McCarthy by some officials of the Wisconsin American Legion.

A few important letters or miscellaneous material appear in the Thomas Amlie Papers (S.H.S.W.); Donald Anderson Papers (S.H.S.W.); Dottie (Druckery) Anderson Papers (Dottie Anderson's home, Shawano, Wisconsin); Edwin R. Bayley Papers (S.H.S.W.); Charles E. Broughton Papers (S.H.S.W.); Marquis Childs Papers (S.H.S.W.); Herman L. Ekern Papers (S.H.S.W.); Roy Empey Papers (S.H.S.W.); Edwin B. Fred Papers (University of Wisconsin Archives, Madison, Wisconsin); Otis Gomillion Papers (in possession of Mrs. Bernadine Gomillion, Milwaukee, Wisconsin); Walter Goodland Papers (S.H.S.W.); Jack Kyle Papers (unprocessed, S.H.S.W.); Marquette University Papers (Marquette University Archives, Milwaukee, Wisconsin); Harold Michael Papers (microfilm, S.H.S.W.); Albert J. O'Melia Papers (S.H.S.W.); Leonard Schmitt Papers (Leonard Schmitt's office, Merrill, Wisconsin); Harold Townsend Papers (Harold Townsend's home, Milwaukee, Wisconsin); and the *Wisconsin State Journal* Papers (unprocessed, S.H.S.W.).

## Published Works: General

No scholarly biography of Joseph McCarthy exists. However, two are presently in preparation: one by Thomas C. Reeves, University of Wisconsin–Parkside, and another by David M. Oshinsky, Rutgers University. The best general work is still Richard Rovere, *Senator Joe McCarthy* (Cleveland and New York: The World Publishing Co. 1959). Beautifully written and at times insightful, Rovere's study is nevertheless inadequate because of its exclusive reliance on newspapers, contemporary printed materials, and his own personal recollections. Robert Griffith, *The Politics of Fear: Joseph R. McCarthy and the Senate* (Lexington: The University Press of Kentucky, 1970), supersedes Rovere's account of McCarthy's Senate career. This award-winning book was the first to incorporate a variety of high-quality sources, and Griffith handles his material with deftness. No historian can write authoritatively on McCarthy, the anti-Communist complex, or partisan politics in the early 1950s without consulting this book. Richard Fried, *Men against McCarthy* (New York: Columbia University Press, 1976) is excellent, particularly on opposition to McCarthy from 1950 to 1952. Fried relied on a huge amount of published and unpublished sources. David M. Oshinsky, *Senator Joseph McCarthy and the American Labor Movement* (Columbia: University of Missouri Press, 1976), chronicles organized labor's response to McCarthy's Senate career, but this book is substantially less impressive than those by Griffith and Fried. An essential recent study is Robert Griffith and Athan Theoharis, eds., *The Specter: Original Essays on the Cold War and the Origins of McCarthyism* (New York: New Viewpoints, 1974). This volume of twelve essays by young scholars concentrates on the anti-Communist activities of major organizations and interest groups—Catholics, conservative intellectuals, liberals, Chambers of Commerce, the CIO, motion-picture industry, and the American Civil Liberties Union. Jack Anderson and Ronald May, *McCarthy: The*

*Man, the Senator, the "Ism"* (Boston: The Beacon Press, 1952), is an unreliable liberal polemic, but portions of it are still necessary for an understanding of McCarthy's early life. Athan Theoharis, *Seeds of Repression* (Chicago: Quadrangle, 1971), condemns the anti-Communist rhetoric and policies of the Truman administration. Two noteworthy articles by an author of a forthcoming McCarthy biography are Thomas C. Reeves, "McCarthyism: Interpretations since Hofstadter," *Wisconsin Magazine of History* 60 (Autumn 1976): 42–54; and Thomas C. Reeves, "The Search for Joe McCarthy," *Wisconsin Magazine of History* 60 (Spring 1977): 185–96.

Other studies that provide some information or unique analysis are Saul Pett, ed., *The AP McCarthy Series* (New York: Associated Press, 1954); Daniel Bell, ed., *The Radical Right* (Garden City, N.Y.: Doubleday & Co., 1963); Earl Latham, *The Communist Controversy in Washington: From the New Deal to McCarthy* (Cambridge, Mass.: Harvard University Press, 1966); Reinhard Luthin, *American Demagogues: The 20th Century* (Boston: The Beacon Press, 1954); James Rorty and Moshe Decter, *McCarthy and the Communists* (Boston: The Beacon Press, 1954); Morris Rubin, ed., "McCarthy: A Documented Record," special edition of *The Progressive* (April 1954); Charles Potter, *Days of Shame* (New York: Coward-McCann & Geoghegan, Inc., 1965); Alan D. Harper, *The Politics of Loyalty* (Westport, Conn.: Greenwood Publishing Corp., 1969); and James T. Patterson, *Mr. Republican: A Biography of Robert A. Taft* (Boston: Houghton Mifflin Co., 1972).

Two popular historical accounts of McCarthy's career are Fred Cook, *The Nightmare Decade: The Life and Times of Senator Joe McCarthy* (New York: Random House, 1971); and Lately Thomas, *When Even Angels Wept: The Senator Joseph McCarthy Affair—A Story without a Hero* (New York: William Morrow & Co., 1973). Both books are of little value to a serious McCarthy scholar.

Unconvincing, but nevertheless the best defense of McCarthy, is William F. Buckley and L. Brent Bozell, *McCarthy and His Enemies* (Chicago: Henry Regnery Co., 1954). Roy Cohn, *McCarthy* (New York: New American Library, 1968), is ghost-written and filled with distortions. For the senator's own account, see Joseph McCarthy, *McCarthyism: The Fight for America* (New York: Devin-Adair Co., 1952).

A number of studies provide perspective on the issue of civil liberties during the McCarthy era. These include Ralph S. Brown, Jr., *Loyalty and Security: Employment Tests in the United States* (New Haven: Yale University Press, 1958); David P. Gardner, *The California Oath Controversy* (Berkeley: University of California Press, 1967); Walter Gellhorn, ed., *The States and Subversion* (Ithaca, N.Y.: Cornell University Press, 1952); Harold M. Hyman, *To Try Men's Souls* (Berkeley and Los Angeles: University of California Press, 1959); and Mary S. McAuliffe, "Liberals and the Communist Control Act of 1954," *The Journal of American History* 63 (September 1976): 351–67.

Relying on election statistics and public-opinion surveys, social scientists have been attracted to the sources of McCarthy's popular support both in Wisconsin and in the nation. The finest study of this kind is Michael Rogin, *The Intellectuals and McCarthy: The Radical Specter* (Cambridge, Mass.: The M.I.T. Press, 1967). For similar studies, besides the previously mentioned one edited by Daniel Bell, consult Louis Bean, *Influences in the 1954 Mid-Term Elections* (Washington, D.C.: Public Affairs Institute, 1954); John Fenton, *Midwest Politics* (New York: Holt, Rinehart and Winston, 1966); Louis Harris, *Is There a Republican Majority?* (New York: Harper and Brothers, 1954); Samuel Lubell, *Revolt of the Moderates* (New York: Harper and Brothers, 1956); James March, "McCarthy Can Still Be Beaten," *The Reporter* (28 October 1952): 17–19; Nelson Polsby, "Towards an Explanation of McCarthyism," *Political Studies* 8 (1960):250–71; Martin Trow, "Small Businessmen, Political Tolerance, and Support for McCarthy," *The American Journal of Sociology* 64 (1958):270–81.

Published Works: Wisconsin

No comprehensive study is available on McCarthy's career in Wisconsin or on his relationship with state groups and residents. Roger Johnson, *Robert M. La Follette, Jr. and the Decline of the Progressive Party in Wisconsin* (Madison: State Historical Society of Wisconsin, 1964) is essential for the 1946 senatorial primary but has little on the McCarthy campaign. A more recent study of La Follette that contains valuable information on the 1946 Senate race is Patrick J. Maney, *"Young Bob" La Follette: A Biography of Robert M. La Follette, Jr., 1895–1953* (Columbia: University of Missouri Press, 1978). Leroy Ferguson and Ralph Smuckler, *Politics in the Press: An Analysis of Press Content in 1952 Senatorial Campaigns* (East Lansing: Michigan State College, 1954), analyzed the comments made by state newspapers on the Fairchild–McCarthy campaign in 1952. For an excellent study of the 1954 recall, see David Thelen and Esther Thelen, "Joe Must Go: The Movement to Recall Senator Joseph McCarthy," *Wisconsin Magazine of History* 49 (Spring 1966): 185–209. Equally excellent is Robert Griffith, "The General and the Senator: Republican Politics and the 1952 Campaign in Wisconsin," *Wisconsin Magazine of History* 54 (Autumn 1970): 23–29. For Wisconsin labor's role in the McCarthy–Fairchild race of 1952, see David Oshinsky, "Wisconsin Labor and the Campaign of 1952," *Wisconsin Magazine of History* 56 (Winter 1973):109–18.

The organizer of the recall tells his own story in Leroy Gore, *Joe Must Go* (New York: Julian Messner, Inc., 1954). David Shannon, "Was McCarthy a Political Heir of La Follette?" *Wisconsin Magazine of History* 45 (Autumn 1961):3–9, answers his question with an emphatic "No." Detailed analyses of voting results in McCarthy's senatorial election victories appear in the previously mentioned studies by Bean, Bell, Harris, Lubell, March, Oshinsky, Polsby, and Rogin. The autobiography of William T. Evjue, *A Fighting Editor* (Madison: Wells Printing Co., 1968), is disappointing because it merely compiles Evjue's columns and editorials that appeared in *The Capital Times* during his long newspaper career.

Some material on McCarthy's geneology is found in Weston A. Goodspeed, Melvin E. Bothwell, and Kenneth C. Goodspeed, *History of Outagamie County, Wisconsin* (Chicago: Goodspeed Historical Association, 1911). An excellent survey of the state's history is Robert C. Nesbit, *Wisconsin: A History* (Madison: The University of Wisconsin Press, 1973).

Unpublished Material

I found a large amount of rewarding material in unpublished works, particularly in Ph.D. dissertations. Donald Crosby, S. J., "The Angry Catholics: American Catholics and Senator Joseph R. McCarthy, 1950–1957" (Ph.D. diss., Brandeis University, 1973), studied the national Catholic reaction to McCarthy. Crosby's published version is *God, Church, and Flag: Senator Joseph R. McCarthy and the Catholic Church, 1950–1957* (Chapel Hill: University of North Carolina Press, 1978). John Addison Ricks III, "Mr. Integrity and McCarthyism: Senator Robert A. Taft and Senator Joseph R. McCarthy" (Ph.D. diss., University of North Carolina at Chapel Hill, 1974), is a detailed analysis of the relationship between the two senators and is particularly useful for understanding the 1952 Wisconsin presidential primary.

Two recent studies that provide rich background on modern Wisconsin history are Carolyn J. Mattern, "The Man on the Dark Horse: The Presidential Campaigns for General Douglas MacArthur: 1944 and 1948" (Ph.D. diss., University of Wisconsin, 1976), and John Edward Miller, "Governor Philip F. La Follette, the Wisconsin Progressives, and the New Deal, 1930–1939" (Ph.D. diss., University of Wisconsin, 1973).

Charles Backstrom analyzed the rise and decline of the Progressive party in "The Progressive Party of Wisconsin: 1934–1946" (Ph.D. diss., University of Wisconsin, 1956). Francis Sorauf, Jr., "The Voluntary Committee System in Wisconsin: An Effort to Achieve Party Responsibility" (Ph.D. diss., University of Wisconsin, 1953), discussed modern political party development up to 1952. However, the Backstrom and Sorauf studies are outdated. A study by Richard Haney, "A History of the Democratic Party of Wisconsin since World War Two" (Ph.D. diss., University of Wisconsin, 1970), is a comprehensive history of the growth of the Wisconsin Democratic party, but it is deficient in its treatment of the McCarthy controversy. A solid study by Karl Meyer, "The Politics of Loyalty from La Follette to McCarthy in Wisconsin: 1918–1952" (Ph.D. diss., Princeton University, 1956), compares popular support for the La Follettes with that of McCarthy. Although dated and unnecessarily lengthy, John Steinke, "The Rise of McCarthyism" (Master's thesis, University of Wisconsin, 1960), is useful for McCarthy's 1946 campaign in Wisconsin. Wayne McKinley, "A Study of the American Right: Senator Joseph McCarthy and the American Legion: 1946–1955" (Master's thesis, University of Wisconsin, 1962), has material on McCarthy's relations with the Wisconsin American Legion.

McCarthy's manipulation of and controversies with newspapers are popular topics with graduate students. By far the finest work on McCarthy and Wisconsin newspapers, and a model for other studies, is Sharon Coady, "The Wisconsin Press and Joseph McCarthy: A Case Study" (Master's thesis, University of Wisconsin, 1965). Unfortunately, Coady carries her analysis only through 1946. Another work on the state press is Robert Harry Pell, "A PME Editorial Criteria vs. Comment on McCarthyism: A Study of Editorial Page Responsibility in the Daily Press of Wisconsin" (Master's thesis, University of Wisconsin, 1963). Studies of the national press that also contain some information on Wisconsin newspapers are Jean Deaver, "A Study of Senator Joseph R. McCarthy and 'McCarthyism' as Influences upon the News Media and the Evolution of Reportorial Method" (Ph.D. diss., University of Texas at Austin, 1969); and Mary Jane Ferguson, "McCarthy v. Pearson: Criticism or Intimidation" (Master's thesis, University of Wisconsin, 1969).

Another popular topic for graduate students is civil liberties during the McCarthy era. James F. Scotton, "Loyalty and the Wisconsin Legislature" (M.A. thesis, University of Wisconsin, 1966), proved invaluable for understanding McCarthyism in Wisconsin. Other studies that provided perspective on this subject were Ronald Wayne Johnson, "The Communist Issue in Missouri, 1946–1956" (Ph.D. diss., University of Missouri, 1973); Alex Nagy, "Federal Censorship of Communist Political Propaganda and the First Amendment, 1941–1961" (Ph.D. diss., University of Wisconsin, 1973); Peter C. Schaehrer, "McCarthyism and Academic Freedom—Three Case Studies" (Ph.D. diss., Columbia University, 1974); and Ingrid W. Scobie, "Jack B. Tenney: Molder of Anti-Communist Legislation in California, 1940–1949" (Ph.D. diss., University of Wisconsin, 1970).

Two other studies dealing with McCarthy in Wisconsin deserve mention. Charles J. Graham, Harold M. Hodges, and Philip S. Anderson, "Characteristics of the McCarthy Supporter" (sociological study, 1954), examined the support for McCarthy in Pierce County, Wisconsin. Graham gave me a copy of their findings. Ted Cloak and Jane Cloak, " 'Joe Must Go': The Story of Dane County in the 1954 Recall against McCarthy" (sociology paper, 1954, Manuscript Library, S.H.S.W.), have interesting observations on the recall movement by two participants.

Unpublished works on McCarthy with only tenuous connections to my topic include Paul Breslow, "The Relation between Ideology and Socio-Economic

Background in a Group of McCarthyite Leaders" (Master's thesis, University of Chicago, 1956); Frank Kendrick, "McCarthy and the Senate" (Ph.D. diss., University of Chicago, 1962); Arthur Peterson, "McCarthyism: Its Ideology and Foundations" (Ph.D. diss., University of Minnesota, 1964); and Immanuel Wallerstein, "McCarthyism and the Conservative" (Master's thesis, Columbia University, 1954).

## Newspapers and Periodicals

Newspapers and periodicals gave McCarthy full coverage and proved indispensible. For McCarthy's career before 1946 I relied on *The Antigo Daily Journal* (1938–1939), *Appleton Post-Crescent* (1938–1945), *The Bonduel Times* (1936), *The Capital Times* (1944), *The Hilltop* (Marquette University yearbook, 1931–1935), *The Manawa Advocate* (1929–1930), *The Marquette Tribune* (Marquette student newspaper, 1930–1935), *Milwaukee Journal* (1942–1944), *Shawano County Journal* (1936–1939), *The Shawano Evening Leader* (1936–1942), *Waupaca County Post* (1935–1936), and the *Wisconsin State Journal* (1944).

Those Wisconsin newspapers studied daily from 1946 to 1957 were the *Appleton Post-Crescent*, *The Capital Times*, *Green Bay Press-Gazette*, *Milwaukee Journal*, *Milwaukee Sentinel*, and *Wisconsin State Journal*.

State newspapers consulted extensively from 1946 to 1957 were the *Ashland Daily Press*, *The Beloit Daily News*, *The Eau Claire Leader*, *Fond du Lac Commonwealth Reporter*, *The Janesville Gazette*, *Kenosha Evening News*, *The La Crosse Tribune*, *Manitowoc Herald-Times*, *Marinette Eagle-Star*, *Oshkosh Daily Northwestern*, *Racine Journal-Times*, *The Sauk-Prairie Star* (1952–1954), *The Sheboygan Press*, *The Evening Telegram* (Superior), *Waukesha Daily Freeman*, *Wausau Daily Record-Herald*, and *Vilas County News-Review* (1952).

Other Wisconsin publications used extensively were *The Badger Legionnaire*, *The Daily Cardinal* (University of Wisconsin), *The Catholic Herald Citizen* (Madison), *Wisconsin Jewish Chronicle*, *The Progressive* (entitled *La Follette's Weekly Magazine*, 1946–1947), and *The Wisconsin Democrat*. Agricultural journals consulted included the *Badger Farm Bureau News*, *Wisconsin Agriculturist and Farmer*, and *Wisconsin Farmers Union News*. Labor-union publications used were the *Kenosha Labor*, *A.F. of L. Milwaukee Labor Press*, *Racine Labor*, *Union Labor News* (Madison), and the *Wisconsin CIO News*.

Newspapers outside Wisconsin studied selectively included the *Chicago Daily News* (1952), *Chicago Tribune* (1951), *The Christian Science Monitor* (1954, 1957), *The Evening Bulletin* (Philadelphia, 1949), *New York Post* (1952), *New York Times* (1946, 1950–1957), *Washington Post* (1950, 1952), and the *Washington Star* (1954).

Useful national periodicals were *Commentary*, *Fortune*, *Look*, *The Nation*, *New Republic*, *The New Yorker*, *The Reporter*, *The Saturday Evening Post*, *Saturday Review*, and *Time*. Wisconsin commentators who contributed to these publications were Edwin R. Bayley, William T. Evjue, Robert Fleming, Graham Hovey, John Hoving, Miles McMillin, and William G. Rice.

## Interviews

I discovered valuable and intimate material on McCarthy's career in interviews with 102 people. I conducted four types of interviews: personal tape-recorded interviews (sixty-eight); telephone tape-recorded interviews (six); personal interviews not tape-recorded (four); and telephone interviews not tape-recorded (twenty-four). All the taped interviews are in my possession, and, at some future date, I intend to donate them to a historical depository.

The following is a list of all the people I interviewed, along with a brief description of the capacity in which they knew or observed McCarthy, the date of the interview, and their residence when interviewed. An asterisk indicates that the interview was tape-recorded.

*Anderson, Donald, publisher, *Wisconsin State Journal* (15 February 1977, Madison).

*Anderson, Dottie (Druckery), McCarthy's secretary in 1939 (1 March 1977, Shawano).

*Baldwin, Karl, friend (3 March 1977, Appleton).

*Bloomquist, Roy, acquaintance (4 February 1977, Clintonville).

*Brown, Gordon, Manawa High School, class of 1930 (3 February 1977, Manawa).

*Catlin, Mark, Jr., assemblyman and Republican leader (24 February 1977, Appleton).

*Cattau, Louis, attorney in Shawano (1 March 1977, Shawano).

*Ceci, Louis, Young Republican leader (4 April 1977, Milwaukee).

*Crane, Harold, acquaintance in Manawa (3 February 1977, Manawa).

*Curran, Charles, Marquette Law, class of 1935 (13 April 1977, Mauston).

*Doyle, James, state Democratic chairman (3 September 1969, Madison).

*Drew, Richard, Marquette Law, class of 1935 (19 May 1977, Waukegan, Illinois).

*Ducklow, Mary Ellen, reporter, *Appleton Post-Crescent* (20 January 1977, Appleton).

*Duffy, John, Democratic leader in Green Bay (18 August 1969, Green Bay).

*Eddy, Loyal, Young Republican leader (11 March 1977, Elm Grove).

*Fellman, David, professor, University of Wisconsin (3 April 1969, Madison).

Fickel, Erwin, Underhill Country School, early 1920s (21 February 1977, Appleton).

*Frei, Lorraine, acquaintance in Shawano (1 March 1977, Shawano).

*Frei, Peter, resident of Mrs. Edith Green's boardinghouse (1 March 1977, Shawano).

Goetz, Ione (Norton), Manawa High School, teacher (18 April 1977, San Antonio, Texas).

*Gomillion, Bernadine, wife of Otis Gomillion, McCarthy's close friend and bodyguard (10 March 1977, Milwaukee).

Graves, Clarence, Democratic leader in Shawano (2 March 1977, Eland).

*Greeley, George, Republican leader and McCarthy staff member in Washington (28 August 1969, Madison).

*Gwin, Hugh, Marquette Law, class of 1935 (13 May 1977, Hudson).

Gyzinski, Irene, Marquette Law, class of 1935 (23 March 1977, Milwaukee).

Hagene, Margaret, secretary of McCarthy Club, 1944 (1 June 1977, Ephraim).

*Hanratty, Charles, Marquette Law, class of 1935 (11 March 1977, Milwaukee).

Hansen, Irving, acquaintance, Waupaca (10 February 1977, Waupaca).

*Harland, Robert, Marquette Law, class of 1935 (5 April 1977, Milwaukee).

*Hart, Edward, attorney, Waupaca (3 February 1977, Waupaca).

*Heenan, James, neighbor of McCarthy family (10 February 1977, Grand Chute).

Henning, Dorothy, Manawa High School, class of 1930 (4 February 1977, Manawa).

*Hershberger, Leo, Manawa High School, principal (3 February 1977, Manawa).

Hobart, Helen, acquaintance, Waupaca (27 April 1977, Waupaca).

*Honkamp, Elmer, Outagamie County Republican and district attorney (10 February 1977, Appleton).

*Hood, Wayne, state Republican chairman (10 September 1969, La Crosse).

Horwitz, Rosalie Stein, Marquette Law, class of 1935 (4 April 1977, Milwaukee).
Howlett, Patrick, court reporter (7 January 1977, Appleton).
*Ingraham, Mark, dean, University of Wisconsin (1 April 1969, Madison).
*Jasper, Claude, Republican leader (22 June 1977, Phoenix, Arizona).
*Kelley, George, Manawa High School, class of 1930 (18 March 1977, Royalton).
Kenney, Warren, Marquette Law, class of 1935 (17 May 1977, Waupaca).
*Kiermas, Ray, close friend, office manager in Washington (7 April 1977, Marco Island, Florida).
*Knowles, Warren, Republican state senator, lieutenant governor, and governor (10 March 1977, Milwaukee).
*Koehler, Herman, attorney, Shawano (18 March 1977, Shawano).
*Kohler, Walter, Jr., Republican governor (5 September 1969, Sheboygan).
*Kools, Mary (Hoolihan), Underhill Country School, teacher (21 January 1977, Appleton).
*Korb, Thomas, close friend and adviser (24 March 1977, Milwaukee).
Kores, Joseph, Marquette, boxer (12 May 1977, Green Bay).
Kriofske, Joseph, Marquette Law, class of 1935, FBI agent (23 March 1977, Milwaukee).
*Luberg, Leroy, administrator, University of Wisconsin (3 April 1969 and 15 February 1977, Madison).
*Lucey, Patrick, Democratic leader and governor (28 August 1969, Madison).
Mackesy, Lillian, reporter, *Appleton Post-Crescent* (29 March 1977, Appleton).
*McCarthy, Stephen, Joe's brother (3 March 1977, Appleton).
McKinnon, Arlo, attorney, friend (23 March 1977, Milwaukee).
*McMillin, Miles, political reporter, *The Capital Times* (2 September 1969, Madison).
*Meisner, Grover, Democratic leader in Shawano (1 March 1977, Wittenberg).
*Meyer, Harry H., mayor of Shawano (1 March 1977, Shawano).
*Middleton, Charles, friend in Shiocton and Milwaukee (22 February 1977, Clintonville).
*Morack, Llewellyn, friend and stockbroker (11 March 1977, Milwaukee).
Mortenson, Melda, Manawa High School, class of 1933 (10 April 1977, Manawa).
*Mullarky, Clifford, Marquette Law, class of 1935 (21 January 1977, Clintonville).
*O'Connor, Bernard, Marquette, boxer (4 May 1977, Skokie, Illinois).
*O'Konski, Alvin, Republican congressman (4 March 1977, Rhinelander).
Ozanne, Robert, director, School for Workers, University of Wisconsin–Madison (15 July 1977, Madison).
*Papka, Roman, Marquette Law, class of 1936 (25 April 1977, Milwaukee).
*Parnell, Andrew, attorney, Appleton (21 January 1977, Appleton).
Peterson, Maurice, Manawa High School, class of 1930 (9 February 1977, Merrill).
*Peterson, Talbot, Republican leader (22 February 1977, Appleton).
*Philipp, Cyrus, Republican national committeeman (25 April 1977, Milwaukee).
Radtke, Mrs. Carl, Underhill Country School, early 1920s (21 February 1977, Appleton).
Reardon, Mary, Joe's cousin (10 February 1977, Appleton).
*Reed, John, McCarthy's driver, 1939 (12 April 1977, Shawano).
*Reiske, Francis, Marquette Law, about 1936 (5 April 1977, Milwaukee).
*Remmel, William, McCarthy lived with him in Waupaca (3 February 1977, Waupaca).
*Renk, Wilbur, Republican leader, member of board of regents (3 September 1969 and 24 May 1977, Sun Prairie).
*Rice, William G., Democrat, professor at University of Wisconsin (2 April 1969, Madison).
*Rubin, Morris, editor of *The Progressive* and *The McCarthy Record* (14 April 1969, Madison).

Scanlan, Bernard, acquaintance in Shawano (21 February 1977, Shawano).
*Schmitt, Leonard, Republican candidate, Senate primary, 1952 (5 September 1969, Merrill).
*Schroeder, Henry, Marquette Law, class of 1935 (25 May 1977, Jefferson).
*Shortridge, Albert, bodyguard (5 April 1977, Milwaukee).
Sinykin, Gordon, friend and adviser of Robert M. La Follette, Jr. (11 November 1970, Madison).
Sipple, Emory, friend (24 May 1977, Madison).
Stadler, Mary (McDermott), Manawa High School, teacher (20 April 1977, Janesville).
*Sturm, Paul, Manwa High School, class of 1930 (18 March 1977, Manawa).
*Tegge, Lloyd, Young Republican leader (24 March 1977, Milwaukee).
*Testin, Honor (Walch), Manawa High School, class of 1930 (29 January 1977, Manawa).
*Thompson, Carl, Democratic leader (10 April 1969, Stoughton).
*Townsend, Harold, chairman, McCarthy Club, 1946 (10 March 1977, Milwaukee).
*Van Hoof, Gerard, attorney and friend (24 January 1977, Little Chute).
*Van Straten, Henry, friend (7 February 1977, Stephensville).
*Van Susteren, Urban, close friend (4 September 1969 and 22 March 1977, Appleton).
*Voy, Mae (Beyer), secretary for Eberlein and McCarthy (18 March 1977, Shawano).
*Wagner, Helen (Ludolph), court report in Shawano (21 April 1977, Shawano).
Walstead, Elliot, state Democratic chairman (4 April 1977, Milwaukee).
*Weeman, Alan, acquaintance, Shawano (18 March 1977, Shawano).
Werner, Francis, attorney and friend (26 January 1977, New London).
*Wyngaard, John, political columnist (30 December 1969, Madison).
One confidential interview.

I also found useful information in the lengthy tape-recorded interviews by Robert Griffith of Miles McMillin and Morris Rubin for the Cornell University Oral History Program. Griffith conducted his interviews in 1967, and both McMillin and Rubin lent me a copy of the typescript of their respective interviews.

## Government Publications

Government publications were not as important for this study as they are for other aspects of McCarthy's career. *The Wisconsin Blue Book* (1952 and 1954), published by the state of Wisconsin, was helpful. I also used the *Congressional Record* (1947–1954). The Tydings report is contained in U.S., Congress, Senate, Committee on Foreign Relations, State Department Loyalty Investigation: *Senate Report 2108*, 81st Cong., 2d sess., 1950. For the Hennings report, I used the volume reprinted and distributed by Americans for Democratic Action, *Investigations of Senators Joseph R. McCarthy and William Benton*, Report of the Subcommittee on Privileges and Elections to the Committee on Rules and Administration, 1952.

# Index